STEVE SIMS

planning and delivering
leisure services

planning and delivering
leisure services

Peter J. Graham
Northeastern University

Lawrence R. Klar, Jr.
University of Massachusetts

ШСb

Wm. C. Brown Company Publishers
Dubuque, Iowa

CREDITS

For permission to reproduce the photographs on the pages indicated, acknowledgment is made to the following:

Agency of Development and Community Affairs, Montpelier, Vermont: 124
Concord (MA) Recreation Department: 100
Jayfro Corporation: 248
Magic Mountain: 274
New Games Foundation: 2
The Quaker Oats Company: 162
U.S. Bureau of Outdoor Recreation: 218
U.S. Department of Health, Education and Welfare, Administration of Aging: x
Virginia Rotundo: 186
Dan Walsh, Winchester (MA) Star: 22
Worcester (MA) Parks and Recreation Department: 44, 74

Consulting Editors

Parks and Recreation
David Gray
California State University, Long Beach

Physical Education
Aileene Lockhart
Texas Woman's University

Health
Robert Kaplan
The Ohio State University

Copyright © 1979 by Wm. C. Brown Company Publishers

Library of Congress Catalog Card Number: 78–73156

ISBN 0–697–07384–X

Printed in the United States of America

*To Barbara,
Janelle, Terry, Jim,
and Our Parents.*

Contents

planning and delivering
leisure services

Preface

One of the major impacts of the technological revolution has been a great increase in the amount of free time available to most Americans. As a result, there has been extensive expansion in a variety of leisure related services. Budgets for municipal recreation and park departments have grown significantly; voluntary, non-profit agencies such as the YWCA and Boys' Club continue to grow in number and in levels of participant involvement; and, agencies which were not primarily developed to provide leisure services have become actively involved in recreation programming. Notable examples of the latter include school systems, police and fire departments, correctional institutions, and hospitals.

The tremendous growth in participation rates in recreation partially relates to a gradual changing of values toward leisure. At one point in our history, work was clearly the dominant influence in peoples' lives. Play and recreation were seen as rest from work, as restorative so the individual would be refreshed for more work, as a reward for work, or as a combination of these factors.

While work certainly remains a dominant influence in contemporary society, and will undoubtedly be so for some time to come, greater importance is being placed upon leisure pursuits which are being viewed in a new light. Recreation is no longer viewed in relation to work. Although much of the old thinking persists, recreation is increasingly perceived as a vehicle capable of positively influencing the self-image of participants, as a tool for rehabilitation, as a social means for contributing to a reduction of racism, and as a means by which people can enhance the quality of their lives by satisfying many of their basic personal needs through involvement in leisure pursuits.

As people continue to seek and value leisure involvements, the various roles of leisure professionals become increasingly important. They are being placed in a position of influence with participants of all types and can be singularly responsible for the human effects of a given program by creating an environment which enables participants to realize their expectations, or one in which other, less desirable outcomes occur.

It is, therefore, essential that planners and administrators fully understand their roles from several different perspectives. First, a basic foundation, or *raison d'etre,* must be clearly established so that the *function* of leisure services is fully understood. Once this framework is established, the specifics of providing services will have a greater likelihood of contributing to desired goals.

Second, the nature of human motivation and behavior must be clearly identified so that programming efforts are accurately directed toward fulfilling human needs. In other words, understanding the psychology of people is an essential element involved in the effective delivery of leisure services.

Third, planning and program effects must be understood from a sociological perspective. A complete leisure services delivery system will be integrated with the efforts of many community serving agencies. This will ultimately sensitize leisure service practitioners to community needs and problems related to such areas as vandalism, delinquency prevention, public health needs, social and recreational needs of special groups within the community, as well as a variety of other factors which affect community solidarity.

Finally, there are many specific planning considerations which must be addressed before activities and programs should be put into operation. These include such matters as community organization techniques, implementing legislative mandates such as providing equal opportunities for minorities and females, understanding the impact of agency values in relation to program outcomes, and the procedures involved in evaluating programs to insure that desirable outcomes do, in fact, occur.

There is, of course, a final phase which will not be addressed in this text; it centers around developing the technical skills at the face-to-face leadership level necessary to actually conduct program activities. This is an area which requires considerable knowledge and complete study in its own right, apart from the broader focus of overall program planning and administration of the leisure service delivery system. Many resources are presently available to the activity leader which will provide technical knowledge in such areas as sport, arts and crafts, drama, dance, campcraft, and so forth.

This book was written on the premise that the major need in leisure services today is the development of a body of knowledge which incorporates philosophical, psychological, and sociological factors in a delivery system which is effectively responsive to human needs. Accordingly, we have placed a strong emphasis upon the application of humanistic principles presented from the perspective of the practitioner who, in his or her studies of leisure services, would rightfully pose the question, "How will this help me to become a more effective practitioner in the field?"

The first chapter of this text establishes a basic philosophical framework and point of departure. The second and third chapters respectively address goals and objectives, and methods of evaluation in leisure services. The fourth chapter, on community organization, is also linked very closely to planning considerations and presents approaches for strengthening agency-community ties.

Chapter five focuses upon activity and program selection with an emphasis upon the *process* of program development rather than the actual procedures involved in leading various activities. Leadership and supervision are discussed in chapter six. The emphasis is upon organizational development, motivation, and staff-subordinate relations rather than leadership or supervision of participants.

The important area of volunteers is presented in chapter seven. Aspects of managing effective volunteer programs are discussed in a manner consistent with concepts presented in the preceding chapter of leadership and supervision. In chapter eight, the techniques employed in public, community, and media relations are examined. Again, the focus is toward the need for creating an atmosphere conducive to the development of positive human interactions.

In the American way of life, competition plays a significant role. The concepts of competition along with the planning and delivery of competitive leisure service programs are explored in chapter nine. Both positive and negative characteristics of a variety of tournament structures are discussed. Emphasis is placed upon the need to provide a healthy, well-balanced competitive program.

Chapter ten is concerned with the scheduling of leisure service programs and the development and maintenance of administrative records. Scheduling is approached from the perspective of meeting community and administrative needs through efficiency. Various forms of administrative data are discussed with stress placed upon the need to generate qualitative as well as quantitative information.

Chapter eleven reviews a variety of legal situations associated with leisure service programming and administration. The thrust of this chapter is to provide basic information concerning legal responsibilities and legislative enactments directly effecting leisure service programs.

The book concludes with an Appendix which provides the reader with a sequential approach to the development and scheduling of recreational activity tournaments. The material included in this Appendix supplements that presented in chapter nine.

Although this text clearly represents the thinking of both writers, the principal responsibility for the preparation of the first six chapters rests with Lawrence R. Klar, Jr. Primary input for chapters seven through eleven and the Appendix came from Peter J. Graham.

We would both like to thank several people in particular for their guidance and support in this undertaking. A special expression of appreciation is extended to David Gray for the many hours he spent editing and assisting us in our revisions. We are extremely fortunate to have his thoughtful and stimulating insights. We are also grateful to William

Randall, and other colleagues at the University of Massachusetts and Northeastern University, for their help in sharing ideas and suggestions for change. We would also like to thank Janice Lang who assisted us greatly at all times on behalf of the publisher.

And, to our respective families, we especially wish to express our appreciation for their support and patience which were so vital to the completion of this project.

Peter J. Graham   Lawrence R. Klar, Jr.
Boston   Amherst

planning and delivering
leisure services

Philosophical Considerations in Leisure Services

Objectives   After reading and comprehending this chapter, you should be able to:

1. Describe and explain the differences between leisure as activity, free time, and state of mind.
2. Define and compare leisure, free time, leisure time, discretionary time, recreation, recreation activity, recreation experience, self-actualization, Being, and peak experiences.
3. Explain the importance of understanding the psychology and sociology of people to effectively deliver leisure services.
4. Explain how program policies influence recreation experiences among participants.
5. Explain the purposes and importance of registration and certification in leisure services.

Defining Leisure and Recreation

A number of views have been advanced which relate to the various philosophies of leisure and recreation. Positions most frequently accepted will be presented briefly and then synthesized into a single approach designed to be specifically relevant to the practitioner. There are clearly no "right" and "wrong" positions when considering philosophical views; however, some are more readily and effectively applied in the actual presentation of leisure programs than others. With this in mind, our discussion is not intended to offer an abstract, purely theoretical perspective; rather, it is specifically designed to be used for the establishment of a working basis for those concerned with meeting human needs through the delivery of leisure services.

Concepts in Leisure

The three primary ways in which leisure has been defined incorporate the notions of time, activity, or that which has been termed, state of mind. Defining leisure in terms of time is the simplest and most commonly accepted approach (Kraus, 1971). According to this view, leisure is perceived as free time, time free from obligation. It is discretionary time to do what one chooses. It is time free from such requirements as eating, resting, and working.

Within this approach, no value judgment is generally made regarding the use of free time. Free time can be used for either positive or negative purposes but, in either case, it is regarded as leisure. When defining leisure according to time, the terms *free time, leisure time, discretionary time,* and *leisure* become synonymous.

Others (Neumeyer and Neumeyer, 1958) have viewed leisure in terms of *activity,* which takes place *during* free time, but is not in itself equated with free time. Instead, activities which are pursued during free time become leisure activities with one important qualifier; it is generally held that such activities must be of a positive nature. Free time activities which contribute to healthy personal adjustment, provide relaxation or enjoyment, and are socially acceptable, are considered leisure activities. Work is perceived as the antithesis of leisure; leisure is pursued more for its own reward while work is seen as a life necessity, tied closely to rewards of an economic nature.

One problem with viewing leisure as activity is that opinions of what constitutes appropriate leisure activities vary widely within the general population. For some, leisure is passive in nature, including such activities as reading an enjoyable book, strolling lazily along a wooded path, sitting quietly by a bubbling brook, or sipping lemonade while chatting quietly with good friends. Those viewing leisure in this light would probably define the more active pursuits such as rock-climbing, basketball, and competitive running as recreation, a term to be discussed more fully in a later section. Other activities such as jogging, hiking, or swimming, might fall in between and be more difficult to categorize.

Categorizations become even more difficult when one must decide if activities are positive in nature. Activities perceived as healthy, worthwhile endeavors by one person may be viewed as detrimental by others. For example, it is doubtful that activities such as dancing, gambling, and card-playing would be perceived as positive pursuits by some people. Differences in basic values may thereby prevent a common acceptance of the term leisure as activity.

The third approach, viewing leisure as a state of mind (de Grazia 1962; Peiper, 1952) has its roots in Aristotelian values and is probably the most difficult of the three views to grasp since it is the most abstract. This does not diminish its value, however, as many of its elements are central to contemporary leisure ideals which will be apparent shortly.

The classical position holds that leisure has nothing to do with time nor work except that there must be freedom to pursue that which one truly wishes to be doing (de Grazia, 1962). But having free time alone is not leisure; participating in a free time activity does not insure leisure.

Leisure occurs only when an individual is totally involved in a pursuit which is fully gratifying in its own right. It can involve virtually any pursuit, passive or active, difficult or easy. The major consideration is that there be total commitment and involvement, and that satisfaction be independent of external factors such as recognition from other people, monetary benefits, and so forth.

In the purest sense, leisure occurs through meditation, contemplation, music, art, or by being close to nature in the spirit of such transcendentalists as Thoreau and Emerson. More broadly speaking, leisure can involve any pursuit in which there is no thought other than the involvement itself, which can mean fully experiencing the exhileration of scaling a mountan peak, sharing in the joyful play of one's children, or being totally engrossed in the task which one has chosen to perform.

In either the broad or narrow sense, however, one element remains essential: there must be a total loss of awareness or sense of obligation to time. The state of mind view of leisure is completely independent of time. Paraphrasing Sebastian de Grazia (1962), modern day proponent of the classical view, to experience leisure, we must be fully extricated from the clock, from a sense of obligation, from external influences; preoccupation with "outside" concerns, particularly those imposing time constraints, prevents the leisure state from occurring. The challenge of the classical view is to convert free time, which exists for everyone in varying degrees, to leisure, a transformation which, according to de-Grazia, few of us have been able to achieve.

It is our position that the simplest and perhaps most common view of leisure should be adopted by leisure service agencies which is that of viewing leisure as free time. From this perspective, the most important component is the idea of being free to choose to do what one wishes. No value judgment is made relating to the quality of one's use of leisure time; it can be positive or negative for the individual, acceptable or unacceptable to society. What constitutes enjoyment for one person may be regarded as drudgery by another; what is boring to some may be gratifying to others.

By adopting this position, several pitfalls are avoided. First, as Kraus (1971) has pointed out, if one assumes that leisure must be a positive or "good" experience, who makes this determination? Second, and closely related, Kraus has emphasized that there are no known universal activities which can be labeled leisure for everyone. Identifying activities as leisure or non-leisure becomes extremely difficult given the variety of preferences and perceptions which exist throughout society. Finally, the abstract, narrow constraints imposed by the classical view are avoided. For example, since leisure in the classical sense is a state of mind, a municipal agency cannot *do* leisure, which is a concept, not a tangible entity. (Although an agency cannot *do* free time either, agency personnel can easily identify their role as one of providing opportunities for people who voluntarily come to the agency during a period of time which is discretionary, that is, free from obligation.)

The leisure service practitioner is concerned with providing services for people during their free time which logically connects the terms *leisure activities* and *free time activities*. By treating these terms synonymously, a view is adopted which is easily understood by the public, practitioners in the field, and the various political bodies responsible for allocating funds for activities and programs. Value judgments are thereby avoided and barriers in communication minimized.

Definitions of Recreation

Many definitions of recreation have been formulated by numerous individuals and there are certain elements which tend to repeat themselves. For example, recreation is widely viewed as positive, occurring during free time, voluntarily chosen, personally satisfying, and activity oriented. In many respects, recreation and leisure are often defined quite similarly.

Following along lines very closely related to the classical view of leisure, David Gray (Gray and Pelegrino, 1973) has offered a perspective which views recreation as a state of mind, a view which we will consider before advancing our own. Gray has adopted a definition of recreation which is psychological in nature; that is, recreation is defined purely in terms of what the participant experiences:

Recreation is an emotional condition within an individual human being
that flows from a feeling of well-being and satisfaction. It is characterized
by feelings of mastery, achievement, exhileration, acceptance, success, personal
worth, and pleasure. It reinforces a positive self-image. Recreation is a
response to esthetic experience, achievement of personal goals, or positive
feedback from others. It is independent of activity, leisure, or social acceptance
(Gray and Pelegrino, 1973; p. 6).

It is what occurs *within* an individual which determines whether or not recreation occurs. A trip around the golf course, for example, would not be considered recreation if the golfer felt depressed and let down due to a poor performance. A basketball game would not be considered recreation for the individual feeling angry because the team was playing below expectations. Painting would not be recreation if the artist felt frustrated at being unable to capture a desired mood on the canvas.

Participating in an activity does not in itself insure recreation; it is the psychological response felt by the individual which is the determinant. According to Gray's view, recreation would occur when a person experiences the tranquility and beauty of nature which leads to a feeling of inner calm and personal sense of well-being. Recreation would occur when a tennis player feels a deep sense of enjoyment because of the beautiful day, the companionship of his or her partner, and the excitement of the play, and these factors collectively contribute to a sense of personal happiness and satisfaction with self and others.

There is an apparent drawback to Gray's definition, however. Should *all* positive feelings be categorized as recreation? Is the scientist's moment of discovery recreation? Or the student's feeling of satisfaction with a term paper well done? If we assume that recreation is independent of either leisure or activity, virtually all satisfying experiences become labeled recreation which seems too far reaching and presents barriers to communication since that is not the context in which most people view recreation. Practically speaking, this definition will not be easily applied as it now stands since it incorporates so many types of experiences.

The psychological focus provided by Gray, however, is important and should be uppermost in the minds of leisure service practitioners. But it may not be appropriate to view recreation apart from leisure or activity since the leisure service practitioner is so intricately involved with each of these elements. Regardless of one's philosophical leaning and personal perspective of what leisure is or is not, society at large has come to hold conceptions of recreation which tend to be consistent. Most people, for example, would have no difficulty identifying activities such as golf, swimming, shuffleboard, arts and crafts, chess, and handball as recreation activities. These activities are frequently offered by recreation agencies; thus recreation has become institutionalized to the point that we all have a common understanding of the services associated with recreation agencies and the type of pursuits in which they are involved. However, although society views recreation primarily in terms of activity provided for people during their free time, this does not in itself provide the leisure service professional with a foundation sufficient for maximizing the effectiveness of leisure services.

Interrelating Leisure and Recreation

The many ways of looking at leisure and recreation need to be reduced to a model which can be easily used by practitioners involved in the leisure service delivery system. While the following discussion does not embrace each and every possible situation related to leisure and recreation, and more importantly, it does not diminish the validity of other viewpoints, it does offer the practitioner an approach which can be readily followed and put into use in day-to-day programming. Equally important, it provides a language readily understood by political bodies responsible for funding programs. By avoiding abstract, esoteric terms, program funding possibilities may be greatly enhanced.

Rather than add another definition of recreation to the list, two components of recreation will be suggested as more easily used alternatives. The first is *recreation activity* which, very simply stated, relates to those activities sponsored by leisure service agencies for people seeking enjoyment during their free time. A *recreation activity* is determined by mutual consensus; it is any activity which is identified as such by the sponsoring agency and is perceived, accepted, and shared in the same context by a constituency.

For example, maintaining a vegetable garden is not generally considered a recreation activity in the same manner as tennis; however, if a municipal recreation department offers a gardening program as a part of its summer offerings and it is accepted by a constituency, it becomes a recreation activity. More obvious and less controversial recreational activities include golf, baseball, creative dance, and swimming. These are not necessarily recreation activities at all times (professional dance, for example), but are easily accepted as such when sponsored by leisure service agencies.

Certainly many agencies which do not have the primary purpose of providing leisure services also sponsor recreation activities and it is implicit that they are included with leisure service agencies in our discussion. For simplicity's sake, however, it is easier to speak primarily in terms of the leisure service profession.

While the idea of a *recreation activity* relates predominantly to institutionalized recreation, a second aspect of recreation follows along psychological lines very closely akin to Gray's thinking. In an effort to use Gray's view of recreation, we will use the term **recreation experience,** rather than recreation. A *recreation experience* occurs as a direct outgrowth of involvement in a *recreation activity*. It is an emotional condition in which a state of inner satisfaction and feelings of well-being are experienced within the individual. The principal difference between recreation, as defined by Gray, and a *recreation experience,* is that the latter is *not* independent of either leisure or activity; it is directly related to both.

A *Recreation Experience* is a positive emotional response to participation in a *recreation activity*, defined as such by the individual or by a sponsoring agency or organization. Responses associated with the recreation experience include feeling good about self and others, experiencing a sense of inner calm or personal satisfaction, or feeling an enriched sense of self-worth which results from motivators of either an intrinsic or extrinsic nature. There is a clear absence of stress and tension which produce anxiety; the joy of *re-creative* experience is achieved. The essence of the classical view of leisure is achieved.

This avoids the broadness of Gray's definition which categorizes virtually all positive experiences as recreation, a definition not easily operationalized by the practitioner since most people perceive recreation in narrower terms. We have, however, retained the psychological component presented by Gray, but in a narrower context. Using the terms *recreation activity* and *recreation experience,* the practitioner is able to easily communicate the specific nature of programs while maintaining a consciousness of the quality of programs from the point of view of the participant's feelings. Thus, we have leisure service agencies sponsoring *recreation activities* for people who are electing to participate during their *leisure (free) time* and who are seeking personal satisfaction through a *recreation experience.*

Self-Actualization and the Recreation Experience

In this discussion, the concept of recreation has been narrowed to two components: *recreation activity* which takes place during free time and relates to programs sponsored by leisure service agencies, and *recreation experience,* which denotes positive feelings experienced by participants involved in recreation activities. A recreation experience of course, can occur in varying degrees depending upon the level of satisfaction experienced, much the same as other feelings which may be of stronger or weaker intensity. This is consistent with the theory of self-actualization advanced by Abraham Maslow (1968; 1971) which will be briefly presented and integrated with the idea of a recreation experience.[1]

Maslow's theory assumes that human beings have certain needs, arranged in levels, which must be satisfied progressively. The first and most critical requirements center around one's *physiological needs* such as eating, sleeping, breathing, and so forth. *Safety needs* occupy the second level of the hierarchy which include protection from danger and deprivation. The third level relates to *social needs* such as the need for belonging, for sharing experiences with others, and loving and feeling loved by others. *Ego needs* occupy the fourth position in the need-hierarchy. Ego needs include feelings of self-acceptance, self-confidence, achievement, social status, and recognition by others. Finally, the need for *self-actualization* constitutes the highest need level. The need for self-actualization simply means having a need to realize one's full potential and living life to the fullest, which is also synonymous with another of Maslow's terms, *Being.* Maslow's theory can be expressed in the form of a pyramid which symbolizes the flow of the need-hierarchy as shown in Figure 1-1. While Maslow does not define self-actualization in a one-sentence or one-paragraph format, he spoke extensively about the nature of self-actualized people. Self-actualization is complex and multi-faceted in scope, but the following characteristics of the self actualized individual summarize the most common elements described by Maslow (1968; p. 26):

1. Abraham Maslow, *Toward a Psychology of Being,* 2nd Edition. New York. D. Van Nostrand Company, 1968. By permission.

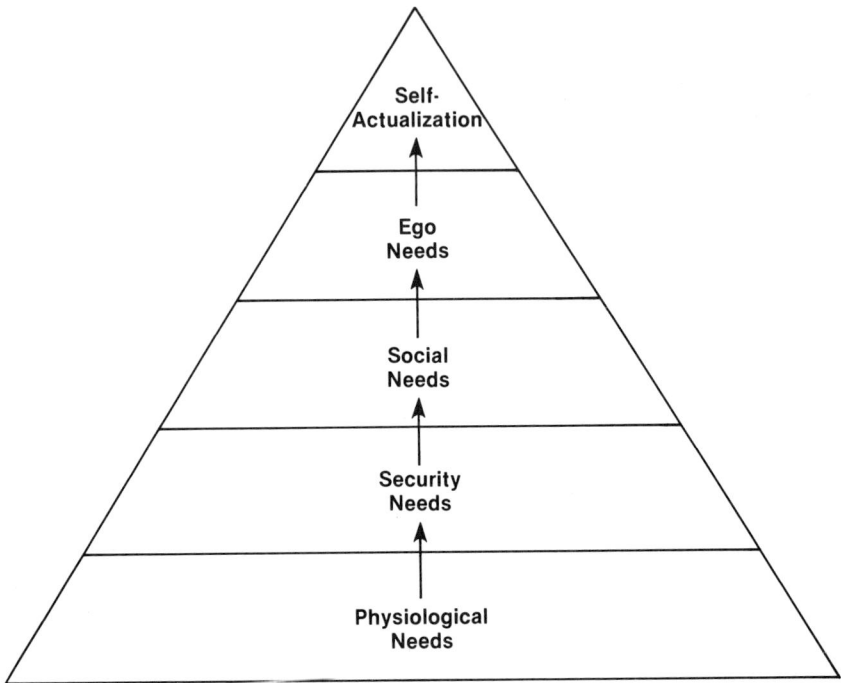

Figure 1.1 Maslow's Hierarchy of Needs

1. Superior perception of reality
2. Increased acceptance of self, of others, and of nature
3. Increased spontaneity
4. Increase in problem-centering
5. Increased detachment and desire for privacy
6. Increased autonomy, and resistance to enculturation
7. Greater freshness of appreciation, and richness of emotional reaction
8. Higher frequency of peak experiences
9. Increased identification with the human species
10. Changed (the clinician would say, improved) interpersonal relations
11. More democratic character structure
12. Greatly increased creativeness
13. Certain changes in the value system

Maslow (1968, p. 46) went on to describe the process of growth toward self-actualization and forces which can inhibit growth:

Every human being has (two) sets of forces within him. One set clings to safety and defensiveness out of fear, tending to regress backward, hanging on to the past, *afraid* to . . . take chances, afraid to jeopardize what he already has, *afraid* of independence, freedom and separateness. The other set of forces impels him forward toward wholeness of Self and uniqueness of Self, toward full functioning of all his capacities, toward confidence in the face of the external world at the same time that he can accept his deepest, real, unconscious Self.

Accordingly, we must choose between the rewards of safety and security, and the more promising, but seemingly riskier, delights of growth. Safety needs are more powerful than growth needs and must be satisfied before higher needs can be addressed, but it is fulfillment of the higher level needs which leads to the self-actualizing process.

It is an oversimplification to say that a person is either self-actualized or not self-actualized. Self-actualization may occur in varying degrees in all of us; on a continuum, some people are more or less self-actualized than others. Furthermore, regardless of the need level exerting the greatest force at a given time, self-actualizing experiences can occur for anyone. Maslow has called such occurrences *peak experiences* and although people who are high self-actualizers seem to have more peak experiences than others who are less self-actualized, peak experiences can occur for anyone.

In terms of our focus, feelings accompanying the *recreation experience,* the *peak experience, self-actualization,* and *Being,* are virtually synonymous. Each relates to situations in which an individual feels a sense of inner satisfaction as an outgrowth of a particular experience. From a leisure services perspective, participants will hopefully experience such satisfaction through involvement in the various agency program offerings, even those who have not reached a high level of actualization.

An additional reference to Maslow clarifies the extent to which self-actualizing concepts interrelate with leisure service ideals. He described a process appropriate for people of all ages, which contributes to the enrichment of personal growth. The process, which embodies the essence of Maslow's theory, includes the following (1968, pp. 57-8):

1. The healthy, spontaneous child, in his spontaneity, from within out, in response to his own inner Being, reaches out to the environment in wonder and interest, and expresses whatever skills he has,
2. To the extent that he is not crippled by fear, to the extent that he feels safe enough to dare.
3. In this process, that which gives him the delight-experience is fortuitously encountered, or is offered to him by helpers.
4. He must be safe and self-accepting enough to be able to choose and prefer these delights, instead of being frightened by them.
5. If he can choose these experiences which are validated by the experience of delight, then he can return to the experience, repeat it, savor it to the point of repletion, satiation, or boredom.
6. At this point, he shows the tendency to go on to more complex, richer experiences and accomplishments in the same section (again, if he feels safe enough to dare).
7. Such experiences not only mean moving on, but have a feedback effect on the Self, in the feeling of certainty ("This I like; that I don't for *sure*"); of capability, mastery, self-trust, self-esteem.

8. In this never ending series of choices of which life consists, the choice may generally be schematized as between safety (or, more broadly, defensiveness) and growth, and since only that child doesn't need safety who already has it, we may expect the growth choice to be made by the safety-need gratified child. Only he can afford to be bold.

9. In order to be able to choose in accord with his own nature and to develop it, the child must be permitted to retain the subjective experiences of delight and boredom, as *the* criteria of the correct choice for him . . .

10. If the choice is really a free one, and if the child is not crippled, then we may expect him ordinarily to choose progression forward.

11. The evidence indicates that what delights the healthy child, what tastes good for him, is also, more frequently than not, "best" for him in terms of far goals as perceivable by the spectator.

12. In this process the environment (parents, therapists, teachers) is important in various ways, even though the ultimate choice must be made by the child:
    a. It can gratify his basic needs for safety, belongingness, love and respect, so that he can feel unthreatened, autonomous, interested and spontaneous and thus dare to choose the unknown;
    b. It can help by making the growth choice positively attractive and less dangerous, and by making the regressive choice less attractive and more costly.

13. In this way the psychology of Being and the psychology of Becoming can be reconciled, and child, simply being himself, can yet move forward and grow.

Integrating Concepts

In developing a basic philosophy of leisure, certain assumptions about human nature must be made and integrated with principles that can be adopted by those individuals developing and implementing leisure service programs. With this in mind, the main concepts in our philosophical framework include *leisure, free time, recreation activity, recreation experience,* and *self-actualization (Being) ideals.* These terms can be interrelated graphically in the following manner:

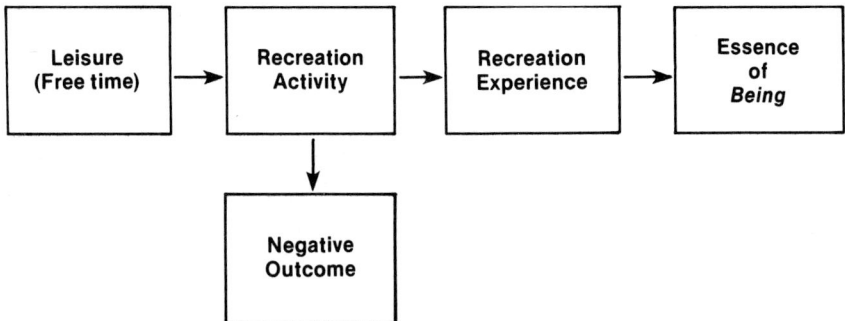

Figure 1.2   Leisure, Recreation and Being

It must also be remembered that within leisure there exists the possibility of choosing non-recreation pursuits which also have the potential of fulfillment in the sense of self-actualization ideals which can be similarly depicted as follows:

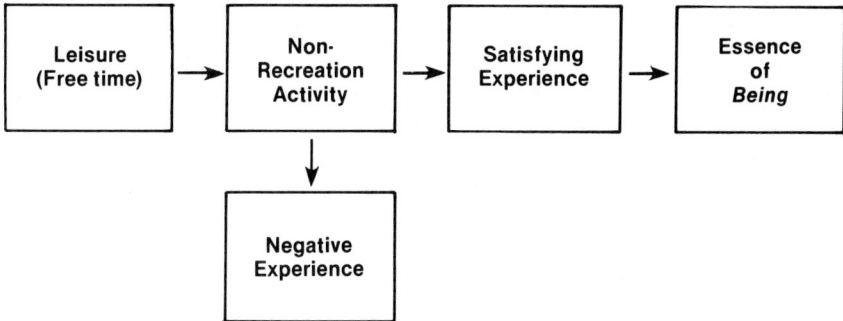

```
┌──────────────┐     ┌──────────────┐     ┌──────────────┐     ┌──────────────┐
│   Leisure    │     │    Non-      │     │  Satisfying  │     │   Essence    │
│  (Free time) │ ──► │  Recreation  │ ──► │  Experience  │ ──► │     of       │
│              │     │   Activity   │     │              │     │   Being      │
└──────────────┘     └──────┬───────┘     └──────────────┘     └──────────────┘
                            │
                            ▼
                     ┌──────────────┐
                     │   Negative   │
                     │  Experience  │
                     │              │
                     └──────────────┘
```

Figure 1.3   Leisure, Non-Recreation and Being

In either case, the possibility of a negative outcome exists, as does the potential for a fulfilling experience. The chief concern of the recreation practitioner, of course, is the nature of participant experiences while engaged in recreation activities. Specifically, the challenge today is to develop and conduct programs which contribute to the occurrence of actualizing experiences for all participants.

The Importance of Agency Values

We have assumed that involvement in leisure service (recreation) activities provides the opportunity for participants to experience recreation ideals to the fullest, that is, in the sense of a recreation experience, or *Being*. For this to occur values must be established which foster an environment that is non-threatening to participants. People must feel that they can enter into an activity without fear of embarrassment or ridicule from others. While this seems apparent enough, all too often would-be participants abstain from becoming involved due to a fear of failure or fear of performing to a lesser degree than others who may be more skilled in a given pursuit. The perceptive recreator is able to emphasize the rewards of participation itself and mutual acceptance of participants regardless of ability levels. With an accepting environment comes a willingness of participants to *choose* to become involved, to *dare* to try new experiences, to *grow* in confidence and self-acceptance, and to become fully involved to the point that a recreation experience is possible. Without such an environment, self-doubts and self-consciousness will most certainly act as barriers to the growth process described in our basic philosophical framework.

Important opportunities for facilitating the growth process among participants exist even before a program is offered; for example, participants can be actively involved in the planning process itself. By involving people in the early phase of leisure service programs, the opportunity for making decisions, contributing creatively to the outcome of planning efforts, and feeling a sense of achievement as a result of contributing to the finished product are given to them. At the same time, the likelihood of continued involvement in the activity will be greater since those involved from the start will feel a vested interest in its success.

In addition to planning considerations, great care must be taken to insure that values associated with programming approaches are handled properly in a manner which contributes to the frequency of recreation experiences among participants. For example, the agency's values associated with the use of reward systems must be carefully assessed to insure that the outcome for all participants is positive. If children are placed on teams to participate in a scavenger hunt and prizes are awarded to the winning team, particularly prizes which are highly desired by the participants, those who do not fare so well may feel quite let down. Obviously, this can occur in any competitive event ranging from sports, pet and costume contests, to talent shows and chess tournaments. If the rewards for winning an activity become more important than the participation itself, the loss may be great, as Maslow (1968, p. 31) has cautioned:

Activity can be enjoyed either intrinsically, for its own sake, or else
have worth and value only because it is instrumental in bringing about a
desired gratification. In the latter case it loses its value and is no longer
pleasurable when it is no longer successful or efficient. More frequently, it is
simply not enjoyed at all, but only the goal is enjoyed.

Experience has shown that participation is often increased when prizes are awarded for excellence or winning, and programs are generally regarded as successful when attendance is high. The truly successful program, however, may be the one in which participants derive their gratification and meet needs through involvement itself, through sharing meaningful experiences with others, or through feelings of achievement and mastery which are relative to the self, rather than others. This is clearly a value judgment, but the recreator who can facilitate such outcomes, which tend to be inner-directed comes far closer to leisure service ideals than one who is unaware of various program effects and is more concerned with numbers alone.

The task for the practitioner is not easy, however, and the process of putting philosophical ideals into practice can be difficult. The mechanics of implementing programs are demanding and often require the full attention of available personnel. Daily tasks necessitate checking out equipment, supervising several areas at once, administering first aid to children with scraped knees, responding to telephone calls, and preparing posters announcing the next week's activities. The list seemingly goes on endlessly, often creating situations in which personnel are unable to interact with participants to the extent that they would wish.

One obvious solution to this problem is the addition of staff members. Realistically, however, this is unlikely, especially during times of economic austerity. In all likelihood, staff members will be required to resolve the difficulty with existing personnel and volunteer resources.

With or without additional staff members or volunteers, however, the basic mood established by an agency is a function of the values which have been adopted, and participants are affected even in situations where direct contact is minimal or non-existent. For example, the atmosphere surrounding a Pee Wee Hockey program can vary widely depending upon the pre-program values which are adopted by the administrators, officials, and coaches who are involved. Values which place great importance on winning, hitting the opponent hard to intimidate him or her, and playing the best players most of the time, especially "when it counts," can be adopted and will significantly influence the program; players will be rewarded for behavior which is consistent with these values and the tenor of play will be predictably aggressive. The results for many are apt to be inconsistent with the *expressed* values and goals of the agency sponsoring the program.

An alternative value system might specify that all players must, without exception, play an equal amount of time regardless of the score or situation in a given game, that players will concentrate on the skill of handling the puck and passing well to teammates rather than checking opponents, and that a game well played is considered more important than the outcome, that is, the final score. Participants involved in the second program will certainly be involved in an activity more closely aligned with the stated ideals of leisure services than those in the first.

An additional example will further bring out the importance of pre-program planning in relation to values. A game requiring umpires or referees, such as basketball, can be directly influenced by the attitude and style of those officiating the contest. The official who calls fouls closely, frequently, and decisively and who allows virtually no arguments over his or her calls will probably have a much smoother, less aggressive game than the official who is laissez-faire or passive in the officiating role. In the latter case, when fouls are rarely called, physical contact is increased, play grows gradually poorer and rougher, and tempers are more likely to flare-up out of frustration.

Program Policies and Values

Such factors as the amount of time each participant must be allowed to play, the manner in which games will be officiated, and the use of awards, if any, may seem to be purely "mechanical" aspects of a program. But if not carefully handled, such factors can damage the effectiveness of a program, even a program staffed with outstanding leaders. Planners and administrators should give careful consideration to such areas to insure that a climate is established which supports the values and ideals expressed by the sponsoring agency or organization.

Unfortunately, in many instances decisions relating to these factors are left to the discretion of those involved at the leadership level. This generally leads to inconsistency among leaders, many of whom are inadvertently ineffective at the expense of the participant. Ineffective leadership is then identified as "the problem." The problem, however, may instead be administrative in nature if basic policies were not formulated and properly transmitted to those working at the leadership level.

Policies do not "make" a program. They should however, set the stage and provide a foundation for the leisure service practitioner. Therefore, clear policy guidelines should be developed which reflect the values and intent of the organization, even if a portion of the guidelines address areas which seem to be rather specific in nature. Examples of recreational sports program policies which might fall under this category include the following:

1. All participants will play an equal amount of time in each game for which they are present.
2. All participants will have the opportunity to play at least three different positions during the season.
3. All participants will receive participation awards at the end of the season, but awards for playing excellence and winning the league championship will not be offered.
4. Special recognition will be given at the end-of-the-season banquet to players for: (1) excellent sportsmanship, (2) cooperativeness with fellow teammates, (3) helping lesser skilled players, and (4) self-determination. (It is anticipated that recognition in one or more of these areas can be received by each participant, not a select few.)

Program policies such as these are intended to serve only as examples of steps which can be taken which will have a direct impact on participants and can be influenced *before* a program is initiated. The essential point is that planners and decision makers should be fully aware of the importance of program policies and the extent to which their presence or absence may have a direct impact on each participant.

Above all, there must be an understanding of how such factors influence opportunities for each participant to experience the exhilaration of the recreation experience.

Professional Standards

Slowly but surely, standards and guidelines are being developed by state and professional organizations. Two major thrusts involve voluntary registration and certification. Certification is similar to licensing in that legislation is passed which requires practitioners to demonstrate competency in their field, usually by meeting certain educational requirements and/or passing an examination.

Voluntary registration is similar, but is not backed by legislation. Most employers do not state that an employee in leisure services must be registered, but often those who are have an advantage when competing for jobs.

The National Recreation and Park Association (NRPA) has established standards for voluntary registration. State recreation and park associations/societies have adopted the national plan, and have been accepted into it. In Massachusetts, for example, a state plan has been formulated and adopted by NRPA which includes registration for the following levels: (1) Master Professional, (2) Professional, and (3) Technician. Within those categories are six examinations:

1. Park and Recreation Professional
2. Therapeutic Professional (non-administrative)
3. Therapeutic Professional (administrative)
4. Recreation Technician
5. Park Technician
6. Therapeutic Technician

As the trend toward registration increases, leisure service practitioners will continue to be affected. Employers who feel that the various registration plans have merit and offer a valid indicator of professional ability and potential, will look toward registered individuals in their recruitment efforts. Ultimately, the quality of practitioners will be raised as standards become clearer and employers' expectations are more closely aligned with those standards.

Summary

If leisure service practitioners hope to effectively meet the expanding leisure needs of people in contemporary society, there must be a clear understanding of their role. This includes gaining an understanding of the function of leisure along psychological and sociological lines, developing sound planning approaches, and insuring that relevant agency values and goals become an integral part of the total delivery system.

To facilitate this process, agency personnel must identify a basic framework from which decisions can be made. We have suggested that *leisure, free time, discretionary time,* and *leisure time* should be regarded synonymously. *Recreation activity,* from an agency perspective, is any activity sponsored by agencies for people seeking pursuits during their free time. It is any activity identified as such by the sponsoring agency and accordingly accepted in that light by the public. A *recreation experience* occurs as an outgrowth of involvement in a recreation activity. It is an emotional response to that involvement which produces feelings of inner satisfaction and a sense of well-being. It is similar to Gray's (1973) psychological definition except that it is not independent of activity; rather, it is a direct outgrowth of involvement in a recreation activity.

A recreation experience is also basically synonymous with Maslow's (1968) ideal of self-actualization or Being. Peak experiences and recreation experiences, for example, elicit highly similar, positive psychological responses in people.

To create an environment which provides maximum opportunities to experience the feelings stemming from a recreation experience, agency personnel must insure that their expressed values and ideals become a part of every aspect of the delivery system. Outcomes should not be left to chance. Once the purpose of a program or activity has been identified, specific steps must be taken during the planning and implementation stages to insure effectiveness. Developing clear program policies and communicating those policies to all members of the staff can enhance this process and contribute to developing a climate in which recreation experiences may occur for participants. With this in mind, the ideals associated with leisure service programming may become realities.

Study Questions

1. Could an agency adopt the classical view of leisure as its basic approach? Would there be limitations to this approach since it tends to be rather abstract? Why, or why not?
2. Many people perceive leisure in terms of certain types of activity. What are the strengths and weaknesses of this approach?
3. What are the strengths and weaknesses of Gray's definition of leisure? Do you support his view?
4. Your authors have defined recreation activity from an institutional perspective; what are the strengths and weaknesses of this approach from the vantage point of the practitioner? The public? Those controlling the allocation of financial resources?

5. Why is Maslow's theory of self-actualization relevant to leisure service practitioners?
6. What is meant by program policies? How might their absence or presence influence the effectiveness of programs?
7. How do agency values influence program policies?
8. Is it critical for activity and program leaders to be aware of agency values and its philosophical framework? Why or why not?
9. What is meant by a humanistic perspective in leisure services and what is its significance?
10. Registration and certification plans are increasing throughout the country—how might this strengthen the leisure service field? Are there disadvantages to this trend?

References

de Grazia, Sebastian. *Of Time, Work, and Leisure.* Garden City, N.Y.: Doubleday & Company, Inc., 1962.

Gray, David, and Pelegrino, Donald. *Reflections on the Recreation and Park Movement.* Dubuque, Ia.: Wm. C. Brown Company, Publishers, 1973.

Kraus, Richard. Recreation Today: *Program Planning and Leadership.* Santa Monica, Calif.: Goodyear Publishing Company, Inc., 1977.

Kraus, Richard. *Recreation and Leisure in Modern Society.* New York: Appleton-Century-Crofts, 1971.

Maslow, Abraham H. *The Farther Reaches of Human Nature.* New York: The Viking Press, 1971.

Maslow, Abraham H. *Toward A Psychology of Being,* 2nd Edition. New York: D. Van Nostrand Company, 1968.

Murphy, James F., and Howard, Dennis R. *Delivery of Community Leisure Services: An Holistic Approach.* Philadelphia: Lea & Febiger, 1977.

Neumeyer, Martin, and Neumeyer, Esther. *Leisure and Recreation.* New York: Ronald Press, 1958.

Peiper, Josef. *Leisure: the Basis of Culture.* New York: Mentor-Omega Books, 1952, 1963.

Related Readings

Brennecke, John H., and Amick, Robert G. *The Struggle for Significance.* Beverly Hills, Calif.: Glencoe Press, 1971.

Brightbill, Charles K. *The Challenge of Leisure.* Englewood Cliffs, N.J.: Prentice-Hall, Inc., 1960.

Brightbill, Charles K., and Mobley, Tony A. *Educating for Leisure-Centered Living.* New York: John Wiley and Sons, 1966, 1977.

Butler, George D. *Introduction to Community Recreation.* New York: McGraw-Hill, 1976.

Carlson, Reynold E.; Deppe, Theodore R.; and MacLean, Janet R. *Recreation in American Life.* Belmont, Calif.: Wadsworth Publishing Company, 1972.

Dulles, Foster Rhea. *A History of Recreation*. New York: Appleton-Century-Crofts, 1965.

Dumazedier, Joffre. *Toward A Society of Leisure*. New York: The Free Press, 1967.

Ellis, M. J. *Why People Play*. Englewood Cliffs, N.J.: Prentice-Hall, Inc., 1973.

Furlong, William Barry. "The Flow Experience: The Fun in Fun." *Psychology Today* June (1976): 35-38, 80.

Gobel, Frank. *The Third Force*. New York: Grossman Publishers, Inc., 1972.

Godbey, Geoffrey, and Parker, Stanley. *Leisure Studies and Services: An Overview*. Philadelphia: W. B. Saunders Company, 1976.

Gray, David E., and Seymour Greben. "Future Perspectives." *Parks and Recreation* July (1974): 27-33, 47-56.

Haworth, J. T., and Smith, M. A. (eds.) *Work and Leisure*. Princeton, N.J.: Princeton Book Company, Publishers, 1976.

Holcomb, J. L. "Leisure: The Actualization of the Self." *Physical Educator* 30:1(1973): 38-39.

Holt, John. *Freedom and Beyond*. New York: E. P. Dutton & Co., Inc., 1972.

Hormachea, Marion N., and Hormachea, Carroll R. *Recreation in Modern Society*. Boston: Holbrook Press, 1972.

Kando, Thomas M. *Leisure and Popular Culture in Transition*. St. Louis, Mo.: The C. V. Mosby Company, 1975.

Kaplan, Max, and Bosserman, Philip. (eds.) *Technology, Human Values and Leisure*. New York: Abbingdon Press, 1971.

Klapp, Orrin E. *Collective Search for Identity*. New York: Holt, Rinehart and Winston, Inc., 1969.

Knapp, R. R. *The Measurement of Self-Actualization and Its Theoretical Implications*. San Diego, Calif.: Educational Testing Service, 1971.

Kozol, Jonathan. *Free Schools*. Boston: Houghton Mifflin Company, 1972.

Lancy, David F., and Tindall, B. Allan. (eds.) *The Anthropological Study of Play: Problems and Prospects*. Cornwall, N.Y.: Leisure Press, 1976.

Lindner, Staffan Burenstam. *The Harried Leisure Class*. New York: Columbia University Press, 1970.

Maltz, Maxwell. *Psycho-Cybernetics*. Englewood Cliffs, N.J.: Prentice-Hall, Inc., 1960.

Maslow, Abraham H. "Defense and Growth." In *The Psychology of Open Teaching and Learning*, edited by Melvin L. Silberman, Jerome S. Allender and Jay Yanoff. Boston: Little, Brown and Company, 1972.

Maslow, Abraham H. *Motivation and Personality*. New York: Harper and Row, 1954.

McClain, E. W., and Andrews, H. B. "Some Personality Correlates of Peak Experiences—a Study in Self-Actualization." *Journal of Clinical Psychology* 25 (1969): 36-38.

Meyer, Harold D.; Brightbill, Charles K.; and Sessoms, H. Douglas. *Community Recreation*. Englewood Cliffs, N.J.: Prentice-Hall, Inc., 1969.

Maul, Terry L. "An Investigation of the Relationship Between Self-Actualization and Creative Thinking Processes." Unpublished doctoral dissertation, University of California at Berkeley, 1970.

Moore, James. "The Relationship Between Leisure Attitudes and Self-Actualization." Unpublished doctoral dissertation, Oregon State University, 1974.

Murphy, James F. *Recreation and Leisure Service: A Humanistic Perspective.* Dubuque, Ia.: Wm. C. Brown Company Publishers, 1975.

Murphy, James F.; Williams, John G.; Neipoth, E. William; and Brown, Paul D. *Leisure Service Delivery System: A Modern Perspective.* Philadelphia: Lea & Febiger, 1973.

Neulinger, John. *The Psychology of Leisure.* Springfield, Ill.: Charles C. Thomas, Publisher, 1974.

Neulinger, John. "Leisure and Mental Health." *Pacific Sociological Review* 14 (1971): 288-300.

Parker, Stanley. *The Future of Work and Leisure.* New York: Praeger Publishers, 1971.

Piers, Maria W. (ed.) *Play and Development.* New York: W. W. Norton & Company, Inc., 1972.

Sapora, Allen V., and Mitchell, Elmer D. *The Theory of Play and Recreation.* New York: Ronald Press, 1961.

Sears, Pauline S. *In Pursuit of Self-Esteem.* Belmont, Calif.: Wadsworth Publishing Company, 1964.

Staley, Edwin J., and Miller, Norman P. (eds.) *Leisure and the Quality of Life.* Washington, D.C.: American Association for Health, Physical Education and Recreation, 1972.

Goals and Objectives

Objectives After reading and comprehending this chapter, you should be able to:

1. State the difference between goals and objectives.
2. State the concepts central to the psychomotor, cognitive, and affective domains.
3. Write complete psychomotor, cognitive, and affective objectives.
4. Explain the relationship between statements of objectives and the process of evaluating programs.

Introduction

Virtually all agencies and groups providing leisure service programs operate on the assumption that participants will have an enjoyable experience and will benefit socially and emotionally from their involvement. Most of the time, however, the actual evaluation of a program is based on the number of participants and subjective assessments of program quality. Although subjective perceptions are highly valuable and are frequently accurate, from a professional standpoint, subjectivity alone leaves many questions unanswered. Participants may turn out for programs in large numbers and seem to be enjoying the experience, but does the practitioner actually know if there are carry-over effects to other areas of the participants' lives? Does the evaluator know the extent to which healthy values are being adopted or the extent to which the recreation experience is being attained? To answer questions such as these, it is necessary to begin with carefully formulated goals and objectives.

It is the integration of the practitioner's professional philosophy of leisure and basic assumptions about human nature, which provide the foundation for establishing the goals and objectives that shape the delivery of leisure services. Failure to develop clear goals and objectives prevents one from knowing where one is going, or if and when one has arrived, since a destination has not been charted.

Defining Goals and Objectives

Although goals and objectives are often used interchangeably, we will make several important distinctions between these terms and clarify the role of each from an agency perspective. By separating functions inherent in each term, semantic complications will be avoided thereby enhancing communication among persons involved in the development of goals and objectives in the leisure service field.

Goals

Once agency personnel have a clear understanding of their leisure philosophy, goals can be formulated which reflect that philosophy. Similarly to Murphy and his associates (1973), we have defined a goal as follows:

A goal is a statement of *intent* which is very broadly expressed, and is probably immeasurable, very similar to an ideal. A goal is timeless, expressing a desired outcome, but one which may actually not be possible to achieve, at least in the short run. It represents a long-range challenge for society which embodies a vision for the future, a better way of life, a way of looking to what may be presently theoretical, but which may someday be possible to attain even by another generation yet to come.

In formulating goals, philosophical biases immediately emerge. A behaviorist, for example, may have very different points of focus if Skinner's (1972) model is adopted compared to an individual advocating Maslow's (1968) assumptions. Or, an administrator who feels that participation in recreation activities is an end in itself may emphasize different goals than a counterpart who views participation as a tool or a vehicle for other things, apart from one's enjoyment in an activity itself.

Since an increasing number of leisure service professionals have adopted a highly humanistic set of values (Murphy and Howard, 1977), it is from that perspective that we will focus. Within that framework, simplified goals might be expressed as follows:

1. Equal opportunities in recreation will be provided for all.
2. Recreation will enhance character development.
3. Recreation will develop a sound body and mind.
4. Recreation will enhance one's appreciation of the arts.
5. Recreation will reduce racial and cultural barriers.
6. Recreation will develop self-actualizing citizens.

These statements are quite broad, and in reality are probably unattainable for all. As stated, there is little likelihood that they can even be evaluated. There are, however, a number of advantages to formulating these and other goals. First, the public is made aware of the overall values and basic philosophy of the agency. This can give people a strong sense of common identity with the agency when goals are adopted which

Chapter 2

reflect values similar to their own. Second, goals provide direction to agency staff members. By being aware of agency goals, they are reminded of potential outcomes and the fact that all service efforts should move toward the theoretical attainment of these outcomes. Third, goals serve as a powerful public relations tool. Statements of goals can be used to enhance the identity of the agency in the public eye, thereby generating enthusiasm and excitement in the community which may, in turn, strengthen the potential for continued or increased agency financial, political, and social support. Finally, agencies which have developed sound goals will be in a position to move into the next phase of the delivery of leisure services: the development of program objectives which support their expressed goals.

Objectives

Unlike goals, objectives are statements of intent which are tangible, attainable outcomes. They are specific in nature, measurable, and restricted by time limits. Objectives should be consistent with goals; that is, the attainment of objectives should contribute to the ideal of achieving goals.

Objectives which are specific, measurable, and expected to be attained within a predetermined time period give clear direction to the leisure service practitioner. In fact, the success of a given program then rests upon the attainment of those objectives. Programs cannot be said to be successful according to any type of objective criteria *unless* objectives are specified, evaluated, and attained.

The challenge, then, is to develop objectives which are consistent with established goals and which are clearly measurable. Unless behavioral objectives are developed, the ultimate assessment of these objectives will be extremely difficult. It is at the time that behavioral objectives are developed that agencies must determine their approach to meeting objectives and the manner in which services will contribute to desired outcomes.

It is not only essential to carefully develop program objectives but it is of equal importance for objectives to be properly stated and evaluated. Too often objectives are stated in a manner which is broad, vague, or even immeasurable. It is also not unusual for objectives to be formulated and then totally ignored once the program is initiated. Objectives are only as valuable as the manner in which desired outcomes are expressed and the extent to which they are then evaluated either during or at the conclusion of a given program.

The Formulation of Behavioral Objectives

The initial wording of objectives must be carefully considered if the objective is to conform to the specified criteria. Mager (1962, p. 11) has offered suggestions for selecting certain phrases while avoiding others.[1]

Words Open to Many Interpretations	Words Open to Fewer Interpretations
to know	to write
to understand	to recite
to appreciate	to identify
to *really* appreciate	to differentiate
to *fully* appreciate	to solve
to grasp the significance of	to construct
to enjoy	to list
to believe	to compare
to have faith in	to contrast

Mager also summarized criteria which should always be applied when formulating objectives. Whenever possible, it is desirable to incorporate each element of the criteria for objective writing since a completely stated behavioral objective automatically solves the problem of how it is to be evaluated. All too frequently, this is not done. In many instances, the desired outcome may be stated but the conditions and parameters are often omitted and the question arises, "Now that the objective has been stated, how will it now be assessed?"

To avoid this problem, objectives should be carefully written, ideally including each of the following elements (Mager, 1962, p. 53):

1. A statement of . . . . objectives is a collection of words or symbols describing . . . . your intents.
2. An objective will communicate your intent to the degree you have described what the (participant) will be DOING when demonstrating his achievement and how you will know when he is doing it.
3. To describe terminal behavior (what the [participant] will be doing):
   a. Identify and name the overall behavior act.
   b. Define the important conditions under which the behavior is to occur (givens or restrictions, or both).
   c. Define the criterion for acceptable performance.
4. Write a separate statement for each objective; the more statements you have, the better chance you have of making clear your intent.

By initially formulating concrete, behaviorally based phrases, it becomes clear what is expected of the individual about whom the objective relates, and the evaluation process is influenced accordingly. By including the conditions under which the performance will take place, the level of accomplishment, the evidence of the accomplishment, and

1. *Preparing Instructional Objectives,* Second Ed. by Robert F. Mager. Copyright 1962 by Fearon Publishers, Inc. Reprinted by permission of Fearon-Pitman Publishers, Inc.

the time in which the accomplishment must take place, the direction of the evaluation process has been determined.

The following exemplifies the difference between a well written and a poorly written objective related to beginners learning the game of chess.

Weak:

The objective of the program is
1. to familiarize all participants with the game of chess.
2. to teach participants the game of chess.

Strong:

1. At the conclusion of a three-week program introducing the game of chess, each participant will *show* the correct movement of pieces *as evidenced by* his or her ability to *play a complete game* with the instructor *without violating the rules* governing the movement of pieces.
2. At the end of the first week of a program introducing the game of chess, each participant will *demonstrate* the concept of checkmating the other player *as evidenced by* attaining a score of at least *80 percent* on a *written test* which presents ten graphic chess problems requiring that black checkmate white in one move.

The weakly written objectives raise many questions since they are quite vague. At what point is one "familiarized" with the game? At what point has one "been taught" the game? What standards have been specified? How will the objectives be assessed? What skill level is expected by what point in time?

The failure to consider these and other points at the time of formulating the objectives leaves the programmer with many considerations yet to be resolved. In addition, anyone reading such "objectives" will gain little or no insight into the actual expected outcomes of the program. In cases where program funding is dependent upon ascertaining approval from a board or political body, this is clearly undesirable. Thus, to increase communication and insight into the *specific* expectations of a given program, the vagueness of the first two statements should be avoided.

The second pair of objectives leaves little room for misunderstanding. Specific directions and expectations have been included for the program leader who is responsible for providing the direct leadership or for administrators/supervisors who may be responsible for evaluating program effects. By incorporating the elements central to writing sound behavioral objectives, agency personnel will not only know their destination but will also know if and when they have arrived.

Bloom (1956a) has categorized objectives into three areas which have distinct characteristics of their own, but are not always mutually exclusive. The three areas or domains are: (1) cognitive domain, (2) affective domain, and (3) psychomotor domain. Although focusing primarily on educational objectives, Bloom's discussion is of considerable importance to the leisure service practitioner, and the concepts are easily transferable.

Psychomotor Domain

The psychomotor domain incorporates elements related to physical movement and motor skills. In leisure services, it would include physical skills such as running, jumping, and throwing.

Specifically, psychomotor elements might center around how far participants can run or swim in a given time period, how far a ball can be thrown, how accurately an archer can perform, or how effectively a tennis ball can be served. The list is virtually endless, but in most cases objectives would be directed toward increasing physical skills believed to improve performance in specific recreation activities. Examples of psychomotor objectives incorporating Bloom's criteria for writing behavioral objectives include the following:

1. Within three weeks, each participant in a community basketball program for elementary school children will be able to dribble a basketball the length of the court in ten seconds without double dribbling or palming the ball (as judged by the program director).
2. At the completion of a six-week swimming program, each participant will have reduced his or her pre-program time in the 100-meter free-style swim by at least 15 percent.
3. At the completion of a six-week period, each participant in the teen center bicycling program will complete a 30-mile cycling trip in one day without experiencing health difficulties.
4. By the end of the first week of a youth tumbling program, each participant will be able to correctly execute a forward roll, (as judged by the program leader).

In each case, the desired behavior, time parameters, quality of execution, and method of judging are clearly implicit. The extent to which objectives were, or were not reached, will be self-evident assuming a high confidence level in those judging behavior in instances where behavior must be assessed by a qualified individual.

Traditionally, those involved in leisure services and physical education have tended to emphasize objectives centering around the psychomotor domain since changes in physical capabilities are relatively easy to determine. The importance of assessing psychomotor advancements is important, of course, and should be continued. There is a growing need, however, to expand efforts in the cognitive and, more importantly in leisure services, in the affective domain; therefore, since these areas have generally not received the attention they deserve, they will be explored more fully in our discussion.

Cognitive Domain

The cognitive domain specifically relates to mental processes which include: (1) awareness, (2) knowledge, (3) comprehension, (4) application, (5) analysis, (6) synthesis, and (7) evaluation. (Bloom, 1956) These elements depicted in figure 2.1, form a taxonomy or a hierarchy in which steps must be reached sequentially.

To *synthesize* information, there must first be awareness, knowledge, comprehension, and the ability to apply and analyze the material. To have *knowledge* of material, there must first be awareness, and so forth. Understanding the progressive relationship between these terms, and the

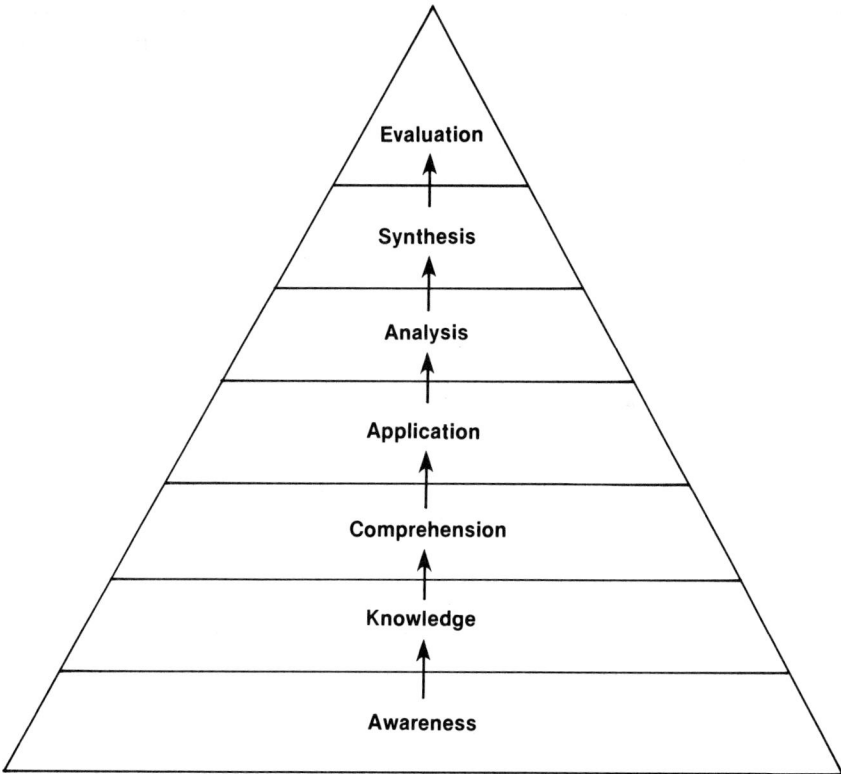

Figure 2.1 (Adapted from TAXONOMY OF EDUCATIONAL OBJECTIVES: THE CLASSIFICATION OF EDUCATIONAL GOALS: HANDBOOK I: COGNITIVE DOMAIN, by Benjamin S. Bloom, et al. Copyright © 1956 by Longman Inc. Previously published by David McKay Company, Inc. Reprinted by permission of Longman Inc.)

steps necessary for reaching each level can be quite helpful to the practitioner facing the task of formulating objectives. Specifically, the desired level to be achieved can be established in advance by considering such factors as the degree of difficulty involved in mastering each level, the nature of the population being served, the number of available resources, the time available for conducting the program, and so forth.

Cognitive objectives may be important in a number of ways. For example, a recreation specialist may be involved with children experiencing learning disabilities who have never been exposed to a certain craft activity such as leatherwork, an activity believed to have therapeutic value for the participants. Prior to actually beginning the leatherwork program, participants must begin the cognitive process by becoming *aware* of the fact that leather can be worked in such a way that a product emerges. They must then develop a *knowledge* and *comprehension* to the extent that tools, leather and a product are connected so that in the *application* phase, materials are used properly. Thus, the recreation therapist can develop objectives which will hopefully allow the participant to be able to create his or her own leathercraft. Accordingly, the following objective might be formulated:

By the end of a three-week program in leatherwork, each participant will have made a zipper-opening leather change purse capable of properly holding coins (as judged by the program leader).

The objective is admirable, but in itself may be too advanced for the group in our example. It may be necessary to utilize **intermediate objectives** which might be as follows:

1. At the end of the first two hours of the leatherwork program, each participant will demonstrate the use of three leatherwork tools without sustaining injury. (This includes awareness, knowledge, and moderate comprehension.)
2. At the end of one week of involvement in the program, each participant will be able to demonstrate the proper use of at least 6 out of 10 leatherwork tools as evidenced by properly selecting the correct tool required to make a piece of leather conform to the shape depicted in a photograph. (This includes awareness, knowledge, comprehension, and rudimentary application of the use of tools in relation to leather.)
3. By the end of the third leatherwork session, each participant will be capable of selecting the proper leather pieces and tools necessary to complete a selected craft. (This includes awareness, knowledge, comprehension, application, analysis.)
4. At the end of the leatherwork program, each participant will complete a leatherwork project (conforming to standards established in

advance by the program staff) without requiring the cognitive assistance of the staff. In addition, each participant will be able to assess the extent to which his or her project conformed to the standards set by the staff. (This includes awareness, knowledge, comprehension, application, analysis, synthesis, and evaluation.)

5. Each participant will retain a basic knowledge of leatherwork by completing three additional leatherwork projects on his or her own during the six months following the completion of the program. (This assesses the permanency of change.)

What has been demonstrated is an approach utilizing *progressive objectives* designed to lead the participant to a point of independence in terms of being capable of effectively utilizing leatherwork materials and tools. Progressive steps may be necessary for the participant to move from having little or no awareness of the activity to a point of familiarity and ability which enables him or her to satisfactorily perform the activity. The use of progressive objectives permits participants to gradually develop cognitive skills to the point that they can fully conceptualize and evaluate the nature of the activity and final product. At the same time, progressive objectives provide check-points to insure that participants have mastered each level before continuing on to the next.

Our examples of cognitive objectives have adhered to the criteria for developing behavioral objectives. This allows them to be readily evaluated by performing tasks which are observable by qualified evaluators.

Written tests may also be administered requiring that the participant attain a specified score for the objective to be met. The expectation should vary depending upon the participants, importance of the knowledge to be gained, and so forth. Since a written test is often impractical or undesirable to administer, it may be preferable to develop criteria for assessing accomplishments through observation. This often requires careful planning in advance to insure that the criteria are applied objectively and consistently. This will be discussed more fully when evaluation concepts are presented and considered.

Affective Domain

The affective domain focuses upon psychological aspects of the individual which include their feelings, attitudes, and values. Krathwohl (1956) has formulated a taxonomy of the affective domain which consists of the following components in hierarchal form: *receiving, responding, valuing, organization,* and *characterization* (Figure 2-2).

To clarify the steps involved in the affective process, let us again refer to the leatherwork program mentioned earlier and assume that the children in the program have never been exposed to any recreation activity of this nature. Thus, they hold no particular feeling related to crafts.

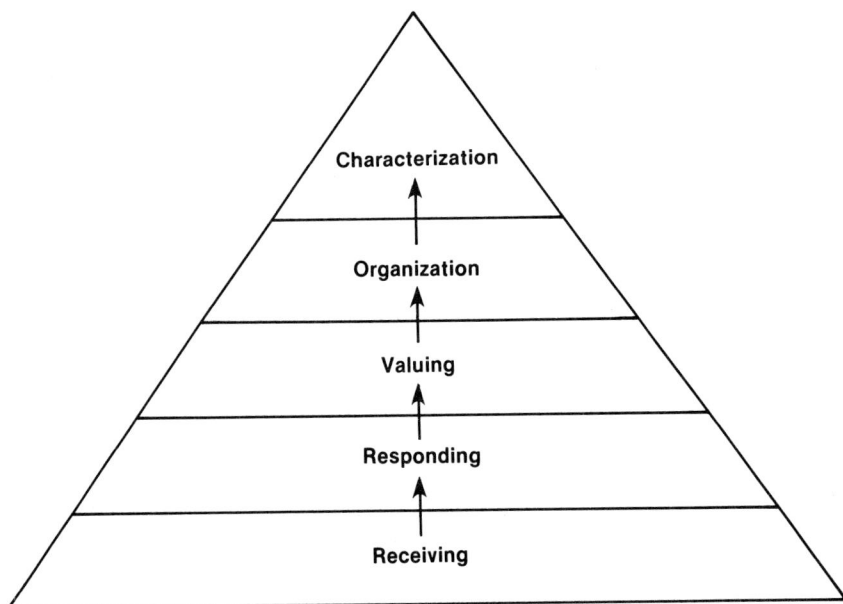

Figure 2.2 (Adapted from TAXONOMY OF EDUCATIONAL OBJECTIVES: THE CLASSIFICATION OF EDUCATIONAL GOALS: HANDBOOK 2: AFFECTIVE DOMAIN, by David R. Krathwohl, et al. Copyright © 1964 by Longman Inc. Reprinted by permission of Longman Inc.)

Hypothetically, in other words, since there is no awareness, attitudes related to the value of crafts have not been formed.

The first step in the process must be to expose each child to the idea of the activity and for this to occur, the child must enter into the *receiving* level; that is, he or she must first receive information about leatherwork. Values are not yet affected at this level, however. The second phase requires the children to *respond* to the information by asking questions, watching curiously in anticipation of more information, and so forth. At this point, an attitude or feeling is beginning to develop. (The point of crossover from receiving to responding is vague, of course, and the precise transition point is not important.) As interest grows, the child may begin to *value* the activity and what it potentially offers. Interest grows if enjoyment is gained from involvement in projects, talking with others about the program, and reading about other crafts. If the activity takes on exceptional importance to the child, that is, he or she becomes fully committed to the activity and a belief in the value of that activity, he or she may try to involve others in the same activity. In other words, the commitment is so strong that there is a desire to bring others into the experience. At this point, the child has evolved to the *organization level* of the taxonomy and has formed attitudes and feelings which are unlikely to change. (This process does not necessarily occur immediately or over a short period of time. It may well extend over many years as is the case when an individual becomes dedicated to a hobby over a lifetime.) Finally, the *characterization level* (usually after adult maturity is reached) occurs when the value or attitude has become an essential component of the individual's life philosophy and that life philosophy has stabilized.

The above example has carried the child completely through a lifetime which, of course, is beyond the scope of most leisure service practitioners. The elements of the taxonomy which are of the greatest concern to the recreator are *receiving, responding,* and *valuing.*

Recreators must be as concerned with the affective domain in the delivery of leisure services, as the cognitive—probably more so since so many of the expressed benefits of recreation and leisure revolve around feelings and attitudes central to the concept of a recreation experience. In other words, it is the affective domain which relates primarily to the recreation experience (*feelings* of well-being, *state* of *inner-*satisfaction, *emotional* condition).

Because the affective domain centers around intangible aspects of the individual (as opposed to concrete components indicating knowledge, in the cognitive domain), it may be more difficult to formulate affective objectives which are measurable. But if the leisure service professional continues to place psychological rewards at the top of the list of benefits derived from recreation, affective objectives must be formulated, put into action, and evaluated to clearly determine program outcomes and quality.

The leatherwork program involving handicapped children can again be used to exemplify how the process of formulating carefully stated affective objectives might be approached. Let us assume that the agency staff members believe that leatherwork can offer a positive experience for the children who participate. More specifically, they believe that the experience can (1) enhance the self-image of participants if they are successful in mastering leatherwork tasks and (2) help to reduce feelings of aggressiveness among the participants. Behavioral objectives might be developed as follows:

1. The participant will experience an increase in feelings of self-worth as a result of his or her involvement in the leatherwork program as evidenced by a favorable change of at least ten percent in pre-and post-test scores on a semantic differential scale (measuring self-image.)

2. There will be a reduction in aggressive feelings experienced by program participants as evidenced by fewer incidents of aggressive behavior, observed by staff members, among program participants

compared to non-program participants during the six-week program period.

In both cases, objectives relating to the affective domain have been approached indirectly since measurement attempts relate to internal aspects of the individual. A written test has been selected in the first instance to obtain an indication of changes in self-image among participants. Very briefly stated, the objective can be evaluated by testing both participants and non-participants prior to the commencement of the leatherwork program and then again at the conclusion of the program. In the example, a semantic differential scale capable of measuring self-image was selected as one of the many types of measures of personal well-being. This scale and others will be discussed more fully in a later chapter.

If the objectives were met, one indicator would be a positive change in self-image scores among program participants and little or no change in scores among those who were not involved in the program. This would imply that the program itself influenced the change, if other factors can be shown to have had no influence. Great care must be taken in ruling out other factors, as will be shown later, but if the proper techniques are utilized to compare the two groups, an indirect measure of self-image can be obtained.

In the second example, which focuses upon aggression, a group of non-participants has also been utilized to provide a standard for comparison. If staff members involved with both groups record all aggressive incidents which occur in their respective groups throughout the duration of the program period, the groups can be compared. One indicator of a reduction of aggressive *feelings* experienced by program participants is a reduction of aggressive *behaviors,* particularly in relation to what would have occurred had they not participated in the leatherwork program. Those who were not involved in the program provide a standard representing the aggressive behavior level which would have existed for the leatherwork participants had they not been involved in the program.

There are many aspects of the affective domain which are of importance to the leisure services practitioner. The following list is far from complete, but suggests a variety of areas which are in need of further exploration:

1. A change in self-image
2. A reduction of aggressive feelings
3. An increased capacity for close contact with others
4. Less need for power and toughness
5. Less feelings of tension and anxiety
6. An increase in self-confidence in front of others
7. A reduction or elimination of racist feelings

8. An increase in respecting and understanding others
9. Feeling a sense of achievement and accomplishment when completing specific tasks
10. Feeling a sense of unison and companionship among fellow group members
11. Feeling a sense of exhilaration similar to feelings associated with peak experiences
12. Feeling cared for and appreciated by others
13. Feeling confident in one's ability to attempt tasks without fear of failure

Invariably these types of desires, all related to the affective domain, are verbalized by leisure service practitioners in one form or another. Because it may be difficult to assess specific results, very little is actually done beyond merely articulating statements of (hoped for) intent. If careful thought is given to each objective area, however, outcomes *can* be assessed, particularly if the *evidence* of desired outcomes is identified and incorporated into the objective according to the criteria previously presented. When the evidence of the desired behavior is stated in the objective itself, the evaluation process should be self-evident.

The desired outcome and standard of performance will vary from one situation to the next, but indicators which might follow the statement ". . . . as evidenced by . . . ." in an objective include:

1 . . . . changes in test score results on pre- and post-test scores of the _____ scale.
2 . . . . an increase in the number of times participants voluntarily share materials with each other (as observed by staff members).
3 . . . . a decrease in the number of arguments which take place between players (of a given sport) and officials.
4 . . . . the extent to which participants voluntarily choose to play with peers of a different race.

If such statements are included in the objective itself, the evidence of the expected outcome becomes clear to those who will evaluate program effects. The only task remaining is determining the method to be used to assess the outcome; that is, selecting the specific test to measure self-image, identifying the staff members who will observe and record the behavior under consideration, or formulating the survey (questionnaire) to be administered at the conclusion of a program.

To repeat, components of the affective domain are frequently difficult to assess but represent an essential area of focus in the leisure field. With this in mind, the discussion which will focus on program evaluation will pay particular attention to identifying psychological measures which can be used by leisure service practitioners for measuring components of the affective domain.

Integrating Domains

We initially stated that the psychomotor, cognitive, and affective domains are not mutually exclusive; rather, they are generally closely interrelated. In our leatherwork program we saw how objectives might be formulated assessing each of the three areas. Although each area was discussed separately, involvement in one domain frequently produces change in the others.

The development of new skills in the game of badminton, for example, may initially be related to obvious psychomotor changes. But the increase in psychomotor ability may not occur without cognitive change as well. In other words, increasing one's skill in badminton may be contingent upon *learning* new body positions when completing a stroke, *learning* how to alter one's grip when executing a backhand stroke, or *knowing* how to position oneself when waiting for the return. The combination of learning proper techniques and increasing one's ability to execute a newly learned skill may lead to a subsequent change in attitude. A classic example of such a change takes place if one realizes that badminton is far from being a "simple backyard game" easily played by anyone; instead, it is an activity which can be physically demanding and played at extremely high skill levels. Motivation will be an important factor influencing the level at which one wishes to play. In our badminton example, each of the three domains has been affected—new knowledge was acquired, physical skills were increased, and an altered way of viewing the activity evolved.

Many times, each domain will be influenced through involvement in leisure service programs. However, evaluation measures should not be consolidated. Objectives should be formulated which are separately directed toward each domain and evaluated on an individual basis. It is through the process of individually evaluating components of each domain that multiple effects of a given program will be identified. In the long run, separating each area and using many different objectives within each area will clarify the specific points of concern for the practitioner involved in the program and greatly simplify the evaluation process.

Additional Areas for Developing Objectives

Although the psychomotor, cognitive, and affective domains are the most frequently discussed facets of developing objectives, the leisure service practitioner has other concerns. Accordingly, two additional points of focus will be considered: (1.) institutional objectives and (2.) community impact objectives.

Institutional Objectives

The leisure service agency must fill many of its own needs before it is able to reach optimum effectiveness. It must, for example, have adequate staff, materials, areas and facilities, financial support, and so forth. Deficit areas may limit services considerably depending upon the severity of the shortcoming.

If problem areas are identified, agency administrators may wish to express solutions to problems in the form of specific objectives. For example, a community of 50,000 population may have only one park in the central area of the city. If it becomes apparent to the municipal park and recreation administrators that several peripheral parks are needed to effectively meet park-related needs of citizens in the outlying areas, the acquisition of new parks may become an objective of the agency. The objective might be expressed in the following manner:

Within five years, three new park areas will be developed, one each in the Greenwood, Fernwood, and Pinewood areas of the city; each park will meet the specifications suggested by the National Recreation and Park Association in terms of proper acreage, facilities, multiple-use standards, (and so forth).

It may be necessary, of course, to develop sequential objectives since achieving the entire objective all at once would be quite an ambitious undertaking for most communities. Intermediate objectives might be formulated which involve: (1) acquiring the land for each park at different time points over the five-year period; (2) developing each park separately, in a predetermined order; or (3) developing all three parks simultaneously, but in stages over an extended period of time.

There are many other situations which could warrant the development of objectives. A few examples would include the addition of new staff or programs, purchasing new equipment, passing a bond for a new area or facility, or decentralizing services, such as in a store-front operation.

If needs are carefully identified, and if objectives are then developed, the direction for meeting objectives will be clarified and priorities can more easily be identified. The process is similar to the system of Management By Objectives, advanced by Odiorne (1965), or the PERT (Program Evaluation Reviewing Technique) format, discussed by Williams (1972).

Unlike the domains discussed in the previous section, the wording of objectives is relatively simple. The basic ingredients of an agency objective include the outcome desired and the time in which the objective should be reached. Depending upon the nature of the agency's need, the means for achieving the objective might or might not be specified. If a new community center is needed in a town or city, the objective might be expressed in one of at least two ways:

1. By the end of the next fiscal year, the municipal park and recreation department will have a new community center under its operation.
2. By the end of the next fiscal year, the citizens of the city will have passed a municipal bond for the purpose of building a new community center to be operated by the municipal park and recreation department.

The objective expressed in the first manner specifies the desired outcome and is the first step in the process. The second objective is preferable if agency personnel are at a point at which the method can be expressed. In all likelihood, the agency would begin with objective one, explore various means by which the objective might be achieved, and evolve to objective two after considerable exploration of various alternatives. The important point is that agencies should think in terms of formulating objectives to meet their own needs, and the evaluation of agency effectiveness should be partially in terms of the extent to which its own objectives are realized.

Community Impact Objectives

Community impact objectives may center around a wide variety of community concerns. They could be directed toward reducing vandalism, crime or delinquency; increasing citizen involvement in community affairs; reducing the number of fires in a forest area; increasing the beauty of an area by reducing the amount of litter left behind by people; or decreasing the number of racial incidents in an area. Community impact objectives address social issues rather than agency-support concerns. They differ from the psychomotor, cognitive, or affective domains by focusing on the result of behavior on community life.

For example, vandalism may be a problem at a youth center in the downtown area. Those responsible for the center may wish to begin a new program designed to instill community pride in the center. The objective is to reduce vandalism costs to the city. Although individual attitudes will have been influenced if the program is successful, thereby categorizing the objective in the affective domain, the principal point of emphasis is on community life rather than on each individual. Outcomes will be assessed in dollars and cents rather than changes in attitudes among the participants. If the objective is to be reached, affective changes will have occurred. But the affective changes will only be indirectly evident, reflected in the extent to which the pattern of vandalism was actually altered.

Attempts to reduce vandalism could follow many lines: new lighting could be installed, police security could be tightened, or additional staff could be hired. In each case, it will be the amount of vandalism that is assessed, regardless of why any change occurred.

Objectives might also be used in combination. For example, in a program for teenagers, objectives might be developed which focus upon enhancing the self-image of the participants (affective domain) as well as reducing incidents of vandalism in the area of the community in which the youths reside (community impact objective). It could be hypothesized that anti-social behavior stems in part from how one feels about oneself; positive changes in self-image would therefore produce constructive changes in behavior.

Either objective could be developed independently or simultaneously with the other. Each provides a special area of focus and would be evaluated separately. A shortcoming of community impact objectives is that the reasons for changes must be inferred. But if a new program is developed, and comparisons are made between those who are involved and those who are not, a carefully controlled study can point strongly to the idea that it was involvement in the leisure service program which produced the environment for change. Ideally, community impact objectives will be used in conjunction with affective objectives so that many of the whys leading to change will be clarified and more fully understood.

Summary

Formulating carefully stated goals and objectives is a critical phase of the leisure service system. Goals and objectives represent the bridge between the philosophical foundation of the agency and the means by which ideals are realized, the programs themselves.

A distinction should be made between the terms *goal* and *objective.* A *goal* tends to be a timeless, broadly stated, visionary ideal. It may be abstract, probably not easily measured, and is a highly valuable vehicle for conveying the philosophy and ideals of the agency. Goals can set the mood of the staff by framing the key concerns of the agency. They also may serve as a highly effective public relations tool.

An *objective,* unlike a goal, is quite specific, measurable, and expected to be attained within a specified time period. An objective clarifies exactly what is expected of the participant. It delineates not only what is expected, but also the level of proficiency which is expected if the objective is to be fully reached.

Since situations and people vary considerably, intermediate objectives may be used, forming steps leading toward a final objective. Each intermediate objective should be carefully evaluated to insure it has been attained before continuing to the next level.

Objectives generally fall into one of three domains: (1) *psychomotor,* which focuses on the physical capabilities and improvements of the participant; (2) *cognitive,* which centers chiefly around thinking and knowledge skills; and (3) *affective*, which examines psychological dimensions in people such as their feelings, attitudes and values. Objectives related to each area should be separately stated, so that changes which occur can be distinctly identified.

Two additional areas were suggested that are important to the leisure service practitioner: (1) *institutional objectives* in which expectations of filling agency needs are expressed, and (2) *community impact objectives*, which state the manner in which programs are expected to affect community variables, such as vandalism, juvenile delinquency, and inter-group harmony and cooperation. Neither of these two categories quite conforms to the first three more commonly used domains but are important to the leisure service agency.

If agency personnel fail to develop sound behavioral objectives, express them weakly, or ignore them once they have been stated, there is little likelihood that the effects of programs will be identified. This means that no matter how beneficial recreation services are *claimed* to be, assessments of effectiveness will remain speculative at best. If leisure services are to effectively meet human needs, and if the leisure services practitioner wishes to serve the community in a professional rather than haphazard manner, the development of carefully stated objectives must be an integral part of program planning. The alternative is to offer programs on a cafeteria style basis, which, if used alone, may prevent the essence of the recreation experience from fully emerging.

Study Questions

1. How are goals and objectives different? What is the practical value of each?
2. How do psychomotor, cognitive, and affective domains differ from one another?
3. What steps are involved in (1) gaining knowledge (cognitive skills) and (2) developing attitudes (affective domain)?
4. What are the criteria necessary to write a complete behavioral objective?
5. How would a completely stated objective be written relating to the (1) psychomotor, (2) cognitive, and (3) affective domains?
6. What are intermediate objectives and how are they used?
7. What are agency objectives and why are they important?
8. What are community impact objectives and why are they important?
9. How might affective and community impact objectives be used simultaneously within the same program? Must they be used together?
10. How would one write a complete (1) agency objective and (2) community impact objective?

References

Bloom, Benjamin S., et al. *Taxonomy of Educational Objectives: Cognitive Domain.* New York: David McKay Company, Inc., 1956.

Krathwohl, David R., et al. *Taxonomy of Educational Objectives: Affective Domain.* New York: Longman, Inc., 1956.

Mager, Robert F. *Preparing Instructional Objectives.* Palo Alto, Calif.: Fearon Publishers, 1962.

Maslow, Abraham H. *Toward A Psychology of Being.* New York: D. Van Nostrand Company, 1968.

Murphy, James F., and Howard, Dennis R. *Delivery of Community Leisure Services: An Holistic Approach.* Philadelphia: Lea & Febiger, 1977.

Odiorne, George S. *Management by Objectives: A System of Managerial Leadership.* New York: Pitman Publishing Corporation, 1965.

Skinner, B. F. *Beyond Freedom and Dignity.* New York: Alfred A. Knopf, 1972.

Williams, John G. "Try PERT for Meeting Deadlines." *Park Maintenance.* September (1972):10-12.

Murphy, James F.; Williams, John G.; Niepoth, E. William; and Brown, Paul D. *Leisure Service Delivery System: A Modern Perspective.* Philadelphia: Lea & Febiger, 1973.

Related Readings

American Association for Health, Physical Education, and Recreation. *Goals for American Recreation.* Washington, D.C.: American Association for Health, Physical Education, and Recreation, 1964.

Atkin, Myron J. "Behavioral Objectives in Curriculum Design: A Cautionary Note." *The Science Teacher* 35(1968): 27-30.

Bannon, Joseph J. *Leisure Resources: Its Comprehensive Planning.* Englewood Cliffs, N.J.: Prentice Hall, Inc., 1976.

Bannon, Joseph J. *Problem Solving in Recreation and Parks.* Englewood Cilffs, N.J.: Prentice Hall, Inc., 1972.

Benedict, Larry Gordon. *The Goals Gap in Education Evaluation, Identification and Development of Methodology.* Amherst: University of Massachusetts Press, 1973.

Berryman, Doris L. *Recommended Standards with Evaluative Criteria for Recreation Services in Residential Services in Residential Institutions.* New York: New York University School of Education, 1971.

Buhler, Charlotte (Malachowski). *The Course of Human Life: A Study of Goals in the Humanistic Perspective.* New York: Springer Publishing Co., 1968.

Berry, Brian S. L. and Jack Meltzer (eds.). *Goals for Urban America.* Englewood Cliffs, N.J.: Prentice-Hall, Inc., 1967.

Eisner, Elliot W. "Educational Objectives Help or Hindrance." *School Review* 75 (1967): 250-260.

Eiss, Albert F., and Harbeck, Mary B. *Behavioral Objectives in the Affective Domain.* Washington, D.C.: National Science Teachers Association, 1969.

Gold, Seymour M. "Goals That Count." *Parks & Recreation* January (1974): 38, 60-62.

Humble, John W. *How to Manage Objectives.* New York: AMACOM, 1973.

Humble, John W. *Management by Objectives in Action.* London: McGraw-Hill, 1970.

Kast, Fremont E., and Rosenzweig, James E. *Organization and Management: A Systems Approach.* New York: McGraw-Hill Book Co., 1974.

Mager, Robert F. *Preparing Instructional Objectives.* Belmont, Calif.: Fearon Publishers, Inc., 1975.

Mager, Robert F. *Goals Analysis.* Belmont, Calif.: Fearon Publishers, Inc., 1972.

Odiorne, George S. *Management Decisions by Objectives.* Englewood Cliffs, N.J.: Prentice-Hall, Inc., 1969.

Odiorne, George S. *Management by Objectives: A System of Managerial Leadership.* New York: Pitman Publishing Corporation, 1965.

Schaller, Lyle E. "The Pros and Cons of Goals and Expectations." *Mayor & Manager.* May-June (1969): 12-16.

White, Harry James. *Systems Analysis.* Philadelphia: W. B. Saunders, 1969.

Young, Stanley. *Management: A Systems Analysis.* Glenview, Ill.: Scott Foresman & Co., 1966.

Research and Evaluation

Objectives   After reading and comprehending this chapter, you should be able to:

1. State four purposes of research and evaluation in leisure services.
2. Describe characteristic limitations of social research relating to testing in the field, conducting attitudinal or behavioral research, and researcher biases.
3. Define and compare exploratory, descriptive, and experimental research procedures.
4. State the conditions under which causal relationships can and cannot be implied in research studies.
5. Explain the importance of control groups in the design of research studies.
6. Describe the basic purposes of four personality inventories and potential uses of each.
7. Describe the basic purposes of two attitudinal scales and potential uses of each.
8. Describe the observation method of evaluating leisure service programs and its basic strengths and weaknesses.
9. State the relative importance of evaluating leisure service programs.

Introduction

Program evaluation is considered to be one of the most important aspects of the leisure service delivery system. Although progress in developing effective evaluative research systems in leisure services has been slow, the need for improving such systems has been emphasized by a variety of writers (Kraus and Curtis, 1973; Bannon, 1976; and Murphy and Howard, 1977). One point appears certain—unless program effects are identified through the research process, the extent to which services are delivered in a professional manner, consistent with predetermined, desired outcomes, will remain unknown.

As we indicated earlier, one of the most common approaches to evaluating program effectiveness has been to identify the number of participants in a given program and to conclude that the most successful programs are those with the greatest participation. In many instances there will undoubtedly be a relationship between numbers of participants and program success; however, this is a quantitative indicator that does not explain the *effects* of a program in human terms.

For example, a community may establish two volleyball leagues which attract 100 participants in each league. On the surface, the leagues may be viewed as equally successful in terms of community involvement. But if one league is plagued by numerous forfeits, arguments with officials, and disputes among participants, and the other league experiences none of these problems, there are certainly differences in program effectiveness between the two leagues. Consequently, the participants in each league may be affected differently—the *quality* of their experience may be quite varied.

To determine if this has been the case, measures assessing the number of participants (quantitative) must be supplemented with measures in the affective domain (qualitative). Therefore, the majority of evaluative techniques which will be presented in this chapter will center around qualitative concerns. The purpose of such research is to attempt to accurately assess qualitative dimensions of human behavior and to express them in quantitative terms.

Before exploring quantitative and qualitative techniques in further detail, several purposes of the evaluation process should be considered. First, as we indicated earlier, it is the evaluation of programs which insures that services are being delivered in a professional manner, and helps identify areas in program design which are in need of revision.

Second, the evaluation should test objectives. If objectives are developed which can be measured, and they are individually assessed according to a predetermined system, the evaluation process will offer insights into the extent to which desired outcomes were or were not achieved.

Third, a better understanding of human nature can come through evaluative research. Answers to such questions as Why do people play? What human needs do leisure services meet? and What is the nature of the recreation experience? will probably remain speculative in the absence of carefully conducted evaluations and research projects.

Fourth, evaluations provide the practitioner with utilitarian data which can be presented to the public or to the legislative body responsible for budget approvals. If the benefits of leisure services can be identified through carefully conducted research, there may be a greater likelihood of receiving appropriate funding on a continuous basis.

There are, however, limitations to any social research endeavor and they must be carefully considered as one designs an evaluation project. Some of the more common pitfalls will be briefly presented.

Limitations of Social Research

Testing in the Field

No matter how desirable it may be to identify the effects of a given program, one must avoid the "human guinea pig" syndrome. There is a limit to what one should ask of people who are participating in a program for enjoyment during their free time. It would be unreasonable to expect a group of senior citizens, or anyone else for that matter, to complete a lengthy psychological inventory at the completion of a bingo night. It may well be quite helpful to know what type of person is attracted to bingo, but the risk of alienating the participants is great in this particular situation.

A more common example involves testing special populations. Since there is so much interest in such groups as the economically disadvantaged, racial minorities, and the handicapped, over-testing is not unusual. People who are repeatedly asked to be a part of test groups may resent this, feeling that they are being exploited rather than helped or served.

Testing in the field can also be difficult if there is simply no reasonable way to handle the logistics or mechanics necessary to administer a written instrument or to conduct a personal interview. There may be insufficient personnel available in the agency, potential respondents may be unwilling to relinquish their time while involved in a given activity, or they may feel that their attitudes and beliefs are no one else's business. Most importantly, perhaps, they may be so involved in what they are doing that it would be highly inappropriate to interrupt. Needless to say, such an interruption would detract from the intent and effectiveness of the program.

Many of these problems can be avoided, of course, by anticipating them in advance. Care can be taken to select times for personal contact which do not overly inconvenience those involved in a given program.

For example, people are often waiting their turn to participate or are resting in between activities and would not object to offering their input at those times. The purpose of the research project can be explained in such a way that people are more than willing to contribute. In particularly lengthy test or interview situations, contact with people can be made in advance so they will be able to arrange to participate at their own convenience. Proper planning and considerable finesse will go a long way toward increasing the likelihood of satisfactory results.

Researcher Bias

In most types of research, the researcher has certain hopes and expectations which are being tested. The leisure service practitioner, for example, would hope that program participants would show evidence of having benefited from involvement in the program. Unless careful controls are developed, the results can be either intentionally or inadvertantly slanted to insure a favorable outcome. Since this problem is so difficult to avoid, program leaders and directors should probably not be involved in the evaluation of their own programs. If this cannot be avoided, the process should be carefully monitored throughout the study period, preferably by someone without a vested interest in the results of the evaluation.

Attitude vs. Behavior

There is considerable controversy surrounding the issue of whether or not social research should utilize surveys and questionnaires to assess attitudes and values, or whether human behavior should be studied by observation and by talking to people (Deutscher, 1973). For example, LaPiere (1934-1935) severely criticized the use of surveys and attitude scales more than forty years ago and is still cited by contemporary writers (Deutscher, 1973, p. 21):

The questionnaire is cheap, easy, and mechanical. The study of human behavior is time consuming, intellectually fatiguing, and depends for its success upon the ability of the investigator. The former method gives quantitative results, the latter mainly qualitative. Quantitative measurements are quantitatively accurate; qualitative evaluations are always subject to the errors of human judgment. Yet it would seem far more worthwhile to make a shrewd guess regarding that which is essential than to accurately measure that which is likely to prove quite irrelevant.

On the other hand, participant observation has certain serious problems associated with it as Becker and Geer (1957) have identified: (1) reliability is a problem since we are not certain that the observer has reported what was actually observed; (2) selective perception may create biases among observers; (3) some types of activity are not subject to public observation; and (4) the observer may, by his or her presence, alter the outcome of the activity.

Certainly both approaches have their merits and shortcomings. Different situations may call for changes in methods. Examples of both approaches will be suggested in this chapter so that depending upon the situation, type of knowledge desired, and style of the evaluator, an appropriate choice can be made.

Additional Considerations

There are many other problems the social scientist faces, too numerous for elaboration in this discussion. Statistical design, test reliability and validity, and data analysis represent but a few additional areas of difficulty which must be addressed. There is no question that well conducted research requires a high degree of skill and not all practitioners have developed the ability to undertake rigorous evaluative studies. This may intensify the need for strengthening relationships between those working in the field and those in the university and college communities. The more the practitioner is familiar with the evaluation process, the greater the likelihood that such relationships will develop and, most importantly, the more willing he or she will be to undertake such research either independently, or in partnership with others who hold similar interests.

Types of Research

There are basically three types of research which we will consider in our discussion of program evaluation. These include: (1) exploratory studies, (2) descriptive studies, and (3) experimental studies. Each has different characteristics and uses, but they share the common features of searching for new insights into areas of interest and ultimately contributing to the development of a body of knowledge capable of providing explanatory and predictive powers. It should be noted that the thrust of the discussion which follows stems largely from the work of Selltiz, Jahoda, Deutsch, and Cook (1959) and Selltiz, Wrightsman, and Cook (1976). Both texts are highly recommended to the reader who wishes a deeper understanding of the research process.

Exploratory Studies

In most cases, exploratory research is conducted without initially formulating hypotheses; that is, the researcher is not generally setting out to test a specific question or issue. As the name implies, the research is exploring an area of interest.

Studies are not merely "hit or miss," however. Selltiz and her associates (1959) have suggested three systematic approaches to exploratory research. The first involves a review of the literature. The researcher's job is to learn more about the subject but also to develop hypotheses based on what has been learned. In other words, by studying what has been written about a given area of interest, the reader will not only learn what is known about the area, but questions about what is not known will inevitably be raised which can then be phrased in an hypothesis format. Even if it is found that little or no research has been completed in a given area, there are generally related topics of interest which emerge that stimulate a desire for further exploration and study.

The second approach involves in-depth discussions with others in the field who have had practical experience in the area of interest. It is not necessary to meticulously design a random sample of practitioners to do this; rather, the researcher may base his or her selection on the availability of practitioners as well as their professional reputations. Nor is there a specific number of practitioners required to constitute a sample. In fact, at some point, additional interviews will probably not provide new information. If the right approach is taken, experienced practitioners will stimulate the researcher's thoughts to a point that new knowledge will be imparted and directions for study will emerge.

The third area is termed insight-stimulating research which involves the selective study of areas which have not already been thoroughly researched. The purpose is to generate rather than answer questions. The work of Abraham Maslow (1968) stemmed largely from this method. He began by asking people about their feelings, particularly in relation to times when they felt especially happy or satisfied. This involved extensive conversations and groupings of responses which ultimately enabled him to identify personal characteristics of "healthy" people, synthesize those characteristics into a theoretical framework, and articulate the theory of self-actualization.

Such an approach is highly experiential and may focus on individuals, groups, or entire communities. At the least, new insights will be gained about people and situations of interest, and further areas of exploration and rigorous study will become apparent.

Each approach to exploratory research is important to the leisure service practitioner if he or she hopes to learn what questions need to be asked, what questions have not yet been asked, and whether or not questions in their own minds have been addressed by others. In fact, some forms of exploratory research must undoubtedly precede all other types of systematic inquiry.

Descriptive Studies

Descriptive studies attempt to answer specific questions in which one or more hypotheses have been formed. Examples include identifying certain attitudes held by program participants, determining socio-economic characteristics of participants in a senior citizens program, and determining the racial make-up of park users. In the first instance attitudes toward fair play might be compared among softball players in two differently organized leagues. In the second example, the practitioner may wish to determine the income and occupational levels of senior citizens using the senior center so that he or she might better understand the type of individual being served or to learn if any gaps may have unknowingly evolved. Finally, a study might be directed toward determining if the use of a community park by minority persons is proportionally representative of the minority population in the total community.

Descriptive research *describes* phenomena as they exist. It is a means of identifying occurrences *after the fact,* which is quite different from experimental research which will be discussed in the following section. Unlike experimental research, one is generally unable to identify cause and effect relationships. Descriptive research can certainly identify relationships but not necessarily what *caused* the relationships to occur. For example, there is clearly a relationship between golf and minority group participation in that activity. The low representation of blacks on the professional circuit and on the average course frequented by "duffers" is readily apparent. We would obviously be in error, however, if we concluded that skin color or race influenced golfing ability. More likely is the fact that minorities are disproportionally represented in the lower income levels which has created barriers for participation in what is generally recognized as an expensive sport. In other words, if one were to speculate on the *cause* of this pattern, economics rather than racial characteristics would be the prime source of influence.

Since many relationships can be identified through descriptive research, one must *always* be cautious when attempting to show cause and effect. In fact, some believe that causal relationships should virtually *never* be inferred as a result of descriptive research (Selltiz, Wrightsman, and Cook, 1976). As we will see when discussing experimental research, there is good reason for such a statement. At this point it is sufficient to emphasize that descriptive research, which can include surveys, questionnaires, attitude scales, psychological inventories, the acquisition of demographic and socioeconomic data, and a variety of other information gathering approaches, describes occurrences after they have taken place which makes it difficult to be sure what caused or produced the final result.

Experimental Research

Experimental research is probably the most difficult to conduct but is also the most fruitful if executed properly. The purpose of experimental studies is to test causal hypotheses. This is accomplished by carefully identifying all (hopefully) of the variables which are believed to be associated with the occurrence of a given event, and then *controlling* those variables in the study. By controlling or manipulating a variable, it simply means identifying the extent to which it is influencing the outcome of the experiment. This will be clarified as we continue.

Two "determining" conditions must be differentiated in experimental research; **necessary** and **sufficient** conditions. Both are related to causality.

A *necessary* condition is one which must *always* occur for a given phenomenon to take place. For example, oxygen is a necessary condition for human life. It must be present or we would not live.

A *sufficient* condition is one which *always* follows a given occurrence. Whenever X occurs, Y will always follow. For example, so far as we know, prolonged interruption and deprivation of sleep will always (eventually) be followed by anxiety. Sleep deprivation, then, is a sufficient condition of anxiety. This does not mean that anxiety results only from extreme loss of sleep; anxiety certainly occurs even among the most rested of individuals. It does mean that anxiety will always be a product of sleep deprivation.

A situation is generally not caused by only one condition nor do situations generally produce only one effect. It then becomes the task of the researcher to identify as many contributory variables as possible and to attempt to determine the relative impact of each variable on the outcome of the event under study. We suspect, for example, that successfully accomplishing certain achievements enhances the self-image of most people. But other factors also influence self-image and the more of these which can be identified, the greater the likelihood that the practitioner will create a favorable environment in his or her program area. Unfortunately, no single variable has been found which is a necessary condition for insuring a positive self-image in people, but the list of variables believed to have a contributory influence is lengthy.

Social research will always be complicated by the fact that the researcher can only determine the *probability* of causal relationships. No matter how accurately a relationship may be gauged, in social research there is always a probability that the findings occurred by chance and that, in fact, there is actually no relationship at all. Findings become strengthened when relationships are studied repeatedly by different researchers and a high degree of corroboration is found. Of equal importance, of course, is that great care is taken in formulating and executing the study design itself.

The Experimental Design

There are certain elements which must be considered when conducting experimental research. A critical factor centers around the time order in which events occur. If one hopes to conclude with reasonable authority that X caused Y, one must insure that X took place before Y and led to its occurrence. A comparison of descriptive and experimental designs will help clarify this. Descriptive studies cannot control for the time order of events since conditions are always assessed after they have happened. A study of attitudes toward the environment among campers may accurately assess their values and feelings but cannot determine if the camping experience caused the resulting attitude or if people with certain attitudes were attracted to the camping program.

On the other hand, if the researcher wishes to determine if camping *causes* a change in attitudes toward the environment, a research project can be designed to control the time order of key variables (attitudes toward the environment and the camping experience itself). To oversimplify, environmental attitudes can be measured before the camping program begins, the program can be completed by the participants, and their attitudes can again be measured at the completion of the program. Assuming other important controls are exercised, any change in attitudes which emerge can, with a reasonable degree of certainty, be attributed to the effects of the program itself. In this example, the time order of events was controlled; the pre-test, the program itself, and the post-test constituted a series of events which permitted this. *Controlling for the time order of events is so important that causality cannot be implied without it.*

A second essential element of experimental research is concerned with identifying other possible causal factors, or contributory variables. Even though an apparent cause-effect relationship may emerge through carefully conducted research, other factors may either have contributed to the occurrence or actually be the primary cause. For example, if an evaluation of a Girl Scout camp program revealed that the participants increased their capacity to develop close interpersonal relationships with their peers, it might be concluded that: (1) participation in Girl Scout camp programs improves interpersonal relations or (2) that participation in social activities produces this result. It may be, however, that the outcome resulted from the skill of the camp leader and that not *any* leader would have facilitated the same outcome. Unless the same pattern is consistently found by evaluating a variety of similar programs, one cannot be certain which variables produced the desired change. In fact, as a side note, leisure service evaluators must face this problem repeatedly; is it participation in the activity itself or the quality of the leadership which is of the greatest value in a program? Since it is often a combination of both, determining the relative importance of each becomes a difficult challenge.

The third major consideration is *concomitant variation* which simply means the extent to which X and Y vary *together*. The relationship between watering a geranium and the flowers it will produce is evident; they clearly vary together. The concomitant variation of sunlight and flowers is also clear. The point is that the researcher must establish the extent to which phenomena are related and change in relationship to each other.

Research and Evaluation

A word of caution is in order, however. One can be easily misled as an example will show. If one were studying plant life and noticed that first the flowers of an unwatered, potted African Violet withered and died, and then the leaves quickly followed, it might be erroneously concluded that without flowers the plant could not survive. It would seem as if the death of the flowers *caused* the ultimate loss of the entire plant. We know, of course, that there is a limit to the length of time a plant can survive without water and recognize the absence of water as the cause of the problem in this example. Since people and life situations are so complicated, the researcher must utilize extreme caution to avoid falling into the trap of misidentifying the cause of concomitant variations.

It must be emphasized that the basic purpose of experimental research is quite similar to that of descriptive study. In experimental research, however, these three elements—time order of occurrence, ruling out or identifying other possible causal factors, and concomitant variation,—*must* be considered. Since descriptive research focuses on events after they have occurred, and the descriptive design format is less stringent, descriptive studies generally have less power than experimental. While both types are necessary, it is our opinion that the greatest growth of knowledge in the leisure service field will come through well-conducted experimental study.

The design of the experimental study will be briefly presented to clarify why it is so much more discriminating than nonexperimental research. It will also be evident that unless the experiment is designed quite meticulously, the findings may be more deceiving than useful.

Experimental Controls

Let us assume that we are interested in evaluating the effects of a given leisure service program in relation to participant values. Specifically, we will hypothetically asume that we would like to know if involvement in a backpacking program for an eight-week period will have a positive effect on the environmental attitudes of youngsters between fifteen and eighteen years of age. If the program is "successful," the environmental attitudes of the participants should be enhanced by the end of their involvement in the program. We will assume that a written test will be utilized to assess environmental values. The following research designs exemplify the importance of controlling all factors which the researcher believes might influence the outcome of the project.

TESTING AFTER THE PROGRAM

In this method, the youths are subjected to the entire program and their attitudes are assessed at the conclusion. Obviously in this case very little will be learned about the extent to which the program influenced attitudes since attitudes were not assessed prior to their involvement in the activity. This design would be appropriate only if base information were already available so that it could serve as a reference point and source for later comparison.

One method for accomplishing this is to include a second group of youths (control group) who are believed to be identical in all respects to the youths attending the program (experimental group), except that *only* the experimental group participates in the program. If both groups are tested at the conclusion of the backpacking program, differences which emerge may be logically connected to the program itself.

A second group is not needed if the researcher is certain of the starting point of the individuals under study. For example, the researcher may wish to identify the amount of knowledge a new group of back-packers can assimilate in a two-day period. If the youngsters who will be in the program have never backpacked before, it can be assumed that they began with little or no knowledge about the proper method of loading a pack, the materials they will need to take on a trip, and so forth. If the youths are tested at the end of the two-day training period, the proportion of material which was learned can be compared to the total amount of information which was presented. The percentage of information assimilated can then be calculated for the group as a whole or for any given individual.

The greatest limitation to testing after the program is that it becomes difficult to rule out other causal variables. In other words, it is difficult to be sure that participants' attitudes can be attributed only to the fact that they were in the program. In most types of research projects additional controls are needed.

TESTING BEFORE AND AFTER THE PROGRAM

In this case, the youths are given a test before the backpacking program begins and are then tested again at the conclusion of the program. Pre- and post-test results can then be compared and related to the effects of the program itself.

This method provides base information but, in itself, does not rule out other factors. How would one know for instance, if the pre-test sensitized the participants to environmental issues in such a way that they began reading related articles in the newspaper, watching television specials, and talking to friends or teachers about key issues which they had previously ignored completely?

Again a control group will help. The control group can also be tested before and after the project period, but would not be involved in the program itself. If the pre-test has a sensitizing effect on the subjects, it will become apparent through a change in the attitudes of individuals in the control group. If there is a change in both groups, the difference in change between the two groups must be examined. In other words, the scores of the control group may increase but if scores increase to a greater extent among those in the experimental group, the difference can be attributed to the program itself.

There is another method for eliminating potential effects of pre-tests. The pre-test can be administered to *only* the control group. It is then *assumed* that the results of the pre-test would have been the same for the experimental group. This can only be done if there is a high degree of certainty that the groups were initially similar in relation to the variables under study.

The best way to insure that the groups are basically equal is to form the groups randomly. This means that if 50 youths apply for entry into the program and only 25 can be accepted, those who are selected should be identified through completely random means which can be accomplished simply by drawing numbers out of an envelope. It would then be necessary to ask the 25 youths who were not accepted to take a pre-test, and they would become the control group in the study. The element of randomness is extremely important to insure that the two groups are initially similar; otherwise later comparisons become highly suspect.

If this condition is met, both groups may be tested after the project period. The scores of the experimental group are recorded, from which the pre-test scores of the control group are subtracted. Since pre-test sensitizing could not take place for the experimental group which did not take a pre-test, the difference between the scores is then indicative of any change which resulted from participation in the program. The greater the difference in scores, the greater the change.

There are other complicating factors which could lead the researcher to utilize two, three, or even more control groups to control all the factors believed to be potential influences. Although more complex, they should not be avoided simply in the interest of expediency. The reader wishing to explore additional aspects of the proper use of control groups in experimental designs will find the work of Selltiz and her associates (1959; 1976) quite helpful.

Evaluative Research Instruments

The selection of the specific instrument for evaluating program effectiveness should be determined at the time program objectives are formulated. In fact, it is highly desirable to identify the instrument in the objective itself. As a rule, this decision will be influenced by practical concerns related to: (1) funds, time, and the logistics of actually obtaining data, and (2) which instruments are available that relate to the study area of interest.

In this section, we will briefly describe several instruments which could prove useful to the leisure service evaluator. The questionnaires and scales which have been selected are meant only to be representative of what is available; the list is obviously far from exhaustive.

Types of Instruments

For the purpose of this discussion, two broad categories of measuring instruments will be considered: (1) personality measures, and (2) attitude scales. Within both categories, we will focus on scales which, for the most part, have withstood the test of time and are widely accepted.

PERSONALITY MEASURES

There are several instruments which have become "tried and true" measures of personality and personality adjustment. These include the Minnesota Multiphasic Inventory, the California Psychological Inventory, and the F-Scale. We will also discuss the more recently developed Personal Orientation Inventory which has also received considerable attention and usage.

Minnesota Multiphasic Personality Inventory (MMPI) — The MMPI is a measure which categorizes people psychiatrically and is probably the most commonly used of any of its type (Allport, 1961). It is quite elaborate and includes 550 separate items which focus on both normal and abnormal characteristics of personal adjustment.

Some of the more frequent measures of adjustment included in the MMPI are depression, paranoia, schizophrenia, introversion-extroversion, the masculinity-femineity (Welsh and Dahlstrom, 1956). The items are answered in a true or false format. Sample items include the following (Hathaway and McKinley, 1956, pp. 75-6):

1. During the past few years I have been well most of the time.
2. I am in just as good physical health as most of my friends.
3. I enjoy many different types of play and recreation.
4. I work under a great deal of tension.

The detailed use and interpretation of the MMPI can be explored by referring to either *An Atlas for the Clinical Use of the MMPI* (Hathaway and Meehl, 1951) or *Basic Readings on the MMPI in Psychology and Medicine* (Welsh and Dahlstrom, 1956).

It must be kept in mind that the MMPI is a lengthy, taxing instrument. Its use in leisure services would undoubtedly be somewhat limited to certain situations, such as in a therapeutic setting or possibly in connection with a school program which involves a "captive" audience. It is, however, a powerful tool and can serve as a vehicle for gaining considerable knowledge about personality and personal adjustment. Practical uses of this and other measures of personality will be considered later in this chapter.

California Psychological Inventory (CPI) — The CPI focuses on more "healthy" or normal characteristics of the individual. It includes 480 items which assess the following characteristics: sociability, social presence, self-acceptance, responsibility, socialization, self-control, communality, achievement through conformity, achievement through independence, intellectual efficiency, flexibility, dominance, psychological-mindedness, capacity for status, femineity, sense of well-being, good impression, and tolerance (Gough, 1957, p. 50). Approximately 200 of the items were abstracted from the MMPI; all CPI items utilize a true or false format.

Unlike the MMPI, it is intended to be used primarily for non-psychiatrically disturbed individuals. The scale may be administered to less adjusted people but was not designed with this in mind; the emphasis is upon dimensions of social living and social interaction, thrusts which are of key importance to the leisure service practitioner.

Again this is an instrument which is lengthy and requires substantial thought by those completing it. It is, however, a powerful instrument and should not be avoided simply because it requires time and effort on the part of those involved in the evaluation process. Parsimony frequently leads to a loss of information and should not be the main determinant, particularly if it leads to a loss in content.

F-Scale — The F-Scale, developed by Adorno, et al. (1950), is designed to measure authoritarianism in people. Specifically, subscales of the instrument assess conventionalism (rigid adherence to conventional, middle-class values); authoritarian submission (submissive, uncritical attitude toward idealized moral authorities of the ingroup); authoritarian aggression (tendency to be on the lookout for, and to condemn, reject, and punish people who violate conventional values); anti-intraception (opposition to the subjective, the imaginative, the tender-minded); superstition and stereotypy (the belief in mystical determinants of the individual's fate; the disposition to think in rigid categories); power and toughness (preoccupation with the dominance-submission, strong-weak, leader-follower dimension; exaggerated assertion of strength and toughness); destructiveness and cynicism (generalized hostility, villification of the human); projectivity (the disposition to believe that wild and dangerous things go on in the world) and sex (exaggerated concern with sexual "goings-on") (Adorno, et al., 1950, pp. 255-7).

Subjects completing the instrument must respond to a series of statements by indicating the extent to which they agree or disagree with the item. Responses include the following: strong support, moderate support, slight support, slight opposition, moderate opposition, and strong opposition.

Examples of statements in the instrument are as follows (Adorno, et al., 1950, pp. 255-6):

1. Obedience and respect for authority are the most important virtues children should learn.
2. The businessman and the manufacturer are much more important to society than the artist and the professor.
3. People can be divided into two distinct classes: the weak and the strong.
4. No weakness or difficulty can hold us back if we have enough will power.

One immediate advantage to the F-Scale is that it is quite short in comparison to the MMPI or CPI. Subscales of the F-Scale are as short as three items and only eight items in length at the most. Scoring is also quite simple since numerical values from one to six can be assigned to each of the six response choices enabling each set of subscales to be totalled individually or collectively. According to Allport (1961, p. 434), "The findings have been so timely and so impressive that psychologists have devoted much zeal to analyzing, checking, criticizing, and modifying both the original scale and the theory involved." The F-Scale consists of items which should be of more than passing interest to the leisure service practitioner. Relationships between power and toughness, and competitive attitudes or competitive behavior could be easily studied using the F-Scale to assess power and toughness characteristics of various populations. In this case, unlike the MMPI and CPI instruments, simplicity and depth can be accomplished simultaneously.

Personal Orientation Inventory (POI) — The POI was designed by Shostrom (1966) based primarily on the theory of self-actualization developed by Maslow (1954), but also on the work of May, et al. (1958), Reisman (1950), and Perls (1947; 1951). The instrument, which includes 150 items, consists of two major scales, inner-directed support and time competence, plus ten subscales which are utilized in different combinations, occasionally repeating items. The subscales are: self-actualizing value (measures affirmation of a primary value of self-actualizing people); existentiality (measures ability to situationally or existentially react without rigid adherence to principles); feeling reactivity (measures freedom to react spontaneously or to be oneself); self regard (measures affirmation of self because of worth or strength); self acceptance (measures affirmation or acceptance of self in spite of weaknesses or deficiencies); nature of man (measures degree of the constructive view of the nature of man, masculinity, femineity); synergy (measures ability to be synergistic, to transcend dichotomies); acceptance of aggression (measures ability to accept one's natural aggressiveness as opposed to defensiveness, denial, and repression of aggression); and capacity for intimate contact (measures ability to develop contactful intimate relationships with other human beings, unencumbered by expectations and obligations) (Shostrom, 1966, p. 6).

The questionnaire consists of 150 paired statements to which the respondent indicates for each pair which statement is more true for him or her. Time for completing the entire instrument generally ranges from fifteen to thirty minutes. Samples of items are as follows (Shostrom, 1963):

1. a. I am bound by the principle of fairness.
   b. I am not absolutely bound by the principle of fairness.
2. a. My feelings of self-worth depend on how much I accomplish.
   b. My feelings of self-worth do not depend on how much I accomplish.
3. a. Man is naturally cooperative.
   b. Man is naturally antagonistic.
4. a. For me, work and play are the same.
   b. For me, work and play are opposites.

There is a coded answer key for each scale which allows responses to be scored quite easily. One or all of the scales can be utilized depending upon the information which is desired.

There are several reasons why the POI should be of special interest to those involved in the delivery of leisure services. First, it focuses primarily on healthy characteristics of personal adjustment which places the emphasis on *positive* concerns in a manner consistent with the tenets of the field itself. Second, it is relatively easy to administer and score. Third, it specifically focuses on elements associated with the recreation experience, that is, self-actualizing and peak experiences, intrinsic motivation, and feelings of well-being. Finally, it is a rather unthreatening instrument which people apparently enjoy or do not mind completing (Klar, 1974; Moore, 1974).

In summary, the MMPI, CPI, F-Scale, and POI each have strengths and can be quite useful in evaluating and researching leisure related phenomena. Specific uses of these scales will be considered following a discussion of attitudinal measures.

ATTITUDINAL MEASURES

Semantic Differential — The semantic differential is an attitude scale developed by Osgood, Suci, and Tannenbaum (1957) and can be applied to any phenomenon of interest. The scale consists of a series of bi-polar (opposite) adjectives between which a seven-step (generally) continuum is presented. Examples include:

Good _____ _____ _____ _____ _____ _____ _____ Bad

Happy _____ _____ _____ _____ _____ _____ _____ Sad

Successful _____ _____ _____ _____ _____ _____ _____ Unsuccessful

At the top of the form on which the adjectives appear, a term or concept is presented, such as the term *camping*. Subjects are then instructed to indicate the meaning of the term by selecting the points along the continuum which most appropriately represent their feelings about it.

Any topic, object, or person can be selected as the point of focus. Other areas could include (1) myself, (2) my friends, (3) my family, (4) school, (5) work, and (6) recreation. In addition, an added dimension can be injected by asking the respondent to indicate the meaning of a term, collecting the answer sheets, and then asking the respondent to indicate what the term should mean to them under *ideal* conditions. This would permit a comparison of the *real* and *ideal* meanings of terms.

The semantic differential scale is not composed of a specific set of items which one must always include in a survey instrument. Virtually any pair of bi-polar adjectives may be used and virtually any term may be selected as the point of focus. It is, therefore, flexible, easy to administer, and can be as long or as short as one needs. Scoring is also quite simple since each of the steps in the continuum separating the paired adjectives can be given a numerical value which will allow totals to be readily computed. Most importantly, extensive skills are not needed, yet important aspects of the affective domain can be assessed.

Likert-type Scale — The Likert-type scale provides an additional type of attitudinal measure which is also quite flexible and relatively simple to interpret. Devised by Likert (1932), it consists of a series of statements to which the respondent may agree or disagree, usually along a five-point continuum as follows: strongly agree, agree, undecided, disagree, or strongly disagree. Some variations delete the *undecided* category or increase or decrease the number of choices. In fact, some versions allow only an *agree-disagree* choice.

A Likert-type scale does not refer to a particular test; rather it describes the format of the scale and method for developing items. This means that a list of statements cannot be formulated simply because they *appear* to be logical and meaningfully related. The process for item development is straightforward, but it is time consuming. In-depth discussions of the methodology have been offered by Selltiz, Wrightman, and Cook (1976) and by Likert (1932) in his original study reported more recently by Fishbein (1967).

An example of a scale which was developed to assess attitudes toward competition in recreation is the Competitive Recreation Activities (CRA) scale (Klar, 1974). The final instrument included 44 items which utilized the following format:

1. I am hesitant to be supportive of competitive recreation activities.
2. Competitive recreational programs spoil the fun of the activity itself.

3. I enjoy recreation best when it is competitive.
4. The greatest pleasure in a recreation program is the competitive experience.

It is important to emphasize that items were not accepted on the basis of *apparent* relevance; a process requiring several testings was required. Two points are important to consider then. First, it is preferable to utilize a scale which has already been developed through the correct process. Only if an appropriate scale is not found should one embark on the task of designing an original instrument. Second, despite the fact that it should not be done, some scales are developed which have not followed the Likert process. The reader should approach the findings of such studies with considerable caution; the validity and reliability of these scales are highly suspect.

Utilization of Personality and Attitude Scales

The researcher must identify the questions which he or she wishes to explore and then select the most appropriate and practical measuring device to incorporate into the study. To exemplify this process, we have listed each of the instruments presented in this chapter and suggested issues for which each might be appropriately utilized.

MMPI and CPI Scales

1. Do participants in community recreation programs tend to be of a certain personality type?
2. Are institutionalized juvenile delinquents who participate in the institution's recreation programs different in personality type than those who choose not to participate?
3. Are participants in drama programs of a different type of personality than those involved in recreational sports?
4. Do changes in personality occur as a result of becoming a "confirmed jogger"?
5. Are personality and leisure values related and, if so, in what way?
6. Are the leisure patterns of children related to the personalities of their parents?
7. Are coaches of youngsters' recreational sports teams, such as Little League, of a certain personality type?
8. Do the personalities of leisure service practitioners fall predominantly in what would be considered a "healthy" range?

F-Scale

1. Are those involved in competitive recreation programs more authoritarian than those who are not?

2. Is rigidity characteristic of individuals who limit their recreational pursuits to only one or two activities?
3. Do participants value toughness and power to a greater extent after they have participated in organized competitive recreation programs?
4. Are prison inmates who are in facilities with extensive recreation programs less rigid and authoritarian compared to inmates located in facilities offering little or no comparable opportunities?
5. Do leisure service practitioners become more or less authoritarian as they acquire increasing years of experience in their profession?

Personal Orientation Inventory

1. Are participants in cultural and fine arts programs more self-actualized than nonparticipants in these programs?
2. Are participants in organized recreation programs able to establish intimate contact with others to a greater extent than those who do not participate?
3. Are joggers more self-actualized than non-joggers?
4. Are self-actualization and leisure attitudes related?
5. Are self-actualization and competitiveness in recreation related?

Semantic Differential and Likert-Type Scales

1. To what extent are leisure attitudes and behavior consistent?
2. How do leisure attitudes differ among various groups of people such as senior citizens, children, racial minorities, athletes, and teachers?
3. Are inner-city children more fearful of the wilderness than rural children?
4. Do attitudes toward the environment change after one participates in a nature program?
5. Do attitudes toward other racial groups change following one's participation in an integrated recreation program?

It should be apparent that the uses of these instruments are many. It is also clear that we know the answers to very few of these questions and this list of queries is far from complete. Hopefully, as a greater number of people who are involved in the leisure service delivery system become aware of the need for addressing these and other important areas, research and evaluation efforts will become more commonplace. In the meantime, those who conscientiously make the effort to evaluate the effects of their services will certainly stand out and reap the benefits which are sure to follow.

Observation of Participants

Although program assessment through observing behavior can limit one's insights in a number of respects, used in combination with the personal interview it can be quite informative. Many inferences can be made from what is observed and the observer can then use interviews to clarify what the participant was feeling during the period of observation.

Let us assume, for example, that the administrators of a four-week camp program wish to determine if cooperative interactions occur more frequently among campers who are involved in a special program than among campers who are not. Campers in unit A will participate in the special program and campers in unit B will not. The fifteen girls in each unit will be compared in an experimental project.

During the first week of camp, the intent is to place the campers of unit A in three situations which require them to solve a problem through concentrated teamwork. This will involve: (1) building a rope bridge across a stream, (2) designing a fitness trail and constructing it, and (3) constructing a dam in the stream to produce a pool for swimming. During the remaining weeks of camp, the behavior of the girls in unit A will be observed and recorded. The fifteen girls in unit B will also be observed during the same time period to serve as a control group. They will participate in the scheduled camp activities, but not the three special teamwork projects performed by the girls in unit A. The girls will be randomly assigned to their respective units.

A check-list can be developed which includes the specific behaviors which camp counselors will record as it is observed. One check-list would be prepared for each camper, by name, and carried on a clip-board by each counselor. A sample check-list is as follows:

Cooperative Behavior Check-List (Camper's Name)	Date:					
Helps another camper when asked.						
Helps another camper without being asked.						
Helps counselor when asked.						
Helps counselor without being asked.						
Asks another camper for assistance.						
Shares personal belongings with others.						
Offers food to others first during meals.						
Apologizes sincerely to others when in error.						
Participates in completing group chores without being asked.						

A number of other cooperative behaviors could be added, of course, and the content would change in other situations depending upon the type of behavior which is examined. It is advisable to have at least several people involved in developing the list to avoid listing ambiguous behaviors which are difficult to observe.

There are at least two approaches which can be adopted with this system. First, the counselors can record behavior and use it as a guide for offering special counseling to the girls, particularly those in either unit who may exhibit uncooperative behavior. If this is done, however, the effects of the three teamwork projects will be difficult to assess since changes in behavior may be due to the counseling rather than the projects. Used in this manner, the check-list would become a tool for counseling rather than an analytical instrument which is part of an experimental research project. This can be a powerful approach, however, apart from a research project. Many insights into human behavior and feelings can result if open dialogues take place following the observation periods.

Second, the experimental approach can be followed. In this case, unusual efforts to counsel the campers should be avoided to insure an accurate test of the effects of the teamwork projects. This does not mean that the counselors' roles are changed or diminished; rather, the counselors must attempt to interact with campers as they would in the absence of a check-list system. The more closely this is followed, the greater the likelihood of attributing differences in the two units to the teamwork projects.

At least three problems should be apparent. First, counselor biases are likely to be present. Those in unit A may interpret cooperative behavior quite liberally without realizing it. Or, if any sense of competition is felt among the counselors in the two units, one or both sets of counselors may intentionally inflate their observations. Second, the counselors in both units may become sensitized to the importance and desirability of cooperative behavior to a point that they are unable to interact with the campers as they would had the project not been undertaken. Third, continually recording behavior can be a nuisance for counselors. It requires constant attention which can be tiring.

Despite these limitations, the check-list system of recording behavior is relatively simple, does not require extensive training other than carefully discussing the types of behaviors which must be observed, and the tabulation of data is not complicated. It also serves as a constant reminder of the objectives of the program in relation to each individual participant.

The observation method is subject to criticism due to the subjective factors which are unavoidable; however, subjectivity can also be an asset. It was certainly effective for Maslow (1968) as he combined observation and interview techniques which led to his articulation of the theory of self-actualization. Whether used on its own strengths or as an exploratory tool to stimulate further research, its impact can be great on leisure service practitioners in any setting.

Quantitative Evaluations

The majority of the discussion thus far has centered around qualitative concerns in the affective domain rather than the more traditional and more commonly used quantitative measures. Although we clearly feel that the emphasis in program evaluation should focus on qualitative measures to a much greater extent, we would also suggest that quantitative measures should be a key determinant in deciding whether or not a program should be offered or continued. This apparent contradiction will be resolved shortly, but first two of the more important quantitative measures will be considered.

Numbers of Participants

This measure includes all people who participate in a given program or activity. It could be expressed in terms of the average number of people per day or per week, the gross number during a given period of time, or the number of different people attending an event or continuous program. Some tally systems can be confounded when the same people return to a particular program many times over a period of days. Total figures will not reflect the number of different people who are involved. In such cases, the average daily attendance is probably a more meaningful figure than gross participation during the program period.

There is sometimes a tendency for administrators to utilize inflated attendance figures in their reports. It is impressive, for example, to report that two-hundred children participated daily in after-school programs offered by the recreation department. This sounds more impressive than stating that approximately twenty children participated in each of ten different school programs. Both figures are certainly correct; however, the first indicator could be deceptive, particularly if mentioned out of context. The point is that attendance figures should be used to help and guide the practitioner. Although reporting favorable participation rates has public relations value and may be reinforcing to the administration, little help is offered to anyone if a "true" picture is not presented and if programs which are poorly attended, are concealed, or misrepresented.

Cost of Services

Certainly recreation programming is influenced by economic factors and it would be short-sighted to focus only on program quality to justify its continuation. Even the finest program cannot generally be justified if the cost is disproportionally high in relation to other agency offerings.

Generally a cost per capita is calculated and programs are compared partially on that basis. For example, a soccer program may cost five hundred dollars for one hundred children over a six-week period. The cost per capita (cost per child) would be five dollars. At the same time, a competitive swim program may involve only twenty children at a total cost of one thousand dollars for the same period of time, creating a cost per capita of fifty dollars. It is clear to see that in times of economic hardship there might be a tendency to cut back programs which reach fewer people at a greater cost; a basic concept in leisure services is to reach as many people as possible with the resources which are available.

Fortunately for many specialized programs, the cost per capita is not the only yardstick for evaluation. Such programs as drama, competitive swimming, and ceramics can be expensive, but they are often highly valued and continued despite somewhat higher costs.

Program Priorities and Quantitative Measures

To return to our apparent contradiction, we must basically conclude that demands for leisure service programs must be based substantially on the *number* of people who ask for and participate in activities of their choice. It is unrealistic to offer a program for five people if another program which would attract a sizeable number of participants would need to be reduced in resource support or even canceled. In other words, it is the responsibility of the practitioner, particularly in a tax-supported agency, to be sensitive to the requests and participation patterns of the greatest number of people.

A pitfall must be avoided, however. It is not enough to provide programs *only* in response to participant patterns since there is also a responsibility to offer quality programs. As we stated earlier, two competitive recreational leagues may each attract many participants, but one may be characterized by fun, cooperation, and good feelings while the other is not. The demand for both programs may be equal, but the agency is not properly fulfilling its role in the league plagued with difficulties. Therefore, the challenge is to attempt to simultaneously focus on both quantitative and qualitative indicators of program effectiveness.

There is, of course, a relationship between qualitative and quantitative indicators. Those programs which are the "better" ones tend to attract the greatest number of participants. Acceptance of this idea is the reason why so many practitioners rely *solely* on participation rates to justify program offerings. The best approach, however, is to concentrate on the type of qualitative factors that lead to effective programs which, in turn, meet the needs of those who are involved to such an extent that participation rates are high. As a general rule, quality increases quantity; the converse may or may not be the case.

The process of program evaluation can be tedious and difficult, particularly when it involves research of a social nature. But it is inappropriate to conclude that human research is so complex that it should not be attempted. It is also unsatisfactory to assume that programs which attract the largest numbers of participants are successful and need no additional evaluative treatment. Hopefully, the ideals, values, and tenets which are basic to leisure services will continuously be examined by practitioners and programs will be appraised regularly through evaluations of all types. Ultimately, the field will emerge as a cogent discipline in which leisure related human needs are fulfilled *and* we know how, when, and why this occurs.

Summary

The evaluation of leisure services is as essential as the planning, leadership, and actual delivery phases of the system. It contributes to the professional development of the field, tests objectives, expands our knowledge of human behavior and motivation, and provides concrete data which help to guide and justify program development and the continuation of existing services.

The three basic approaches to program evaluation include exploratory studies, descriptive studies, and experimental research. Each attempts to provide new insights which lead to the development of a body of knowledge in relation to human behavior in leisure services.

Only the experimental research format provides a consistent basis for implying causal relationships. It is essential to control the time order of relevant events and other variables which could influence outcomes to be certain that relationships which are found to exist are, in fact, varying together in a clearly identifiable manner.

One or more control groups are frequently required to provide a standard for later comparisons. If possible, group allocations should be determined by random means.

There are numerous instruments which are designed to assess personality and personal adjustment. Several of the more commonly used scales are the Minnesota Multiphasic Psychological Inventory (MMPI), California Psychological Inventory (CPI), and F-Scale. The more recently developed Personal Orientation Inventory (POI) has come into increasing use and is particularly relevant to leisure services since it places a central emphasis on the process of self-actualization.

Two frequently used instruments in attitudinal measurement are the semantic differential and the Likert-type survey. They do not require extensive skill to administer or interpret although the process for design-ing an original Likert-type scale can be cumbersome. Existing scales should be used if at all possible.

Quantitative measures of program effectiveness are extremely im-portant to the practitioner who must be responsive to participation pat-terns and program popularity. The cost of programming per capita must also remain an important consideration. Ideally, however, the develop-ment of quality programs, that is, those which best meet human needs, will be the principal goal. If a high standard of quality is attained, high participation rates should be the natural consequence.

Program evaluation is not an easy process but it is essential if the leisure service practitioner hopes to understand program effects. As Gray (Gray and Greben, 1974, p. 50) has emphasized:

We must evaluate everything we do in human terms. The critical
questions are not, "How many were there?" or "Who won?" The critical
question is, "What happened to Jose, Mary, Sam, and Joan in this experience?"

If the leisure service practitioner can begin to find answers to this key question, numbers will inevitably take care of themselves.

Study Questions

1. What are the basic purposes of research and evaluation in leisure services?
2. What difficulties are faced when conducting social research?
3. What are the basic approaches to research and what are the characteristics of each?
4. What is meant by *causality* in research? Can causality be implied in exploratory and descriptive research?
5. What is meant by the terms *necessary* and *sufficient* conditions? How do they relate to causality?
6. Can causal relationships in social research be established with total centainty? Why or why not?
7. How does one control the time order of events in research and why is this important?
8. What are some of the conditions in which one or more control groups would be used in evaluating program effects?
9. How might personality and attitude scales be used in evaluating or researching the effects of leisure services? How can they be used with other variables of interest?
10. Why is the POI especially appropriate for use in leisure services?
11. What are the weaknesses of the observation method of program evaluation? How can this technique be useful despite its limitations?

12. Are participation rates indicative of program quality? Why or why not?

13. How are qualitative and quantitative indicators of program effectiveness related?

References

Adorno, T. W.; Frendel-Brunswick, E.; Levinson, D. J.; and Sanford, R. N. *The Authoritarian Personality*. New York: Harper & Row, Publishers, 1950.

Allport, Gordon W. *Pattern and Growth in Personality*. New York: Holt, Rinehart and Winston, 1961.

Bannon, Joseph J. *Leisure Resources: Its Comprehensive Planning*. Englewood Cliffs, N. J.: Prentice-Hall, Inc., 1976.

Becker, Howard S., and Geer, Blanche. "Participant Observation and Interviewing: A Comparison." *Human Organization* 16:3 (1957): 28-32.

Deutscher, Irwin. *What We Say/What We Do*. Glenview, Ill.: Scott, Foresman and Company, 1973.

Fishbein, Martin (ed.) *Readings in Attitude Theory and Measurement*. New York: John Wiley & Sons, Inc., 1967.

Gough, H. G. 1957. *Manual for the California Psychological Inventory*. Palo Alto, Calif: Consulting Psychologist Press, 1957.

Gray, David E., and Greben, Seymour. "Future Perspectives." *Parks & Recreation* July (1974): 26-33, 47-56.

Hathaway, S. R., and McKinley, J. C. "Article 7, Scale 2, (Depression)." In *Basic Readings on the MMPI in Psychology and Medicine*. Edited by George S. Welsh and W. Grant Dahlstrom. Minneapolis: University of Minnesota Press, 1956.

Hathaway, S.R., and Meehl, P. E. *An Atlas for the Clinical Use of the MMPI*. Minneapolis: University of Minnesota Press, 1951.

Klar, Lawrence R., Jr. "The Relationship Between Competitive Recreation and Personal Adjustment." Unpublished doctoral dissertation, Oregon State University, 1974.

Kraus, Richard G., and Curtis, Joseph E. *Creative Administration in Recreation & Parks*. St. Louis, Mo.: C. V. Mosby Company, 1973.

LaPiere, Richard T. "Attitudes vs. Actions." *Social Forces* 13 (1934-1935): 230-37.

Likert, Rensis. "A Technique for the Measurement of Attitudes." *Archives of Psychology* 21:140 (1932): 44-53.

Maslow, Abraham. *Motivation and Personality*. New York: Harper & Row, Publishers, 1954.

May, R.; Angel, T.; and Ellenberger, H. *Existence*. New York: Basic Books, 1958.

Moore, James E. "The Relationship Between Self-Actualization and Leisure Attitudes." Unpublished doctoral dissertation, Oregon State University, 1974.

Murphy, James, and Howard, Dennis R. *Delivery of Community Leisure Services: An Holistic Approach*. Philadelphia: Lea & Febiger, 1977.

Osgood, C.; Suci, G.; and Tannenbaum, P. *The Measurement of Meaning.* Urbana: University of Illinois Press, 1957.

Perls, F. *Ego, Hunger and Aggression.* London: George Allen and Unwin, Ltd., 1947.

Perls, F.; Hefferline, R.; and Goodman, P. *Gestalt Therapy.* New York: Julian Press, 1951.

Reisman, David; Glazer, N.; and Denney, R. *The Lonely Crowd.* New York: Doubleday Books, 1951.

Selltiz, Claire; Jahoda, Marie; Deutsch, Morton; and Cook, Stuart W. *Research Methods in Social Relations.* New York: Holt, Rinehart and Winston, 1959.

Selltiz, Claire; Wrightman, Lawrence S.; and Cook, Stuart W. *Research Methods in Social Relations.* New York: Holt, Rinehart and Winston, 1976.

Shostrom, Everett L. "Personal Orientation Inventory Manual." San Diego, Calif.: Educational Testing Service, 1966.

Shostrom, Everett L. "Personal Orientation Inventory." San Diego, Calif.: Educational Testing Service, 1963.

Welsh, George S., and W. Grant Dahlstrom (eds.) *Basic Readings on the MMPI in Psychology and Medicine.* Minneapolis: University of Minnesota Press, 1956.

Related Readings

Agnew, Neil M., and Pyke, Sandra W. *The Science Game.* Englewood Cliffs, N.J.: Prentice-Hall, Inc., 1969.

American Alliance for Health, Physical Education and Recreation. *What Recreation Research Says to the Practitioner.* Washington, D.C.: American Association for Health, Physical Education and Recreation, 1975.

Bales, R. F. *Personality and Interpersonal Behavior.* New York: Holt, Rinehart and Winston, 1970.

Blalock, H. M., Jr. *Causal Inferences in Nonexperimental Research.* Chapel Hill: The University of North Carolina Press, 1961.

Buros, Oscar K. (ed.) *The Seventh Mental Measurement Yearbook.* Hyland Park, N. J.: Gryphon Press, 1972.

Burton, Thomas. *Recreation Research Methods; A Review of Recent Studies.* Birmingham, Ala.: University of Birmingham, 1968.

Campbell, A., and Converse, P. E. (eds.) *The Human Meaning of Social Change.* New York: Russell Sage Foundation, 1972.

Clausen, Aage R. "Response Validity in Surveys." *Public Opinion Quarterly* 32 (1968 69): 588-606.

Edwards, A. L. *Techniques of Attitude Scale Construction.* New York: Appleton-Century-Crofts, 1957.

Fishbein, M., and Ajzen, I. *Belief, Attitude, Intention and Behavior.* Reading, Mass.: Addison-Wesley, 1975.

Forem, Jack. *Transcendental Meditation* (Chapter 5: Self-Actualization). New York: E. P. Dutton Company, Inc., 1973.

Gray, David. "Toward an Improved System of Attendance Measurement." *California Park and Recreation Magazine* (August 1967): 12.

Guttman, Louis. "A Basis for Scaling Qualitative Data." *American Sociological Review* 9 (1944): 139-150.

Hare, Van Court. *Systems Analysis: A Diagnostic Approach.* New York: Harcourt, Brace & World, 1967.

Hatry, Winnie, and Hatrie, Fisk. *Practical Program Evaluation for State and Local Government Officials.* Washington, D.C.: The Urban Institute, 1973.

Hillway, Tyrus. *Introduction to Research.* Boston: Houghton Mifflin Company, 1964.

Hubbard, Alfred. *Research Methods in Health, Physical Education and Recreation.* Washington, D.C.: Association for Health, Physical Education and Recreation, 1973.

Nagi, Saad Z., and Corwin, Ronald G. *The Social Contexts of Research.* New York: John Wiley and Sons, Inc., 1972.

Neulinger, John. *Psychology of Leisure.* Springfield, Ill.: Charles C. Thomas, Publisher, 1974.

Neulinger, John. "Leisure and Mental Health." *Pacific Sociological Review* July (1971): 288-300.

Neulinger, John, and Miranda Breit. "Attitude Dimensions of Leisure." *Journal of Leisure Research* 1:3 (1969): 255-261.

Nienaber, Jeanne, and Wildavsky, Aaron. *The Budgeting and Evaluation of Federal Recreation Programs.* New York: Basic Books, Inc., Publishers, 1973.

Ontario Research Council on Leisure. *Analysis Methods and Techniques for Recreation Research and Leisure Studies.* Toronto: Ontario Research Council on Leisure, 1977.

Rosenthall, Robert. *Experimenter Effects in Behavioral Research.* New York: Irvington Publishers, Inc., 1976.

Shaw, M. E., and Wright, J.M., *Scales for the Measurement of Attitudes.* New York: McGraw-Hill, 1967.

Shostrom, Everett L. "An Inventory for the Measurement of Self-Actualization." *Educational and Psychological Measurement* 34:2 (1964): 207-218.

Sze, William C., and Hopps, June G. *Evaluation and Accountability of Human Services Programs.* Cambridge, Mass.: Schenkman Publishing Company, 1975.

Thurstone, L. L. "The Measurement of Social Attitudes." *Journal of Abnormal and Social Psychology* 26 (1931): 249-269.

Weiss, Carol H. *Evaluation Research: Methods of Assessing Program Effectiveness.* Englewood Cliffs, N.J.: Prentice-Hall, Inc., 1972.

Wessler, R. L. "Experimenter Expectancy Effects in Psychomotor Performance." *Perceptual Motor Skills* 26 (1968): 911-917.

Witt, Peter A., and Bishop, Doyle W. "Situational Antecedents to Leisure Behavior." *Journal of Leisure Research* 2:1 (1970): 64-77.

Wood, George C., et al. *Evaluating Your Community Education Program.* Pendell Publishers, 1977.

Wuebben, Paul L.; Straits, Bruce C.; and Schulman, Gary I. *The Experiment as a Social Occasion.* Berkeley, Calif.: The Glendessary Press, Inc., 1974.

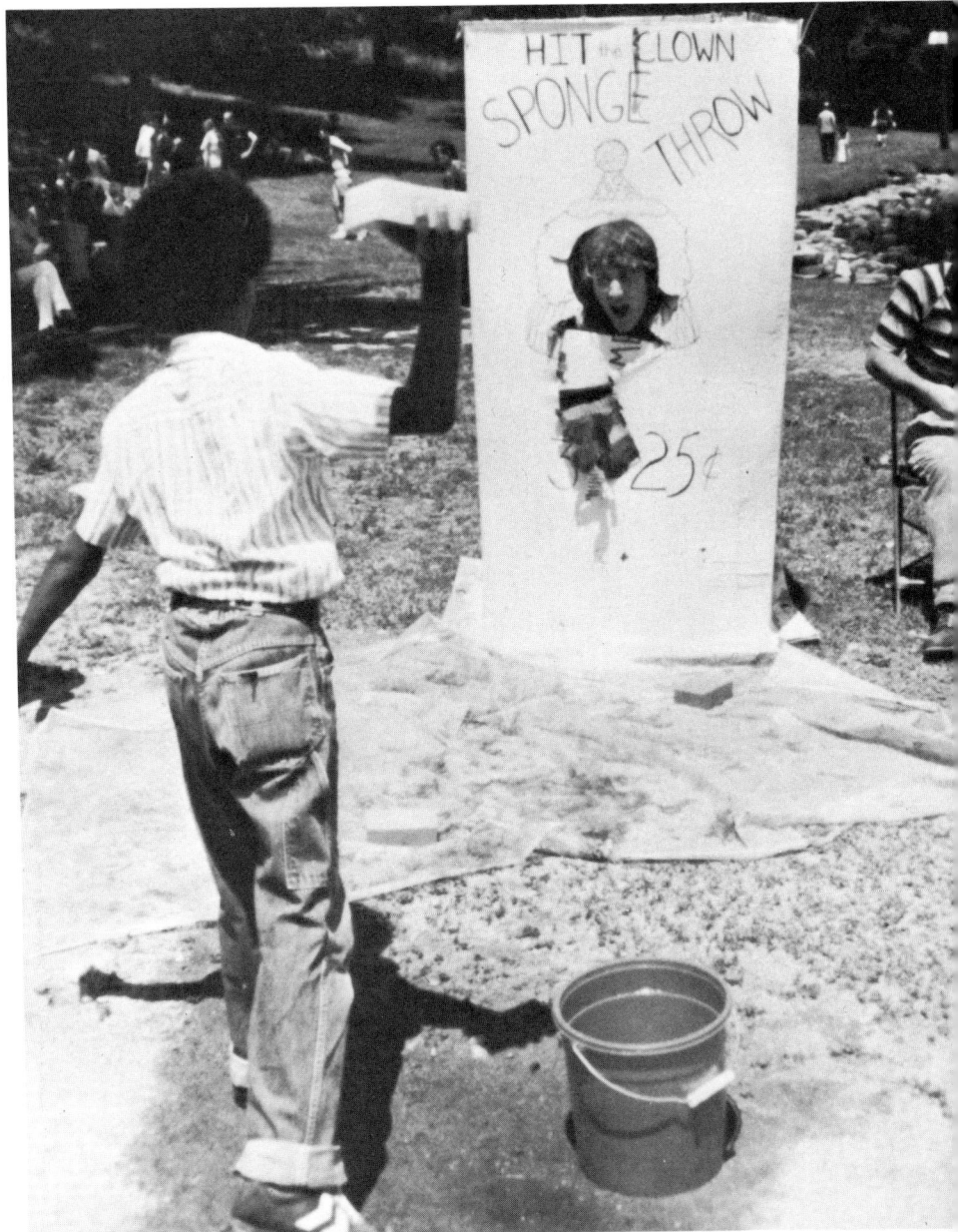

Community Organization

Objectives   After reading and comprehending this chapter, you should be able to:

1. Differentiate between a cafeteria style of programming and the enabler approach, relating each to process and program concerns.
2. Identify differences between programming **with** and **for** people and how each approach influences participant commitment to programs.
3. State the importance of community programming surveys in relation to actual participation outcomes.
4. State the extent to which popular programs are not necessarily synonymous with effective programs.
5. Explain the importance of inter-agency cooperation when dealing with deep-rooted social problems.
6. Differentiate between beautiful program areas and facilities, and areas and facilities offering beautiful (effective) programs.
7. Define the leisure service practitioner's role as a community organizer.
8. Graphically and verbally depict the community organization process as it relates to the leisure service practitioner.

Introduction

*Effective delivery of leisure services
must begin with an understanding of the
needs of the people to be served.*

This appears to be a simple statement; yet, in practice, it is one which is frequently misunderstood or ignored to the point that programs do not become effective. Any one of several factors may contribute to such ineffectiveness. First, programs are often based upon knowledge of *past* successes. This approach can be appropriate but if utilized solely in itself, any social changes which have occurred will be missed, thus producing an obsolete program that will likely be destined to failure. If planned programs are based on past patterns a year in advance, operating funds may be "locked in" preventing shifts in programming emphasis as the preferences among community residents change. It is always difficult to abandon yesterday's success, even when once "tried and true" programs become obsolete.

Second, and closely related, if communication is weak between practitioners and the public, the changing needs and preferences of potential participants will not be identified at times when interests in new areas may be peaking. Should this occur, a golden opportunity for immediately offering responsive programs will be missed.

Third, weak communication and a low level of interaction between practitioners and the public will invariably limit the involvement of participants in the planning and implementation phases of programming. This leads to a substantial loss of resources which might have added considerable depth and creativity to the agency. Such situations also fail to provide opportunities for the public to become involved in ways which could facilitate the growth process so vital to upward movement, movement potentially leading to a self-actualizing life-style.

When the needs of people are misperceived by those providing programs, the leisure service delivery system seriously fails to reach full potential. This failure becomes costly to the supporting community in terms of economics as well as personal growth. It is also costly to the practitioner since it is doubtful that true rewards of professional service can be realized in the wake of moderate to low effectiveness.

With these concerns in mind, the following discussion focuses on the role of leisure service agencies in the community organization process. It is our belief that community organization is as essential for the leisure service practitioner as it is for the social worker and therefore must be fully utilized for the delivery system to approach a desirable level of effectiveness.

Examining Ineffectiveness

It is often a simple task to identify programs which result in failure, but causes for failure are not as easily determined, particularly if they are related to the *process* of providing services rather than the manner in which activities are presented at the face-to-face level. A brief discussion of situations in which program success was not achieved, coupled with a discussion of related problem areas, will provide a foundation for establishing principles which can enhance program development through community organization processes.

A New Teen Center

There was tremendous excitement in the Recreation Department in a small, affluent city of approximately 35,000 population. The new teen center was to open in two weeks and staff had been hired to manage the facility and provide programs for teens who previously had no facility they could call their own. This had been perceived as a problem in the community because the older teens in particular had expressed a need for a center for some time.

The center opened on schedule and during the first few weeks attendance was high. The facility, which had ping-pong and pool tables, reading and music rooms, a dance area, and various games such as chess, checkers, and monopoly was used extensively. However, toward the end of the first few weeks attendance figures began to drop rapidly and within a few short months only ten or fifteen youths frequented the center on a given day. Most of those who attended were between the ages of 13 and 15.

The staff was bewildered. It had planned and advertised a variety of programs ranging from tournaments and dances to special events such as outings to professional sports events and backpacking trips. In addition, free music lessons were available (especially guitar, recorder, and flute) but only a handful of teens became involved.

Within a year the center director resigned to take a job elsewhere as did most of the original supporting staff members. Several center directors were hired in the course of the next two years but none were able to alter the picture. The older teenagers rarely used the center and the attendance among the younger set remained relatively low.

Adult citizens in the community and the recreation staff members attributed the poor support of the center to the teens themselves. In fact, they concluded that the youths were apathetic, misguided, and beyond the reach of "the establishment." An easy conclusion to draw — except that too many other communities offered programs to their teens which were thriving and generally conducted in far less elaborate facilities. Although it is possible to let the blame rest with the youths, this hardly seems plausible.

What caused the problem? Judging from what is known about the process adopted by the recreation staff members, the principle stated at the beginning of this chapter of developing ". . . understanding of the needs of the people . . ." was virtually ignored, albeit unintentionally. It was *assumed* that the elaborate center, in itself, would attract participants. It was *assumed* that the departmental staff would correctly identify and offer activities which would be of interest to the youths. Frequently, planners and programmers will be correct in their assumptions but this was not the case in this particular vignette.

The major error of the department staff centered around a failure to establish a working relationship with the clientele to be served. The staff remained virtually isolated during both the planning and implementation stages. As a result, the participants had little or no vested interest in the success or failure of the center since everything had been done *for* them.

Murphy (Murphy, et al., 1973), referred to programming of this nature as *cafeteria style programming.* This is an approach in which a variety of programs are offered to the public and program continuation is primarily contingent upon community responsiveness reflected in the form of past participation patterns. Thus, programs are generally offered again only if the numbers of participants are sufficient to warrant continuation. "Cafeteria style" administrators tend to assume that their role does not extend beyond the basic requirement of offering and conducting activities, a rather narrow definition of "success."

Frequently, advocates of cafeteria style programming hold the view that the only task of the leisure service practitioner is to develop many programs which, largely through trial and error, lead to the identification of the "best" activities—"best" being defined in terms of popularity. Those adhering to this approach tend to steer clear of analyzing program effects, particularly effects relating to the psychology of the participant. Rather than play "armchair psychologist," the cafeteria style programmer assumes that if people wish involvement in a given program, they will support that program in sufficient numbers and therefore program continuation should be determined on that basis alone.

The principal limitation of this view, of course, is that the values and ideals expressed by most leisure service agencies go well beyond the cafeteria approach. Such values and ideals do *not* focus only upon large participation rates; rather, they clearly purport to enhance self-image, build character, develop healthy interpersonal relations, heighten creativity, increase self-confidence, and so forth. But the cafeteria style planner will probably never know if such values and ideals are achieved since they are not really part of the criteria employed for program selection and continuation.

The counterpart to cafeteria style programming was also discussed by Murphy (Murphy, et al., 1973). It is as concerned with *process* as it is with *program* considerations. This style, referred to as the *enabler* approach to the delivery of leisure services, is one in which practitioners specifically see their role as facilitators for meeting human and community needs. The enabler judges the effectiveness of a given program, not only by the number of participants in a program, but also by the quality of the participant's experience. This means that the *role of the recreator,* and the *function of recreation,* must be clearly established at the onset in terms of expected outcomes, and that success is dependent upon the extent to which those outcomes are achieved. Certainly, counting numbers of participants continues to be an important criterion but the evaluative process must not stop there. The enabler's evaluation centers around whether or not community problems are being effectively addressed and whether or not the recreation experience becomes a reality for participants. Most importantly, perhaps, the enabler actively involves people *with* the planning and implementation of programs. In contrast, the cafeteria style approach is to program *for* people.

An important difference between the cafeteria and enabler approaches is consciousness. The proponent of the former style stands back from the program, sees that large numbers of people are participating, and says, "This is a successful program." The enabler, however, becomes involved with participants to the extent that he or she possesses an awareness of what is occurring *within* the participant and *within* the community. When a child who had been unable to interact with others without being aggressive and hostile begins to modify that style of behavior and develop a more positive view of self as well as others, the enabler may then say, "For this child, this is a successful program."

Returning to our teen center problem, it was readily apparent that a cafeteria style approach had been unsuccessfully implemented by the staff. There was virtually no interaction between staff and public, particularly during the planning phases. No sense of commitment to the center was felt by the teens. Everything had been done for them, rather than by or with them. This leads to our first principle in leisure service programming:

Principle I. Programming with rather than for people may facilitate a strong sense of commitment to the program among participants.

Caution must be exercised at this point lest this principle be taken for granted. It appears, in fact, that common sense alone would bring one to this point; yet it cannot be overemphasized, particularly in light of the number of times it is violated in practice. The implementation of this principle is much more difficult than it appears. There are processes, however, which, if conscientiously followed, can effectively overcome potential difficulties. These processes are considered in the latter portion of this chapter.

A New Community Program

During the peak of the economic boom in the early 1970s, an upper-middle class housing development laced with meandering canals, lovely neighborhood parks, and considerable undeveloped open green space, sprang up near a large metropolitan area. The development was especially conducive for leisure based activities. Both the developers and the citizens of the new community were conscious of the need for instituting leisure service programs, particularly for the teen population. They concluded that leisure service professionals should be hired on a consultant basis to recommend program directions based on the desires of the population.

Consultants were employed and they carefully created a survey instrument designed to allow respondents to express their feelings toward a wide array of activities. Opportunities for responding to "open-end" items were ample. Virtually all of the teens participated in the survey and the results were tabulated. A number of program areas emerged pointing to directions of priority. Based on this data, programs were developed and implemented but from the day the center opened, there was very little participation. Another failure.

A basic violation occurred in this example which may help to explain why the programs failed to meet the needs of the community. Although a questionnaire was completed by most of the teenagers in the new area, their "true" preferences were not accurately assessed. In surveys of this nature, it is all too easy to suggest an extensive list of program areas which "sound good" at the time the survey is conducted. It is also possible that preferences are indicated based upon perceptions of what others like and dislike. However, for the survey participant there is absolutely no commitment, so why not be extravagant in responses? By failing to involve the teens in the *process* of program development in a way which would create a sense of caring about the outcome, the first principle was violated—programs were ultimately offered *for* rather than *with* people.

A second principle now emerges, which is closely aligned with the first, but warrants separate consideration in its own right:

Principle II. Providing programs on the basis of what people say they want offers no assurance of initial participation or continued involvement of participants.

Conducting a survey, or merely asking people what they think they would like allows people to remain uncommitted. Certain degrees of success may be experienced through the use of this method but, by and large, it is weak if used alone. The power of the survey emerges when it is used as a preliminary springboard for continuous involvement *with* the population to be served. But it is merely paying lip service to the enabler approach if survey results are used exclusively to proceed on a cafeteria style basis.

A Correctional Facility Program

To an increasing extent, administrators of correctional institutions are recognizing the need to provide healthy leisure service programs for inmates. Accordingly, in a western state, a recreation director was recruited for a summer to administer a program for approximately 100 young men between 18 and 25 years of age. The inmate response was gratifying as they were eager to add to their leisure time options. On the basis of what the population said they wanted, the following activities were established as ongoing structured programs: basketball, ping-pong, pocket billiards, track and field, and rock music.

Although participation was consistently high, a problem quickly emerged — there were repeated arguments and near-fights, especially in the basketball program. Tensions ran high both on and off the court. Subgroups began to form into a "we-they" configuration. All in all, the positive values to be derived from involvement in recreation activities remained a hazy ideal. What had happened? A third principle can be introduced which relates to what had occurred:

Principle III. Offering programs based on popularity offers no assurance that participants are actually benefiting from their involvement.

The heart of the issue is basic—the values of toughness, aggression, and power, all common to institutional life, were the dominant reinforcers in the programs. Winning and "being best" were the most prized rewards, rather than participation itself.

This syndrome is not peculiar to correctional institutions. It is notably common in the inner city but occurs in virtually any environment. Activities which reinforce existing undesirable patterns of behavior must therefore be approached with extreme caution. It may, of course, be necessary to begin with programs which are clearly based upon popularity alone, but once relationships between participants and staff members are strengthened, directions capable of influencing positive social and psychological changes can be explored. This is a process which requires considerable interpersonal skill and will be considered more fully in a later section.

Programs for the Aged

In a community of approximately 100,000 population, a senior citizens program was developed utilizing schools as central facilities for conducting programs. The programs were carefully planned and offered by exceptionally dynamic leaders. Those senior citizens who attended had been actively involved in developing and sustaining programs. A deep sense of pride evolved which was enjoyed by staff and participants alike.

Despite the success of the program for those who were involved, the staff members were troubled by the fact that neither Chicano nor black senior citizens had ever become involved. Almost every participant was white and had a reasonably comfortable level of income. Thus, the on-site effectiveness of the program meant nothing to a substantial portion of the population. A fourth principle will shed light on this frequently found situation:

Principle IV. Offering a program, no matter how outstanding, is not enough in itself if there are economic, geographic, or psychological barriers which inhibit citizen involvement.

In this particular community, most of the minorities did not live in the vicinity of the schools used for the programs. For lower income group members, the absence of inexpensive transportation presented a substantial financial problem. Many did not own an automobile and the community had no bus service. The absence of a public transportation program clearly presented an insurmountable barrier for this group.

In addition, there were formidable psychological barriers. Interviews later revealed that seniors in this group felt that the program was *by* whites, *for* whites. They felt no identity with "the program across town." Their values were different, their past experiences were culturally divergent, and their insecurity in an unfamiliar environment was a problem. For this group, the program represented another failure.

How might this have been avoided? Certainly an obvious step related to the selection of program sites which would have circumvented the geographic barrier. But even this may not have been sufficient. For the program to be effective, our preceding principles of leisure service programming should have been utilized. Again, as we will later discuss, through a process of effective community organization many of the pitfalls described in this brief case study can be avoided.

A Response to Urban Crisis

During the late sixties and early seventies, many cities were torn with racial and political unrest. Riots erupted all too frequently, police-community relations were at an unprecedented low point, and there was a general disillusionment with governmental processes, particularly among the economically disadvantaged. A major source of discontent centered around perceived and real inequities in the delivery of leisure services. It was pointed out by Kraus (1968) for example, that the lack of adequate recreation services available to the economically disadvantaged was identified by black leaders as a major cause of the tremendous unrest, which has been termed the urban crisis of the sixties.

In an attempt to respond to such inequities, numerous federal and state governmental agencies allocated millions of dollars to cities and counties for the purpose of developing anti-crime and delinquency prevention programs, many of which were related to leisure services. In Atlanta, Georgia, for instance, a police station wagon was fully equipped with a PA system and records. A radio disc jockey was assigned to the vechile so that it could be dispatched quickly to an area where "trouble might be brewing." Once at the scene, street dances could be instantly initiated thereby creating a pleasant diversion (National League of Cities, 1968). In other cities, recreation directors, many with little or no professional preparation or experience, were hired directly from lower economic communities. This type of employment policy was instituted in response to community demands for economic and self-determination.

The intent was sound but the outcomes were questionable. Leaders hired in this way rarely had the knowledge and the skill to function as a leisure service practitioner. The in-service programs which were implemented to teach them the complexities of their new roles only scratched the surface. Programs which initially involved the community were frequently not sustained. In general, regressions occurred which were predictable since the leaders, through no fault of their own, did not have the understanding of leisure service concepts to sustain a truly community-based comprehensive leisure service delivery system.

Still other approaches involved the busing of lower income youngsters to national park and forest areas as a means of broadening their appreciation of the environment while at the same time hoping to magically produce substantial personality alterations which would lead these youngsters away from delinquency related values and life-styles. Again the intent was commendable and these programs no doubt had a number of favorable effects, but it is doubtful that deep-rooted changes occurred among the participants if their involvement was limited to one or two such excursions. In instances where environmental programs were integrated with a variety of other services, benefits were often dynamic and long-lasting, but more frequently than not, such programs were offered only once or twice and were not integrated with other agency services.

As important as the need for change was, history has shown that, at best, these types of approaches were no more than "Band-Aid" attempts which only temporarily responded to symptoms. Thus, an additional leisure service programming principle became evident:

Principle V. Offering programs designed to solve deep-rooted social problems may be demanding too much of the leisure service delivery system and its capabilities if such programs are not integrated with other supporting forces on a sustained basis.

This is not to say that the leisure service practitioner cannot have a great impact on social problems — quite the contrary. But it is doubtful that societal problems can be attacked through leisure programs alone. A well-orchestrated, comprehensive effort will be more effective in the long run. Such an effort may be spearheaded by leisure service agencies but it must also involve a variety of other community based agencies and groups.

A Beautiful Community Park

After five years of diligent planning, a community of almost 100,000 population had finally acquired a park. It was a park of which residents could be proud. A multi-purpose building had been erected and was available to community groups for meetings, for employees of the Park and Recreation Department to offer programs to small groups of participants, and for the storage of sports equipment and games to be used by members of the community at the park site.

For many months the park received extensive use by the citizenry and very few problems were evidenced. There was no vandalism, a variety of groups shared the park simultaneously without any difficulty, and everyone appeared quite content. By the end of the first year, however, the park had become so popular among the local teenagers that many of the neighboring residents begain to complain that the teens were "taking over" the park. Youths would gather in small to medium-sized groups and "hang around" on weekends, after school, and in the evening, sometimes until 10 p.m. when the park curfew came into effect.

The teens were not violating any laws but tension in the immediate area of the park continued to grow. The chief of police began receiving telephone complaints from local residents. In response, he ordered patrol officers to go into the park regularly to "check things out." It did not take long for a resentment toward the officers to develop among the youths. Derogatory comments by the youths to police officers became increasingly commonplace. This prompted officers to clear the area, sending the teens on their way. The park staff sided with the officers, afraid that the youths would begin committing acts of vandalism. A volatile situation developed in which park employees regularly requested police assistance whenever groups of more than four or five gathered without being involved in a specific program.

Police-youth tensions grew to the point that the officers went out of their way to find reasons to force the youths to leave the park. Finally, officers apprehended eight youths who were smoking cigarettes in the park. The officers were within proper boundaries since the youths were below the legal smoking age, but this incident served only to increase tensions and the youths "retaliated" by refusing to go into the park. They moved their gathering places to street corners in the downtown area, or they found an older teen with a car and left the area altogether.

Eventually, the image of the park was restored. It continued to be carefully patrolled by the police department and park staff and its beauty was preserved. As far as the teenagers were concerned, however, the park was a pretty place to view, but it provided nothing for them. For this group, a failure occurred which stemmed from another important concept:

Principle VI. Effectively maintaining beautiful areas and facilities may have little bearing on the extent to which the leisure service delivery system meets human needs.

In effect, a wall was constructed to keep a particular group out of the park so the park's beauty and reputation would be maintained. But this action ultimately led to the exclusion of an important segment of the population. Gray (1973) has referred to this type of approach as the "Tyranny of the Chain-Link Fence." Those advocating protective barriers, whether in the form of rules, fences, or patrols, believe that they are fulfilling their most essential function: the control and protection of the facility. The essence of this approach was expressed by Gray as follows:

The most deleterious effect of the chain-link philosophy is on the deployment of staff. Such a philosophy holds that the primary concern of the staff is to operate the center. It identifies the primary tasks as surveillance of grounds to assure compliance with rules, safety, proper use of facilities and control of equipment; development of a schedule for use of the facility; planning and execution of a program of activities with the staff in face-to-face leadership roles; coordination of maintenance activities to insure the readiness and sanitary condition of the premises. Such a philosophy rewards facility managers and holds that what happens on the center is what counts. (p. 288).

The difficulties involved in maintaining areas and facilities should certainly not be underestimated nor taken for granted. The challenge, however, is to carry out the important function of preservation in a manner which simultaneously meets the needs of the population. In other words, the purpose of the facility should never be forgotten.

In our case study, the facility was, in fact, preserved for a large segment of the population, and this is important; but it was accomplished at the expense of another significant group. Alternatives which utilized community organization concepts could have been incorporated into the problem-solving process, possibly preventing the outcome just described. The challenge might have been met if the counterpoint to the chain-link fence philosophy had been adopted through positive people-to-people interaction. It is essential, as Gray (Gray and Pelegrino, 1973) has recognized, that community centers and parks not remain isolated islands, withdrawn in their own little spheres. Centers ". . . cannot continue to serve a small, clean orderly segment of the community while there is violence in the streets and expect the populace to continue to support it." (p. 289).

Community Leadership through Leisure Services

Identifying and unifying appropriate community resources for the purpose of ultimately developing a *coordinated* leisure service delivery system can ititially be a difficult process, but highly rewarding in the long run. It basically involves "spinning a web" that connects otherwise isolated resources. The greater the number of bonds, the stronger the capability.

But before the web can be developed, the leisure service practitioner must ask, "Why do I need involvement with other agencies? How will it enhance the delivery of services?" The response can be found in the philosophical framework that guides the agency, a philosophy ultimately expressed in terms of the role of the recreator and purpose of the agency.

The advocate of the cafeteria style approach, for example, would probably not be comfortable with community organization concepts since the role of the recreator would be extended beyond an acceptable point; that is, it would be viewed as extending too far into the realm of other agencies.

The enabler, on the other hand, can readily welcome a community-wide, web-spinning process and remain consistent with his or her basic purpose. The enabler is concerned with addressing social problems and enhancing personal growth among participants. These concerns are so important that great effort will be expended to determine the extent to which leisure services are positively affecting them. Inevitably, the enabler realizes that involvement in recreation activities, in and of itself, meets only a portion of the individual's needs. In a lower income area of the inner-city, for example, the practitioner becomes aware of health problems among participants which the leisure service agency is not equipped to address. Providing a temporary diversion from hunger and poor health touches only a small portion of an individual's life when so much more should be done. If self-actualizing experiences are to become realities for participants, lower needs related to safety and security must first be addressed. Self-actualization will remain a meaningless ideal if such basic needs are ignored. Focusing on program activities alone ignores necessary steps of the hierarchy.

If leisure service agencies hope to maximize the benefits derived from involvement in recreation activities by members of a given community, then the *total* person must be considered and this cannot realistically be accomplished by a single agency. Why not integrate the efforts of the many available resources which provide community services? A reasonable notion, but a difficult connection to complete. No matter how conscientious the individual, it is not always easy to know where to begin nor how other groups should be approached. Fear may exist that the personnel of one's own agency may view efforts to involve other agencies as threatening or extraneous to the immediate program. Many will also harbor a fear of being rejected by members of other agencies. Time is also a limitation; community organization requires considerable effort and it is all one can do to maintain one's own program much less become involved with other agencies which offer distinctly different services.

Such limitations notwithstanding, these obstacles can be diminished. If these and other hurdles can be overcome, the long-range dividends can be substantial. In fact, with the absence of a total community approach, citizens will unfortunately receive services in piecemeal fashion from a variety of fragmented agencies. Consequently, the initial investment is much too important to simply overlook or avoid.

But it might also be asked whether or not a leisure service agency is an appropriate spearhead for a community organization movement. In reality, it probably matters little which agency takes the initiative so long as leisure service agencies become involved in the process. However, leisure service agencies enjoy an advantage shared by few others. They serve the public from a *positive* perspective. This means that leisure services are sought by participants who wish an enjoyable experience. They do not come to fill a *deficit need* as might be the case for one seeking services from the unemployment or welfare office, or the county health clinic. Leisure service agencies are more involved with *growth needs* and are thus perceived in a more favorable, supportive light.

Serving in a capacity which *attracts* participants is especially important since other agencies frequently have difficulty reaching those in greatest need. This may also be true for the leisure service agency as well, but large numbers of citizens who may be in need of assistance from various social service agencies will not seek help from them, yet will become involved in leisure service programs. Once the contact is solidified by the leisure service practitioner, the opportunity to involve that person with other community resources is enhanced to the extent that strong bonds between agencies have been established. It is not enough when one sees a family in need of services to simply suggest an agency to them which might provide assistance. Bureaucracy is intimidating and it is unlikely that a family, especially one which is probably unfamiliar with agency and governmental processes, will take the necessary step to acquire help.

The alternative is to have inter-agency ties so strong that a referral can be personalized. A specific staff member's name can be given to the family so they have a personal contact. A quick telephone call to a familiar ally in another agency can help break the ice so that the family visitation is expected. In the event the visit is never made, a staff member from the second agency may initiate a personal follow-up action. As time goes on, members of both agencies will be aware of each other and will collaborate whenever opportunities for service arise which are of mutual concern.

There may be a point at which the family no longer requires the services of the assisting agency, but could nevertheless continue their involvement in leisure service programs. Consequently, the leisure service practitioner, as a result of having been successfully involved in an effective referral process, may be in a position to further advise the family in other areas of concern as well, if and when such a need arises. This is not to be construed as creating a counselor role for the practitioner; rather it suggests a role in which there is an awareness of the *total* person and a willingness to go beyond activity programming alone. When leisure services are sought by the public, and agency-community relations are favorable, the leisure service practitioner is in a highly favorable position to serve as a catalyst for the community organization process.

Community organization, once initiated, becomes a continuous process always subject to change as the need for new directions is identified. But the basic process remains stable and once it is implemented it can unify the resources required to effectively respond to meeting human needs. The details of implementation may vary from one community to another due to political factors, economic conditions, leadership differences, and

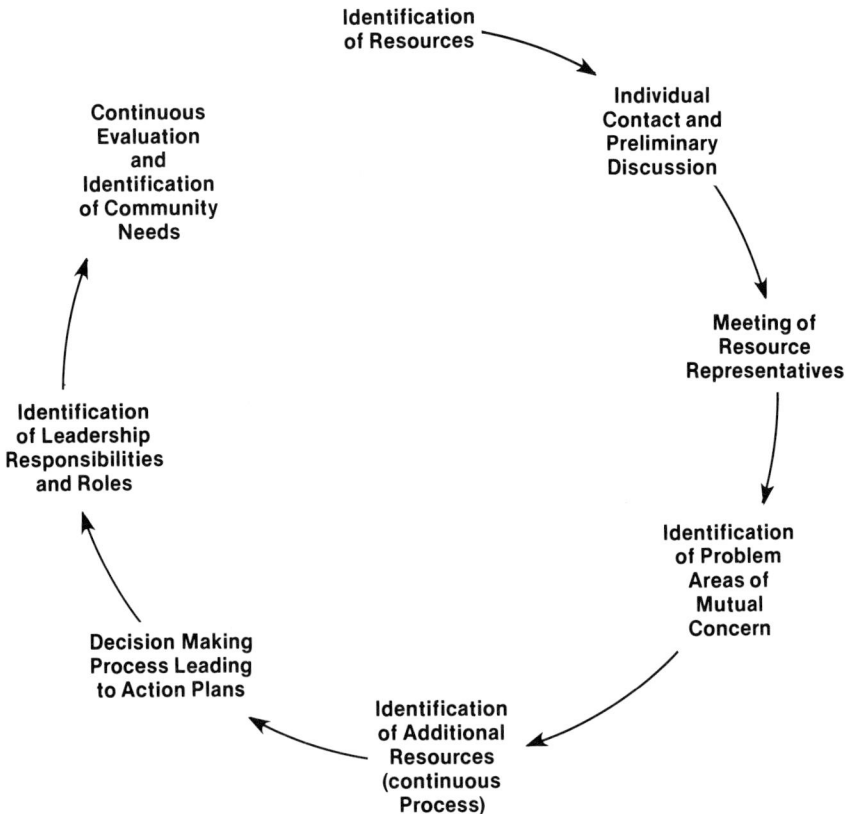

Figure 4.1   The Community Organization Cycle

so forth, but the steps described in Figure 4-1 can serve as an overall guide capable of adoption in virtually any community. The discussion which follows examines this process assuming that the major leadership would be provided by personnel from one or more leisure service agencies.

Integrating Community Services

The first step must be to carefully identify existing community resources which might be an asset in a coordinated, community-wide effort. Although far from exhaustive, and certain to vary among communities, the following list will identify agencies which could provide valuable depth to the community organization process:

School Guidance Counselors
County Public and Mental Health
  Services
Law Enforcement Agencies
Fire Department
Welfare Office
Unemployment Office
State and County Park
  Departments
Probation and Court Offices

Service Organizations and Clubs
Colleges and Universities
Voluntary, Non-profit Agencies
Local Merchants
Industry
Volunteer Bureau
State Extension Service
Church Organizations
Newspaper, Radio, and Television
  Media

Once a preliminary list of agencies has been prepared, it is probably best to narrow the field initially keeping in mind that at a later time the number of involved agencies can be extended. Contact must be made with staff members from each of the selected agencies. Initial contact should be made on a personal basis at which time concepts related to community organization can be discussed. It is important, however, not to expect any type of firm commitment by an agency during the exploratory meeting. Any specific commitment as well as the nature of involvement should be determined by those who actually meet and develop ideas directed toward the formulation of a new approach.

Decisions relating to which agencies should be initially approached must be carefully considered. It is suggested that the agencies which should be contacted first are those having personnel who would be the most receptive to leisure service ideals and to extending their involvement in the community. For example, agency personnel who have previously interacted with leisure service staff members would be logical choices for initial contact. So, too, are those agencies which have traditionally exhibited a willingness to expand their roles in innovative and creative ways.

It may be self-defeating to attempt to initially involve agencies which are not amenable to change. If, for example, the administrators of a local law enforcement department perceive their role as exclusively protecting the community from a monitoring and enforcement perspective, their input at an inter-agency meeting may be quite negative thereby putting a damper on planning ideas. Law enforcement agencies were intentionally selected as an example since it is not unusual for police and public safety department officials to hold to the view that "social work" is not a law enforcement role. Progressive departments have rejected this outmoded view in the belief that a great deal can be done at the preventive as well as enforcement level. Such departments are generally eager to unite with other community resources and become quickly involved at the onset. Others, however, must be approached much more cautiously—probably after other agencies have come together, have begun to formulate their approach, and have actually initiated one or more new, cooperatively sponsored programs. In any case, it is essential that law enforcement agencies become involved in the process at some point; otherwise, social and community problems cannot be fully addressed. Due to the importance of acquiring police involvement, the following guidelines are offered to facilitate the process:

1. Law enforcement officials must not be asked to replace existing responsibilities with new obligations; rather, they should be asked to *extend* their role in a manner which will ultimately lead to an increase in the effectiveness of their departments.

2. Law enforcement officials must not be put on the defensive through criticism of existing approaches, whether warranted or not. Emphasis should not be on past or present limitations but on increasing the effectiveness of all community service agencies through new approaches. Placing importance on positive factors is essential and cannot be overemphasized.

3. Ultimately, as many law enforcement officers as possible should be involved in the effort. In the past, some departments have agreed to appoint one or more Police-Community Relations officers to work with other community resources, but the remainder of the department continued to perform duties in the usual manner. Two problems typically arose. First, beat or patrol officers often felt that the Police-Community Relations officers were shirking their duties by wasting time meeting with community groups, speaking to students in the schools, and so forth. They were not perceived as doing "respectable" police work. Consequently, many problems related to morale and inter-officer relations were generated. Second, and of equal importance, police-community relations officers were viewed as "the exception" by many members of the community at large. Citizens felt that these officers were merely paying lip-service to meaningful Police-Community Relations since roles had not changed for the majority of law enforcement officers in the

department. It is therefore essential to encourage law enforcement administrators to allow all officers in the department to become involved in those processes which appropriately extend their roles.

4. It may be helpful to have information about other communities that have effectively involved law enforcement officials in inter-agency programs. Through this approach, potential objections may be averted while at the same time specific ideas may be presented which lend structure and direction to possible areas of involvement.

5. Law enforcement officials may be more willing to enter into a cooperative effort if they perceive that their work may be simplified. If all agencies, including law enforcement departments, are willing to explore new means of providing cooperative services to the community, efforts in controlling crime and delinquency may be aided in the long run.

It is important to consider how each and every agency which might potentially become involved would benefit. Once that has been explored and clarified, methods of involving others will become clearer. In addition, the direct benefits to be gained by the community will simultaneously become addressed. The benefits afforded different agencies may vary widely but certain patterns will emerge which can serve as a starting point.

Far from all-inclusive, the following exemplifies how actual benefits from interagency cooperation can accrue. In addition, sample areas are presented which might be discussed in an effort to generate interest for agencies to become a part of a widespread community approach.

1. Law enforcement and probation officers will become aware of resources which can offer alternatives to the juvenile and criminal justice systems, alternatives which may be more effective, particularly in light of dismally high recidivism (re-arrest) rates.

2. Agencies involved in counseling and social-welfare functions will be in a position to make better decisions about their clientele if they understand more about their "total needs." Input from several agency representatives can provide this type of depth.

3. Local merchants who are willing to contribute money or materials to sponsor programs will receive valuable visibility in the community, visibility which may increase their effectiveness as a retail enterprise. This can be true for industry as well.

4. Church organizations will be able to extend their involvement with individuals or groups in ways which are consistent with the tenets of their doctrine. Such action may lead to increased involvement among community residents in the church, an involvement which could be of life-long value to those choosing such a direction.

5. Increased interagency participation by voluntary agency personnel could ultimately involve a greater portion of the community in their own specialized programs. This would extend the opportunities for agency goals and objectives to be directed toward a greater constituency.

6. Governmental agencies would increase their visibility and involvement with community residents thereby creating opportunities to become more sensitive to citizen needs. Services, which may be bogged down with bureaucracy, can become more personalized.

7. Volunteers who are involved in a coordinated, interagency effort have important opportunities to meet their own personal needs while providing meaningful service to others.

8. Service organizations and clubs could have greater opportunities to carry out their principal function, that is, providing services to the community.

9. By establishing a community sanctioned, organized coalition of agencies through community organization processes, many community resources will not only be willing, but anxious to participate. There is generally an awareness that involvement in such efforts strengthens the thrust and scope of their own particular group or organization.

10. Each group or agency which becomes involved in a coordinated effort has the opportunity to interact with resources from other groups and agencies in a new manner, perhaps on a first-time basis. Gaining insights into the roles and functions of others is invariably a valuable experience.

The list of benefits could go on for some time. The point is that these and other potential values should be carefully identified and considered before the process is actually initiated. Sensitivity to the needs of other agencies and groups will greatly increase the likelihood of leisure service practitioners effectively drawing community groups together.

Earlier, a number of case examples were highlighted in which difficulties were experienced in one form or another. At this point, it may be helpful to draw from the *success* of a neighborhood area of approximately 10,000 people which was geographically isolated from the remainder of the city of more than 100,000 population. The area was bounded by highways on all sides, had its own name which had been designated by the original developer, and was perceived as "different" from the remainder of the city by most of its residents. Although many in the community had lived there for years, more than half could be considered transient, not an atypical situation in a highly mobile society.

The area was economically depressed but not poverty-stricken. The average income per family in 1972 was approximately $7,000 a year, considerably lower than the $13,500 average for the city as a whole. Many social problems existed such as high crime and delinquency rates, vandalism, and a high drop-out rate in the high school.

The school board district decided to employ a Community School Director to provide educational and recreational services. Several elementary schools were used as bases of operation. The schools were made available to the director during non-school hours. With no additional staff support, the Community School Director was able to provide tremendous increases in services to the community by the end of the first year:

1. Using only volunteers, free classes were offered in automotive repair, music, specialized crafts, gymnastics, and various other activities.
2. The municipal Recreation Department began to extend programs into the elementary schools and provided the staff necessary for program delivery.
3. The County Mental and Public Health Departments came into the schools on a regular basis and provided counseling and educational services of all types, depending upon the needs and requests of the community.
4. Faculty from the local two-year community college offered accredited courses in the elementary schools which overcame transportation barriers in the area since residents were within walking distance of a school.
5. After receiving only minimal initial support, the teenagers developed and sustained programs almost entirely on their own. They were able to benefit as much by this process as they were as participants in the activities themselves.
6. Local law enforcement officers who were assigned to patrol the area stopped in regularly at the schools when programs were in process to informally interact with the participants. This strengthened community relations tremendously, particularly among teenagers. Numerous barriers were reduced after they had opportunities to interact with officers under non-threatening conditions. Officers who came to know the youths on a different level were later able to personalize the handling of youngsters who came to their attention. In other words, in situations requiring the intervention of police officers, all youths were not necessarily treated the same since new insights entered into the decision making process.

7. Local merchants often provided support in the form of refreshments, materials, and prizes for special events which were developed by the Community School Director.
8. A pre-school program was developed using federal funds and fees (based on a sliding scale according to one's ability to pay) at no cost to the community. Many working mothers were able to utilize the school for their children.
9. The Juvenile Probation Officer responsible for youths in the area visited one of the schools every week, meeting with youths as a group, thus increasing his contact and involvement with them while strengthening his relationship with the Community School Director.
10. A representative from the State Unemployment Department worked closely with the Community School Director in an effort to increase job opportunities for area residents seeking employment.
11. Representatives from schools, voluntary agencies, governmental agencies, and the municipal recreation department met monthly to discuss individual cases which had come to their attention. They made every effort to insure that the best possible services were being provided by adopting a multiple agency approach.
12. Staff members responsible for providing radio, television, and newspaper coverage in the city were actively involved with the Community Schools program. Publicity and announcements of events were always assured and as a result public relations were strengthened.

Not all of the problems of this community were solved, nor is it likely that they will be, but the benefits experienced by the community were extensive and certainly greater than had been possible prior to the arrival of a community organizer, the Community School Director. He operated from a base very similar to that of leisure service practitioners, especially those in municipal and voluntary agencies, except that he had even less supporting staff resources. The role he played could be adopted by many who are involved in a leisure service agency. It is the role of catalyst, leader, and organizer. It requires sensitivity to human needs, sensitivity to the needs of other agencies, and a great deal of skill, time, patience, and belief that it will work.

Leisure service agencies wishing to take a major role in mobilizing community resources must be willing to fully support staff members by allowing time for the process to evolve. The scenario cannot be written in advance since it may develop quite differently from one community to another, but if the leaders are tactful and skilled in interacting with others, diverse groups can be effectively united. It takes organization, sometimes arbitration, and always considerable effort to insure continuous communication among agencies. All of these elements appear to be logical enough on the surface, but each requires great thought and planning.

Understanding that the delivery of leisure services must be coordinated with a total community system is the first step leading to increased effectiveness for all involved. Developing insights into the nature of human and societal needs, coupled with the ability to plan and develop programs *with* the community is a process which can significantly increase the professional stature and credibility of the leisure service field.

Summary

There has been considerable controversy surrounding what a leisure service practitioner should or should not be (Murphy, et al., 1973). Roles vary from the cafeteria style programmer to the enabler, or somewhere in between. Both approaches are needed but it must be kept in mind that the cafeteria style programmer may tend to limit involvement with the community to activity programming alone.

A common pattern of such programmers is to present a wide variety of activities from which community residents may pick and choose. The continuation of programs tends to depend upon which activities are attended in the greatest number.

While the cafeteria style programmer is often quite successful in attracting many participants, little is revealed about the quality of programs and the extent to which the inner person is affected by involvement in them. The enabler, however, focuses as much attention on the recreation *process* as the mechanics of providing activities. Not only are numbers of participants used as an indicator of program success, but so are such factors as:

1. Are leisure services throughout the community integrated to avoid duplication?
2. Are there objectives established for programs and are they evaluated in humanistic terms?
3. Are steps being taken to meet the basic needs of participants, such as at the physiological and safety levels of Maslow's hierarchy, before attempting to address higher and probably more-difficult-to-meet needs.
4. Are participants involved in the planning and decision making of programming in such a way that a commitment to the success of the program is generated?
5. Are the resources in the community fully utilized so that the *complete* person is being considered and served in an integrated rather than fragmented fashion?

The enabler and the community organizer share a common outlook and are basically one and the same; one cannot fulfill the role of enabler without also being aware of the need for integrating community resources. Although the enabler role certainly seems to be a logical approach for those involved in leisure services, it is actually not adopted as much in practice as one might suspect. This is due largely to the effort that is required and the feeling that there simply is not enough time available for such extensive involvement. For those who have been able to "make time," however, the pay-offs have been great for agency and participant alike. It is as if the work required increases in mathematical proportions but the actual benefits increase geometrically.

The observations of Minzey (1972, p. 153) clearly synthesize the challenge and the capabilities of the community organization process. Speaking specifically about community education which utilizes Community School Directors to develop and delivery services of all kinds, his comments are applicable to all agencies concerned with meeting human needs:

> Even the practice of community education which is primarily program oriented results in benefits to the community. Certainly there are advantages to providing for the educational or recreational needs of a community, even if all the problems of the community are not solved.
>
> The real promise of community education, however, comes in that aspect called process. For unlike most current endeavors of social engineering which attack the symptoms of our problems, community education provides a system for involvement of people in the identification and solution of their problems . . . . And even if the final result is less than desired, a technique for returning to participatory democracy to our communities may be merit enough . . . .

By combining *program* and *process* in leisure services, there can be rewards from involvement in programs as well as from being a part of their development. By integrating community services, there is a greater likelihood that the *total* person will be more effectively served. By understanding the full scope of community organization, the likelihood of attaining agency objectives will most certainly be increased.

Study Questions

1. What is the difference between cafeteria style programming and the enabler approach? Why is each important?
2. What is the difference between program and process in leisure services?
3. What are the advantages and disadvantages of programming (a) with and (b) for people in leisure services?

4. What dangers are involved in using activity preference surveys as a basis for program planning?
5. Why should or shouldn't programming be primarily based on popularity, that is, numbers of participants?
6. What barriers may exist which inhibit citizen involvement and participation in leisure programs?
7. To what extent might leisure service programs help solve social problems?
8. What is meant by the "Tyranny of the Chain Link Fence," and why is it significant to leisure service practitioners?
9. Why might leisure service agencies be logical choices to take the leadership as community organizers, spearheading the efforts of a variety of community agencies and resources?
10. Which agencies in your own community would you involve in a total delivery system and what roles might each play?

References

Gray, David E. "Tyranny of the Chain Link Fence." David Gray and Donald Pelegrino. In *Reflections on the Recreation and Park Movement*, Dubuque, Ia.: Wm. C. Brown Company, Publishers, 1973.

Kraus, Richard. *Public Recreation and the Negro: A Study of Participation and Administrative Practices.* New York: Center for Urban Education, 1968.

Minzey, Jack. "Community Education: An Amalgam of Many Views." *Phi Delta Kappan* November (1972): 150-153.

Murphy, James F.; Williams, John G.; Niepoth, E. William; and Brown, Paul D. *Leisure Service Delivery System: A Modern Perspective.* Philadelphia: Lea & Febiger, 1973.

National League of Urban Cities. *Recreation and the Nation's Cities: Problems and Approaches.* Washington, D.C.: Prepared for the Bureau of Outdoor Recreation, Department of the Interior, 1968.

Related Readings

Aetshuler, Alan. *Community Control: The Black Demand for Participation in Large American Cities.* New York: Pegasus, 1970.

Anderson, Carl L. *Community Health.* St. Louis: The C. V. Mosby Company, 1969.

Bakacs, Tibor. *Urbanization and Human Health.* Budapest: Adademia, Kiadó, 1972.

Bannon, Joseph J. (ed.) *Outreach: Extending Community Service in Urban Areas.* Springfield, Ill.: Charles C. Thomas, 1973.

Berridge, Robert. *The Community Education Handbook.* Midland, Michigan: Pendell Publishing Co., 1973.

Buell, Bradley. *Community Planning for Human Services.* New York: Columbia University Press, 1952.

Campbell, Ronald, and Ramseyer, John A. *The Dynamics of School/Community Relations.* New York: Allyn & Bacon, 1955.

Cavan, Ruth S. "Negro Family Disorganization and Juvenile Delinquency." *The Journal of Negro Education* 3:28 (1959): 230-239.

Cohen, A. K. *Delinquent Boys.* Glencoe: The Free Press, 1955.

Dahl, Robert A. *Politics, Economics, and Welfare: Planning and Politico-Economic Systems Resolved Into Basic Social Processes.* New York: Harper & Row, Inc., 1953.

Glueck, Sheldon and Glueck, Eleanor. *Family Environment and Delinquency.* Boston: Houghton Mifflin Company, 1962.

Goetschius, George W. *Working with Community Groups: Using Community Development as a Method of Social Work.* London: Routledge & Kegan Paul, 1969.

Golany, Gideon. *New-Town Planning: Principles and Practice.* New York: John Wiley & Sons, Inc., 1977.

Goldstein, Bernard. *Low Income Youth in Urban Areas.* New York: Holt, Rinehart and Winston, Inc., 1967.

Grier, William H. and Cobbs, Price M. *Black Rage.* New York: Basic Books, Inc., 1968.

Hawn, Peter (ed.) *Community Politics.* London: J. Calder Publishers, 1976.

Heller, Celia S. *Mexican-American Youth: Forgotten Youth at the Crossroads.* New York: Random House, Inc., 1966.

Howe, Louise Kapp. *The Future of the Family.* New York: Simon and Schuster, 1972.

Illinois Youth Commission. *Delinquency Prevention through Community Organization.* Division of Community Services, 1956.

Janowitz, Morris. *Community Political Systems.* Glencoe, Ill.: Free Press, 1961.

Kahn, Alfred J. *Planning Community Services for Children in Trouble.* New York: Columbia University Press, 1963.

Keve, Paul W. *Imaginative Programming in Probation and Parole.* Minneapolis: University of Minnesota Press, 1967.

Kvaraceus, William C. (ed.) *Negro Self-Concept: Implications for School and Citizenship.* New York: McGraw-Hill Book Company, 1965.

Lippitt, Ronald and Eva Schindler-Rainman, *The Volunteer Community: Creative Use of Human Resources.* Fairfax, Va.: NTL Learning Resources Corporation, 1975.

Liturch, Eugene. *School, Family and Neighborhood: The Theory and Practice of School-Community Relations.* New York: Columbia University Press, 1974.

MacCallum, Spencer Heath. *The Art of Community.* Menlo Park, Calif.: Institute for Humane Studies, 1970.

MacIver, Robert M. *The Prevention and Control of Delinquency.* New York: Atherton Press, 1966.

Molloy, Larry. *Community/School: Sharing the Space and the Action.* New York: Educational Facilities Laboratories, 1973.

Nelson, Lowry. *Community Structure and Change.* New York: Macmillan Publishing Co., 1960.

Nesbitt, John A.; Brown Paul D.; and Murphy, James F. (eds.) *Recreation and Leisure Service for the Disadvantaged*. Philadelphia: Lea and Febiger, 1970.

Neumeyer, Martin H. *Juvenile Delinquency in Modern Society*. New York: D. Van Nostrand and Company, 1952.

Nye, F. Ivan. *Family Relationships and Delinquent Behavior*. New York: John Wiley & Sons, Inc., 1958.

Pinkney, Alphonso. *Black Americans*. Englewood Cliffs, N.J.: Prentice-Hall, Inc., 1969.

Presthus, Robert Vance. *Men at the Top: A Study in Community Power*. London: Oxford University Press, 1964.

Roth, Robert (ed.) *Person and Community: A Philosophical Exploration*. New York: Fordham University Press, 1975.

Saleman, Graeme. *Community and Occupation: An Exploration of Work Leisure Relationships*. London: Cambridge University Press, 1974.

Suttles, Gerald D. *The Social Construction of Communities*. Chicago: University of Chicago Press, 1972.

Totten, William. *The Power of Community Education*. Midland, Mich: Pendell Publishing Company, 1970.

Warren, Roland L. *The Community in America*. Chicago: Rand McNally, 1972.

Weaver, Robert Cliffton. *The Urban Complex: Human Values in Urban Life*. Garden City, N.Y.: Doubleday, 1964.

Williams, John E. and Morland, J. Kenneth. *Race, Color, and the Young Child*. Chapel Hill, N.C.: University of North Carolina Press, 1976.

Activity Selection and Programming

Objectives After reading and comprehending this chapter, you should be able to:

1. Identify the tasks generally performed by leisure service activity leaders in both functional and philosophical terms.
2. Prepare an activity notebook following the format suggested in this chapter.
3. Identify key planning considerations related to providing leisure activities for youths, senior citizens, handicapped individuals, and those in correctional settings.
4. Describe the importance of the activity leader as a role model for participants.
5. Explain problems related to program stereotyping in leisure services and be able to present a rationale for modifying activities and programs to avoid such problems.
6. Outline characteristics typically associated with youngsters of varying ages.
7. Describe the limitations and strengths of leisure activity preference surveys.

Introduction

In one sense, the selection of recreation activities is one of the easier tasks faced by the leisure service leader or programmer. Numerous books, manuals, magazine articles, and films are available which present specific activities and how they should be conducted. Frequently, in fact, activity areas are extensive enough to warrant the formulation of entire publications for separate areas of interest. Such areas might include (1) arts and crafts, (2) human movement, (3) games, (4) sports, (5) outdoor activities, (6) indoor activities, (7) drama, and (8) activities for special populations.

It is not the availability of activities which generally presents the leader with difficulties; it is insuring that (1) activities are appropriately matched with population groups and (2) the process involved in delivering activities fosters an environment consistent with the ideals and values of the agency.

As the selection of activities and programs is discussed, it will be with both of these points in mind. Each activity area will not be examined, however, since the "how to" aspect of activity leadership is available elsewhere. We will attempt to develop broad concepts which can be applied in a variety of settings. In addition, pitfalls will be discussed which, if not avoided, may significantly reduce the effectiveness of the program.

A point of controversy should first be addressed. It is not unusual, particularly among those in academic circles, for criticism to be launched at academic programs which place a heavy emphasis on skill courses in the curriculum. Critics suggest that colleges and universities should prepare planners and large-scale programmers who are equipped with an understanding of supervisory and managerial skills as well as depth in the social and behavioral sciences. They feel that learning to conduct face-to-face activities leaves the student technically competent but limited in terms of understanding the full scope of the delivery system.

Proponents of the skills approach argue, however, that face-to-face leadership is the most frequent point of entry into the field and that to be effective at that level, program leadership skills must be acquired. The feeling is that growth in the other areas will come with time and experience.

Our own opinion is that the latter view does not adequately prepare the practitioner for advancement; it fails to provide the tools necessary for one to be effective at supervisory and administrative levels within an organization. An increasing number of academic programs are moving to a more balanced position in recognition of this concern. In any case, it must be emphasized that activity *is* a critical component of the delivery system. Participants become involved with leisure service agencies primarily to participate in a given activity. Ultimately, other services may also be sought, but activity will continue to be the major motivating influence. While the "best" balance between skills and theory courses may continue to be debated, it is our feeling that those who are involved in *any* aspect of the delivery system will function more effectively if they have not overemphasized activity skills to the exclusion of conceptual and planning areas. At the same time, those at all levels must be concerned with delivering activities at the highest skill level possible. Therefore, both philosophical and technical components of the delivery system must be addressed to effectively meet the needs of diverse groups and individuals within a community.

Qualities of the Effective Activity Leader

The effective activity leader is one who has many areas of involvement beyond having the ability and the knowledge to lead activities. In many cases he or she will carry the primary responsibility for: (1) overseeing volunteers, (2) recording participation rates, (3) developing publicity announcements and activity schedules, (4) performing routine first-aid, (5) repairing equipment, (6) providing supervisors with information related to future needs, (7) cooperating with staff members from other agencies in multi-agency programs, (8) resolving interpersonal differences between participants, and (9) reinforcing behavior and situations which contribute to an atmosphere leading to the occurrence of recreation experiences. Thus, the activity leader must develop along several fronts by acquiring technical knowledge, an understanding of the essence of the recreation experience, and an awareness of professional standards related to leisure services. In addition, these elements must be bonded togther with personal strengths and characteristics which enhance one's effectiveness as a practitioner in a human service discipline.

Philosophical Values

As we mentioned earlier, it is essential that *all* leisure service practitioners understand the philosophy and values of their agency. It is not enough for agency ideals to be concerns only of supervisors and administrators. Activity leaders set the final stage for allowing those ideals to become a reality. Therefore, leaders should always be aware of the extent to which their actions and approaches are affecting individuals within the program *in relation to agency expectations and ideals.*

Establishing sound behavioral objectives, of course, will greatly assist one in making such determinations. If objectives have not been developed by the agency, the activity leader may wish to develop his or her own. This should preferably be done with other leaders and one's supervisor to insure acceptance of basic approaches and consistency among leaders.

Since many activity leaders are seasonal and part-time, it is particularly important to insure that agency values and expectations are repeatedly reinforced. Pre-service and in-service training programs, plus continual on-site interactions between supervisors and leaders, will greatly help the process.

It is not enough for an agency to be satisfied with high participation rates alone; the star programs will be those in which leaders are as conscious of quality as they are of quantity.

Activity Leader Strengths

The list of desirable qualities associated with the effective activity leader is virtually endless; however, the following strengths, suggested in part by Kraus and Bates (1975) and Vannier (1977), are particularly important:

1. Concern for individual needs and feelings
2. Vitality and enthusiasm
3. Creativity, particularly in planning activities and ways to involve individuals who may be reluctant to participate for one reason or another
4. Flexibility in dealing with people, new ideas, new activities, modifying traditional activities, and so forth
5. Responsible commitment to one's duties and to participants
6. Ability to plan activities and to anticipate circumstances which might alter the smooth delivery of services
7. Awareness of objectives
8. Technical knowledge of the various activities to be provided
9. Ability to emphasize cohesiveness among participants
10. Tendency to "think positive," to search for constructive solutions to problems, rather than to rely on autocratic, rigid, or basically punitive courses of action

There is no magic formula, of course, but in general, the motivated, concerned leader who understands people and activity skills will excel over those who restrict their involvement to the techniques of providing activities. Many of the points suggested above will be expanded upon as the discussion continues.

TECHNICAL KNOWLEDGE

As a rule, leaders who are confident in their jobs are aware of many different types of activities and know them in detail. They also know where to obtain information related to new ideas, techniques, and ways to modify existing programs. In addition to seeking such information from books, periodicals, activity kits, and so forth, they are able to utilize the strengths of participants and involve them to introduce new ideas.

The number of references available to activity leaders which provide detailed descriptions of games, sports, special events, arts and crafts, outdoor activities, and so forth is extensive. Frequently, however, no single source provides the variety that is so often desired by leaders. The tendency is to repeat that which is familiar and available in one or two accessible references, such as one owned by the leader or in the agency library. In fact, it is not uncommon for an agency to develop its own manual which becomes the key source for leaders and programmers. If all books written on activity skills and leadership were purchased by a single agency or individual, the cost would be considerable; as a result, many excellent activity ideas are missed.

Activity File — One technique for overcoming this problem is to develop a comprehensive activity file, accumulated over a period of time, from many sources. An individual, for example, could begin a notebook system (or index card system) in which exciting program ideas are recorded. Extensive use of the library would save costs and provide a central source for easily obtaining materials. Careful selection of activities would allow one to develop a reference which only included high quality activities. In time, the notebook would grow and include "the best" from a large universe.

The organization of the notebook is quite important and should be carefully planned. The following system is suggested as one approach:

1. Activities should be listed by topic, such as

   a. outdoor games
   b. indoor games
   c. waterfront activities
   d. social activities
   e. arts and crafts
   f. drama, dance, and singing activities
   g. nature programs
   h. sports

   Subcategories of each major area might also be formed. Within waterfront activities, for example, one might include synchronized swimming activities, swimming games, boating games, and racing events.
2. A comprehensive bibliography should be formed which includes references from which activities were selected.
3. Each activity should be coded to identify the source from which it was selected. The coding may be numerical or by the author's name.
4. An additional coding system should be devised to indicate for which populations a given activity is appropriate. Codings should be included on the page describing the activity. In addition, color-coded tabs which extend beyond the pages may be added to allow a search for population-specific activities. Color codings might be as follows:

   a. pre-school youth   blue
   b. elementary school youth   red
   c. junior high school youth green
   d. high school youth   orange
   e. adults   brown
   f. senior citizens   lavender
   g. handicapped/retarded   yellow
      groups

   If the color-coded tabs are consistently lined up, activities for specific groups within each activity area can be quickly identified.
5. Each activity should be coded by a qualitative index. In other words, although it is assumed that all activities included in the notebook are of high quality, it may be helpful to indicate those which are especially effective.

Eventually, the notebook could be expanded into multiple volumes. If the development of such a notebook were undertaken by an agency, or several agencies, rather than an individual, each activity area could be encompassed in a notebook of its own.

Agencies and individuals must exercise caution when forming notebooks. It would be tempting to reproduce descriptions of activities directly from the original, or to copy the material verbatim. Copyright restrictions preclude this and must be observed. If the essence of ideas are recorded, however, this should not be a problem.

An activity notebook will not guarantee effective leadership but will provide important material for leaders of all types. It could be especially helpful to agencies which experience a high rate of turnover among leaders due to seasonal or part-time demands for leadership.

Again care must be exercised, however. It would be quite simple for agency administrators and supervisors to rely exclusively on the "tried and true" which could stifle the creativity of new leaders and simultaneously fail to be responsive to changing trends in the community. If opportunities for new input are continuously encouraged, and if all staff members develop strong ties with those in the community, the activities notebook can become a dynamic force, reflecting creative energy rather than a set mold gathering dust on the shelf.

Programming for Diverse Groups

We will direct our attention to several key groupings although other categories may certainly be identified. These include: (1) age and sex factors; (2) recreation in corrections; and (3) therapeutic recreation.

Age and Sex Factors

YOUTH GROUPS

It is unrealistic to expect characteristics of children to always be consistent within age groupings since growth and maturity rates vary considerably. Certain patterns have been identified, however, which provide a basic understanding of developmental stages and various needs associated with them. The leisure service practitioner can strengthen programs by being aware of typical trends, and insuring that activities are planned using that knowledge. In the following discussion, based partially on guidelines provided by Schurr (1975), youth characteristics and needs will be presented with implications for leisure activity programming.

Youth 6-8 Years. Youth in this age group tend to be energetic, curious, imitative, and individualistic, that is, able to play easily alone but are weak in sharing with others. Physical capabilities tend to be becoming more refined but large motor skill capabilities are dominant.

A key aspect of children in this age group relates to their relatively short attention span. Energy and curiosity levels are so high that a wide variety of activities requiring short, understandable explanations are recommended. Active games are quite appropriate such as running, relay-races, ball-handling, obstacle courses, dance, and activities which allow the participant a degree of self-testing. Interpersonal comparisons should be avoided so that success is defined in terms of the self.

Limits in relation to others begin to be defined during these years. Activities which enhance cooperation, sharing, and empathy for others are highly appropriate.

Role modeling is an important characteristic of these youngsters and significantly influences the identity forming process of "who am I?" This should be one of the greatest concerns of the activity leader since he or she becomes a part of the modeling process through example. This is a prime reason why the values and ideals of the agency must not only be carefully formulated, but also must be promoted by staff members at all levels. For example, the following factors can have a direct impact on the role modeling process:

1. The manner in which leaders handle disputes or differences of opinion.
2. The way in which leaders react to winners and losers of an event.
3. The extent to which leaders encourage shy, quiet youngsters and offer them support.
4. The ability of the leader to approach discipline problems positively; that is, attempting to constructively resolve problems rather than resort to punishment or removal of participants from the program.

In terms of skill development, the leader should focus on achievements related to the self, rather than on interpersonal comparisons; participants are well aware of "who is best." The strong leader will use activities to strengthen the individual's skill but also his or her self-confidence, feeling of mastery, sense of achievement, and pride in knowing there has been continuous improvement.

This is an exciting age group, frequently difficult to handle, but easily managed and motivated if activities are wisely selected, continually varied, and skilfully led. Unfortunately many leaders become frustrated when youngsters at this age become "wild" and disorderly. Rather than continue what has been scheduled, perceptive leaders will realize that the needs of the participants are obviously not being met by what has been structured and a new approach is needed. A shift to a new activity, perhaps one which allows for a greater expression of physical energy, may be quite helpful. Leaders can trap themselves if they insist that participants must always comply with a predetermined schedule of events. A "have fun *my* way, or else" attitude can certainly be self-defeating.

A positive, flexible attitude must be communicated to youngsters this age. This is essential for any group, but especially for youths who are developing so many attitudes and values, likes and dislikes, related to their leisure life-style. The child who is willing to try new activities without fear of failure and self-consciousness will develop a broader base for later years. We all know people, for example, who attempted an activity as a youngster, did poorly, which produced feelings of inadequacy and embarrassment, and never again became involved in that particular pursuit. Hopefully, the effective leader will be aware of this potential and provide the type of support and encouragement which will minimize this problem.

A suggestion might be helpful at this point. There is a tendency for leaders to exclude activities which they themselves cannot perform skilfully since they do not wish to appear clumsy in the eyes of participants. People are quite tolerant and understanding, however, and if presented in the right spirit, the skill level will not be as important as involvement in the activity. Most importantly, the leader will serve as a model, willing to undertake an adventure, regardless of ability in relation to others. As a result, participants will follow this lead and realize that one need not feel self-conscious or of lesser worth simply because one is not highly skilled in a particular undertaking.

In discussing the next age groups, it should be kept in mind that many of the principles relating to younger children are also applicable to older youths. Thus, leadership considerations for various groups of all types are not mutually exclusive.

Youth 9-12 Years. Youngsters in this age group have become more coordinated and in need of being involved in activities requiring increasingly more difficult skills. Differences in physical ability become more apparent with boys playing more vigorously and competitively than girls. Stereotype male-female interests begin to take shape as teachers, parents, and leisure service practitioners help to perpetuate the process.

Boys and girls begin to sharpen intellectually and enjoy taxing games and the application of strategy. Creative thinking and the desire to explore things in greater depth become more apparent.

As youths move toward the junior high school years, the need to conform and feel accepted by others increases sharply. Feelings of insecurity and uncertainty in group situations become quite strong. New awarenesses of the opposite sex begin to emerge which increases feelings of self-consciousness. Such feelings often lead to expressions of antagonism between the sexes and sensitivity to group pressure. Generally this decreases considerably during high school years.

Given the fact that group norms exert an especially strong influence, and the self-image is highly vulnerable during this period of self-consciousness, the role of the activity leader is very challenging. In all probability, the leader will have the greatest success by planning programs which sometimes integrate boys and girls and sometimes do not. In either case, the following concerns should be incorporated into the planning process:

1. The strength of the *group* should be built upon since group spirit and allegiance are so strong. Activities which strengthen cooperation and interpersonal skills are highly appropriate. Even in competitive activities intra-team spirit and cooperation can be emphasized without negating the worth of those on other teams. Pride in collective accomplishments should be emphasized rather than individual effort, although certainly individual excellence can be appropriately recognized as well.
2. Efforts should be made to minimize the importance of individual errors to offset already-existing fears of personal failure. This requires developing a strong interpersonal support system and providing encouragement regardless of performance.
3. Coeducational activities should be selected which allow boys and girls to be comfortable with each other. Activities which do not place individuals in threatening positions are particularly appropriate. For example, an activity such as a scavenger hunt can be planned in which teams of boys and girls together are formed. This requires a cooperative, team effort for maximum effectiveness. As boys and girls join forces and get to know each other better, much of the self-consciousness which exists can be reduced and replaced by good feelings associated with knowing one has been accepted by others.

Youth 13-17 Years. The teen years provide exciting, adventurous times for youngsters. Teenagers begin to strengthen their identity, self-image, and sense of "who am I?" as they move toward adulthood and greater independence. They will be greatly affected by early childhood experiences. Attitudes and feelings toward others begin to stabilize.

Perceptions and earlier experiences related to leisure strongly influence recreation participation and the style of one's involvement. Peer pressures remain strong as does the need to conform. There is little likelihood that one will participate in an activity in which one is not reasonably proficient if there is a fear that others will form a critical, non-accepting judgment which will lead to a certain element of rejection.

Providing leisure services for teenagers can be quite difficult since a principal focus of teens is toward each other. Frequently, the strongest motivator for participation is simply to be with each other such as at a dance or non-structured drop-in center. Structured activities, if provided too frequently, may not be appropriate for at least two reasons. First, teenagers are striving to be independent and in control of their own situation. Structured activities present constraints which require conformity to adult standards and rules. The desire for self-determination may be so strong that such programs will be rejected. Second, many structured activities do not easily lend themselves to informal interaction among participants. "Hanging around," for example, is a common teen activity which has appeal simply because interaction occurs easily and at a pace appropriate for the mood.

This does not mean that *only* unstructured activities should be available to teenagers. Many youngsters in this age group have a strong desire to become involved in dramatics, sports, crafts, and so forth, and expect a great deal of structure in the program.

Process is probably as important to many teenagers as the actual programs. Thus, the manner in which programs are developed can be critical to success or failure. As was discussed in the fourth chapter, the leader can frequently be most effective as a facilitator who adopts a role similar to the Community School Director within the Community Education system. As a facilitator, the leader responds to the desires of participants by involving them in the conception, planning, and implementation of programs. A commitment to the program is demonstrated through involvement; the result is generally a stronger sense of participation since participants have a vested interest in the outcome of *their* program.

The activity leader need not be passive in his or her role as facilitator when working with teens or any other group. Considerable interest in an idea can be stimulated by the leader as easily as from the teens themselves. Ultimately, the fine tuning of the idea should be undertaken by the teens, and the leader can take a supportive rather than directive role.

The more perceptive activity leaders have the ability to use one teen program as an effective springboard for others. For example, it may be that a teen center has become extremely popular largely due to several programs which include: (1) informal, regularly scheduled drop-in hours; (2) a tape library of rock music that has been developed by teenagers who tape-record music from the personal records of those who attend the center; (3) a physical fitness room which includes weight-training equipment and tumbling mats; (4) a leader who provides an evening and late afternoon fitness program, including jogging; and (5) a room with a coffee house atmosphere in which refreshments are available for purchase and folk music is played quietly in the background over a small stereo system. Effective leaders will not rest on their laurels and assume that because the center is experiencing success they need only maintain the present programs. First, the leader should strengthen personal ties with participants. Trust and confidence must be strengthened if new directions are to be pursued. Second, during the hours of high participation, the leader should interact with participants and identify additional areas of interest to the teens. The germ of an idea can be reinforced by the leader to strengthen enthusiasm and generate discussion by others. In this way, the initial program provides the opportunity for interaction which can lead one into the *process* of developing new programs. Finally, the strong leader will seek ways to directly involve more participants in strengthening existing programs, even those which are already successful. Teenagers seek and respond well to being given responsibility. The effect can be a new commitment to an existing program and insurance that the program will continue to flourish.

As a general rule, it is important to create an environment conducive to self-determination by teens. One approach is the development of a teen advisory board which addresses various concerns ranging from activity programming to insuring that their peers responsibly maintain the program. The selection of officers should be carried out entirely by the membership and should probably be reconstituted at least annually. It is also highly recommended that adult members of the community be invited to participate as members of the advisory board, even as nonvoting participants. This has several advantages. First, if the teens come under criticism for any reason, whether justified or not, they will have the basic support of board members who will be able to represent the teen position to others in the community and to insure that others understand that although there may be occasional problems, the value of the program far exceeds them. Second, adults may be capable of tapping community resources in the form of people or materials, resources which could strengthen existing capabilities. Third, if volunteer adults are providing input into the program, there may be a stronger degree of confidence in the program among political figures who are responsible for budget allocations. Such confidence can also help to insure that teen programs may be carried out in facilities other than their own, such as in a school cafeteria, auditorium, or gymnasium.

If a number of teens in the community do not participate in the programs of a given agency, it is not necessarily a reflection of program or agency quality. Many teenagers meet their needs in other ways and do not gravitate toward agency offerings. In a highly mobile society, particularly in urban areas, this is frequently the case since so much may be available elsewhere. In fact, it is not unusual for even the most popular of teen centers to find that when youngsters reach driving age, they spend far less time in the program.

On the other hand, leaders can increase the desirability of a program by concentrating on process, as well as programs, by creating opportunities for teenagers to take on responsibilities and shape their own direction. While the facility in which one operates teen programs is important, the most effective programs are frequently strong as a result of being centered around creative processes rather than an elaborate structure. If the emphasis is placed on *people* and a creative environment is developed, powerful programs can develop in even the simplest of facilities. Perhaps the most essential ingredient for success is to truly listen to the views and ideas of teenagers, to realize that their standards and norms may have changed from those which existed in past years, and to allow them as much freedom to grow in their own way as possible. The element of trust, combined with constructive leadership, can lead to a process which contributes significantly to responsible, mature outcomes for those who are involved.

LEISURE ACTIVITY SELECTION FOR GIRLS AND BOYS

A brief survey was recently developed (Klar, 1978) relating to activity selection for girls and boys between the ages of six and thirteen. Before reading ahead, you should complete the survey on the following page so that this discussion may be applied to your own results.

Activities are grouped according to a stereotyped pattern as follows:

1. Items 3, 6, 9, 12, and 15 are typically associated with boys.
2. Items 2, 5, 8, 11, and 14 are typically associated with girls.
3. Items 1, 4, 7, 10, and 13 are typically considered appropriate for boys and girls.

To determine the extent to which you "crossed over" traditional lines, score your survey as follows:

1. Begin by horizontally totaling the number of checks you recorded for items 3, 6, 9, 12, and 15. The maximum score possible is 20 since there are five items and four possible choices for each item.
2. Repeat the process for items 2, 5, 8, 11, and 14.
3. Repeat the process for items 1, 4, 7, 10, and 13.
4. The three figures reflect the extent to which you feel that *both* sexes might approximately participate in (1) typically male oriented activities, (2) typically female oriented activities, and (3) activities generally considered to be appropriate for both.

Note that scores reflect only choices related to the sex of participants. You may now tally the check marks vertically to identify age-related patterns as follows:

1. Vertically total the check marks for both columns (a) and (b). The maximum score possible is 30 since there are two columns with fifteen items per column.
2. Repeat the process for columns (c) and (d).

LEISURE ACTIVITY SELECTION FOR GIRLS AND BOYS

Fifteen leisure-related activities are included in the following list. Please determine for whom you would offer each activity, if you were able to create the **ideal overall program** which would best meet the needs of youth between the ages of **six** and **thirteen years.**

Youth Groups

A. Girls 6-9 years   C. Girls 10-13 years
B. Boys 6-9 years   D. Boys 10-13 years

Please indicate your programming selections on the following checklist. If you feel that a given activity is not appropriate for any of the groups, the choices in that category should be left unmarked.

ACTIVITY	A Girls 6-9	B Boys 6-9	C Girls 10-13	D Boys 10-13
1. Volleyball				
2. Modern Dance				
3. Ice Hockey				
4. Relay Races				
5. Sewing				
6. Football				
7. Leatherwork				
8. Figure Skating				
9. Wrestling				
10. Candlemaking				
11. Cooking				
12. Shop (woodwork)				
13. Softball				
14. Knitting				
15. Baseball				

3. The first figure represents the number of activities that you feel are appropriate for youngsters between the ages of six and nine. The second figure represents the number of activities that you feel are appropriate for youngsters between the ages of ten and thirteen.

Theoretically, *all* of these activities could be appropriate for both sexes of any of the stated ages. There is no reason why girls cannot derive pleasure from hockey or wrestling; that is, no reason that stems from characteristics innate in girls. Any barriers which exist stem from socialization processes which have evolved over the years. The reasons for this development are many and go beyond the realm of our discussion. The point is that times have changed and we must re-think traditional practices. There are a number of reasons why we feel that the most progressive (and valid) response to this survey would be one which includes *all* activities for *all* youngsters.

First, as we mentioned, the reasons boys and girls gravitate toward certain different activities are rooted in our social system, not based upon something inherent in the physiological or psychological make-up of boys and girls.

Second, if there is value to be derived for boys participating in male-oriented activities, there is no reason why girls would not experience the same benefits if they were also able to participate in those activities. The same is true in reverse. Cooking programs need not be reserved for girls when the rewards associated with this activity might just as easily be shared by boys. If an activity has value for one group, it can also have value for the other.

Third, even age should not be a barrier for participation. We often underestimate the capabilities of youngsters and may wait too long to involve them in certain programs. Consider the point, for example, that activities which are pursued by high school and college age students are frequently those which were gratifying during their younger years. In fact, activities with which they are unfamiliar in the early years may be avoided completely in later life. This pattern of rejecting participation in certain activities begins as early as the fourth and fifth grades; therefore, why not extend opportunities usually reserved for "older" youngsters to those who have just begun their years in school?

This leads to a fourth point. Some activities may not be appropriate for all youngsters if dangers are involved. For example, it is unlikely that six year olds would be advised to operate a lathe or power drill in a woodwork program. Certainly, however, hammer, nails, screwdriver, and handsaw can be managed with minimum risk as has been demonstrated in "junk playground" programs. The point is that activities can be modified greatly to accommodate younger participants, weaker participants, and so forth. Other examples include:

1. Lowering the net or using a lighter ball to begin a volleyball program for six to eight year olds.
2. Offering "T-Ball" in place of baseball which enables batters to hit the ball from a stationary standard positioned at home plate. Although pitching skills are not developed, the pace of the game is lively and all other aspects of the game can be experienced.
3. Offering hockey to both sexes and all ages but minimizing the physical contact aspects of the game. (This is quite common in many communities. Programs are offered to youngsters as young as four years old, boys and girls alike in the same program.)

Fifth, if traditional approaches are to be changed, offerings may need to be packaged a little differently. A cooking program might not initially appeal to some boys; however, if the activity were to center around making pizzas in conjunction with a dance program, a shift in appeal could be easily envisioned. This program was successfully carried out in a teen-center in an East Bay city near Oakland, California. The participants were what one might term "tough" and certainly not the average youngster one would associate with apron and spatula. Intuitively, it would seem that the possibilities for positive growth are far greater in this type of program than they might be in a boxing program which, by its very nature, emphasizes antagonism rather than cooperation, and seems to reinforce "toughness" rather than changes in one's self-identity.

The survey which you completed is meant only to serve as a catalyst for introspection and dialogue. Results should not be used to compare people or to create an environment which fosters defensiveness. Hopefully, it can be a springboard for considering new ways to view activity selection. Needless to say, personal biases will influence that process, but it is safe to suggest that new opportunities can be extended to boys and girls alike if we dare to try.

Finally, the survey may also be used as a training tool for subordinates who are responsible for activity selection in their respective programs. It might be useful, for example, to be used as a part of a pre-service or in-service training program. In any case, it is becoming increasingly important that leisure service practitioners address these issues. Opportunities for dialogue leading to new approaches should be a continuous part of the communication process within all agencies wishing to remain responsive to our rapidly changing society.

ACTIVITY SELECTION FOR SENIOR CITIZENS

When one thinks in terms of activities typically associated with our older population, bingo, choir, gardening, and shuffleboard come to mind. How frustrating to be perceived as weak, passive, and limited in one's interests and capabilities!

As with teenagers, senior citizens have a stake in what should be available to them and how it should be presented. Very simply, consider the following activities which, in fact, are actually offered by progressive leaders and certainly do not reflect stereotyped programming:

1. Canoeing and hiking programs
2. Square dancing which surely would physically tax most of us
3. Bus trips (in excess of 1500 miles one-way) which offer none of the amenities of a cruise
4. Slow pitch leagues in which those in their eighties regard those in their sixties as "wet behind the ears"
5. Tennis programs which attract participants in their nineties
6. Marathon races which attract people of virtually all ages and are frequently won by participants well out of their thirties and forties

The list could go on indefinitely; yet, misconceptions related to the capabilities and interests of senior citizens persist. Innovative leaders can help to reverse this tendency and some are doing so quite effectively. In one instance, for example, seniors into their eighties played musical chairs with all the enthusiasm of people one-eighth their age. Would this be an activity typically offered by most senior center directors?

There is always the question of risk to the participant and issues of potential liability. But if all programming selections are based upon fear, we find ourselves back to the bingo and shuffleboard syndrome. Not that these activities should be criticized in any way — but much more is possible if we are willing to expand our thinking. We are all willing to take certain risks at one time or another and senior citizens are no exception. Many activities include risks which do not prevent us from participating regardless of our age. The sensitive and innovative leader will attempt to leave the decision to participate or not participate up to the individual in the program. Most of us know our capabilities and the senior citizen is probably especially aware of his or her limits.

Whether dealing with more active programs, passive pursuits, or social functions, it is important to remember that age does not change our *basic* needs. The desires for companionship, achievement, excitement, exploration, and new experiences remain with us. It is true that the potential for loneliness, poor health, depression, and self-depreciation resulting from idleness may exist to a greater extent among the elderly and these tendencies may be reinforced by social stereotyping—but what *is* does not reflect what *must be*. Sensitivity to this problem is essential for the senior citizen program director. On the other hand, if seniors are perceived as having the same basic needs and desire for full participation as any other person, exciting, stimulating, and progressive program offerings are possible.

Activity Selection In Correctional Institutions

Whether providing services in a correctional institution or in an urban area known for high crime and delinquency, certain special factors must be considered—factors which differ from "traditional" settings. In general, particularly in institutions, there is an aura of toughness, aggression, and a tendency to define certain aspects of interpersonal relations in terms of power. Proving one's worth is often manifest by physical acts of violence or boasting of one's illegal pursuits when on the "outside."

Given an environment of toughness, how does the leisure service practitioner select activities which will be of rehabilitative value for those who have gone astray, whether in or out of a correctional setting? Traditionally, activities such as boxing, karate, weight-training, basketball, pool, and ping-pong emerge as popular favorites. In each case, the element of power exists either through competition or physical strength.

We suggest that such activities may not be as constructive as they seem. In fact, they may simply be reinforcing and perpetuating the very values and norms which have partially contributed to the offenders' problems.

There is no solid evidence that involvement in these and other activities has a constructive effect, but we are not suggesting the avoidance of such activities when providing leisure services to offenders. However, rehabilitation generally requires a basic change in the self-image and identity of the offender. Many institutional programs do not offer that opportunity. Recreation activities are used only as rewards, or as outlets for aggression. They are easily used as a source of punishment by being withdrawn at the slightest hint of a problem, or they are viewed as ways to help "pacify" physically tense individuals. Given this view of recreation activities, it is no wonder that they often play a minor role in the rehabilitation process.

The rationale for offering leisure services within correctional institutions is as viable as for other populations. Leisure activity involvement should be viewed as a vital aspect of one's existence, not merely a fringe benefit.

Therefore, more than physical or competitive activities should be included in an overall program. Journalism, art, drama, music, radio and television programming should be explored, as resources permit. Inmates should be a part of the decision making process and have opportunities for self-determination, creativity, and responsibility. What better use of one's leisure could those advocating rehabilitation expect?

Realistically, institutions will not do away with the more aggressive activities but there can be expansions into new areas. Some institutions have already accomplished this and with excellent results, particularly in relation to upgrading daily prison life.

It is pointless to consider rehabilitation in the true sense without including leisure behavior in the process. But the *type* of recreation activity provided within institutions is extremely important as is the philosophy behind the choices. Those involved in providing leisure services in correctional settings must seek to develop programs in the same manner that one would adopt in the community. Both participation *and* process must be points of focus.

We would also encourage institutional administrators to provide opportunities for inmates to participate in leisure activities outside of the facility. It is true there are certain risks, but learning to adjust to daily living cannot take place within the confines of a cell block. Administrators of the California Youth Authority have provided such opportunities for some time now, and fully support the process. Hopefully others will also begin to adopt a more realistic and creative view of the importance of leisure pursuits in relation to personal adjustment. There is certainly little to lose and a great deal to gain.

Therapeutic Recreation Programming

There are a number of excellent books, pamphlets, and other publications which provide considerable depth in activity leadership for special populations, particularly the physically or mentally handicapped. Rather than extract from such sources, we will suggest that a great deal can be learned about the essence of the recreation experience by studying special populations, particularly the mentally handicapped.

At the risk of generalizing, we believe that no other group exhibits certain aspects of self-actualization than among those who are mentally handicapped. Retardation may limit one's ability to function completely independently, but not one's ability to experience life to the fullest. The following characteristics, typically associated with this population, exemplify our point. In general, it is not uncommon for the mentally handicapped to

1. be unaware of feelings of self-consciousness and embarrassment;
2. become fully involved in what they are doing, whether leisure or work related, often oblivious to other people or things;
3. exhibit unrestrained glee, anger, or sadness, without regard to acceptability; that is, feelings are expressed openly and honestly, as they are experienced;
4. appreciate and value all personal accomplishments and to accept personal credit for those achievements in a way which strengthens feelings of self-worth and confidence;
5. appreciate the value of warm relationships with others and to be able to communicate warmth and affection through touching, facial expression, and dialogue, without feelings of self-consciousness so often experienced by non-handicapped individuals.

It is certainly true that all of these characteristics are not present in every mentally handicapped individual at all times. The extent to which they *are* exhibited is remarkable. This is important because we have easily visible examples of *behaviors* which are associated with *feelings* which relate closely to the components of the recreation experience. The essence of those feelings embodies the notion of an intrinsic focus. In other words, all visible evidence would suggest that the primary reason for participation is for *personal satisfaction* and that satisfaction is derived from participation in the activity itself in terms of what the activity actually offers.

This leads us to a key point: if the principal motivation for this special population is primarily intrinsic in nature insofar as involvement in recreation activities is concerned, why are trophies and prizes used so extensively in special programs? The use of awards is common in programs ranging from the Special Olympics to a Saturday morning bowling outing.

Two immediate effects are readily apparent when this occurs. There is a likelihood that a shift will occur moving the point of focus from the delight which was experienced as a participant to over-valuing the importance of the award. This is a risk when providing activities for any group but the risk of *undoing* the actualization process seems greater.

Second, the potential for hurting the feelings of those who do not receive awards is high. This is especially damaging to individuals who may not fully understand the rationale underlying the use of prizes and only know the feeling of disappointment produced by being "left out."

Of all people served by leisure service practitioners, mentally handicapped individuals may be the least appropriate for award systems. Instead, we should build on strengths which are more related to self-actualization and the intrinsic components of the recreation experience. Perhaps the pupil can serve as the mentor. . . .

Activity Preferences and Participation

A basic principle in leisure services states that programming and activity selection should be determined by finding out what people want. It is not unusual, for example, for leisure service practitioners to develop a survey which includes a list of activities to which respondents indicate their preferences. Decisions related to activity selection may then be based upon expressed desires.

Used alone, however, activity preference check-lists can be misleading. As was true in the example presented earlier, people have a tendency to be quite liberal when completing surveys in the comfort of their homes and tend to include much more than they can realistically undertake. When this occurs, participation rates in programs based upon surveys easily fall below expectations.

Surveys are important, however, if used in conjunction with other planning techniques. For example, volunteers or citizens interested in helping to develop programs might be identified through an item on the survey. Proper follow-up could lead to the formulation of one or more action committees composed of individuals who are genuinely committed and willing to be involved.

Door-to-door surveys can often be more effective than those in which surveys are mailed. Returns are higher which produces greater representation. They are time-consuming, of course, and considerable training is necessary if interviewers are to be effective. Interviewers can obtain a great deal of information, however, and in the long run, will report data which more accurately reflect citizens' true feelings. At the same time, personal contact may facilitate a greater willingness among citizens to make a commitment supportive of specific activity areas.

Surveys can be effective tools for sensitizing the public about agency purposes and programs. This in itself can lead to increased participation in existing programs. The process can be further strengthened by scheduling one or more public meetings as a follow-up to the survey. Ideally, the interest stimulated by the survey, in conjunction with effective publicity announcing meetings, will lead to increased citizen participation and input. In the final analysis, programs will be more sensitive to public desires which will be reflected in increased involvement.

Surveys take time to construct and administer but provide an important mechanism for maintaining contact with the public. If they are used as a tool to grow and to increase efforts to be responsive to a constituency, they can be of great value. If surveys are administered with less intensity and without follow-up, they can weaken an agency. This is especially true if agency administrators feel that they have fulfilled their responsibility by conducting a survey but then blame the public for failing to attend a program which had been supported "on paper." A survey is a tool; the challenge for those providing leadership in leisure services is to use it as a part of the planning process, but to utilize human service skills to extend beyond the tabulation of check-marks.

Summary

The quality of activity leadership is an extremely important component of the leisure service delivery system. Knowledge of the technical aspects of leading various activities and interpersonal skills is essential. In addition, each leader must fully understand the purpose and ideals of the agency and the importance of properly representing agency values in all aspects of leadership. Strengths in leadership, activity knowledge, and human relations will be of rising importance. (This will be especially true as registration and certification processes become more widespread.)

Effective activity leaders will be keenly aware of characteristics associated with different age groups. Serving as a planner, decision-maker, and daily role model, this awareness can assist the leader in carrying out individualized programs.

There has been considerable stereotyping in programs for many groups. Activities for boys and girls frequently follow separate lines; youngsters are excluded from many activities on the premise that they cannot handle them; senior citizens are viewed as weak, only able to participate in passive pursuits; and in correctional settings, inmates are repeatedly offered activities which do little to change individual quests for power, toughness, and perhaps an artificial sense of self-worth that restricts adjustment when returning to the community. If approached properly, either through modification of activities or by introducing activities previously not offered to specific groups, great strides can be made to reduce stereotyping in leisure services. This can open new vistas and allow experiences which have been valuable to one group, to be shared by others.

Much can be learned from the mentally handicapped in relation to characteristics associated with the recreation experience. Practitioners should question the use of awards in programs for this group and build upon inner rewards, rather than those extrinsic in nature.

Identifying the leisure activity preferences of those in the community is essential. Surveys provide an excellent vehicle for the process but should not be used alone. Surveys can be an important part of planning but should be viewed primarily as a springboard for fuller agency-citizen interaction.

Study Questions

1. What are the key responsibilities of the leisure activities leader? How broad do you feel his or her role should be?
2. Why is it important for the activity leader to be aware of agency values and philosophy? To what extent do you think this is the case (in actual practice)?
3. How might a leisure activities notebook help you as a leader? As a supervisor? As a member of the community? As a member of a church or service organization?
4. Are the only effective leisure service programs those in which participants are involved in the *process* of program development? To what extent is *process* important for various groups?
5. Why were mentally handicapped individuals referred to as visible examples of self-actualization in action? Do you agree?
6. Is the use of awards appropriate for mentally handicapped individuals? If awards are used, how might potential problems be avoided?
7. What would you recommend for a balanced program in a correctional facility and why?
8. Is the leisure activity preference survey a valuable means for assessing citizen desires? Is it generally an accurate indicator of preferences and a valid predictor of subsequent behavior?

References

Klar, Lawrence R., Jr. "Leisure Activity Selection for Boys and Girls." Amherst, Massachusetts: Leisure Studies and Resources Program, University of Massachusetts. Mimeographed survey, 1978.

Kraus, Richard G., and Bates, Barbara. *Recreation Leadership and Supervision.* Philadelphia: W. B. Saunders Company, 1975.

Schurr, Evelyn L. *Movement Experiences for Children.* Englewood Cliffs, N.J.: Prentice-Hall, Inc., 1975.

Vannier, Maryhelen. *Recreation Leadership.* Philadelphia: Lea & Febiger, 1977.

Related Readings

Adams, Ronald C.; Daniels, Alfred N.; and Rullman, Lee. *Games, Sports and Exercises for the Physically Handicapped.* Philadelphia: Lea & Febiger, 1972.

American Association for Health, Physical Education and Recreation. *Desirable Athletic Competition for Children of Elementary School Age.* Washington, D.C.: AAHPER, 1968.

Blake, O. William, and Volpe, Anne. *Lead-up Games to Team Sports.* Englewood Cliffs, N.J.: Prentice-Hall, Inc., 1964.

Boyd, Neva L. *Handbook of Recreational Games.* New York: Dover Publications, Inc., reprint 1975.

Batcheller, John, and Monsous, Sally. *Music in Recreation and Leisure.* Dubuque, Ia.: Wm. C. Brown Company Publishers, 1972.

Arnold, Nellie D. *The Interrelated Arts in Leisure.* St. Louis: The C. V. Mosby Company, 1976.

Beson, Kenneth R., and Frankson, Carl E. *Arts and Crafts for Home, School, and Community.* St. Louis: The C. V. Mosby Company, 1975.

Broer, Marion. *Efficiency of Human Movement.* Philadelphia: W. B. Saunders Company, 1973.

Cochran, E. V. *Teach and Reach That Child.* Palo Alto, Calif.: Peck Publications, 1971.

Corbin, Charles. *A Textbook of Motor Development.* Dubuque, Ia.: Wm. C. Brown Company Publishers, 1973.

Corbin, Charles. *Inexpensive Equipment for Games, Play, and Physical Activity.* Dubuque, Ia.: Wm. C. Brown Company Publishers, 1972.

Corbin, H. Dan. *Recreation Leadership.* Englewood Cliffs, N.J.: Prentice-Hall, Inc., 1970.

Danford, Howard G. *Creative Leadership in Recreation.* Boston: Allyn and Bacon, 1964.

Frye, Virginia and Martha Peters. *Therapeutic Recreation.* Harrisburg, Pa.: Stockpole Books, 1972.

Gerhardt, Lydia. *Moving and Knowing—The Young Child Orients Himself in Space.* Englewood Cliffs, N.J.: Prentice-Hall, Inc., 1973.

Havighurst, Robert J. "The Leisure Activities of the Middle-Aged." *American Journal of Sociology* (September, 1957): 152-162.

Hyatt, Ronald W. *Intramural Sports Programs: Their Organization and Administration.* St. Louis: The C. V. Mosby Company, 1975.

Kenyon, Gerald S., and Loy, John W. (eds.) *Sport, Culture and Society: A Reader on the Sociology of Sport.* New York: Macmillan, 1969.

Kosarin, Sol. *Juvenile Delinquency: A Remedy Through Music.* New York: Vantage Press, 1956.

Kraus, Richard. *Therapeutic Recreation Service: Principles and Practices.* Philadelphia: W. B. Saunders, 1973.

Kraus, Richard (ed.) *Reader's Digest Book of 1000 Family Games.* New York: Reader's Digest Books, 1971.

Lowry, Thomas Power. *Camping Therapy: Its Uses in Psychiatry and Rehabilitation.* Springfield, Ill.: Charles C. Thomas, 1974.

Mobley, Tony A., Light, Stephen S., and Neulinger, John. "Leisure Attitudes and Program Participation." In *Parks & Recreation* (December 1976): 20-22.

Monsour, Sally; Cohen, Marilyn; and Lindell, Patricia. *Rhythm in Music and Dance for Children.* Belmont, Calif.: Wadsworth, 1966.

Newsweek. "The Graying of America." February 28 (1977): 50-65.

National Recreation & Park Association. *Creative Recreation Programming Handbook.* Arlington, Va.: NRPA, 1977.

O'Morrow, Gerald S. *Therapeutic Recreation: A Helping Profession.* Reston, Va.: Reston Publishing Co., 1976.

Richardson, Hazel A. *Games for the Elementary School Grades.* Minneapolis: Burgess, 1972.

Sherif, M.; Harvey, J. O.; White, B. J.; and Hood, R. *Theoretical and Experimental Studies in Interpersonal and Group Relations.* Norman: University of Oklahoma Press, 1954.

Shivers, Jay S. and Calder, Clarence R. *Recreational Crafts: Programming and Instructional Techniques.* New York: McGraw-Hill Book Company, 1974.

Sidentop, Daryl. *Developing Teaching Skills in Physical Education.* Boston: Houghton Mifflin Company, 1976.

Simon, Paul (ed.) *Play and Game Theory in Group Work: A Collection of Papers by Neva L. Boyd.* Chicago: University of Illinois at Chicago Circle, 1971.

Smith, Bert Kruger. Aging in America. Boston: Beacon Press, 1973.

Stanley, Dennis; Waglow, Irving; and Alexander, Ruth. *Physical Education Activities Handbook for Men and Women.* Boston: Allyn and Bacon, 1973.

Straub, William F. *The Lifetime Sports-Oriented Physical Education Program.* Englewood Cliffs, N.J.: Prentice-Hall, Inc., 1976.

U.S. News & World Report. "How Americans Pursue Leisure." May 23 (1977): 60-66, 69-76.

Supervision and Leadership Effectiveness

Objectives   After reading and comprehending this chapter, you should be able to:

1. Identify differences between personal power and position power.
2. State the major responsibilities of the leisure service supervisor.
3. Explain the processes involved in recruiting, interviewing, and selecting new employees.
4. State the purposes of pre-service and in-service training programs.
5. Describe the purposes and process of employee evaluations.
6. Define the process of Management By Objectives.
7. Describe the evolution of contemporary management and organizational development theories.
8. Differentiate between **successful** leadership and **effective** leadership.
9. Describe the process of diagnosing group capabilities and adapting leadership style to the situation.
10. Define **leadership style** in the context of the leadership model presented.

Introduction

Leadership in this chapter will be considered primarily in relation to staff-subordinate interactions rather than activity leader-participant relationships. Many concepts apply at both levels since the motivation of followers is central to both situations, but we will limit our discussion to subordinate-leader aspects within agencies.

We will begin by considering the broad roles and duties of the supervisor including many responsibilities which are characteristic of both administrators and supervisors, depending on the particular structure of the agency. This will be followed by a discussion of planning approaches related to staff-subordinate relationships. Essentially, this includes the application of management by objectives as a technique for sound planning. After considering several key theories of leadership, a model will be suggested for diagnosing situations and selecting courses of leadership action appropriate for those situations. Finally, the model will be applied in various ways to exemplify its breadth and capabilities.

One point must be emphasized at the onset. There are clearly no "instant solutions" for solving leadership problems. Many theories have been developed to guide the leader, and each has its own particular strengths and weaknesses. The reader must ultimately select and develop his or her own style of leadership. Hopefully gaining an understanding of various theories will strengthen that process.

Leadership in a work setting implies that one individual is given certain responsibilities and duties which involve influencing others. This may include serving as facilitator, director, controller, or change agent. As Hersey and Blanchard (1977, p. 10) have pointed out, this does not mean that the supervisor controls people in a negative sense:

"Control and manipulation have become negative connotations . . . (but) if in your job as manager, you are concerned about the people for whom you are responsible—their cohesiveness, commitment, and the kind of rapport they have with you, then you are concerned with controlling behavior. . . . It really is not important what you call it; perhaps you can think of a better word—call it facilitating, training, having an impact, whatever. But remember, if you accept the role of manager or leader, you accept with it the responsibility of having an impact on the behavior of other people."

By definition, the supervisor has been placed in a position of influence over others. This is referred to as *position power* rather than *personal power* (Etzioni, 1961). *Position power* is that which comes with the job itself and is basically determined by the policies and procedures established by the organization. In the military, for example, a captain is given certain powers over enlisted personnel and these powers are clearly specified, primarily in written form, through regulations.

Personal power, however, has to do with the ability of the leader to gain the respect, admiration, and loyalty of subordinates through his or her actions. Interpersonal effectiveness and personal leadership skills lead one to a position of influence that transcends power which is inherent in the position itself. Ideally, the supervisor, who automatically has position power, will earn respect and commitment from subordinates by developing relationships which reflect the influence of personal power.

Personal power also involves mastery of certain technical details associated with one's job. Interpersonal effectiveness alone, no matter how dynamic, may not be sufficient if the supervisor lacks knowledge about the type of work performed within the organization. In a municipal park operation, a supervisor of park technicians would be less than successful if he or she lacked knowledge about natural resources, administrative procedures within the organization, or problems associated with preventive maintenance of equipment. Theoretically, as we will discuss shortly, technical knowledge is not necessary for effective leadership; realistically, however, it can often be an asset in helping the leader gain the respect of subordinates and to provide a deeper understanding of the problems faced by others at all levels.

At this point we must offer a word of caution. It is not unusual for supervisors in leisure services to have supervisory responsibilities for areas and facilities, as well as personnel. It is also not unusual for supervisors of areas and facilities to fall into the trap of emphasizing preservation and maintenance factors to an extent that negatively affects program effectiveness. As Gray (1968, p. 288) has stated:

On many municipal recreation centers, the most conspicuous design element of the physical plant is a chain-link fence. It is never quite clear whether its purpose is to keep the staff in or citizens out. . . . The chain-link fence which surrounds their professional world limits their service to the confines of the center, supports a come-to-us philosophy, limits their professional role, restricts the horizon and the concepts of service of the recreation movement.

No matter how important the facility, problems associated with vandalism and "normal wear and tear" should not be solved by merely enacting stricter rules or developing bigger and stronger protective barriers. Such measures, particularly if used alone, will generally lead to greater protection but will also serve to keep people out. A beautiful park or attractive community center is diminished in value if preservation is at the expense of participation and involvement.

The challenge, therefore, is for supervisors to create an atmosphere which *involves* people, not excludes them. Preservation must be *with* people's commitment, not against. The "tyranny of the chain link fence" can be a far greater price to pay than one might suspect and must constantly be guarded against at all levels.

Responsibilities of the Leisure Service Supervisor

Concerned with technical and human concerns, the supervisor faces a variety of tasks and responsibilities. Specific roles will vary among agencies, but the following responsibilities are typically associated with the leisure service supervisor:

1. Serves as liaison between face-to-face leaders and upper management and is directly involved in program planning
2. Provides leaders with logistical support such as equipment, supplies, maintenance, and arrangement of transportation for special trips and outings
3. Participates in the preparation of budgets, especially in an advisory capacity
4. Stimulates interaction between program leaders and the media, particularly local newspapers and radio stations

5. Handles routine discipline problems
6. Becomes involved in planning and conducting pre-service and in-service training programs
7. Insures that safety standards are always properly maintained
8. Insures the proper maintenance of records of various types such as participation rates and patterns, employee attendance, accident reports, maintenance schedules, and programs offered
9. Evaluates subordinate effectiveness and counsels on the quality of individual performance, professional development, and factors related to morale
10. Interprets organizational policy to subordinates

These and other duties involve responsibilities related to: (1) the public, (2) subordinates, (3) co-workers and administrators, (4) program areas, and (5) facilities. In essence, then, the supervisor not only "supervises," but also fulfills many responsibilities associated with lower-level administration (Kraus and Bates, 1975). As a rule, administrative duties increase with the size and complexity of the agency but will constitute a portion of one's supervisory responsibilities in virtually all agencies.

Thus, the broad areas typically associated with the leisure service supervisor include: (1) program and staff development (Sterle and Duncan, 1973), and (2) lower level administration and technical support (Kraus and Bates, 1975). In the discussion which follows, we will examine several of these areas, beginning with the process of recruiting, screening, and hiring new staff.

Recruitment of New Employees

Recruitment of qualified personnel can be a taxing, yet exciting process. If carried out effectively, it can generate a number of benefits apart from the actual acquisition of a new employee.

First, seeking new employees for key positions generally requires agency administrators and supervisors to re-examine the scope of the vacant position. Decisions should be made to look for qualities in the new employee which are either similar to those characteristic of the employee being replaced, or to alter duties and responsibilities in such a way that different strengths are sought. Duties incorporated in the position, areas of responsibility, and interdepartmental relationships within the agency may be altered considerably as a result of reassessing the scope of the vacant position. In general, this provides a time for introspection and reevaluation by the administration.

Second, opportunities for dialogue among existing agency employees are created as a natural part of self-examination. Staff and line members alike should be encouraged to communicate their feelings and concerns;

most importantly, those in positions of influence should be receptive to new ideas rather than merely paying lip-service to them.

Third, recruitment efforts increase agency visibility. Depending upon the situation, position announcements will be disseminated locally and perhaps nationally as well. If prepared properly, the reputation and image of the department will be enhanced through the process.

Finally, if high-caliber applicants apply for the vacant position, the credibility of the agency or department may be enhanced. Quality individuals tend to seek quality organizations — the attraction of such individuals could generate greater support among key persons with influence, such as town or city managers, council members, board members, and so forth.

DISSEMINATING JOB ANNOUNCEMENTS

The method for disseminating information on position vacancies frequently depends upon the level of the position. Positions for part-time activity leaders are generally announced only in the local area. Notices may be placed in the newspaper and may also be sent to nearby colleges, universities, or high schools. Higher level positions should be announced more extensively to increase the likelihood of attracting high-quality applicants. State recreation associations, colleges and universities in other states, and the National Recreation and Park Association all represent important sources of contact.

Attracting high-quality individuals from "traditional" sources is often not sufficient in itself. It is essential to extend into areas where high-caliber minorities may be reached. All too often employers feel that openly announcing position vacancies meets fair employment standards; however, efforts to recruit minority applicants must involve more than the traditional approach. This does not imply that standards must be compromised; rather, that if the concept, "equal opportunity" is to apply, opportunities to become *aware* of openings constitutes the first step. Agency administrators must insure that minority organizations are aware of job positions, and that recruitment is extended into areas known to consist of minority residents.

Finally, the way in which job announcements are prepared can be quite important. How often, for example, might an announcement read similarly to that depicted in Figure 6-1?

This hypothetical announcement tells very little about the position itself or the local community, and certainly provides little opportunity for public relations which could lead to elevating the identity of the agency. Several specific points bear consideration:

1. Applicants want as much information as possible, particularly if they reside some distance from the community announcing a position vacancy.

```
┌─────────────────────────────────────────────────────────────┐
│                         (Town)                               │
│                                                              │
│                      (Department)                            │
│                                                              │
│  Position: Recreation Supervisor                             │
│                                                              │
│  Duties: Supervise and coordinate recreation activities and  │
│                                                              │
│          sport programs for groups of all ages.             │
│                                                              │
│  Salary: $13,000-$14,500 starting salary.                    │
│                                                              │
│  Qualifications: Masters degree in Parks and Recreation or   │
│                                                              │
│                  related field, plus three years experience. │
│                                                              │
│  Closing Date: April 1                                       │
│                                                              │
│  For further information contact:                            │
│                                                              │
│              J.B. Abel, Superintendent                       │
│                                                              │
│              Parks and Recreation Department                 │
│                                                              │
│              15 A Street                                     │
│                                                              │
│              City Hall, Room 10                             │
│                                                              │
│  An equal opportunity employer.                              │
│                                                              │
└─────────────────────────────────────────────────────────────┘
```

Figure 6.1 Hypothetical Position Announcement

2. All of us tend to respond more favorably if the strengths of the community are mentioned. This could include proximity to recreation areas, the existence of cultural centers, and geographic points of interest. Although areas such as Denver, San Francisco, and Boston have attractions which surpass most cities, each community has its own strengths, and these should be highlighted.

3. The phrase, "masters degree in Parks and Recreation or *related field,*" is used frequently and tends to draw mixed reactions among professionals. Many feel that the field in which one obtained a degree is not as important as the ability and quality of the particular individual. Others feel, however, that positions of responsibility in leisure services should be filled with people educated specifically in the field and that we are selling the field short if we believe that "anyone" can do the job. This point is certainly debatable; however, it is in the best interest of the leisure service profession to insure that qualifications are properly established for all positions and that those qualifications are met in full. The determination should be based on *substance* rather than degree labels. We have no answer which will resolve the issue of whether or not positions *should* be open to "related fields,"

but more often than not, this is the case. However, it should be pointed out that those in leisure services who have developed a strong foundation in the field should have an automatic advantage, not by virtue of a degree title, but by the substance of what they know.

An example of a stronger job announcement model will help. Dade County, Florida, has designed a job description form which broadly describes all positions in the County Park and Recreation Department. Since positions are not necessarily vacant, specific openings are described in detail on an additional sheet. Job inquiries directed to the Park and Recreation Director are answered with the general form and, if an opening exists, is accompanied with a detail sheet announcing the position. The Dade County approach is as follows:

Department of Park and Recreation
Metropolitan Dade County
Miami, Florida

Today, the Metropolitan Dade County Park and Recreation Department is considered one of the top park systems in the United States. The Department has reached that position through hard work, effort, and vision.

We are proud of our reputation and constantly search for the best personnel to continue and develop our programs.

The information on this brochure can assist you in understanding the process of applying for employment in our department. The information is arranged to answer some of the questions a potential applicant is likely to ask.

1. I have just graduated from college with a degree in Recreation. How do I go about applying for a position with Park and Recreation?

In order to apply for most positions requiring a college degree, it is necessary to apply in person at our Central Personnel Office, 2501 Coral Way, and make an appointment to take the appropriate Civil Service examination. A score of 70 or better is required to be placed on an eligible list. Your name will remain on this list for a one-year period. When positions become available, you will be notified by mail to come for an interview.

2. What information do I need to bring when applying to Personnel?

You will be asked to complete a Dade County Employment Application. You will need your social security card. You may be asked to furnish your college transcript.

3. Where is the Personnel Section for the Dade County Park and Recreation Department?

This section is located within the administrative grounds at 50 S.W. 32nd Road, Miami, 33129.

4. What is the future of promotional opportunities in the Dade County Park and Recreation Department?

The Board of Dade County Commissioners has approved a 10-year expansion master plan under the "Decade of Progress" Bond Issue which approves the construction of 18 new parks. One of these projects will be a 734-acre "New Zoo." Thus, promotional opportunities will be ample for many employees.

5. I'm a minority group member, are there many possibilities for employment in the Dade County Department of Park and Recreation?

Definitely: The Dade County Park and Recreation Department strongly encourages, and is actively seeking, application by minority group members. We are an Equal Employment Opportunity Organization.

6. What kinds of positions are available in the Dade County Park and Recreation Department?

These are the kinds of positions you may qualify for on the open-competitive register:

Position	Qualifications
Recreation Leader	Graduate of High School or GED; **and** 1-yr. full-time paid experience in Physical Ed. or Group Recreation, **or,** may substitute for experience—2-yrs. College in Recreation, Phys., Ed., or Fine Arts (music, drama, dance, crafts), or Outdoor Educ. Written exam.
Recreation Center Director I	College degree in Recreation, Physical Ed., Park & Rec. Management, or related. Full-time paid experience in Rec. or Physical Ed. may be substituted for education on a year-to-year basis (not to exceed 2-yrs.).
Recreation Center Director I (Pool Manager)	Graduate of High School or GED and 1-yr. fulltime paid experience as a lifeguard. Age 21-45. All applicants must present the following current certification at the time of application: First Aid Certificate; American Red Cross Water Safety Instructor or YMCA Instructor's Rating; State Board of Health Swimming Pool Operator's Certificate (or, provisional certificate requirements must be completed during the first 6-mo. of employ.)
Park Services Officer I	Degree in Park Management, Recreation Admin., or Business Administration; **and** 1-yr. fulltime paid Admin. or Management experience; resume at time of application; written exam.
Administrative Officer I	Degree in Business, Management, Gov't., Psychology, Sociology, Human Relations, Math, Physical and Biological Sciences; **or,** a Bachelor's **and** completion of a county admin. internship; **or,** 1-yr. full-time paid satisfactory experience in a county generalized public service information program. Prefer professional or administrative experience. Resume. Written exam.
Administrative Officer II	Education: same as above; **and** 2-yrs. paid full-time experience; **or,** a Masters in above-named curricula **and** 1-yr. post-grad. experience or internship training in a government agency. Resume. Written exam.
Park Manager I (Clubhouse Operations)	High School graduate or GED; 4-yrs. fulltime paid managerial experience in Hotel or Restaurant operation. May substitute college coursework in Administration or related area on a year-for-year basis. Complete resume at time of application.
Landscape Architect I	Degree in Landscape Architecture; sample of work must be submitted at interview along with a complete resume at time of application.
Landscape Foreman II	2-yrs. paid full-time supervisory experience in Landscape development including the use of tree cranes, tractors, and similar heavy equipment. Written exam.
Zookeeper I	Some experience in custodial care and feeding of wild or domestic animals, reptiles or birds is desired.

We sincerely hope that the above information will make the application process to our department simple and productive.

We, at Dade County Park and Recreation, wish you much success in pursuing your career in the Park and Recreation field.

enc: Dade County Brochure
      Employment Handbook

SAMPLE JOB DESCRIPTION
DADE COUNTY, FLORIDA
Recreation District Supervisor

Nature of Work

This is administrative and supervisory work in assisting in the direction of the overall recreation services for a geographical district of the county.

Work involves responsibility for the operation and maintenance of all recreational facilities within the area of assignment. The employee plans, assigns, and reviews the work of subordinate Recreation Directors, Supervisors, and related personnel engaged in carrying out a full and varied recreation program. As supervisor of a district the incumbent assists in the administration and coordination of the county wide recreation program under guidance and direction of the Recreation Superintendent. Work is performed in accordance with predetermined policies and programming, but the employee exercises considerable independence in determining work methods and procedures to carry out assigned objectives. Administrative supervision is received from the Recreation Superintendent who reviews work principally for program effectiveness and the attainment of desired results through personal consultation and analysis of written reports, program curriculum, and participation data.

Illustrative Tasks

Plans, organizes, staffs, directs, and coordinates the work of a large group of recreation personnel within a recreation district, engaged in carrying out a full and varied program; reviews work for completed objectives, supervises the development of a wide variety of general recreation activities including playgrounds, community youth centers, aquatics, athletics events, and diversified group interest programs.

Confers with the superintendent in planning the effective use and development of recreation areas and makes suggestions concerning plans and designs of playgrounds, buildings and related facilities.

Assists in research and related studies on community needs in the county in order to promote and maintain maximum participation in the program.

Receives and reviews reports from the district's line organization and takes necessary action or recommends suitable action; reviews and evaluates various recreation personnel assigned to the district through field visitation, analysis of reports, and through conferences and meetings.

Prepares reports on district's activities; conducts correspondence regarding the various phases of the program; prepares preliminary budget for superintendent's review.

Meets with interested civic groups and organizations concerning their needs in relation to the district recreation services and facilities.

Performs related work as required.

Knowledge, Abilities and Skills

Thorough knowledge of the objectives and principles of public recreation, including considerable understanding of the activities which make up a community recreation program.

Considerable knowledge of the recreation facilities and equipment needed in a large population area.

Considerable knowledge of the recreation interests and activities in a community and skill in incorporating these within a community recreation program for all ages.

Ability to plan, supervise, and direct the activities of a large group of recreation personnel in a manner conducive to full performance and high morale.

Ability to work with and obtain the cooperation of civic groups and the general community.

Ability to prepare and submit clear and comprehensive reports.

Ability to analyze a variety of information and to exercise a marked degree of independent judgment in arriving at conclusions.

Desirable Experience and Training

Thorough experience of a progressively responsible nature in an organized public recreation program; and graduation from an approved college or university with major course work in physical education or recreation.

SCREENING AND INTERVIEWING APPLICANTS

Invariably, individuals who do not meet quite all of the specified requirements for a given position will submit applications. These are relatively easy to identify (unless they have not responded honestly, which would generally be detected at a later time) and should be eliminated from consideration. Courteous letters of rejection should be sent as soon as ineligibility is determined.

All other applicants who meet the specified qualifications require further attention. A point of controversy should be mentioned, however. As a general rule, not all candidates for a position can realistically be interviewed if the number is especially large; however, some communities *require* that all qualified applicants be given the opportunity for a personal interview. If the latter is the case, attention must be given to the basic requirements of the position by making them stringent enough, yet clearly related to job requirements, to keep the number of qualified individuals to a manageable number. In some cases where the number of applicants is exceptionally large, a lottery system has been used to select from among all who are fully qualified, such as those seasonally employed by the National Park Service. There can be no single rule for developing job requirements or for limiting the number of qualified applicants; therefore, this must be worked out in each agency.

Civil service agencies and agencies which administer written exams to formulate lists of qualified applicants do not face this problem. In most cases, only the top three applicants are interviewed under the "rule of three" which requires an appointment from among the three candidates at the top of the eligibility list.

Interviewing is not always considered to be a supervisory function. If not, those responsible for interviewing should obtain supervisory input to insure that job related lines of questioning are pursued during the interviews.

Once the technical qualifications for the position have been determined, the interview procedure must be arranged. Briefly, the following factors should be considered:

1. The interview panel should consist of the same individuals for everyone being interviewed for the same position.
2. If technical information is to be covered in the interview, individuals knowledgeable in the concepts to be covered should constitute the panel, at least in part.
3. The same basic questions should be asked of all applicants.
4. Sexist questions should be completely avoided.
5. Interviews should be long enough to allow the applicant to relax and communicate fully his or her capabilities and personal attributes.
6. A system of objectively scoring each applicant should be devised prior to the commencement of the interviews. Each interviewer should utilize the same system.
7. Applicants should have the opportunity to respond to open-ended questions.
8. Applicants should have the opportunity to ask any questions which they may have about the agency, community, or job duties.
9. Each applicant's personal philosophy of leisure services and basic approach to people should be carefully considered since understanding the relationship between the leisure service delivery system and human needs is essential for practitioners at all levels.

Pre-Service and In-Service Training

The *pre-service* training program, coupled with an initial orientation period, generally incorporates one or more of three broad job-related areas (Sterle and Duncan, 1973, p. 106):

1. Putting the employee at ease
2. Explaining his (or her) job and its importance
3. Creating a real interest in the role and efforts of the agency

It is primarily designed to familiarize employees with the job and surrounding environment, and to introduce them to what will be required to effectively perform their jobs. This should include sharing information related to the agency's goals and philosophy, its policies and procedures, safety, liability and legal concerns, employee benefits, and so forth. The period of time allocated for pre-service training should be sufficient to enable the new employee to become aware of the basic workings of the agency; eventually, of course, pre-service training elements will become so familiar that they will be taken for granted.

In-service training is for the employee who has been on the job for a period of time. Its purpose is to strengthen skills and to build upon what the employee has learned through experience about the organization and about his or her own effectiveness as a leisure service practitioner, leader, or supervisor.

In-service training is particularly important in agencies employing individuals who have not been trained in the leisure service field. As Kraus and Bates (1975) have pointed out, many are effective leaders and have outstanding personal qualities, but lack an in-depth understanding of the goals and objectives of leisure services.

Even individuals who received a strong foundation in leisure services can benefit from in-service training programs. For example, some of the potential benefits of a well designed program include the following:

1. Leadership skills can be strengthened.
2. New ideas in programming can be explored.
3. New methods of strengthening relationships with other agencies can be identified.
4. Volunteer-employee relationships can be improved, especially by including volunteers in the in-service training program.
5. Exciting speakers and workshop leaders can be invited to participate in the training process which often stimulates new ideas and feelings of increased motivation.
6. Employees will often "feel important" and better about themselves in agencies which are willing to expend time and energy to further develop their staff.

In-service training provides an ideal vehicle for involving senior employees in a meaningful way. For instance, it is not unusual for individuals who have been with an agency for many years to experience a decrease in motivation. This is often coupled with a sense of feeling threatened by new "eager beaver" employees who are young and full of energy. The problem is clearly brought to light in a case study described by Bannon (1972, pp. 210-11):

Can You Teach an Old Dog New Tricks?

You have just accepted a position as director of parks and recreation in Clawsonville. Your predecessor had held the position for the past twenty-five years and has now retired. It is obvious to you that the department has not made much progress during the past ten years. Little was done to develop new programs, long-range planning is at a standstill, and in-service training for the staff does not exist. The three supervisors in the department are all close to retirement and do not show much initiative or desire to improve the situation. Many of the younger staff members are unhappy. This is evidenced by the fact that more than 50 percent of the staff under thirty years of age leave the department each year. Naturally this presents a serious problem, especially at the recreation centers and playgrounds.

One of your first efforts to correct the situation is to introduce an in-service training program for all staff members. The supervisors are naturally opposed to the idea. In their opinion, it is a waste of time. "We've held our jobs for ten years. If we don't know them by now, we never will," says John Stevens, supervisor of the maintenance staff. George Evans, another old-timer and head of the recreation centers, indicates, "I've been through this rigmarole before. I've had workshops until they're coming out of my ears. Frankly, I think it's a waste of time. I think they will be far better off if they leave me alone and let me get some work done around here. Besides, you can't teach an old dog new tricks."

Mrs. Bishop, supervisor of the cultural-arts division, also is unhappy about the training program. She believes that in most cases the people who instruct these programs are out of touch with reality and do not understand the problems of operating a program.

According to the grapevine, the younger staff members are excited about the program and the opportunity of learning new techniques. Some of them feel, however, that the older staff members will try to sabotage the program before it even gets started.

Although there is not necessarily an "ideal" answer for all who encounter this problem, one approach which could be helpful is to ask those who are senior in the organization to assist in designing and presenting in-service training programs. They have a tremendous wealth of knowledge to share and will certainly feel a sense of meaningful involvement if this approach is implemented properly.

Whether developing a pre-service or in-service training program, there are specific steps in planning one should consider. No single list can cover all situations, but the following points should be considered prior to implementing the training process:

1. Formulate the objectives of the program in a manner which involves the staff members who will participate. They are likely to identify areas of concern which could go unnoticed in the absence of dialogue.
2. Insure that each person who will be involved in a leadership capacity understands the stated objectives and his or her role in the program. Programs must also be carefully structured; it is not unusual for agencies to schedule "open-end" sessions which facilitate dialogue but do not deal with specific issues and specific courses of action.
3. Training accomplishments should be evaluated and the resulting feedback should influence subsequent training approaches.

4. It is generally better to follow a relatively strict schedule to insure that all topics are addressed. Topics which are not resolved or are of particular interest can be returned to at another time. Adhering to a pre-determined format and sequence of events tends to hold the interest of participants and communicates a sense of organizational ability and competence among those responsible for presenting the training sessions.
5. An appropriate setting should be selected for the training program. The proper choice will depend upon the nature of the tasks to be accomplished, of course. Sessions may be conducted at the site of a program area or facility, such as a swimming pool, playfield, or gymnasium. If a classroom atmosphere is desired, the area should be comfortable and free of distractions.
6. Outcomes of the training program should be recorded in written form, particularly if new courses of action are identified. Ideally, one outcome of sessions, especially in-service training programs, should be the formulation of concrete objectives pertaining to job effectiveness. These should be accompanied by specific methods for evaluating their attainment. Finally, follow-up sessions should be planned to permit the process to be continuous rather than sporadic.

The reasons agencies most frequently choose not to conduct pre-service or in-service training programs center around time and money. Training sessions require considerable staff time to plan and conduct, time which removes those who are involved from normal duties. Financial costs can also be a deterent. Employees are frequently paid during the training sessions which requires additional salary expenditures. But the dividends resulting from training programs can be far greater than these costs; thus, it is an investment process rather than a loss of time and money. In the long run, benefits can include increased morale among employees, less employee absenteeism and turnover, improvement in skill levels, and a more effectively functioning organization.

Employee Evaluations

The evaluation of subordinates can be an extremely difficult task, particularly involving instances in which a subordinate is experiencing difficulties. But whether an employee is performing admirably or not, the evaluation process should be used as a building tool, a means for increasing capabilities and job effectiveness.

Leader performance evaluations are generally the responsibility of the supervisor and supervisors are evaluated by higher level supervisors or administrators (Kraus and Bates, 1975). Evaluations usually take place on a regular basis, such as following a new employee's first three months with an agency, and every six months thereafter. The specific pattern varies among agencies, but invariably decisions related to retention, tenure, promotion, and salary increases are tied very closely to evaluations. This places the supervisor in a critical role, one which requires considerable attention if it is to be carried out with skill and fairness.

EVALUATION FORMS

There are almost as many types of evaluation forms as there are agencies, but we will suggest an approach which is commonly adopted. The employee evaluation form lists a number of factors relating to the individual and his or her job performance; each factor is then assessed on a continuum such as: (1) Exceptionally Outstanding, (2) Outstanding, (3) Satisfactory, (4) Poor, (5) Totally Inadequate. An example of this system of rating is presented in Figure 6-2.

Such factors may be accompanied by one or more additional sections. For example, additional sections might address the following items:

1. What are the employee's key strengths?
2. What are the employee's key weaknesses?
3. Have areas of needed improvement which were pointed out on earlier evaluations been remedied?
4. Has the employee performed any job or task in a particularly exemplary way?
5. What has the employee done on his or her own to develop more fully as a leisure service practitioner? (Examples could include additional schooling, attending conferences and workshops, attending board/commission meetings, and so forth.)

Finally, a section might be added for any specialized area of concern, such as in a therapeutic setting. Rating topics might include:

1. Knowledge of medical terminology of disorders
2. Knowledge of disorders and their symptoms
3. Ability to prescribe appropriate leisure activities for individuals with differing disabilities
4. Knowledge of the roles of other members of the medical/therapy team
5. Ability to foster a sense of independence in patients

Depending upon the agency and clientele, the list could be varied or expanded. Other settings which use specialized evaluation factors include correctional institutions, camps for the handicapped and mentally retarded, and commercial enterprises. In each case, careful consideration should be given to isolating special areas beyond the general factors evaluated in most agencies.

EMPLOYEE PERFORMANCE EVALUATION

Name _____ Position _____

Date _____ Evaluator _____

Date of Last Evaluation _____

Evaluation Factors	Rating 1	2	3	4	5
A. Personal					
1. Ability to work without supervision	___	___	___	___	___
2. Ability to work with others	___	___	___	___	___
3. Dependability	___	___	___	___	___
4. Ability to constructively influence others	___	___	___	___	___
5. Diplomacy and tact	___	___	___	___	___
B. Task-related					
1. Ability to organize tasks	___	___	___	___	___
2. Quality of written reports	___	___	___	___	___
3. Knowledge of program skills	___	___	___	___	___
4. Planning ability	___	___	___	___	___
5. Initiative	___	___	___	___	___
6. Relations with participants	___	___	___	___	___
7. Willingness to try innovative approaches	___	___	___	___	___
C. Overall					
1. Effectiveness compared to others in a similar capacity	___	___	___	___	___
2. Effectiveness compared to previous performance	___	___	___	___	___
3. Potential and advancement	___	___	___	___	___
4. Overall effectiveness	___	___	___	___	___
Totals					

A = _____
B = _____   A+B+C = _____
C = _____

_____   _____
Evaluator's Signature   Employee's Signature

                                                          _____
                                                          Date

Figure 6.2   Employee Performance Evaluation

In all cases, evaluations should be discussed with the employee and used as a tool to identify strengths and weaknesses, correct problem areas if they emerge, and to reinforce positive attributes of the individual as a person and in the performance of his or her job.

A basic attitude of "think positive" should be adopted by the supervisor. This means that positive solutions to problems should be sought whenever possible. It is easy to reprimand, punish, or threaten, but these behaviors tend to be less motivating than constructive, helpful measures. Most of us realize our own inadequacies and feel worse if they are belabored; criticism can, therefore, lead to greater tension and a reduction in overall performance. On the other hand, praise and helpful suggestions which are accompanied by an expression of confidence in the individual are usually welcome and contribute to improvement. If the evaluation process is looked upon by all as an aid rather than a threat, the overall atmosphere of the agency will most certainly be enhanced.

Management, Leadership, and Motivation

At this point, we will turn more fully to the sensitive area of supervisor-subordinate relations as it relates to employee motivation, job efficiency, and overall productivity (effectiveness) of the agency. This will include a brief examination of managing by objectives, theories of leadership, and a model which will enable the leader of subordinates to effectively diagnose situations and apply the appropriate leadership style for the given situation.

Management By Objectives

The process leading to an effective leisure service delivery system requires a tremendous amount of careful planning and interaction among agency personnel. Since the desired outcome is to effectively serve the community, considerable attention should be given to developing a systematic approach leading to that end.

A framework which provides such a structured format and a planning model is Management By Objectives (MBO), advanced by Odiorne (1965). Very simply, "Management By Objectives is a continual process whereby superior and subordinate managers . . . periodically identify their common goals, define each individual's major areas of responsibility in terms of results expected of each and use these agreed upon measures as guides for each operating department and for assessing contributions of each manager to the work of the entire institution" (Deegan and Fritz, 1975, p. 119).

At least two benefits can result from the use of the MBO model: (1) goals and objectives will not only be clarified but will also be systematically checked before, during, and after the delivery of programs, and (2) those involved at the supervisory and administrative levels will be required to communicate among themselves and with subordinates on a regular basis. This can have a great impact on the morale, motivation, and effectiveness of employees at all levels.

Deegan and Fritz went on to describe the basic components of the process. The first is formulating mutual agreements between superior and subordinate managers. This requires developing a climate which facilitates honest dialogue that produces a commitment to support agreed-upon decisions. Second, common goals must be identified and adopted if such commitment is to be expected. This is essential if personnel at all levels are to understand and agree with what is expected of them. Third, major responsibilities must be clarified so that personnel know *how* to follow through on their commitments. Manuals, job descriptions, meetings, and in-service training programs may all play an important role in properly defining one's responsibilities. Fourth, each employee should be able to determine how well he or she is performing. Thus, specific and realistic personal objectives should be established which become a part of the fifth step, the performance budget. The performance budget provides checkpoints for monitoring progress. Objectives should be put into writing and referred to frequently. The final phase centers around the evaluation of performance and the evaluation should be in terms of established objectives.

Management By Objectives is basically a process by which the delivery of services is carefully mapped out from beginning to end, well in advance of the actual point of delivery. Check points of all types can be established to assist in meeting deadlines and to insure that personnel are maintaining the desired course of action. One example of the MBO planning and implementation processes might be depicted as shown in Figure 6-3.

Of course many problems may occur no matter how well the MBO process is delineated and followed. Differences of opinion may emerge, resources for implementation may not be ideal, or the need for a certain service or program may be mis-diagnosed. But if a reasonable system of problem solving is adopted, difficulties can be minimized.

We cannot devote full attention to the MBO model but suggest that the reader refer to additional sources to gain depth in the process. Specifically, helpful sources have been developed by Lasagna (1971), Levinson (1970), Morrissey (1970), Odiorne (1965; 1969), and Varney (1971).

Leadership and Motivation

A basic concern of all leaders should be identifying the needs of their subordinates and fostering an environment which allows those needs to be met. Although individuals vary considerably in personality, likes,

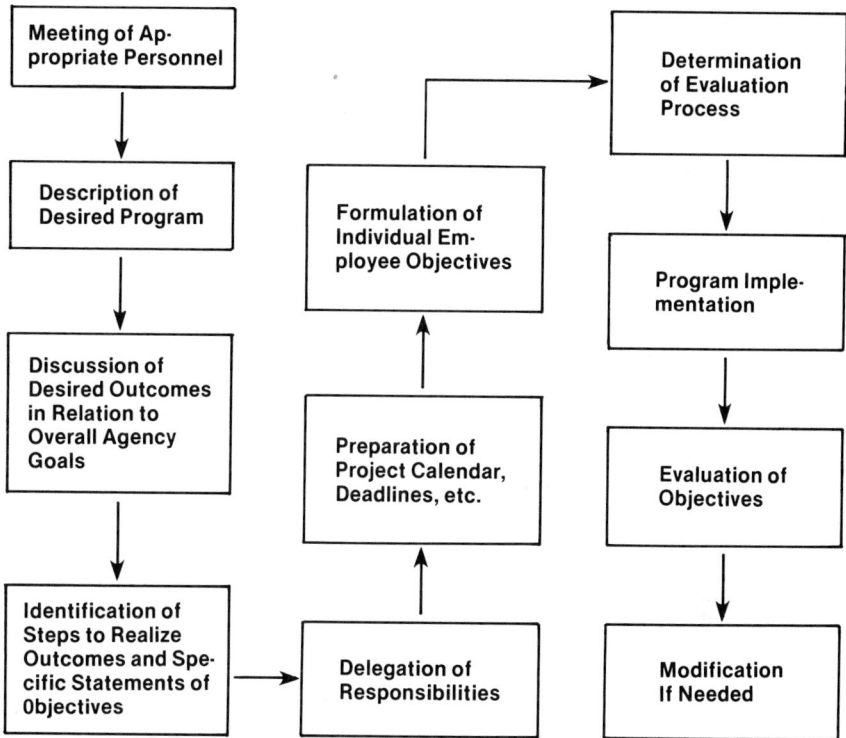

Figure 6.3 Management by Objectives Flow Chart

dislikes, and so forth, research has shown that knowledge about some of the basics of human motivation can help supervisors select courses of action which can greatly strengthen leadership effectiveness.

An important point relating to *leadership effectiveness* and *successful leadership* must be made. The distinction, first suggested by Bass (1960) and discussed later by Hersey and Blanchard (1977), is important. The *successful* leader may be capable of insuring that the job gets done, relying on his or her position power. The job or task is completed but primarily as a result of an authoritarian style of leadership. By this, we are referring to the type of leader who controls and directs in such a way that subordinates have little or no input into the decision making process, and generally are motivated by external pressures. External pressures can include fear of reprimand, fear of being fired, and so forth.

Effective leadership, however, occurs when subordinates not only complete the task appropriately, but do so willingly and find it highly rewarding. The leader who relies on personal power and who fosters a democratic style of leadership is not only considered to be successful, but effective as well. Personal power is more directly related to effectiveness than is position power.

Our purpose is to focus upon variables most closely associated with the development of personal power. Although personality, disposition, and attitude toward people influence one's ability to generate personal power, a number of other factors also enter into the picture. Personal power should not be viewed simply as one's God-given attributes. This will become evident as theories of leadership are presented and a model for effective leadership is described.

THEORIES OF LEADERSHIP

Maslow's Hierarchy of Needs and the Hawthorne Effect. In our earlier discussion, Maslow's (1968) hierarchy of needs was related to participants in leisure service programs. The model has direct application to leader-subordinate relationships.

In earlier years, particularly up to and into the Industrial Revolution, managers tended to assume that employees worked out of a basic need for food, shelter, clothing (physiological needs), and wages, fringe benefits, and property (safety or security needs). In terms of Maslow's hierarchy, the higher level needs (social, esteem, and self-actualization) were virtually ignored. The tendency for leaders to be autocratic (authoritarian) was quite common. Work was viewed as drudgery and the leader believed that strong direction and control were necessary to insure job success; striving for leadership *effectiveness* was not the key concern.

Basic assumptions related to motivation were shaken, however, as a result of Mayo's (1933) study at the Western Electric Hawthorne plant in Hawthorne, Illinois. The study was initially designed to test the effects of lighting conditions on employee productivity.

An experimental group of women who assembled telephone relays was identified. Lighting conditions were varied with the expectation that improved illumination would lead to increased production. A control group of women performing the same task was selected in an environment maintaining constant lighting conditions at a normal level. After a period of time, it was found that productivity in *both* groups increased significantly.

Other variables were also manipulated; for example, employees in the experimental group were given scheduled breaks and shorter work weeks. Productivity in *both* groups continued to rise. Uncertain about the cause, Mayo and his associates decided to explore the impact of removing all that had been given to the experimental group. To the amazement of the researchers, *productivity continued to increase* to an all-time high.

Before continuing further, the reader is encouraged to formulate a theory explaining the results of the study. Why did performance continue to improve in the control group which received none of the benefits of the experimental group? Why did productivity in *both* groups rise to an all-time high after all benefits were withdrawn from the experimental group? How might Maslow's theory be applied?

In fairness to the reader, we must admit that an important element of the study has not yet been described, an element that is central to the entire experiment: the researchers spent considerable time interviewing workers in both the experimental and control groups. The interviewing process had a direct impact on all of the women. They felt that management *cared* about their problems, concerns, and feelings, perhaps for the first time in any depth. Productivity rose because the workers' attitudes changed so dramatically that an actual desire to do well evolved. As Hersey and Blanchard (1977, p. 53) pointed out, "the workers began to feel that management viewed them as important, both as individuals and as a group; they were now participating in the operation and future of the company and not just performing unchallenging, unappreciated tasks."

In essence, it became evident that people were not motivated only to fill physiological and safety needs through the work experience. Higher levels of the Maslow hierarchy took on a new sense of importance in the work arena.

McGregor's Theory X and Theory Y. The work of McGregor (1960; 1966) was directly influenced by the Hawthorne study. Now a classic theory of human motivation, his model describes two basic approaches to the management of employees. They delineate assumptions about human nature as follows:

Theory X and Theory Y Assumptions About Human Nature

Theory X

1. Work is inherently distasteful to most people.
2. Most people are not ambitious, have little desire for responsibility, and prefer to be directed.
3. Most people have little capacity for creativity in solving organizational problems.
4. Motivation occurs only at the physiological and safety levels.
5. Most people must be closely controlled and often coerced to achieve organizational objectives.

Theory Y

1. Work is as natural as play, if the conditions are favorable.
2. Self-control is often indispensable in achieving organizational goals.
3. The capacity for creativity in solving organizational problems is widely distributed in the population.
4. Motivation occurs at the social, esteem, and self-actualization levels, as well as physiological and security levels.
5. People can be self-directed and creative at work if properly motivated.

The Theory Y manager, then, does not see work as only a path to financial remuneration but as a natural part of life, as natural, in fact, as play. This does not mean that work is always *fun*. It simply suggests that the same benefits can be experienced through work that are associated with play, such as feelings of satisfaction, accomplishment, creativity, and a positive sense of self-worth.

Despite the widespread awareness of McGregor's work, and the writings of others who have followed in the same vein, many managers continue to adopt a style of leadership which is more closely aligned with Theory X assumptions. Interestingly enough, *both* the Theory X and Theory Y type managers not only believe their respective assumptions are true but also feel they can "prove" that they are correct. What occurs is a type of self-fulfilling prophecy. The Theory X manager assumes that people are lazy, do not like work, and so forth, and treats them accordingly by controlling and directing their behavior through extremely close supervision and coercive leadership. Employees react negatively to the autocratic, stifling approach by doing as little as possible to "get by," avoiding anything which requires extra responsibilities. The Theory X leader then responds with, "I told you so," and increases efforts to exercise control over subordinates.

The Theory Y leader also finds support in his or her style by treating people as if they are creative, willing to accept increased responsibility, and able to find work a satisfying and enriching experience. When subordinates, "rise to the occasion," the manager's beliefs related to Theory Y are reinforced.

In both situations, the Theory X and Theory Y approaches to management can be *successful;* it is unlikely, however, that the Theory X style will be *effective,* at least in the long run. Given the choice, the potential for developing a strong organizational framework is clearly more likely if one adopts a *positive* view toward human nature. This does not imply a loose organizational system which allows total freedom and fosters weak supervision. This will become apparent when we explore a leadership model which is highly compatible with the Theory Y approach to leadership and management.

Herzberg's Theory of Motivation. Herzberg (1959; 1966) focused on two major categories related to job satisfaction: **hygiene factors** and **motivators.** *Hygiene factors* refer to elements which are not actually part of the job itself such as the working environment, company policies and regulations, salary, staff-subordinate relations, fringe benefits, and interpersonal relations. These aspects of the job may affect job performance but are not components of the job itself; rather, they constitute the environment in which the job is performed.

Motivators encompass elements which are related to the job itself and include such variables as feelings of achievement, challenging work, increased responsibility, growth and development, recognition of one's accomplishments, and opportunities for creativity. Thus, motivators are closely related to *esteem* and *self-actualization* needs on the Maslow hierarchy; hygiene factors correspond more closely to physiological, safety, and social needs.

Hygiene factors can certainly create problems for employees but tend to be less critical to job satisfaction than motivators. We are certainly familiar with people who select occupations which require working under extremely adverse conditions and for relatively small compensation. Yet the level of fulfillment through performing the job may be great. Notable examples include those who accept positions as Peace Corps volunteers, inner-city social workers, and community public health employees. In fact, the clearest example may be volunteers of all types who receive only the reward of personal satisfaction for their efforts.

Referring again to McGregor's model, Theory X managers tend to concentrate primarily on hygiene factors, often to the exclusion of motivators. The conscientious Theory Y manager, however, places the greater emphasis on motivators, but not to the exclusion of hygiene factors.

It must be emphasized that hygiene factors *are* important and can be responsible for retaining or losing employees. There is a limit, for example, to how much adversity one can accommodate in even the most rewarding occupation. In fact, a single hygiene factor, such as salary, can be all-important, particularly if an employee is paid well below his or her counterparts employed by other agencies, and a similar position is available elsewhere. This means that lower-level needs (hygiene needs) must be met and maintained at an acceptable level, but even if met, do not have the power of motivators to fully enrich the work experience.

Leadership Style and Effectiveness

The chief concern of the leader or manager is to contribute to making his or her agency an effective one, rather than one which is only successful. We have assumed that effective organizations are those composed of personnel who find their work enriching and satisfying, and are therefore, highly motivated. These are generally employees who can simultaneously meet personal needs as well as the needs (goals and objectives) of the organization.

There are many traits generally associated with leaders, such as impressive appearance, speaking ability, perseverance, discretion, and so forth (Sterle and Duncan, 1973, p. 10). It is clear, however, that not all individuals possessing these and other similar strengths are leaders; nor do all leaders possess the same traits. Frequently the *situation* partially determines how leaders emerge. The most promising of leaders may never emerge as such if there is no room for advancement, if there is discrimination, and so forth. Therefore, it is safe to suggest that personal attributes *and* the situation have their impact on determining who emerges as a leader and how this is accomplished. Furthermore, both variables will influence the extent to which a leader will be effective in the leadership role.

Our emphasis in this discussion will not be on *how* leaders emerge but to what extent leaders can be effective in *varying* situations. Thus, we will focus on "leaders" who are identified as such by virtue of supervisory or administrative positions. They are those individuals who have position power in their jobs. The challenge is for those with position power to exercise influence primarily through *personal power* in such a way that subordinates are motivated to better serve their agency and those who are served through it.

Leadership Style

Leadership style, as Hersey and Blanchard (1977) have emphasized, is not how the leader *believes* he or she leads. Nor does style relate to how the leader *desires* to lead. Leadership style relates to the *behavior of the leader* (supervisor or administrator) *as perceived by others.* In other words, the manner in which followers view their supervisor *is* the leadership style of that supervisor, regardless of the motives and perception of the supervisor.

A supervisor, for example, may believe that she has an "open-door" policy and has made a point of telling her staff that they are always welcome to come in to share ideas. If subordinates follow her lead but find that their ideas are always rejected, no matter how diplomatically, they may begin to perceive her as rigid and autocratic in style. The supervisor and follower perceptions are not in alignment, but it is the followers' perceptions which "count" and will subsequently influence their level of motivation. Therefore, to repeat, **leadership style is as perceived by others,** which may or may not be consistent with the leader's self-perception.

Diagnosing Group Capabilities

We stated that varying situations may influence whether or not a leader will be effective or ineffective. Fiedler (1965; 1967) for example, has recognized that not everyone is comfortable or capable in all situations. He suggests, that whenever possible, leaders should be changed to an environment which suits their style, rather than attempting to change the deep-rooted characteristics of the leader. While this may be desirable, it may also be unrealistic, particularly in organizations which do not easily lend themselves to such flexibility.

We maintain that the leader cannot always be transferred to a different setting and that changes in leadership style can be implemented which allow the leader to be flexible as situations change. This requires that the leader develop diagnostic skills, skills which enable him or her to identify the functioning level of the group, and to exercise leadership influence accordingly.

The process should begin by first analyzing the group's capabilities to perform the tasks of the job. As a general rule, the less able personnel are to successfully perform the task at hand, the more the leader needs to become involved in sharpening those skills. The leader may do this by offering personal help, developing in-service training programs, asking peers to help peers, and so forth. As the capabilities of individuals in a given group increase, the leader's role in task training is less active.

Second, but perhaps simultaneously, the leader must be conscious of employee needs, both individually and collectively. Do employees share the same goals as the agency and are the needs of both being met? If not, there is a need for interaction and dialogue to resolve differences. The presence or absence of hygiene factors and motivators should be examined *with* those who are involved. In other words, group (or individual) feelings related to need fulfillment directly influence capabilities.

Capability, therefore, relates to group or individual skill-level in performing the job itself as well as the extent to which personal and agency needs are met. These variables, which are tied closely to subordinate motivation, will be examined in relation to leadership style.

Leadership Style Alternatives

Naturally, in a broad sense, there are as many styles of leadership as there are leaders. To simplify basic leadership alternatives, however, leadership style is commonly analyzed in terms of a tendency toward task concerns or relationship concerns (Hersey and Blanchard, 1977). Basically, a person who is a task-oriented leader is primarily concerned with productivity or getting the job at hand completed. A totally task-oriented supervisor would advocate "all work and no play" while on the job and could easily be susceptible to an autocratic approach.

The relationship-oriented leader would be concerned with the personal welfare of subordinates, the quality of subordinate interpersonal relations, morale, and leader-follower relationships. The emphasis would be on human dynamics rather than the task of completing the job.

Rarely would a leader be "all tasks" or "all relationships." Most individuals have concerns for both, although in varying intensity. Our purpose is to discuss a system which allows the leader to establish a proper balance under changing conditions.

Leadership Style and Group Capabilities

The leader must constantly appraise the capabilities of the group, keeping in mind that capabilities can change. For example, a group may be extremely capable and self-reliant until a completely new program is introduced. At that point, the group may be unable to perform necessary tasks thereby dropping drastically in capability. Becoming sensitive to such shifts is the leader's first step.

As a general rule, as group capabilities increase, the need for leader intervention decreases, and vice-versa. Since groups can vary in their ability to accomplish certain jobs (a task concern), and in their cohesiveness, ability to get along, and ability to communicate (relationship concerns), the degree and type of leader intervention may vary. The following four situations and suggested leadership emphases exemplify the process.

Assume that four different groups face a problem. Given the capabilities of each group, consider the leadership actions that are suggested for each group.

1. The group is highly cohesive and has demonstrated the ability to solve problems on its own, determine appropriate actions for itself, and effectively implement its decisions.

    Leader Intervention: The leader does not need to guide the process in this instance. The group is capable of working on the problem, arriving at a solution, and implementing it. The leader can always be available if difficulties are encountered, but can show trust and confidence in the group by remaining in the background. Group members then have the opportunity for self-determination, creative expression, and reaping the benefits of *their* actions. This is highly consistent with Theory Y management and generates opportunities for motivators to exert their influence. This situation is ideal for leader and followers alike.

2. The group is highly cohesive and has demonstrated the ability to solve problems on its own and implement solutions, once direction and limits have been established.

    Leader Intervention: A task emphasis would be appropriate to give the group direction, but the leader should then withdraw, allowing the group to continue on its own. Although structure would be required initially, there is no need to continue it through the problem-solving and implementation phases. This situation is faced by leaders repeatedly, but frequently leaders tend to go beyond the step of giving the group direction, and their tendency to over-direct deprives the group of important growth.

3. The group is not cohesive nor do group members work closely together on a daily basis since individuals have separate program areas of responsibility. Group members are quite capable, however, and once given direction, are fully competent in executing the delivery of services.

Leader Intervention: Considerable direction will be necessary to help the group solve problems. The leader may need to make necessary decisions on his or her own, and structure the direction for the group. However, if the leader wishes to increase the capability of the group to solve problems, solutions should be sought collectively and *process* should be emphasized. This may require spending time sharing ideas, feelings, and experiences so that individuals begin to know one another more fully. Social interactions might also be appropriate. A spirit of unity may develop in time which allows group members to communicate more fully and effectively in the future. Thus, a high emphasis on relationship concerns would help the group develop strength in the problem solving process.

An emphasis on task-oriented concerns would be helpful initially, but once the task became defined, structure could be removed. In time, as relationships strengthened, the group would increase in its ability to handle its own decision-making as new tasks were encountered.

4. The group lacks cohesion and is not efficient at delivering services without considerable supervision and guidance.

Leader Intervention: In this case, the supervision must generally be continuous. Decisions may be made autonomously by the leader or by the group under direct leadership. This situation frequently occurs when a new group of seasonal employees is hired by an agency for their first time. It can also occur if a completely new program is implemented. However, as quickly as possible, the leader should create opportunities for the group to become more autonomous, more capable on its own. Little by little, as the group grows in cohesiveness and task effectiveness, less direct leadership (monitoring, directing, defining of tasks) is necessary.

The main thrust of these examples is basic: leaders should strive to allow groups under their supervision to become as autonomous as possible. Implicit in this ideal is that groups can increase in capability in both task and relationship areas.

In the remainder of the chapter, several lengthier case studies will be presented. In each case, the reader should attempt to determine the following:

1. The *root* of the problem, rather than symptoms.
2. The implications if the problem is not resolved.
3. Appropriate courses of action based upon properly diagnosing the group in relation to the problem. (The resolution of the problem may require sequential courses of action.)

Alternative courses of action should be explored as well as multiple causes of the problem. We recognize that case studies cannot generally present *all* elements surrounding a situation; however, they can be utilized to show what one knows. In other words, they should be used as a tool for applying as much as possible, rather than attempting to formulate a minimum "correct" response. In addition, the reader is encouraged to search related references for supporting material.

Case Studies

The Hilltop Center's Downward Slide

As the supervisor of the entire teen program in a city of more than 100,000 in population, you have had many highly exciting programs develop over your five years as supervisor. You have three full-time, year-round supervisors working for you as well as six teen-leaders and many volunteers. It has been almost a year since you have needed to replace any of your paid staff and volunteer turnover has been exceptionally low. Teenagers have been actively involved in conducting their own affairs; in fact, the staff members at each of the three teen centers have formed exceptionally close relationships with the teens at their respective centers. Both you and the lower-level supervisors in your program have relied heavily on the democratic process for problem solving and decision making and have grown to be quite friendly, able to easily discuss things of either a work-related or personal nature.

In mid-April the supervisor of the Lark teen center had the misfortune of sustaining a back injury while on a camping trip and you were informed that he would be away from the job for at least four months, but if all went well, no longer than six months. You carefully discussed the situation with the Superintendent of Parks and Recreation and concluded the following:

1. A full-time replacement was necessary since you were involved in the peak planning period leading up to the summer months.
2. You did not feel that any of the face-to-face leaders had the experience to handle the supervisory position.
3. You and the Superintendent were aware of a city employee (Carolyn Turner) with a degree in Leisure Studies and Resources who was presently working full-time with the senior citizens at the Senior

Center. Carolyn had proven to be absolutely tremendous in her ten months with the City and had worked extensively with teens in her previous position. She had been highly commended by her former administrator for her ability to work exceptionally well with any age group.

4. After speaking to the Mayor and going through the proper channels, Carolyn was transferred to the teen position with the understanding that she would return to the Senior Center within six months, at most.

You were delighted to have Carolyn with your staff and she was welcomed heartily by everyone at the first staff meeting. She was enthusiastic, personable, and eager to begin. Several planning areas were discussed and the meeting broke on a high note.

You sent out memos during the week which notified everyone of the staff meetings scheduled for the next month and indicated that there would be at least two a week due to increased planning needs. Carolyn called you just before the first of the scheduled meetings and asked if she and her staff from the Hilltop Teen Center could pass up the meeting and use the time to work on their own. You felt very uncomfortable with this but since she was so insistent, you agreed.

The next day, you received a rather detailed memo from Carolyn outlining several program concepts she and her leaders had planned for the summer. The report was very complete and included a number of excellent ideas which were quite compatible with your programming views.

The same process occurred several days later — Carolyn called before the meeting and begged off so she and her leaders could use the time among themselves. You strongly encouraged her to join you this time emphasizing that you wanted her ideas to be shared with the other Center supervisors. She was quite insistent and you again went along with her. True to form, she followed up the next day with a nicely summarized report of their planning activities. At this point you began to feel troubled — the regular meetings you called did not "feel" right with part of your staff gone. The others on your staff mildly chided you over the fact that the Hilltop staff members were turning into hermits. The same pattern continued with the following results:

1. Morale began to drop among the other two teen center staff members.
2. You realize that you were partially responsible for this because of your obvious reservations about letting Carolyn and her staff operate on their own.
3. Carolyn and her staff proved to be doing an excellent job, better than had been accomplished prior to her arrival.
4. You became convinced, however, that their success was at the expense of the total program and was breaking down the sense of unity of

your staff. In fact, you felt especially threatened because you feared that (1) Carolyn was making it apparent that she didn't really need you for her to be effective, and (2) she might even eventually work herself into the Assistant Superintendent's position about to open up due to a retirement next year.

5. The drop in morale among the staff members who were not working under Carolyn began to affect their work — absences increased, attendance dropped slowly, arguments seemed to flare up for no apparent reason, and you began to really worry about how this would be perceived by the administration.

6. This caused you to crack down on your staff, including the Hilltop employees. You increased staff meetings, required more paperwork and overall accountability.

7. You finally succeeded in alienating most of the staff from yourself, Carolyn was replaced by the now recovered "regular" supervisor, and things went rapidly downhill after she left. You could get no cooperation from anyone except the recently returned supervisor, but he had lost all feeling for his staff (they were now far more independent and less in need of his direct guidance). The administration was applying pressure to correct the situation.

8. Totally frustrated now, you feel unable to deal with the situation and, in fact, make a commitment to take another position elsewhere.

9. You think you understand how "it" all happened — it is clear to you that, very simply, Carolyn undermined everything you stood for. But two questions continued to nag at you, and you doubt that they can ever *really* be answered: first, where did you initially go wrong —or was it you at all? And, second, although things were a mess when you left, why was the Hilltop program clearly the best of the three at the time Carolyn left, and did not slide with the others until after her departure?

The Three-Month Tailspin

You have just received your master's degree in Leisure Studies and Services from a well-known school and have been hired as the Teen Program Supervisor in a city of 125,000 people. You are one of four supervisors in the city and have seven recreation leaders and seven assistant recreation leaders under your supervision. In addition, approximately 20 volunteers are also involved in teen activities under the direction of the various assistant recreation leaders. The recreation leaders under your supervision in the teen program are civil service employees.

After arriving, you find that the former teen supervisor had been gone for more than two months prior to your arrival but the position was temporarily occupied by the Senior Recreation Leader, Rob Kelly. Rob is a very capable and dependable employee who has been with the department for eight years and is about to complete his B.A. in Leisure Studies and Services after six years of taking college courses on a part-time basis.

Upon your arrival, Rob Kelly was transferred to his former position as head Recreation Director of the city's main teen center. Rob and his staff had done an outstanding job in the center for more than two years, working effectively as a highly cohesive group.

Rob now deeply resents being placed under your leadership for three reasons. First, he feels that he did an excellent job as acting supervisor and he thus "proved himself." Second, he has had eight years of experience in the department and feels that he deserves more consideration based upon his knowledge of the community and his longevity on the job. Third, he feels he has overcome his educational liability since he is about to graduate from college after much hard work while supporting his wife and two children. Although he would not admit it, Rob also resents being placed under the leadership of a younger person, who is still "wet behind the ears."

After three months on the job, you find that teen participation at the center is falling, volunteers are dropping out of the program, and your leaders' morale is distressingly low. Several of your better leaders have feelers out for new jobs.

You feel that you have tried everything. You attempted to socialize with Rob by having a few beers after work on two occasions. It never seemed to get off the ground. In your weekly staff meetings, which included all leaders, you worked hard to develop a feeling of unity and common cause, but to no avail. In fact, the more you encouraged your leaders, the less they responded. Although you have always felt strongly that positive human relations is the key to effective supervision, twice you decided to tighten things up by carefully delineating everyone's duties and your expectations. Again there was no improvement.

You are extremely discouraged at this point. A once-effectively run teen center is on the verge of total collapse, and you feel that it is your fault as the supervisor. Apparently this view is shared by the director of the department. He has advised you that if the situation is not corrected, you will need to look for employment elsewhere.

A Classic Case of Mediocrity

You have been the Park and Playground Program Supervisor in the Leisureville Parks and Recreation Department for the past year and feel that for the most part, things have gone fairly well. The job has been demanding, however, and you have had to spend considerable time training and guiding your three full-time and twelve part-time staff members. This has frustrated you often especially since you feel they *should* be able to do a better job. All of your staff members either have a degree in Leisure Studies and Resources or are working toward it.

Initially you tried to let them have their own freedom to operate but it just didn't work out. For example, when you first arrived you had heard that the supervisor you replaced had been very rigid and autocratic in the way he treated the staff. He called staff meetings often, required detailed activity reports constantly, and spent considerable time watching leaders carry out their programs. In terms of participant response, the programs were successful and high in demand but you felt that this was not an approach which you could follow. Therefore, you decided to let the leaders know at a staff meeting that they could carry out their programs on their own and that if needed, you would certainly help.

After almost a month of trying the "new approach," you realized that things were a mess. Leaders were beginning to be late for work more frequently and you found that on-site programs had been cut back. Rather than organize and lead carefully planned programs as they had done in the past, leaders were merely passing out equipment for participants to pursue their own free-play interests. In two cases, leaders had their "steadies" come to the park site and entire periods were spent visiting with each other.

You learned of the problem when the Superintendent called you in to find out what was going on. You explained your intent and *he* "explained" to *you* that you had better get things straightened out in a hurry. He was displeased, to say the least!

You called another staff meeting, went over the immediate problem with your leaders, and it seemed that you all came to an agreeable understanding. They assured you that the programs would be initiated again and you again emphasized that they were on their own.

Several weeks later, more problems emerged. Boy and girl friends of staff members were still visiting them during work hours and programs were only partially restored and with little enthusiasm or interest.

You decided that things had gone far enough and so you called a staff meeting and laid it on the line and let people know in no uncertain terms that there would be replacements for anyone not able to do the job. You followed your meeting by frequently visiting program sites and by requiring written weekly reports. In a short time, things were "back to normal" and no one had to be fired.

Much as you disliked admitting it, you came to believe that this was a staff that *had* to be closely guided and directed. You hated putting in the necessary time required for closely supervising programs, but at least participation stayed relatively high and the superintendent was happy. You weren't really happy, however, about the fact that leaders rarely suggested new programs and ideas; any changes had to be initiated by you. It also seemed a shame that morale was not especially high—people did their jobs satisfactorily, but just well enough to keep you off their backs. Even though things could be "different," you don't know what else you could have done and at least the programs were "good enough."

Summary

Effective supervision can be best attained if those in a position of influence are able to motivate, direct, and stimulate employees through personal power rather than position power. This can be furthered by developing a solid understanding of human nature and human relations. Basic assumptions about human motivation become critical and research has shown that leaders adopting a Theory Y profile, coupled with the ability to differentiate between motivators and hygiene factors, are often the most successful *and* effective as supervisors.

In addition, the effective leader does not adopt only one leadership style; rather, he or she is able to diagnose the situation in relation to the capabilities of followers, and flexibly adapt his or her style to that situation. Ideally, the leader will strive to increase the capabilities of followers to a point where they can be self-sufficient.

The role of the supervisor extends beyond managing people. Supervisors are frequently involved in recruiting new employees, interviewing them, providing them with pre-service and in-service training, and are required to evaluate them as well. They are also involved in extensive planning which requires that they understand how to structure planning efforts through a mechanism such as Management By Objectives (MBO).

The supervisor, then, must possess a tremendous range of skills to serve as an effective bridge between administrators and face-to-face leaders. In this capacity, he or she has the opportunity to analyze agency effectiveness from a unique perspective and can often be the catalyst which allows the leisure service delivery system to function to the fullest.

Study Questions

1. Does a leader require any more than position power to be effective? Successful?
2. Discuss the basic responsibilities of the leisure service supervisor; toward what or whom are these responsibilities generally directed?
3. What benefits may be enjoyed by an agency which executes a well-planned recruitment program when searching for one or more new employees?
4. What elements should be included in the written description of a job announcement?

5. What procedures should interviewers adopt when conducting the job interview?
6. What are the key differences between pre-service and in-service training programs and what are the potential benefits of each?
7. Draft a sample employee evaluation form. How can the evaluation process be a constructive rather than threatening experience for subordinates?
8. What is meant by Management By Objectives (MBO)? Is MBO a system generally relevant to business and industry rather than leisure service agencies?
9. How does successful leadership differ from effective leadership? Is successful leadership ever justified or preferred?
10. What was the significance of the Hawthorne study?
11. As a result of new information relating to staff-subordinate relations, employee motivation theories, and knowledge about organizational development, most managers clearly implement theory Y principles in their supervisory and administrative roles. *Is there support for this statement?*
12. Motivators, as defined by Herzberg, are the only elements critical to employee morale. *Is there support for this statement?*
13. *Leadership style* encompasses the leader's behavior, attitudes, and hopes centering around meeting agency objectives. *Is there support for this statement?*
14. There may be situations which require the leader to initiate considerable structure for subordinates, regardless of the basic capabilities of subordinates. *Is there support for this statement?*
15. What would constitute the ideal leader in the context of this chapter? Is the ideal attainable?

References

Bannon, Joseph J. *Problem Solving in Recreation and Parks.* Englewood Cliffs, N.J.: Prentice-Hall, Inc., 1972.

Bass, Bernard M. *Leadership, Psychology, and Organizational Behavior.* New York: Harper & Row, Publishers, 1960.

Dade County Department of Park and Recreation. Job Information flyer. Miami, Fla., undated.

Deegan, Arthur X., and Fritz, Roger J. *MBO Goes to College: Management By Objectives.* Boulder, Colo.: University of Colorado Division of Continuing Education, 1975.

Etzioni, Amitai. *A Comparative Analysis of Complex Organizations on Power, Involvement and Their Correlates.* New York: The Free Press, 1961.

Fiedler, Fred E. *A Theory of Leadership Effectiveness.* New York: McGraw-Hill Book Company, 1967.

Fiedler, Fred E. *Engineering the Job to Fit the Manager. Harvard Business Review* 51 (1965): 115-22.

Gray, David E. "Tyranny of the Chain Link Fence." In *Reflections on the Recreation and Park Movement by* David E. Gray and Donald Pelegrino. Dubuque, Ia.: Wm. C. Brown Company Publishers, 1968.

Hersey, Paul and Blanchard, Kenneth H. *Management of Organizational Behavior: Utilizing Human Resources.* Englewood Cliffs, N.J.: Prentice-Hall, Inc., 1977.

Herzberg, Frederick. "One More Time: How Do You Motivate Employees?" *Harvard Business Review* 46 (1968): 53-62.

Herzberg, Frederick. *Work and the Nature of Man.* New York: World Publishing Co., 1966.

Klar, Lawrence R., Jr. "Leisure Activity Selection for Girls and Boys." Amherst, Mass.: Leisure Studies & Resources Program, University of Massachusetts. Mimeographed survey, 1978.

Kraus, Richard G., and Bates, Barbara J. *Recreation Leadership and Supervision: Guidelines for Professional Development.* Philadelphia: W. B. Saunders Company, 1975.

Lasagna, John B. "Make Your MBO Pragmatic." *Harvard Business Review* 49 (1971): 64-69.

Levinson, Harry "Management by Whose Objectives?" *Harvard Business Review* 48 (1970): 125-134.

Maslow, Abraham H. *Toward A Psychology of Being.* New York: D. Van Nostrand Company, 1968.

Mayo, Elton. *The Human Problems of an Industrial Civilization.* New York: The Macmillan Company, 1933.

McGregor, Douglas. *The Human Side of Enterprise.* New York: McGraw-Hill Book Company, 1966.

McGregor, Douglas. "Conditions of Effective Leadership in Industrial Organization." *Journal of Consulting Psychologists* 8 (1960): 56-63.

Morrissey, George. *Management by Objectives and Results.* Reading, Mass.: Addison-Wesley Publishing Co., 1970.

Odiorne, George S. *Management Decisions by Objectives.* Englewood Cliffs, Prentice-Hall, Inc., 1969.

Odiorne, George S. *Management by Objectives.* New York: Pitman Publishing Corp., 1965.

Sterle, David E., and Duncan, Mary R. *Supervision of Leisure Services.* San Diego: San Diego State University Press, 1973.

Varney, Glenn H. *Management by Objectives.* Chicago: Dartnell Corp., 1971.

Related Readings

Argyris, Chris. *Increasing Leadership Effectiveness.* New York: John Wiley & Sons, Inc., 1976.

Argyris, Chris. *Management and Organizational Development: The Path from XA to YB.* New York: McGraw-Hill Book Co., 1971.

Argyris, Chris. "Interpersonal Barriers to Decision Making." *Harvard Business Review* 44:2 (1966): 84-97.

Argyris, Chris. "Creating Effective Relationships in Organizations." *Human Organizations* 17 (1958) 34-40.

Burke, W. Warner. *Current Issues and Strategies in Organizational Development.* New York: Behavioral Publications, Inc., 1977.

Cartwright, Dorwin and Zander, Alvin. *Group Dynamics: Research and Theory.* New York: Harper and Row, 1968.

Drucker, Peter F. *The Effective Executive.* New York: Harper and Row, 1967.

Fiedler, Fred E., and Chemers, Martin M., with Mahar, Linda. *Improving Leadership Effectiveness: The Leader Match Concept.* New York: John Wiley & Sons, Inc., 1976.

Fernandez, John P. *Black Managers in White Corporations.* New York: John Wiley & Sons, Inc., 1975.

Francis, Dave and Woodcock, Mike. *People at Work: A Practical Guide to Organizational Change.* San Diego: University Associates, Inc., 1975.

Guilford, Joan S., and Gray, David E. *Motivation and Modern Management.* Reading, Mass.: Addison-Wesley Publishing Co., 1969.

Hare, A. Paul. *Handbook of Small Group Research.* New York: Free Press, 1969.

Jones, John E., and Pfieffer, J. William (eds.) *The 1977 Annual Handbook for Group Facilitators.* San Diego: University Associates, Inc., 1977.

Kirschenbaum, Howard. *Value Clarification: An Advanced Handbook for Teachers and Trainers.* San Diego: University Associates, Inc., 1977.

Kemp, Gratton C. *Perspectives on the Group Process.* Boston: Houghton Mifflin Co., 1964.

Ladany, Shaul P. *Management Science Applications to Leisure-Time Operations.* Amsterdam and New York: North-Holland Publishing Co., 1975.

Likert, Rensis and Likert, Jane Gibson. *New Ways of Managing Conflict.* New York: McGraw-Hill Book Co., 1976.

Mali, Paul. *Managing by Objectives.* New York: John Wiley & Sons, Inc., 1972.

Mansell, Richard. "Management by Objectives: Emphasis on Systematic Planning." *Management Strategy* 1:1 (1977): 1-2, 4.

Newport, Gene M. *Supervisory Management: Tools and Techniques.* St. Paul, Minn.: West Publishing Co., 1976.

O'Connell, Brian. *Effective Leadership in Voluntary Organizations: How to Make the Greatest Use of Citizen Service and Influence.* New York: Association Press, 1976.

Patten, Thomas H. *Manpower Planning and the Development of Human Resources.* New York: John Wiley & Sons, Inc., 1971.

Rickards, Tudor. *Problem-Solving Through Creative Analysis.* New York: John Wiley & Sons, Inc., 1974.

Sargent, Alice G. *Beyond Sex Roles.* St. Paul, Minnesota: West Publishing Co., 1977.

Shaw, Marvin E. *Group Dynamics: The Psychology of Small Group Behavior.* New York: McGraw-Hill Book Co., 1971.

Swingle, Paul G. *The Management of Power.* New York: John Wiley & Sons, Inc., 1976.

Weiss, H. W. "How to Understand Managerial Decision-Making." *Management Strategy* 1:2 (1977): 1-2.

Strengthening Programs through Volunteers

Objectives   After reading and comprehending this chapter, you should be able to:

1. Describe the functions of volunteers and the roles they assume within the leisure service program.
2. Explain the values and limitations associated with the use of volunteer personnel.
3. Understand the need for treating volunteers differently from professional personnel.
4. Describe some of the problems encountered by an interviewer.
5. Discuss a variety of organizational management theories and their application to the administration of volunteer personnel programs.
6. Explain the importance of providing volunteer personnel with recognition for their efforts.
7. Identify the values and liabilities associated with the process of volunteer evaluation.

Introduction

Historically, volunteer personnel have played a significantly important role in the development of community leisure service programs. The fact that, "most present-day departments were started through the efforts of volunteers" (Lutzin and Storey, 1973, p. 245), and that, "volunteers traditionally have been an important part of organized recreation and park programs" (Kraus and Bates, 1975, p. 333), make it imperative for leisure service administrators to be knowledgeable regarding who volunteers are, the roles they play, the value of their services, and the processes employed to recruit, select, train, supervise, evaluate, and recognize this special group of leisure service personnel.

Who Are Volunteers

Under most circumstances, volunteers may be described as those individuals who donate their time, knowledge, and abilities without expectation of salary or other financial consideration. Existing among each segment of society, volunteers represent all walks of life. They may be:

1. Parents
2. Program participants
3. Educators
4. Hobby enthusiasts
5. Former recreators
6. Retired persons
7. Activity specialists
8. College/university student interns
9. Professionals from the fields of theatre, music, art, dance, communications, business administration, government, and so forth
10. Representatives of professional, social or service organizations such as military groups, fraternal organizations, P.T.A.'s, Grange, University Women's Club, Sierra Club, and so forth

Almost every person residing in a community possesses skills, knowledge, and interests which can be of benefit to the leisure service program. There is no limitation as to the source of volunteer personnel nor the types and backgrounds of individuals who can make positive contributions to the program.

Volunteer Motivation

Motivation to contribute one's services to a leisure service agency may stem from a variety of reasons. Parents often become actively involved in those activities and programs which are of direct benefit to their children such as Boy or Girl Scouts and organized youth sports leagues. In addition to academic credits, student interns gain valuable professional experience through their association with a community leisure service program. Elder citizens often believe it their civic responsibility to donate their services. Some persons perceive their contribution as a means of "getting a foot in the door" with respect to future salaried employment, while others become involved to gain personal recognition, publicity, and prestige within the community. For many individuals, ". . . the chance to be of voluntary help is in itself a form of recreation" (Meyer and Brightbill, 1964, p. 410).

Volunteer Roles

Volunteers serve community leisure service programs in a myriad of areas. However, volunteer roles may generally be categorized in three major classifications:

1. Administrative and consulting volunteers
2. Skill and activity program volunteers
3. Operational services volunteers

Although similar to those offered by Rodney (1964), the above classifications are more precise in categorizing the nature of the volunteer roles contained therein.

Administrative and Consulting Volunteers

These volunteers usually perform in roles associated with the direct administration of leisure service programs. Some examples of the roles contained within this classification are:

1. Members of the Board of Directors
2. Committee appointees
3. Fund raisers
4. Facility planners
5. Consultants

Skill and Activity Program Volunteers

They are primarily involved only with those facets of the leisure service program which are directly related to their specific area of interest or expertise. This classification includes roles such as:

1. Club leaders
2. Skill or activity program instructors
3. Camp counselors
4. Special event assistants
5. Senior center coordinators

Operational Services Volunteers

These individuals are affiliated with the "nuts and bolts" tasks required for the smooth and efficient operation of a community leisure service program. Contained within this classification are volunteer roles such as:

1. Secretarial
2. Clerical
3. Maintenance
4. Publicity and public relations
5. Financial
6. Legal

Obviously, many more roles could be classified under each category. It is the responsibility of the leisure service director to characterize and categorize each volunteer role as it relates to his or her community program. For example, Bannon (1976) suggests that volunteers represent an excellent source for help in conducting a questionnaire survey. Under which category should these volunteers be classified? Either *administrative* or *operational services* could be appropriate. If the volunteer in question contributed to the design of the study, then he or she would be performing an administrative function. On the other hand, if the individual's role were strictly one of distributing or collecting the survey instrument, then he or she would be performing an operational services function.

When defining volunteer roles in leisure services, it is very important that program directors, when possible, not substitute volunteers for professional personnel. In most situations, the role of the volunteer is one of supplementing and complementing professional employees, rather than one of replacing such individuals. However, it must be recognized that it is not always possible to achieve the "ideal" distribution of volunteer and professional staff. Consequently, it is not uncommon to find volunteer personnel functioning in roles normally thought to be the domain of professional personnel.

Community leisure service administrators must be pragmatists. Decisions related to the assignment of roles to volunteers must be based upon the "real" environment in which the program exists. And given the fact that it is not always possible to employ the number of professionals desired, administrators recognize the value of having volunteers available to fill these roles.

Value of Volunteers

Several values can be derived from the use of volunteer personnel. In many communities, if not most, governmental bodies are being pressured to expand services rendered to the community while maintaining a "no growth" expenditure rate. In response to these pressures, governmental bodies have in turn placed demands upon agencies to increase their service levels while at the same time allocating static or even reduced budgets. To comply with these demands for expanded services (the costs of which tend to exceed the amount of available financial resources), agency directors have become more dependent upon the services of volunteers. "The need for volunteers is greater now than ever before and the work ahead indicates even greater demands" (Sessoms, et al., 1975, p. 147). Without the assistance of volunteer personnel many current community leisure service programs would be sharply reduced in scope or worse, completely eliminated.

Volunteer personnel are frequently sought to provide skills and knowledge not possessed by full-time personnel. For example, an architect residing in the community might be recruited to help with the planning of a new facility or an antique automobile buff might be enticed to organize and administer an antique auto show. Through the judicious use of such individuals, leisure service administrators may increase the effectiveness of their programs in providing for the needs of the entire community.

Volunteers tend to be highly enthusiastic since their motivation to be involved is voluntary. Their enthusiasm can create an atmosphere which helps to promote both interest and participation in their particular activity or program. And volunteers, while providing leisure service opportunities for others, are often fulfilling a personal need to make a positive contribution to the community through the sharing of their skills, knowledge, and abilities.

Another potential value to be gained from the use of volunteers is related to tasks normally assigned to professional personnel. With volunteers being assigned many of the routine, mundane tasks so necessary for the smooth and efficient operation of a program, professional personnel can be relieved from these chores and assigned to more important administrative and supervisory responsibilities. However, some argue that, in reality, the necessity to train and supervise volunteers actually increases the obligations placed upon professional personnel and therefore decreases their ability to perform their "normal" duties.

The fact of the matter is that it is quite possible for such an outcome to occur. But in a well-designed and administered volunteer program such an outcome will only be of short duration. Once volunteers are trained and have become familiar with their assigned duties, they will usually be able to perform their tasks without requiring a significant amount of professional staff time. Consequently, in the long run, the use of volunteers will enable professional personnel to gain some "free" time which can be devoted to the pursuit of other duties. And, in addition, the community in general becomes a beneficiary of the utilization of volunteer personnel because of the expanded recreational opportunities provided by the leisure service program.

Limitations of Volunteers

The use of leisure service volunteers also has its disadvantages. Because of their inexperience in dealing with the various aspects of the total leisure service program, volunteers can potentially contribute to a reduction in the program's overall performance efficiency (this is especially true with respect to first-time volunteers).

Another limitation concerns the commitment volunteers are able to make to the program. In many instances, volunteers are often able to devote only a limited amount of time to fulfilling the demands of assigned roles because of full-time employment, family responsibilities, or other personal commitments. Quite frequently, volunteers tend to perceive their community work as secondary to their other pursuits.

Furthermore, although volunteers tend to enter a program or activity with a great deal of interest and enthusiasm, for some it may quickly subside. Employment, family, or other personal pressures and demands may result in a reduction of their willingness and ability to contribute the time and energy necessary to properly fulfill an assignment. When this situation occurs, the end result is frequently either resignation or a reduction in the quality of the volunteer's performance. In either case, the participants suffer and the reputation of the leisure service program becomes tarnished.

Administrators must hold leisure service volunteers accountable for their performance in different ways than would be used with salaried employees. For example, when a professional staff member is absent without notice or is continually late for assignments, humanistically oriented administrators must treat the individual with respect and as a mature person as suggested by both McGregor (1960) and Argyris (1957); nonetheless, direct action must be pursued to remedy the problem. Yet, in the case of a volunteer guilty of the same violation, the administrator is often required to exercise greater tact and demonstrate more sensitivity than that normally afforded the professional employee. This course of action is necessary for a very pragmatic reason; failure to do so may prompt the volunteer to tender his or her resignation. When a situation of this nature occurs, it is often manifest by an increase in the workload and responsibilities which must be borne by the remaining volunteer and professional staff members.

Another problem relates to the termination or reassignment of volunteers. Once functioning in a role, volunteers are often difficult to remove or transfer, even if their performance fails to meet minimum established standards. For example, how does an administrator effectively deal with the problem of a repeatedly tardy and frequently absent volunteer ceramics program director when no other volunteer qualified in this particular area is available? Such a set of circumstances is referred to as a "lose-lose" situation: no matter what course of action the administrator elects to pursue, it will be considered by many as wrong and will not effectively resolve the problem.

A final limitation centers on the fact that some individuals who volunteer their services have ulterior motives. It is not uncommon, for example, for an individual to consider affiliation with a community leisure service program as a means of gaining political prestige and visibility, power, social status within the community, or an initial step toward securing future salaried employment within the agency. In and of themselves, these motives may not prove detrimental to the agency. But, too often volunteers once having achieved their ulterior motive (or having failed to do so) terminate their relationship with the leisure service program. Such action can lead to a disruption of the normal program operations and the implementation of corrective measures may result in undue pressure being placed upon administrators and program personnel.

Volunteer Program Assets vs. Limitations

Following a thorough analysis of volunteer program assets and limitations, many leisure service administrators have concluded that the potential values which can be derived from such a program far outweigh its limitations and have included volunteer personnel in their programs. On the other hand, numerous administrators have arrived at just the opposite assessment. Consequently, the use of volunteers has been prohibited in their community programs.

We believe that the exclusion of volunteers represents a loss of valuable leisure service resources. Often, the "real" reason behind the prohibition of volunteers can be traced to the program director's fear of being unable to successfully cope with the demands commonly associated with such programs. If this be the case, it is suggested that such administrators seek assistance in at least producing a limited but well-designed experimental volunteer program. Given the benefit of sound administrative leadership and knowledgeable application of organizational development techniques, it is quite possible that the results of such an experimental venture will be sufficient to allay the administrator's fear of such programs.

Recruitment of Volunteers

Effective volunteer recruitment is essential for the successful operation of many community recreation programs. However, before the actual recruitment process can begin, the types and numbers of volunteers required to operate the program must first be determined. The resulting number should be considered as simply a minimum volunteer force as no capable volunteer should be denied the opportunity to render his or her services. After the number and types of volunteers have been identified, the next step is the development of minimum qualification standards for each of the volunteer roles to be filled.

Qualification Standards

These will vary according to the particular role being considered. For example, all persons accepted as volunteers in a leisure service program should be of acceptable character as determined by community standards. However, an individual selected for and assigned to head up the outdoor education program must possess knowledges specific to that particular program while an individual assigned the role of supervising a "teen" dance need not be capable of performing the latest dance steps. It is the responsibility of the program administrator to establish the minimum standards required and qualifications for each specific role.

Recruiting

This can actually commence once the initial two steps have been completed. In the recruiting process, it is not uncommon for the nature of the role to be filled to dictate the manner in which the process is conducted. To illustrate the point, if the board of directors requires the services of a person possessing a solid background in finance, then the search for an appointee would logically focus on individuals associated with the business and banking communities. On the other hand, if a volunteer were needed to direct a phase of the nature program, the search might be directed toward individuals belonging to clubs which sponsor nature programs.

Use of the Media

The mark of an effective administrator is often displayed through his or her skilful use of the media in recruiting volunteer personnel. Published articles, radio announcements, participation in talk shows, and televised broadcasts of feature stories, when properly handled, can be valuable vehicles for the dissemination of a variety of messages, particularly those prepared and designed to stimulate the interest of potential volunteers in the community leisure service program. When any phase of the media is used as a recruiting vehicle, it is very important that the valuable and significant role played by volunteer personnel be stressed. Current volunteer needs should be noted in each recruitment communication. In addition, the name and address of the person or agency to be contacted by volunteer candidates should be included in the text of each message.

The wise leisure service administrator will actively seek opportunities to develop a good working relationship with representatives of the media. Through such interaction, it is possible to "educate" media personnel regarding the goals and objectives of the program. Moreover, the potential for receiving the publicity necessary to insure a successful turnout of volunteers is enhanced.

Finally, a well-designed volunteer recruitment program can also serve as a public relations vehicle. Built into each recruitment message should be a reference to the benefits provided to the community.

Community Surveys

Leisure service administrators should consider each member of the community as a potential volunteer. Each citizen possesses knowledge, skills, and interests which may be of benefit to the community program. Identification of each individual's areas of potential contribution may be ascertained through a community survey. Meyer and Brightbill (1956) suggest that to acquire help in conducting a community-wide survey, the leisure service administrator should enlist the support of one or more community organizations.

Questionnaires are the most common instrument used to gather data pertaining to citizen's leisure interests, knowledge, and skills. When developing a questionnaire, caution should be exercised to keep it as brief as possible without sacrificing necessary data. For a survey of this nature, information such as the respondent's name, address, telephone number, age, particular interests, skills, and knowledge would be deemed as necessary and vital. However, data relative to the educational background and sources of personal references would not be considered as being necessary. Such information can be gathered once the individual has actually been contacted with specific reference to volunteering his or her services.

Community-wide questionnaire surveys can be conducted using one of three methods. First, the instrument can be mailed to each known person in the community requesting that he or she complete the questionnaire and return it either by mail or in person. Second, interviewers can use the telephone to contact all listed subscribers in the community. Using this method, the caller asks the individual each of the questions and then records the responses. Finally, the third method consists of actually interviewing each person at their home, place of business or at one of the agency's facilities.

No matter which method is elected to conduct the survey, a substantial amount of time must be allocated in terms of personnel. It is for this reason that the assistance of community organizations is suggested. Through use of their membership, the personnel time normally devoted to usual program requirements would not have to be curtailed.

Particular attention should be paid to the type and number of people included in the survey. Ideally, each member of the community should be involved in the study. However, this goal is not always possible to attain. Insufficient funds, lack of time and personnel, respondent's failure to cooperate, or citizens possessing unlisted telephone numbers or no telephone at all represent some of the problems which make it all but impossible to realistically include each and every citizen in the study. Nonetheless, program directors should exercise extreme care to insure that no one demographic segment of the population is inadvertently excluded from the study.

Community Organizations

When large numbers of volunteers are required to sponsor and/or supervise a particular event such as a field day or a bike-a-thon, leisure service administrators often solicit support from social or service organizations within the community. It is not uncommon, for example, for a V.F.W. post, teachers' association, or community service organization to co-sponsor a special event with a leisure service agency and through their membership provide the personnel required to conduct the event.

Personal Contact

In the final analysis, the most successful volunteer recruiters are those administrators who solicit on a personal basis. Leisure service directors should make a special effort to address community groups on a regular basis. Woven into each address should be a message about the important role played by volunteer personnel in the operation of the program. Once interest has been stimulated, it becomes significantly easier to attract prospective volunteers. Astute recruiters will contact potential volunteers by means of a personal letter or telephone call—or better yet, in person. The personalized approach increases the potential volunteer's sense of importance and value to the program which may increase the probability of his or her accepting an invitation to serve in a volunteer capacity.

The Volunteer Resource File

Once the study has been completed, the collected data should be used to develop a *volunteer resource file.* The data collected from each survey participant should be recorded on index cards (or stored in a computer data bank). The completed index cards are then filed alphabetically for future reference. However, a more advanced and efficient system is one in which the data are cross-indexed. To install such a system, an index card (in addition to the original) must be created for each interest area or expertise indicated by the respondent. The additional cards are then filed under specific program or activity categories. The cross-indexing system allows individuals to be identified either by name or area of skill.

Once the initial volunteer resource file has been created, additional information such as new names or the addition or deletion of areas of expertise for a particular individual can continually be included. To maintain the file's accuracy and efficiency, the data should be periodically updated.

Selecting Volunteers

Volunteers may be selected by the following:

1. Volunteer program coordinator
2. Leisure service program director
3. Professional activity director
4. Other volunteers
5. A committee

However, no matter who is assigned the responsibility for the selection process, final selection should not commence until all candidates have been screened and their willingness to accept a volunteer role verified.

Following an initial screening of the applications, each individual should be categorized according to ability, skill, etc. *All* persons willing to volunteer their services can usually be used in some capacity within the program. Under normal circumstances, no person seeking to render service should be turned down. Some role, no matter how temporary or minor, should either be found or created to accommodate each volunteer. Candidate selection and assignment can be facilitated by having each applicant complete an inventory form prior to the interview. Included in the inventory should be data relating to personal history, previous volunteer service, recreation experiences, personal references, educational background, leisure interests, areas of expertise, occupational background, and an indication of the days and time available for assignment. Based upon these data, a decision should be made regarding the area or program role in which the candidate could best serve the agency. In formulating this decision strong consideration must be given to providing a role which will best serve the personal needs or desires of the candidate.

Prior to conducting a candidate interview, each interviewer should review the responsibilities associated with the position for which the candidate is being considered. Failure to conduct such a review often results in a poor interview and enhances the potential for erroneous candidate assessments.

No matter how outstanding a candidate may appear, if his or her talents or interests are not compatible with the qualification requirements for a particular position, then he or she should be used in a different capacity. And it should be clearly understood that, when possible, all successful candidates for leadership roles possess at least the minimum established qualifications. For example, all aquatic leaders should, at the minimum, possess a senior life saving certificate. A water safety instructor's certificate would be preferable.

Halo Effect

During the course of the interview, interviewers must be alert not to allow the "halo" effect to influence their assessment of the candidate. The "halo" effect is a phenomenon whereby impressions gained early in the interview play a dominant role in the final assessment of the candidate[1] This phenomenon may be caused by a variety of things. For example, an interviewer may be impressed by a candidate's firm handshake, attire, response to the initial question, or failure to physically meet a particular stereotype associated with the position for which he or she is being considered. Such early impressions may produce either a positive or negative effect upon the interviewer. When the "halo" effect occurs,

1. For a more complete discussion of the "halo" effect, the reader is directed to a paper by Graham (1976) titled "Affirmative Action: Its Effects Upon Intramural-Recreational Sport Department Employment Policies."

the interviewer tends to formulate his or her final assessment of the candidate at that point in the interview and information revealed throughout the remainder of the interview tends to be disregarded.

General Characteristics of Volunteers

Sessoms, et al. (1975), among others, suggest that there are some characteristics, which all leisure service volunteers (as well as professional personnel) should have in common. Among these are:

1. Conscientiousness and ability to attend to details
2. Tact
3. Good moral character and reputation within the community
4. Psychological stability
5. A fertile imagination

Additional characteristics are usually associated with each of the three major volunteer personnel classifications. Some of those, which are not necessarily mutually exclusive, are as follows:

Administrative and Consulting Volunteers

1. A liberal, well-rounded educational background
2. Demonstrated maturity of judgment and ability to comprehend and cope with contemporary social issues
3. Respectability and stature within the community
4. A strong interest in the administrative aspects of community leisure service programs
5. Ability to devote both the time and energy required for the successful completion of all role assignments

Skill and Activity Volunteers

1. Possession of skills and/or knowledge of the assigned activity or program
2. Ability to successfully interact with a wide-range of individuals and groups
3. Ability to perform, teach, and supervise the activity assigned
4. Ability to develop and conduct a program designed to accommodate the varying skill and need levels of the total community (with certain exceptions)
5. Dependability

Operational Service Volunteers

1. Willingness to learn a variety of tasks and to attend to details
2. Ability to successfully complete assigned tasks

3. Dependability
4. Ability to successfully interact with others in a cooperative effort

At some point in the discussion, interviewers should inform the candidate regarding the *level of performance* expected from persons assigned to the particular volunteer role for which he or she is being considered. Knowledge of this information enables the candidate, if successful, to make a mature, fully-informed judgment whether to accept or reject the volunteer appointment. For example, a potential book club discussion leader, after learning that he or she would be expected to be able to direct the discussion of two current books a month, may decide that the assignment would be too taxing. Consequently, the individual may reject an appointment as a leader but might be willing to accept an assistant leader's position which is less demanding.

Training the Volunteer

If volunteer personnel are to contribute to the efficient and competent operation of the community leisure service program, then an effective training program is essential. Volunteer training programs should parallel those provided for professional employees and should consist of three distinct segments:

1. Pre-service training (orientation)
2. In-service training
3. Periodic refresher training opportunities

Pre-service Training

Included should be a thorough orientation to the general policies and regulations governing the leisure service agency. In addition, volunteers should be introduced to those policies and regulations specifically related to their assigned program or activity role. All personnel — volunteer as well as professional — must be willing to accept and abide by established policies and administrative practices, if the program is to operate smoothly. Many volunteers, especially those accepting an assignment for the first time, can benefit greatly in the understanding and implementation of policies and regulations gained through observation of professionals or other volunteers in action. For example, a game room supervisor can learn a great deal in a short span of time if allowed to observe experienced personnel function on the job. And by having things explained while on site, the reason for certain policies become more meaningful in terms of their purpose and application.

Early in the pre-service training period, professional and volunteer personnel should be introduced to one another. Steps should be taken to insure that this initial meeting becomes a mutually rewarding experience. Often a social function, such as a luncheon, can provide an ideal opportunity to initiate the integration process. No attempt should be made at such affairs to distinguish volunteers from professional personnel. Rather, an overt attempt should be made to treat each individual as an equal. One way of initiating this concept is to provide the same kind of name tag for all participants. By placing volunteers and professionals on an equal basis, the fear of the superior-subordinate complex held by some people can be at least temporarily stemmed. During the course of his or her welcoming remarks, the program administrator should include comments regarding the importance of the volunteer to the success of the community leisure service program in addition to mentioning the vital role that the professional staff plays in assisting the volunteer achieve his or her performance objective. By "stroking" each group, the administrator is enhancing the probability of the event becoming a mutually satisfying experience. And, as suggested by Hersey and Blanchard (1977), the use of appropriate personnel management techniques is essential if administrators are to successfully foster cooperative relationships among personnel.

In-service Training Programs

These consist of a variety of undertakings. The primary purpose of such programs is to provide the volunteer with training in those areas identified as being potentially beneficial to both the individual and the leisure service program. All personnel — volunteer as well as professional — require periodic updating regarding developments occurring within or related to the leisure service field. In-service training program offerings may include:

1. A demonstration of the newest innovative techniques used to teach special populations
2. Introduction to new methods of accounting and bookkeeping
3. Instructional seminar on the operation and/or maintenance of office equipment
4. Certification programs in areas such as aquatics
5. Leadership training
6. Development of evaluation and supervisory skills

In recent years, in-service training programs have placed a great deal of emphasis on the development of human relation skills and the acquisition of knowledge related to program evaluation and accountability techniques. In a humanistically oriented leisure service program, it is deemed important for all personnel to be skilled in dealing with people and perceiving their particular needs. It is only through such understanding interaction that the potential of participants to enjoy a positive "recreation experience" will be enhanced.

There are numerous methods for conducting in-service training programs. However, clinics, classes, field trips, seminars, and workshops are the most frequently used.

Refresher Training Opportunities

These opportunities tend to consist of such things as provision of recommended reading lists related to "professional" development, arranging for release time to attend training sessions conducted by other agencies, and the dissemination of information pertaining to available resource materials. Refresher training opportunities are often pursued on the basis of individual initiative. However, it is not uncommon for group involvement to be promoted. For example, if a manufacturer is sponsoring a clinic on the use of office machines or audio-visual equipment at some location in the community, it would be quite appropriate for the leisure service director to make arrangements for a group of volunteers to attend the session. The knowledge gained from participation in the training program would prove beneficial to both the volunteer and the community program itself.

Each of the three facets of the training program is equally important to the success (or failure) of volunteer personnel in achieving their performance goals. However, because volunteers are just that — volunteers, it is extremely important that the training program be designed in such a manner that the volunteer is attracted to it and firmly believes that he or she is gaining from the experience. If the volunteer does not experience a sense of satisfaction by having participated, a drop in attendance may be encountered which could seriously diminish the value of the program.

Supervision of Volunteers

A well-organized program of supervision can be a valuable asset. Through proper supervision, volunteers can be assisted in maintaining and improving their level of performance which, of course, helps to insure the successful operation of the community leisure service program. As suggested by Kraus and Bates (1975) and Meyer and Brightbill (1956), failure to provide effective supervision is often cited as a major contributor to less than satisfactory performances by volunteers.

The nature of supervision afforded volunteers should be of the same high caliber as that provided professional personnel. Many (but certainly not all) volunteers lack the training and background in leisure services possessed by professional personnel. Therefore, a well-organized program of supervision, in conjunction with the various training programs, represents an ideal opportunity to help reduce this "knowledge" gap.

Good programs of supervision can also contribute in other ways. They can be signals to volunteers which clearly indicate that their donated time and efforts are recognized as important and meaningful to the successful operation of the program. Furthermore, astute administrators will vary the amount and type of supervision rendered. As suggested by Argyris (1957), when a volunteer demonstrates growth along the maturity continuum, in this instance measured by his or her demonstrated ability to successfully assume and complete assigned tasks, his or her accomplishments should be recognized by a change in the type or amount of supervision rendered. Treating each individual as a mature person also brings McGregor's (1960) Theory Y into play. In addition, by recognizing one's growth through an alteration of supervision, the individual is encouraged to move toward self-actualization which is in keeping with Maslow's (1954) Hierarchy of Needs Theory.

Prior to actual appointment and role assignment, each volunteer should be provided full information regarding responsibilities and expected performance levels associated with each of the positions available. Once volunteers have accepted a particular role, they should be immediately supplied with their schedule and given information including where to report, to whom they shall be responsible, the type of supervision they can expect to receive, and the nature of their own supervisory responsibilities, if any.

Supervisor-Volunteer Relationship

Supervisors should strive to develop a good working relationship with their subordinates. The role of the supervisor should not be perceived as one of engaging in a leader-subordinate power struggle. Rather, it should be approached as a joint venture designed to enable the volunteer to perform role responsibilities to the best of his or her ability. Ideally, all supervisors should view volunteer personnel under their guidance as competent, intelligent, eager, responsible, mature individuals as suggested by McGregor's (1960) Theory Y.

Supervision Problems

When problems arise in the supervisory process, Kraus and Bates (1975, p. 342) suggest that they can frequently be attributed to:

1. Poor communication
2. Lack of adequate job descriptions
3. Inadequate screening of applicants or inappropriate selection and job assignment
4. Misconceptions held by the volunteer about the agency
5. Conflicts with other staff members

When possible, the clarification of problems should be sought through a conference between the volunteer and the supervisor.

Problems often arise because of some mechanical procedure governing the operation of the program. In many instances, once the source of a mechanical problem is evidenced, it can be rectified. Unfortunately, not all problems are so easily resolved. Those related to personality conflicts or to the inability of a volunteer to meet performance requirements present situations in which the resolution process requires a much more sensitive and sophisticated approach.

As mentioned earlier in this chapter, volunteers must often be treated differently than professional personnel with respect to discipline and performance standards. Nonetheless, leisure service administrators must exercise their authority to insure that the community program operates at the highest efficiency level possible in attempting to meet the needs of the citizens. Therefore, after a thorough and open discussion of the particular personality or performance problem, it is not uncommon for the administrator, volunteer, or both to suggest a change in assignment which often proves beneficial to all parties.

Evaluation of Volunteers

As discussed in Chapter Three, the evaluation of agency effectiveness is a very necessary, but often difficult, process. The evaluation of volunteer personnel must be considered as no less a challenge.

Similar to program evaluation, volunteer performance assessment should be an ongoing, continuous process. The evaluation concept should be conceived and administered as an educational and constructive endeavor, rather than a threatening or negative process.

Distinguishing Evaluation Criteria

One of the primary purposes of the evaluative process should be that of identifying particular assets and liabilities, strengths and weaknesses of the volunteer. However, to effectively accomplish this, a distinction must be made between the criteria used to evaluate volunteers and that employed to assess professional personnel. This distinction is necessary because although certain performance criteria might be the same for each group, there are many areas in which the professional staff should be subjected to a much more thorough and demanding review than that which is applied to the volunteer.

To illustrate the point, assume that two members of the custodial staff are to be evaluated. A volunteer custodian would not be held as accountable for the cleanliness of restroom facilities as would the full-time employee. In the same vein, the professional gymnasium supervisor, under most circumstances, would be expected to maintain greater security and adherence to safety regulations than that accomplished by the volunteer.

Areas of Evaluation

Evaluation of an individual's performance should be restricted to those responsibilities outlined in his or her job description and/or any other mutually agreed upon criteria. This is one basic principle which should be shared by all evaluators. When an individual is subjected to an evaluation focusing on unknown criteria or criteria not agreed upon (or not announced) prior to the start of the period of service being evaluated, then the process must be characterized as being both deceptive and unfair. Any evaluation conducted in this manner represents a threat to the educational concepts upon which the evaluative process is assumed to have been based.

Evaluation Report

Once all the evaluation data have been collected for a particular individual, it should be assimulated into a clear, concise, comprehensive report. It is vital that all evaluation reports be reduced to writing and that a copy be presented to the volunteer. Aside from providing both the agency and the volunteer with the exact information derived from the evaluation, the report represents a practical method of storing information about the volunteer and the program for future reference.

Evaluation Follow-up

Following distribution of the evaluation report, the appropriate supervisor should meet with the volunteer to discuss his or her evaluation. When evaluation conclusions are to be discussed, the supervisor should begin by reviewing the positive findings. This should help to reduce the volunteer's tension and fear of being threatened by the supervisor. If successful in setting the volunteer at ease, the supervisor will usually find that discussion of the negative or less than satisfactory conclusions will become an easier and much more fruitful task.

Supervisors must pursue the discussion of critical assessments with a great deal of tact and sensitivity. The approach must be constructive rather than destructive. The ultimate goal of such discussions should be to determine the cause of the deficiency and once identified to encourage the volunteer to work toward the eradication or lessening of the areas in which deficiencies were noted.

When possible, an attempt should be made to design strategies which will enable the volunteer to capitalize upon his or her strengths. At the same time, individualized programs should be developed which will assist the volunteer in the correction of detected deficiencies. In both instances, the particular needs of the individual as well as the leisure service program must be kept in perspective. For example, if the evaluation report reveals that the volunteer has not been effective in a leadership role and the volunteer not only concurs with the findings but seeks a transfer to a different role, the supervisor should attempt to comply with the request. Although compliance might result in a temporary leadership void, to do anything less would satisfy neither the individual's desire nor the program's need for effective leadership.

Used in an intelligent, humanistic manner, performance evaluations can be a valuable tool in assisting volunteer personnel with the development of their abilities to the greatest potential possible. On the other hand, through improper use the same evaluative process can deteriorate into an extremely destructive instrument — one capable of permanently destroying volunteer morale and effectiveness. To illustrate the point, assume that a supervisor subscribes to the humanistic philosophy and approaches the evaluation process as an educational and constructive venture. In such a situation, the volunteer being evaluated by this particular supervisor will probably derive a great deal of personal benefit from the experience and, regardless of the findings, will be encouraged to continue with his or her assignment. But, if the situation is reversed so that the supervisor represents an individual who believes that the evaluation report can be used to threaten and belittle an individual, then the probability of those volunteers under this person's supervision perceiving the evaluative process as a valuable and fruitful experience becomes rather remote. Given such a situation, it is much more likely that the volunteer will emerge from the evaluation depressed and probably debating whether or not to continue donating his or her services to the community program.

Recognition of Volunteers

Most volunteers do not receive monetary compensation for their services. Consequently, the most viable method available to community leisure service departments wishing to acknowledge individual and collective volunteer contributions is through some form of recognition. Basically, there are two types of recognition: private and public.

Private Recognition

This refers to recognition conferred upon a volunteer by a supervisor or the program director in a very personal manner. Normally, knowledge that such recognition has been bestowed is shared by very few individuals. Private recognition is usually conveyed in the form of a verbal "pat on the back" or a personal letter of recommendation.

Public Recognition

Public recognition, by definition, is designed to be known by large numbers of people. With respect to leisure service volunteer personnel, public recognition may be sub-divided into two segments:

1. Intra-agency public recognition
2. Community-wide public recognition

The major difference between the two segments is the extent to which the information is disseminated.

INTRA-AGENCY RECOGNITION

This type of volunteer recognition is announced only to the leisure service department personnel. News regarding intra-agency recognition is usually disseminated by means of "in-house" newsletters, bulletins, and posted notices. Also, volunteers supervising trips might be recognized for their contribution by providing free admission to the attractions visited. Other volunteers might be provided with free use of the agency's leisure service facilities. As previously mentioned, some agencies regard a letter of recommendation or one of commendation as an appropriate method of providing volunteer recognition.

COMMUNITY-WIDE RECOGNITION

All forms of recognition accorded volunteers which is intended for consumption by the general public are included under this heading. While many of these forms are basically designed for intra-agency purposes, they may also be announced publicly through the media. One popular method of expressing recognition is through agency sponsorship of a social function, possibly a dinner-dance or luncheon, at which each volunteer is cited for his or her contribution and presented with some small gift or token of appreciation. Other agencies might elect to establish a "Volunteer of the Month" award.

Finally, Hersey and Blanchard (1977) suggest that an individual's competency and dependability may be recognized by means of an increase in the program responsibility assigned the individual. In effect, recognition for excellence in volunteer performance is conveyed through a "promotion." From a humanistic as well as management point of view, achievement of volunteer recognition through the application of organizational development techniques is strongly endorsed. However, because the objective of most efforts is that of providing frequent recognition to as many individuals as possible, it recommended that leisure service agencies institute a multi-faceted volunteer recognition program.

Summary

Community leisure service programs can be effectively strengthened through the use of volunteers. However, not all administrators are of this opinion; some prohibit the use of volunteer personnel because of a fear of not being able to successfully cope with the problems associated with such a program. Nonetheless, increasing economic concerns coupled with constant pressure to expand leisure services have resulted in a greater dependency upon the services contributed by volunteer personnel.

Identification of potential volunteers may be facilitated by the use of a cross-indexed volunteer resource file. Information for the file is usually gathered via a community survey employing a questionnaire instrument. Once prospective candidates have been identified for volunteer positions, they must be interviewed, classified in terms of their ability to contribute to the leisure service program, and then assigned a role within the program.

Earle Zeigler's (1954) "Bill of Rights" for the volunteer is as germane today as when originally published with respect to describing what administrators must do to provide for the needs of leisure service volunteers. Contained in Zeigler's proposal are the following articles:

1. The volunteer has the right to expect a continuous program of help, encouragement, and training in order to serve more competently.
2. The volunteer has the right to have his task limited to a definite period so that he may have the satisfaction of a job well-done. We can not usually expect the volunteer to give unlimited time to the recreation program because of the pressures of his regular job.
3. The volunteer has the right to have the opportunity to advance the program by suggesting new ideas, offering service, and sharing in the achievement.
4. The volunteer has the right to understand the time and place at which the service is to be performed, the duration of the assignment, the nature of the duties to be carried on, the individual to whom he is to report, the type of records to be kept, or the materials to be provided.
5. The volunteer has the right to be made to feel that there is a genuine need for the work that he is asked to do. The assigned task must be adjusted to his abilities, must be definite, and should preferably be in writing.
6. The volunteer has the right to see the relationship of his task to the objectives and functions of the department. He has the right to be given a place to work which is properly maintained and in which his associates are sociable and congenial. (p. 100)

Study Questions

1. Who are volunteers and what role do they play in the delivery of leisure services?

2. How would a leisure service administrator attempt to determine the types of volunteer resources existing within the community?
3. What are the assets and liabilities related to the use of volunteer personnel?
4. What are the various facts comprising a successful volunteer recruitment program?
5. What are the general characteristics usually associated with leisure service volunteers?
6. Can you describe the methods used to train volunteer personnel?
7. From a humanistic perspective, how would you explain the philosophy which should permeate the supervision and evaluation of volunteer personnel?
8. In lieu of monetary compensation, how might recognition be rendered in appreciation for volunteer services?
9. How would you describe some of the organizational management concepts leisure service administrators might implement in the management of volunteer personnel programs?
10. Looking toward the future, how would you describe the status of volunteer personnel in community leisure service programs five years from now? in ten years?

References

Argyris, Chris. *Personality and Organization*. New York: Harper and Row, Publishers, Inc., 1957.

Bannon, Joseph J. *Leisure Resources: Its Comprehensive Planning*. Englewood Cliffs, N.J.: Prentice-Hall, Inc., 1976.

Graham, Peter J. "Affirmative Action: Its Effects Upon Intramural-Recreational Sports Department Employment Policies." *27th Annual Conference Proceedings of the National Intramural-Recreational Sports Association* (1976): 29-43. Also ERIC Microfiche no. 129-812.

Hersey, Paul, and Blanchard, Kenneth H. *Management of Organizational Behavior: Utilizing Human Resources*. Englewood Cliffs, N.J.: Prantice-Hall, Inc., 1977.

Kraus, Richard G., and Bates, Barbara J. *Recreation Leadership and Supervision: Guidelines for Professional Development*. Philadelphia: W. B. Saunders, Co., 1975.

Lutzin, Sidney G., and Storey, Edward H. (Eds.) *Managing Municipal Leisure Services*. Washington, D.C.: International City Management Association, 1973.

McGregor, Douglas. *The Human Side of Enterprise*. New York: McGraw-Hill Book Co., Inc., 1960.

Maslow, Abraham H. *Motivation and Personality*. New York: Harper and Brothers, 1954.

Meyer, Harold D., and Brightbill, Charles K. *Recreation Administration: A Guide to Its Practices*. Englewood Cliffs, N.J.: Prentice-Hall, Inc., 1956.

Meyer, Harold D., and Brightbill, Charles K. *Community Recreation: A Guide to Its Organization*. Englewood Cliffs, N.J.: Prentice-Hall, Inc., 1964.

Sessoms, H. Douglas; Meyer, Harold D.; and Brightbill, Charles K. *Leisure Services: The Organized Recreation and Park System*. Englewood Cliffs, N.J.: Prentice-Hall Inc., 1975.

Zeigler, Earle. "Bill of Rights." *Youth Leaders Digest* December (1954): 100.

Related Readings

Cull, John G., and Hardy, Richard E. *Volunteerism: An Emerging Profession*. Springfield, Ill.: Charles C. Thomas, 1974.

Drucker, Peter. *Management: Tasks, Responsibilities, Practices*. New York: Harper & Row, 1973.

Hampton, David R.; Summer, Charles E.; and Webber, Ross A. *Organizational Behavior and the Practice of Management*. Glenview, Ill.: Scott, Foresman and Company, 1973.

Kraus, Richard G., and Curtis, Joseph E. *Creative Administration in Recreation and Parks*. 2nd ed. St. Louis: The C. V. Mosby Co., 1977.

Litwin, George H., and Stringer, Robert A. *Motivation and Organizational Climate*. Cambridge, Ma.: Harvard University Press, 1968.

Michael, Donald N. *The Next Generation*. New York: Random House, 1965.

Rodney, Lynn S. *Administration of Public Recreation*. New York: The Ronald Press Co., 1964.

Romney, George. "Let's Get Involved." *Parks and Recreation*, 10 (January, 1975): 9.

Routh, Thomas A. *The Volunteer and Community Agencies*. Springfield, Ill.: Charles C. Thomas, 1972.

Stenzel Anne K., and Feeney, Helen F. *Volunteer Training and Development: A Manual*. New York: The Seabury Press, 1976.

Stone, Marvin L. "Helping People, An American Custom on the Rise." *U.S. News and World Report*, 77 (September 2, 1974): 29-32.

Public, Community, and Media Relations

Objectives After reading and comprehending this chapter, you should be able to:

1. Explain the process of communication.
2. Discuss the purpose of public relations.
3. State the advantages and disadvantages of using a variety of public relations information dissemination vehicles.
4. Make proper use of the techniques employed in the development of news releases.
5. Describe the concepts of community and media relations.
6. Discuss the need for community involvement in the decision-making process.
7. List the various promotional modes used to generate effective community and media relations.

Introduction

Included among the prime ingredients of most successful community leisure service programs is the need to develop effective techniques which generate positive public, community, and media relations. The term *public relations* is generally used to identify projects and efforts designed to promote leisure service activities and events, to create a positive public image, and to entertain personal requests and to smoothly resolve any individual complaints.

Community relations is a term used to describe those undertakings which attempt to actively involve the community in the development, planning, operation, and evaluation of the leisure service program. The term *media relations* refers to efforts initiated to enhance the working relationship between leisure service personnel and the members of the media who assist in the promotion of the many activities and events associated with community leisure service programs.

Critical to each form of leisure service public relations is the effective use of the communication process. In the course of our daily interactions we communicate with one another constantly. We deliver our messages in a variety of formats; verbal, written, and visual. Nonetheless, communication remains for most people a greatly misunderstood process.

Communication

Today's community leisure service administrator is required to disseminate program information to numerous, diverse audiences. All segments of the community—young and old, teens and adults, healthy and handicapped, rich and poor—must be informed of program offerings, schedule of events, and so forth. Effective delivery of this information requires that a variety of communication vehicles be employed. In this chapter, we will review the different types of delivery vehicles available for the promotion of leisure service activities and events; however, before undertaking such a review it is important that the theoretical construct of the communication be examined.

Communication Process

No matter which method of transmitting a message is selected, the communication process remains the same. Belasco, Hampton, and Price (1975) have divided the communication process into **five phases.** The *first* relates to the formulation of thoughts by the sender. When an individual wishes to communicate with others, it becomes necessary for that individual to decide exactly what is to be conveyed.

Encoding the message into appropriate language represents the *second* phase of the process. Each word (or symbol) used should be as clear and simple as possible. Observance of this practice increases the potential for effective communication. Yet, all too often, simple messages are made needlessly complex. This fault was well illustrated by A. P. Herbert, a British member of Parliament who took Nelson's immortal phrase, "England expects every man to do his duty," and transformed it into a complex version which read:

England anticipates that, as regards the current emergency, personnel will
face up to the issues and exercise appropriately the functions allocated to their
respective occupational groups. (Chase 1957, p. 59)

The *third* phase of the communication process concerns the actual transmission of messages. It is at this point that the sender must decide upon the most efficient and effective mode for delivering the message. Should the communication be dispatched in written, verbal, or visual form? Only after the intended message receiver has been identified should decisions of this nature be made. Once the delivery target has been determined, the communication transmission vehicle deemed to be most effective in reaching the target audience can be utilized. For example, messages pertaining to "teen" activities might be best delivered through announcements broadcast over radio stations featuring "teen" music. On the other hand, messages intended for adults might be more effectively disseminated through the publication of notices in the local press.

Phase *four* relates to the reception of transmitted messages. To receive the transmitted message, the target audience must be aware of the channel of communication which will be used and must have access to that delivery vehicle. To illustrate the point, assume that information regarding the annual Labor Day picnic is to be disseminated through notices published in local newspapers. To insure that the information will successfully reach the intended audience, the leisure service personnel responsible for delivering the picnic information must make sure that:

1. the public is aware of how and approximately when the picnic information is to be announced
2. the information published is accurate, understandable, and legible
3. the newspapers containing the announcement are available to and read by the target audience

The *fifth* phase identified by Belasco and his associates pertains to decoding the message. Were the transmitted words (or symbols) interpreted by the receiver in the same context as intended by the sender? Whenever a message is decoded in a manner different from the original intent, the message becomes distorted. And depending upon the degree of distortion the message may actually become erroneous.

The problems associated with encoding and decoding of communicated messages were brought to the forefront when President Jimmy Carter of the United States visited Poland in 1977. In the text of his historic address to the Polish people, Carter used the phrase, "after leaving the United States. . . ." The American State Department translator encoded the word "leaving" into Polish by using a very old and little used term. Decoding the message in contemporary language, the Polish audience was astonished to learn that President Carter had "abandoned" the United States. (Newsweek, January 9, 1978, p. 20)

Completion of the communication process is dependent upon an additional element. This sixth and final phase is associated with the concept of feedback. Feedback is a term used to describe any response that indicates that a message has been received. Feedback may be visual, verbal, or written.

Process Evaluation

The only way a message sender can determine whether his or her communication has been accurately encoded, transmitted, received, and decoded is through the feedback given by the message's target. If the feedback is consistent with the intent of the message, then it becomes reasonable to assume that the communication process has been successfully executed. On the other hand, if the feedback is of an unanticipated

```
┌─────────────┐      ┌─────────────┐      ┌─────────────┐
│  Message    │ ───▶ │  Message    │ ───▶ │  Message    │
│ Formulation │      │  Encoding   │      │Transmission │
└─────────────┘      └─────────────┘      └─────────────┘
       ▲                                          │
       │                                          ▼
┌─────────────┐      ┌─────────────┐      ┌─────────────┐
│  Feedback   │      │  Message    │      │  Message    │
│     to      │ ◀─── │  Decoding   │ ◀─── │  Reception  │
│   Sender    │      │(Interpretation)│   │             │
└─────────────┘      └─────────────┘      └─────────────┘
```

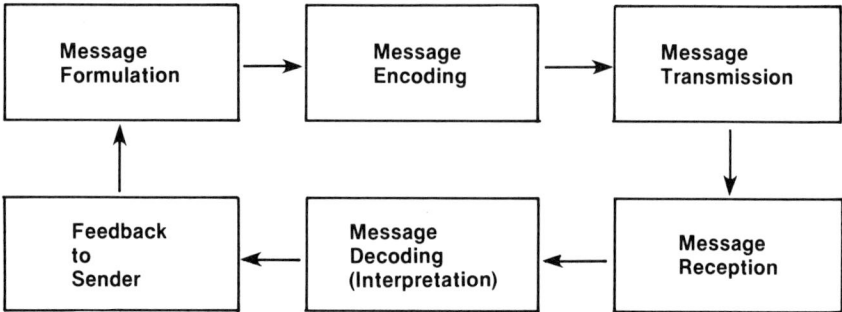

Figure 8.1 Communication Process Model

nature or if the message's target fails to provide any feedback, it might then be concluded that one of the following situations exists:

1. the message was not received
2. the message was encoded incorrectly
3. the message was correctly encoded but incorrectly transmitted
4. the message was accurately encoded, transmitted, and received but incorrectly decoded
5. the message was accurately encoded, transmitted, received, and decoded, but the receiver elected not to acknowledge its receipt
6. The message was accurately encoded, transmitted, received, and decoded, but the receiver either failed to concur with or was not influenced by its content

The communication process sequence is illustrated in Figure 8-1. For the entire process to be successful, each individual phase must be effectively implemented.

Public Relations

The establishment of positive public relations is considered a vital aspect of the leisure service delivery system. In the past, the concept of public relations was limited to the promotion of program activities and events. Today, however, public relations is perceived in a much broader context as a multifarious concept. Kraus and Curtis (1977, p. 234) indicate that public relations has three primary purposes:

1. to disseminate information to the public
2. to alter the public's beliefs and actions through persuasion
3. to coordinate the actions and attitudes of the public and the organization that is serving the public

The Public

Residing within the average community are many citizens who are both knowledgeable and supportive of the leisure service program. However, there are also individuals who oppose the expenditure of tax generated monies to support such "frivolous" enterprises as leisure service activities and events. In addition, there are numerous residents who lack an understanding of the diversity of recreational opportunities available to them on the local level. And, of course, each community has a few residents who basically favor the activities and events sponsored by the leisure service program, but harbor certain personal reservations stemming from inadequate services or some unpleasant incident. Included within this category would be the older citizen who is unhappy about what is felt to be inadequate facilities available for Senior Citizen programs and meetings, or the parent upset because his or her child has had a personal item "ripped-off" at the local community center.

Program Image

Creation of a positive program image among the community residents requires that the program administrator institute a campaign to desseminate leisure service information broadly and regularly. This campaign should be designed to inform all segments of the community about the various activities and events available. Furthermore, the dispersed material should serve to interpret the program's philosophy, goals, objectives, policies, and procedures. Successful program information and interpretation campaigns will assist the general public in understanding the mission of the community leisure service program.

Public Relations Goals

According to Meyer and Brightbill (1956, p. 37), "Public relations has many specific purposes all of which, in one way or another, are aimed at strengthening public acceptance, approval, and support." Program acceptance, approval, and support can be manifest in several ways, such as favorable legislative actions, increased budget allocations, expanded private contributions, an increase in the number of volunteers, a growth in the number of program participants, and so forth.

Included among the desired outcomes of a modern comprehensive community leisure service public relations program, as suggested by Kraus (1977), Meyer and Brightbill (1964), and Kraus and Curtis (1977), are the following:

1. to interpret the program's goals and objectives to the community
2. to explain program policies and to announce plans for new activities, events, facility development and improvement plans, etc.
3. to announce sign-up dates, activity schedules, and general facility use schedules
4. to focus public attention upon a specific activity or special event
5. to educate the public regarding the values and benefits that can be derived through participation in the program's tax supported activities and events

6. to act as a catalyst in stimulating the creation of hobby clubs, special interest groups, and other leisure oriented social functions within the community
7. to encourage citizens to come forth and volunteer their time and skills to the community program
8. to encourage citizens to express their opinions, thereby creating a two-way communication channel
9. to impress upon the public that their leisure service program is up-to-date and that the program administrators continually seek and implement new and innovative program activities, events, and concepts

Determining the Target Market

Prior to launching a public relations effort, the leisure service administrator should make a practice of defining the target market. Similar to the approach used by business executives marketing a new product, the leisure service program director should identify the segment of the public toward whom the public relations effort should be aimed. For example, if a promotional effort were to be directed toward the entire community, then a general public relations approach would be quite appropriate. However, if the target were determined to be a particular segment of the community, then a more directed and specific approach would be required for the public relations thrust. For instance, a public relations project directed to the general population should be delivered through a vehicle which produces a "shotgun" effect. Newspapers and radio announcements are two dissemination modes which produce such an effect. On the other hand, material designed to reach a particular audience, such as school-aged youngsters, might prove more effective if dispersed through school related channels of communication, such as newsletters, posters, public address announcements, school newspapers, or flyers.

As earlier noted there exists within every community a variety of groups to which leisure service public relations efforts must be directed. Each segment is defined by certain established parameters. Community populations may be segmented by age, such as youngsters, "teens," adults, and "seniors;" by affiliation, such as religious, political, occupation, social, civic, charitable, and fraternal; by special characteristics, such as the handicapped, emotionally disturbed, gifted, and unemployed; and, the community-at-large. Each of these population segments represents a different public or audience with whom the leisure service administrator must be concerned.

Public Relations Delivery Modes

There are numerous delivery modes available for leisure service administrators to use in conjunction with their public relations programs. Used singularly, or in combination, each delivery mode is capable of disseminating program information to the target clientele. Kraus and Bates (1975), Sessoms, Meyer, and Brightbill (1975), Kraus and Curtis (1977), and others have identified those communication modes commonly used in public relations campaigns.

NEWSPAPERS

Newspapers represent an excellent public relations vehicle. All sorts of newspapers exist. Most are available though purchase or subscription but others are distributed free of charge. In many communities it is not uncommon to find newspapers with specific religious, political, or ethnic orientation. Others focus on a particular hobby, interest, or profession. And, newspapers written in foreign languages are frequently available, especially in urban areas.

Most communities, regardless of size, take great pride in having their own "local" press. Small town newspapers are usually published weekly, whereas those located in larger communities tend to be printed on a daily basis.

For a newspaper to be effective as a public relations vehicle, it must be both available to and read by the target clientele. To illustrate the point, assume that a Spanish Cultural Festival, which has been designed primarily to attract members of the Spanish-speaking community, is to be promoted through articles and press releases written in English and published in the local press. If the newspapers carrying the promotional material are not read by most of the Hispanic community because of an inability to read English, or for a variety of culturally-related reasons, then this particular public relations effort is not going to be successful in achieving its intended outcome.

If confronted with such a situation, an experienced and culturally sensitive administrator would promote the festival through those newspapers read by the general community as well as through publications known to be popular and widely read within the Hispanic community. And, of course, it is often preferable for such promotional publications to be printed in both Spanish and English.

The need for a multilingual public relations effort has increased in importance with the growth of non-English speaking segments of the population. Leisure service personnel, especially those associated with urban programs, should make extensive use of multilingual information distributing techniques.

Another important factor that the leisure service administrator must take into consideration when using newspapers as a public relations vehicle is that many people tend to read certain sections of the newspaper more carefully and faithfully than others. For example, members of the business community are prone to turn to the financial pages, while sports enthusiasts often focus their attention strictly on the sports pages.

Leisure service administrators should take advantage of these tendencies. When submitting public relations copy for publication, every effort should be made to insure that the copy will be printed in the section of the paper most likely to be read by the target audience. Garden club announcements would probably be best located in the home and garden section of the newspaper, whereas a notice soliciting croquet tournament entries might be more fruitful if located in the sport pages rather than the theatre and entertainment section.

NEWSPAPER COPY PREPARATION

Certain guidelines should be observed when preparing newspaper copy for submission. Adherence to the following procedures will make material more acceptable and will enhance its publication potential.

1. Copy should always be typed, double-spaced and, when possible, restricted to a single page. Strict attention should be paid to providing open space at both the top and bottom of the page and appropriate margins on either side.
2. The article should be accurate and to the point. Paragraphs should consist of brief sentences using simple, easy to understand words. The "lead," or first paragraph, should provide all the basic information, such as who, when, where, why, and how. The story can be expanded in subsequent paragraphs. However, those details deemed least important should be left for the last paragraphs. When copy is "edited" the tendency is to "cut" the last paragraphs until the article is reduced to the desired publication length.
3. One should try to use the names of known people, places, and events. Readers will read an article more thoroughly when they can identify with people and situations which are familiar to them.
4. The author should record his or her name along with the name, address, and telephone number of the agency represented at the top of the page. Also located at the top of the page should be the date when the copy was submitted and the date when the article should be published. Some articles are submitted for immediate release, while others are only to be published on or following a specified date.
5. Centered on the page immediately below the final paragraph should be the symbol "#." This symbol is a signal to the editor that the article has concluded.
6. All copy should be submitted early enough to meet established newspaper deadlines. This means that deadlines for each publication should be known in advance.
7. A carbon or photocopy of all submitted material should be maintained in a file for future reference.

```
            Charles DeFilippo
         Leisure Service Department
            Deep River, Texas
               729-0889

Release Date:                          Date Submitted:
Immediate                              April 14

    The Annual Deep River Model Airplane Contest will be

held at 10:00 am, Saturday, April 22, at the Wing Memorial Community

Center. The public is invited to view the record 374 models enter-

ed and to attend the award ceremonies scheduled for 1:00 pm in the

main showing room.

    George Gregory, last year's Grand Champion, will be

competing in the 12-14 year old division. Cheryl Pierce, Gordon

Watkins, Jean Gomes, and Gerrie Valdez are expected to give Gregory

a strong challenge. Some of the top contenders in the 9-11 year

old category appear to be Richard Garb, Carol Rudenhauer, Josephine

Rivers, Michael Sanchez, Mary Watkins, Gene Kaczka, and Rosalie

Green. Sisters Dede and Rachael Robbins along with Ann Foley,

Freddie Berger, Billy Garcia, and Jose LeClerc will be among those

trying for honors in the 6-8 year old division.

    Judging this year's entries will be Jack Mellon, Pam

Salvadi, Michael Rudenhauer, Lou Berger, Dave Kaczka, Theresa

Valdez, Dan Cruz, Marie Robbins, and Gerrie Reinhardt. Each judge

is an experienced pilot or model airplane builder.

    Members of the refreshment committee are Susan Sheenan,

Jim Clark, Steve LeClerc, Dennis Reinhardt, Linda Amico, and Terri

Kerr. There will be no admission fee and refreshments will be

available at minimal charge.
                               #
```

Figure 8.2 Sample News Release

Figure 8-2 illustrates a typical news release. Note that it follows the suggested guidelines and that it has been submitted for immediate release.

PRINTED MATERIAL

Pamphlets, reports, guides, handbooks, bulletins, flyers, newsletters, posters, schedules, and directories are representative of the types of public relations vehicles included under the rubric of printed materials.

Kraus and Curtis (1977, p. 236) noted that, "The simplest and most effective means of reaching large numbers of people is through printed media, such as newspapers, brochures, and reports."

The use of printed materials in leisure service public relations campaigns has escalated in recent years. This increase coincides with the technological developments that have led to the creation of new, rapid, efficient, and low cost printing and reproduction processes. Leisure service administrators are encouraged to make extensive use of printed materials. Similar to newspapers, printed materials are only effective when written in the languages understood by the various clientele being serviced.

Leisure service administrators must be cognizant of the fact that printed public relations materials, no matter how diversified or widely disseminated, are incapable of successfully reaching every segment of the community. Specifically, individuals handicapped by blindness or illiteracy will not benefit (at least not directly) from the distribution of printed materials. Moreover, many people simply fail to take the time to read printed material. Consequently, program directors should employ audio and visual delivery vehicles in addition to the printed materials used in the public relations campaign.

AUDIO AND VISUAL

Public relations efforts may be disseminated to target audiences through the use of audio and visual delivery modes such as photographs, radio, television, motion pictures, slides, tape recordings, video tapes, film loops, and sound amplifying systems. Once again, the application of technological advancements has resulted in the development of a variety of relatively inexpensive, highly effective audio and visual communication tools.

Photographs. The use of photographs as a public relations tool can be extremely effective. Whether printed in publications or arranged for public review on display boards or easels, photographs convey messages in a very effective and direct manner. Frequently a photograph is able to accomplish communication tasks which otherwise might never be achieved. A photograph of a person beaming with the satisfaction that results from a "recreational experience" communicates the joy that may be gained from participation in the various activities and events sponsored by the leisure service program. The type of message communicated by such a photograph is often extremely difficult if not impossible, to describe and transmit in written or verbal form.

Photographs also make very nice awards. When used in this manner, they generate both short- and long-term public relations benefits. The short-term effect is gained upon presentation of the photograph. The recipient is usually quite pleased to receive the award and tends to have a positive image of the leisure service program. The award serves to strengthen that image. In the future, whenever the recipient views the photograph, pleasant memories are recalled and the positive image of the leisure service program is reinforced. Long-term public relations effects generated by the photograph are virtually limitless, restricted only by the life of the photograph and the frequency of viewing.

Radio. The broadcast of leisure service information over local radio stations represents another valuable public relations delivery vehicle. Most communities are serviced by one or more radio stations. In the United States, each radio station licensed by the Federal Communications Commission is required to provide a specified amount of air time, free of charge, for the broadcast of public service announcements. Consequently, most radio station managers welcome the receipt of announcement copy from public service agencies. In fact, some radio stations use the broadcasting of public service announcements as a marketing tool to attract a greater listening audience.

Leisure service program administrators should take full advantage of free radio broadcast time. All announcement copy should be carefully prepared to insure its accuracy. As a general policy, broadcast releases should be distributed to each radio station that serves the community. In addition, program directors should institute news release distribution procedures to insure that announcements directed toward a particular clientele are broadcast over those radio stations commonly listened to by the target audience. Given the diversity of AM and FM radio stations, the astute administrator will become familiar with the programming formats of the different stations and will acquire a knowledge regarding the listening preferences of the various population segments within the community.

Commercial television. Commercial, community, and closed-circuit television offer additional modes for the dissemination of public relations promotions. Most community residents have direct access to a television set. Studies have shown that the average individual spends a considerable amount of time viewing commercial television, especially youngsters. Thus, leisure service broadcasts, such as news reports, editorials, feature stories, and information announcements are highly effective in reaching a large number of community residents.

Community (public) television. A growing communication medium, it can be very effective as a public relations vehicle, if used wisely. In addition to possessing all the attributes ascribed to commercial television, community television lends itself to more diverse and ambitious undertakings. The community leisure service administrator might, for example, host a weekly talk show focusing upon local issues and areas of interest.

A program of this nature would provide extensive exposure for the various activities and events comprising the community program. Staff members, program participants, government representatives, and other members of the community could be invited to participate in the various discussions.

Community television could also be used to broadcast a variety of leisure service activities, such as arts and crafts instruction, physical fitness programs, and the like. Televising programs of this nature would enable special populations, such as the handicapped and homebound, an opportunity to participate and gain from these activities — activities which otherwise might not be available to these individuals. The versatility of community television as a public relations delivery vehicle is only limited by the imagination of the leisure service staff.

Closed-circuit television. It possesses many of the same features as commercial and community television. Programs originating from one site can be delivered to as many locations as desired. The delivery power of closed-circuit television is restricted only by the number of reception points integrated into the system.

Closed-circuit television can be an especially valuable communication tool, particularly for large city leisure service programs. As an illustration, assume that a significant number of residents in a large city have expressed a desire to learn to play chess. The leisure service administrator would like to provide an instructional program to accommodate the citizen's needs. However, two major problems have stymied efforts to implement such a program. First, a survey of the residents interested in such instruction reveals that they live in all sections of the city rather than in close proximity to one another. Second, in searching for a qualified chess instructor, only one individual was located who is willing to take on the assignment, and that person is only available for one hour per week. The director's problems could readily be resolved if the leisure service program had its own closed-circuit television network connecting each of its community centers throughout the city. If this were the case, then the available instructor could teach a televised class which could be broadcast to each of the leisure service facilities within the community. Depending upon the circumstances, televised instructions could prove to be both popular and successful in providing for certain leisure needs.

Closed-circuit television may also serve to effectively inform viewers of program information, such as activity schedules, facility availability, meeting dates, registration deadlines, and so forth. Information of this nature could be listed on the closed circuit television screen in the same manner as commercial airlines post flight arrival and departure data.

Closed-circuit television is also very effective in providing facility surveillance. The placement of television cameras at strategic locations throughout a facility will significantly expand the programs' security capability. For many individuals, the knowledge that security is being provided for both their person and property is of utmost concern. Thus, the presence of closed-circuit television cameras would serve as a public relations vehicle designed to generate positive feedback from facility users.

Videotapes. The development of sophisticated, but relatively inexpensive and easy to use videotape equipment provides another dimension for the use of television as a public relations delivery vehicle. One very attractive feature of videotape is that once a promotional effort has been recorded, if it fails to meet expected standards, it can be retaped as often as necessary. Another feature is that videotapes require very little storage space and can be easily transported.

When used to record activities, such as the instructional chess program mentioned earlier, videotape can be of immense value to the community leisure program. If the televised chess lessons had been recorded on videotape, they could be played back whenever an individual wished to make up a missed lesson or wished to review a particular strategy. Moreover, if a subsequent instructional chess program were to be programmed, only the tapes would be needed. Through the proper use of a videotape system, leisure service program costs could be substantially reduced.

As home videotape and play-back units become more popular, community leisure service administrators might consider establishing a videotape library. Persons wishing to view a particular concert, theatre production, or instructional lesson could check out the videotape and play it back at their convenience while at home. The establishment of a videotape library could serve to deliver leisure service activities and events to portions of the community not adequately serviced by the typical programming schedule. There are many individuals unable to take advantage of leisure service offerings due to schedule conflicts. For example, workers on night and "swing" shifts could be offered expanded opportunities for participation and enjoyment of activities and events in which, under normal circumstances, they might otherwise be excluded. Also, individuals wishing to participate in two instructional programs offered at the same time could actively participate in one, and later use the videotapes to receive instruction for the second.

Motion pictures. These represent the Rolls-Royce of the public relations delivery fleet. Similar to the famed automobile, motion pictures are usually viewed as a luxury — unfortunately, a luxury that most community leisure service programs are unable to afford.

Professionally produced motion pictures are extremely effective in delivering messages to viewing audiences. The cost of obtaining the professional expertise necessary to produce an effective motion picture, however, makes this public relations medium prohibitive for all but the most affluent of communities. To produce a 16-millimeter motion picture involves the investment of several thousands of dollars and a considerable expenditure of staff time and energy. To offset the financial barriers to motion picture production, program administrators should seek private and/or commercial sponsorship for such promotional ventures.

The second major problem associated with motion pictures relates to the "life" of the film. Although a substantial investment is required to produce a motion picture, no guarantee can be given regarding the length of time that it will remain viable and effective as a public relations vehicle. This uncertainty is due to factors which cannot be effectively controlled, such as leisure activity preferences, equipment designs, hair styles, clothing fashions, and automobile designs. These factors, as well as others, serve to date the film and unfortunately each of these dating factors has a propensity to change significantly within a short period of time. Once a film becomes "outdated" it is virtually impossible, for all practical purposes, to alter the "time frame" to reflect the current "scene." In most instances, the only realistic way to accomplish this task is to remake the entire film.

Slide shows. Offered here is an excellent, flexible, and relatively inexpensive alternative to motion pictures. Although slides lack the "action" associated with motion pictures, a multi-projector slide show can produce a similar effect.

The construction of a slide show first requires the establishment of a theme: What message is the show to convey to the audience? The theme dictates the type of slides which should be used in developing the show. For example, if the intent of a show were to demonstrate to a community finance committee the need for an increase in the maintenance budget, then slides depicting deteriorating facilities would be most appropriate and effective. On the other hand, if the purpose of a slide show were to attract potential participants to a particular activity, slides focusing on the positive qualities of the activity would be most fitting.

Acquisition of high quality slides no longer requires the services of a professional photographer. With the amateur photographic equipment which is currently available, leisure service staff members or community residents are quite capable of "shooting" the slides to be used in the slide show.

A slide show, on the average, should consist of approximately 80-140 slides. This number of slides will produce a show ranging from 20-30 minutes in length. Slide shows requiring a greater length of time run the risk of boring the audience, thereby negating the potential for gaining a positive public relations effect.

Even though a picture (or slide) is capable of saying a thousand words, slide shows are much more effective when narrated. Narrators very familiar with a show's content frequently make their presentation extemporaneously. More often, however, narrators prefer to have a script available — even if it is simply used as a reference.

Slide show scripts should be written in simple, straightforward language. To assist with the reading of the script, the text should be typewritten and double- or triple-spaced. Once the script has been finalized, it is extremely important that the slides be arranged in order so that they are synchronized with the accompanying narration. Integrated into the script should be some indicator (word or symbol) that informs the narrator when to advance each slide.

Finally, to insure an effective narration, the narrator should be provided with adequate reading light and should rehearse as many times as necessary until he or she becomes familiar and comfortable with the script.

Most slide shows are presented using a single slide projector. However, two or more projectors are being used with greater frequency. Projecting the same or different slides on multiple screens in a desired sequence and combination tends to create a sense of "action." The overall "pace" may be controlled by the narrator through the use of a hand-held electronic slide changing unit or controlled by a signal on a taped narration which automatically activates the slide-change device. Slide shows can be highly versatile. Presentations can be developed to display virtually any topic imaginable and can be shown wherever electricity or a battery power-pack is available. And almost any smooth, light-colored surface will serve as a screen upon which to project the slides. Slide show materials are easily transported from one location to another and require very little storage space.

A valuable strength of slide shows is flexibility. Slide shows can be readily altered to meet the needs of different audiences or to accommodate changes in audiences. For example, if the arts and crafts segment of a slide show needed to be changed from rug-hooking to macramé, the necessary changes may be easily accomplished simply by replacing the rug-hooking slides with those depicting macramé. Similar alterations, of course, would have to be made in the script to insure accurate narration of the "new" slide show. This is easily accomplished by developing multiple scripts.

Of the various photographic media available, slide film is the least expensive. Consequently, most leisure service programs should be able to afford the funds required to produce a variety of slide shows over any given year. In fact, administrators should annually or biannually construct a pictorial record of their program's activities and events. Within a relatively short period of time, a substantial number of slides can be accumulated which may then be used to create a slide library. Labeled with the date and place where the slide was taken, as well as the identity of the subject and/or individuals shown, each slide could then be classified and filed in a logical, recorded manner. In this way, the director should have the slides required to construct a slide show which could be made available on very short notice.

Slide-tape shows. Tape-recorded narrations may be used in conjunction with slide shows. Slide-tape shows possess all of the assets associated with the slide show described above; however, the taped narration has a distinct advantage over the "live" production. A mistake made in a "live" narration can prove to be both embarrassing and difficult to rectify. Mistakes made in a taped narration can be discovered, erased, and corrected before the tape is played to an audience. The ability to erase and correct mistakes has made the tape-recorded form of narration quite popular.

A further advantage of the slide-tape format is that once the "perfect" narration has been recorded, it may be used as frequently as desired without the presence of a narrator. As a result, slide-tape shows can be shown by almost anyone—even persons lacking any knowledge of the show's content. All that the projectionist need know is how to operate the audio and visual equipment.

Tape-recordings made to accompany slide shows must contain some type of recorded signal which indicates to the projectionist the appropriate time to advance each slide. Audio signals of this nature usually take the form of a distinctive "beep" or similarly identifiable sound. Once the audio signal is issued, it is usually followed by a short period of silence—enough time to allow for the slide change—before the narration continues.

Through the application of audio technology, a second method of slide changing has been developed for use with tape recordings. At each point in the narration when the slide should be advanced, a very high frequency sound is recorded on the tape. Although this sound is too high to be heard by the human ear, it can be heard by an electronic changing device. When the silent signal is heard by the changing device, the slide projector's changing mechanism activates. Needless to say, only slide projectors equipped with such a device can make use of the automatic tape recorded slide-change signal. Use of this changing technique further reduces the potential for error and simplifies the responsibilities of the projectionist.

Slide-tape shows can be further enhanced through the introduction of music. While recording the narration, background music can be played or, under certain circumstances, music can be used as the primary audio accompaniment to the slides. Incorporating music into the slide-tape format tends to increase the show's appeal and attention gathering power.

Tape recordings. When used in conjunction with a telephone answering system, they can create yet another public relations delivery vehicle. Program information, such as facility-use schedules, starting times for various activities and events, entry deadlines, tournament results, and activity commencement dates can be recorded. Information can then be delivered to individuals who dial the appropriate telephone number which activates the answering service connected to the taped playback system.

The advent of relatively inexpensive telephone answering systems has made this particular public relations system quite popular. Once the answering system has either been purchased or leased, the only other expenditure required to maintain the system is payment of the monthly telephone bill.

As with all other forms of delivery systems, the success of the tape recorded telephone information vehicle is dependent upon the general public's knowledge of its existence. To benefit from the system, the public must be aware of the telephone number required to activate the answering system and the information being provided. Thus, it becomes the responsibility of the leisure service administrator to insure that the scope of the service has been made known throughout the community.

Film loops. Joined together at the beginning and end to form a loop, the film will run continuously when shown through a loop film projector. Many of the prohibitive restrictions associated with motion pictures also apply to the film loop; however, because most film loops are made from either regular or Super 8-millimeter film and are relatively short in duration, their production costs are considerably less than that required to finance a regular motion picture.

Film loops can be extremely effective in promoting the community leisure service program. Film loops can be developed to promote almost any type of activity or event and thus possess the potential to generate a vast amount of positive public relations. The fact that a film loop will run continuously is a desirable asset; no matter when an individual begins to view the film, he or she will be able to see the entire production in a brief and uninterrupted period of time.

For most people, nothing is more aggravating than to attend a function and not be able to clearly hear the announcements, the speech, or the music. When this situation occurs, those affected tend to develop a negative impression of both the function and the sponsoring agency. To insure against such negative reactions, the community leisure service program administrator should make appropriate use of a quality sound-amplifying system.

Sound-amplifying systems. Available in assorted styles ranging from hand-held to massive stationary units, the costs of these units varies according to the type and quality of the system. The type of sound-amplifying system best suited for a particular situation is governed by the nature of the activity or event. For example, if a crowd of closely gathered people is to be given instructions relating to the start of a classic automobile rally, a hand-held amplifying system would probably be sufficient. However, if the same instructions were to be given to a larger crowd or one spread over an extensive area, a larger system would be preferable. On the other hand, if a sound amplifying system were to be used to transmit precise sounds, such as music or singing, an amplifier capable of generating a loud and powerful as well as a clear and sharp sound should be employed.

Leisure service administrators should possess a knowledge of the various sound-amplifying systems available. To employ the wrong type of system in a given situation might prove worse than not using a sound-amplifying system at all.

Exhibits, demonstrations, and instructional clinics. Parents, relatives, friends, and even strangers enjoy the opportunity to observe the efforts of exhibit participants. Through the sponsorship of exhibits, positive public relations can be created for both the participants and the general public. Every effort should be made to involve as many exhibitors as possible. All levels of ability should be included in the exhibit. The opportunity to display one's efforts should not be restricted to only those possessing the very best talent.

Many individuals, especially adults, are reluctant to admit to their lack of either knowledge or skill in leisure activities. Subsequently, these individuals tend to avoid any situation which might lead to the discovery of this deficiency. To assist individuals harboring such fears, as well as others, leisure service administrators should sponsor activity demonstrations, and instructional clinics. When provided with group learning opportunities, many otherwise reluctant citizens will become actively involved. The fact that functions of this nature are group-oriented and attract individuals sharing similar needs provides the participant with a sense of security. Following an initial exposure to an activity, many individuals are stimulated to pursue further opportunities to participate in their newly found leisure interest.

Public speaking. Leisure service administrators should seek and accept every possible public speaking engagement. The opportunity to personally address audiences can result in significant contributions to the creation of positive public relations.

Speaking at public functions allows the audience to personally meet and listen to the individual responsible for providing them with leisure opportunities. This exposure becomes valuable because the administrator is no longer perceived by the audience as just a name; rather, he or she becomes a person, a reality, someone with whom the audience can relate and identify. Furthermore, public speaking engagements enable the speaker to address issues and aspects of the community leisure service program deemed appropriate and of interest to the particular audience. Moreover, public speaking engagements afford the leisure service administrator an opportunity to solicit and respond to questions pertaining to the community program. This type of two-way communication can prove extremely beneficial to both the administrator and the attending audience.

Participants who have enjoyed their involvement in the activities and events sponsored by the leisure service program tend to express their satisfaction through positive word-of-mouth comments. Such positive expressions serve the leisure service program well. In addition, Kraus (1977) has noted that the maintenance of a cooperative, friendly relationship among leisure service personnel, members of the business community, and other community organizations and agencies enhances the local department's public relations campaign.

Community Relations

The development and implementation of a successful community relations program is considered by many leisure service administrators to be a task of significant importance. A community relations program should strive to generate public support for the leisure service program and to provide maximum opportunity for residents to gain "a piece of the action" in terms of becoming involved with the program's development, operation, and evaluation. This requires an administrator who is sensitive to the needs of the public and who possesses the ability to effectively interact and cooperate with a variety of individuals.

Citizen Committees

Numerous avenues exist through which administrators can provide opportunities for citizens to become involved in the development, operation, and evaluation of the community leisure service program. One of the more popular is the establishment of *standing* and *ad hoc* committees. Once these committees have been constituted, the members are presented with a specific charge. For example, committees may be created to review program operating policies and procedures; to plan new programs and facilities; to serve as special advisors to the administrator; to develop and supervise a fund-raising campaign; to evaluate specific activities and events; or, to serve as a grievance board to hear complaints and recommend solutions.

Committees may be established on a neighborhood, district, or community-wide basis. Yet, no matter which geographic structure is employed, one factor remains constant — care must be taken to insure that the committee is composed of individuals who adequately represent residents from all segments of the community. Failure to adhere to this guideline may result in citizen resentment. Individuals believing that their interests are not being adequately represented (or protected) may vent their displeasure through actions that could be disruptive or even violent.

Leisure service administrators should be especially cognizant of the social turmoil evidenced in the United States, and elsewhere, during the late 1960s and early 1970s. These historical protests were the outgrowth of a strong social awareness movement—a movement which demanded that all members of a society be allowed a voice in the decision making process. If committee appointments are truly reflective of the community population, social problems are much more likely to be addressed cooperatively rather than through tension and conflict.

Agency Cooperation

In many communities, the leisure service department is not the only agency that sponsors and promotes leisure and recreational programs. Agencies such as YMCAs and YWCAs, Jewish Community Centers, Police Athletic Leagues, Catholic Youth Organizations, Boys' and Girls' Clubs, fraternal and civic organizations, professional associations, as well as business enterprises often sponsor and promote leisure and recreational activities and events.

Consequently, community leisure service administrators should actively seek to avoid potential conflicts and unnecessary duplication of services. Measures should be developed to avoid scheduling conflicts, competition for participants, and the straining of personal and professional relationships. To achieve this, administrators of the various agencies should establish effective channels of communication and strive to develop strong, cooperative professional relationships.

Successful cooperative planning and scheduling will not only create a sense of good will among participating agencies, it may also result in the expansion and improvement of opportunities afforded community residents to participate in and enjoy leisure pursuits. As an illustration, assume that a community leisure service department has scheduled a cross-country ski tour for the same date that the Boys' and Girls' Clubs have scheduled a similar event. If left unchanged, this scheduling conflict would force each agency to compete for participants. The net result of this conflict and ensuing competition would be the creation of a lose-lose situation. Neither agency would be able to achieve optimum results, and the cross-country skiers would be forced to make a choice between the two programs.

If an effective channel of communication had existed among the agencies mentioned above, the conflict could have been avoided. With cooperative scheduling, the conflict would have been discovered prior to public announcement and two separate dates could have been established. Thus, the competition for participants would have been eliminated and the cross-country skiers would have been allowed an opportunity to participate in both events, rather than being forced to choose one over the other.

Cooperative efforts also extend to the sharing of facilities and equipment. For instance, it is not uncommon for a civic organization to sponsor a community day. To enhance the program, the sponsoring organization might initiate a request to hold the community day at the community park which is equipped with barbeque pits. Furthermore, a request might be submitted to borrow certain recreational items, such as a volleyball and net, softball equipment, and a large cageball. Upon receipt of such request, the leisure service administrator should seek to cooperate to the fullest extent possible. Failure to lend support may create negative attitudes toward the leisure service program in the minds of the organization's membership.

Involving the Business Community

Participation in leisure pursuits is viewed by most individuals as a positive endeavor. Business people are very conscious of this positive attitude held by the public. Consequently, many business enterprises are anxious to become affiliated with leisure activities and events. This involvement frequently takes the form of financial support. In return for the sponsorship of an event or activity, businesses anticipate that they will receive ample and appropriate recognition for their efforts. Aside from providing community residents with an opportunity to engage in leisure pursuits, business enterprises expect to generate a substantial amount of good will throughout the community which ultimately will be translated into increased business.

Administrators of leisure service programs should pursue and encourage business sponsorship of activities and events. At the same time, however, an alert posture must be maintained to insure that all businesses within the community desiring to become sponsors are provided an equal opportunity. Failure to insure fairness and to provide an equal opportunity could result in charges of favoritism and discrimination being lodged by those entrepreneurs unable to gain public recognition as activity sponsors.

Civic, Professional and Fraternal Organizations

Many organizations, such as the Veterans of Foreign Wars, American Legion, Knights of Columbus, Grange, Masons, Junior Chamber of Commerce, Rotary Club, and the Red Cross frequently sponsor leisure activities and events. It is not uncommon for these organizations to become involved with instructional programs, holiday celebrations, community days, and sport programs. For example, the American Legion sponsors an organized baseball program for youth.

It is not unusual for community organizations to assist one another. For example, in Winchester, Massachusetts, the Enka Society, a community-based charitable organization, annually sponsors the Town Fair. Society members volunteer their services to sell tickets and food, to conduct the various games of skill, and so forth. The Society uses the funds generated by this annual event to support, at least in part, a variety of other community programs. The local hospital, Boy and Girl Scout units, The Winchester Leisure Service Department, Police Athletic League, Red Cross, Senior Citizen's Center, and the Visiting Nurses Association have each been beneficiaries of the Enka's efforts.

Leisure service administrators should enthusiastically cooperate with these and other similar organizations. Again, through the coordination of efforts the public is afforded expanded opportunities to engage in leisure pursuits. And, of course, this represents a major objective of leisure service programs. Leisure service administrators who demonstrate a willingness to cooperate with community organization help to enhance the image of their program in the minds of the organization's membership.

Educational Personnel

The community school concept possesses many favorable aspects, but it is also a concept necessitating close cooperation between those involved in municipal leisure service programs and those in the roles of Community School Directors in the public schools. The premise underlying the community school concept is that through the joint use of existing facilities greater efficiency accompanied by a reduction in operational expenses many be achieved. Generally, school facilities are capable of supporting a variety of leisure activities and events. Classrooms, gymnasiums, radio broadcasting and television studios, auditoriums and stages, art and music rooms, vocational shops, and outdoor areas are made available for Community Education programs.

In the average community, 50 percent or more of the tax revenues are expended in support of educational programs. Most educational facilities are used, on the average, eight hours or less per day during the week. During weekends, school vacations, and summer recess, many school facilities are left idle. Thus, in an effort to maximize the use of these facilities, school and leisure service personnel have sought to institute cooperative ventures.

The success of community school programs results in both agencies sharing in the positive image created within the community. The general public is quick to recognize and appreciate programs which promote the efficient use of existing facilities, reduce operational expenditures, and expand the educational and leisure opportunities available to members of the community. Taxpayers are especially sensitive to such efforts during periods of fiscal constricture and escalating tax rates.

Public Officials

Program administrators should be constantly alert for opportunities to extend recognition to public officials for their service and contributions to the community leisure service program. Officials, such as the mayor or town manager; members of the city council or board of selectmen; county commissioners; members of the leisure service board of commissioners; police, fire, and public works personnel; and many other community officials contribute in many ways, either directly or indirectly, to leisure service programs.

Whenever possible and as often as possible, the efforts of public officials should be brought to the attention of the community. By paying tribute to their contributions, two things may be accomplished. First, the public acknowledgement of their efforts constitutes a "stroking" effect which assists the individual in meeting his or her esteem needs. Second, as a result of its association with and avowed support from respected community leaders, the leisure service program gains in prestige.

The recognition of public officials can be accomplished in several ways. News articles praising the individual for his or her contribution can be prepared and released to the community media representatives. Public officials can be requested to serve in highly visible honorary roles, such as Grand Marshal for the annual community parade. At award ceremonies, public officials can be introduced and asked to make the presentations. Photographs of the event can be taken and submitted to the local press. The leisure service department can design an attractive certificate of recognition which can be presented to selected officials at a special awards ceremony.

Community Surveys

The construction and dissemination of survey instruments represents another method for allowing community residents an opportunity to express their opinions. Although community surveys enable administrators to gain valuable information in addition to generating positive community relations, they should be used sparingly. Because the survey method of research has been used so extensively in recent years, "Many Americans . . . have been overpolled, interviewed, queried, and explored through surveys." (Bannon, 1976, p. 128)

Survey instruments must not be deceptive. If the individuals completing the questionnaire have been informed that their identity will not be disclosed, then every precaution must be taken to insure that anonymity is preserved. No tricks or codes designed to identify the respondent should ever be incorporated into the survey without the knowledge of the individual. To do so discredits the credibility of the sponsoring agency and could hinder participation in subsequent surveys. The construction of a survey instrument should reflect a top-quality effort; anything else leading to a weak instrument can easily cast a poor image upon the leisure service program.

Bannon (1976, pp. 132-133) suggests that in addition to the collection of specific data, a community survey usually has additional objectives:

1. To increase community involvement in decision-making and planning
2. To provide the agency governing board, professional staff, and community residents with a better understanding of public parks and recreation
3. To provide supporting data for the governmental units making decisions relative to the planning process

Program directors should closely supervise the administration of all community surveys. Residents selected to participate in surveys should always be treated politely, even if they elect not to cooperate. For example, if a community center visitor is requested to complete a questionnaire and refuses, he or she should be thanked and the interviewer should seek out the next potential participant. Persons refusing to participate in surveys should never be pestered or harassed in hopes that such action might cause them to recant.

Once the community survey has been completed and the data analyzed, the results and conclusions should be made public. The reporting of study results is important because in all too many instances study participants never receive any feedback. In return for the study participant's time and energy, he or she should be extended the courtesy of being able to gain access to the study results, even if they are only reported in summary form. A lack of feedback may be an indication to the survey participants that the study was never completed or that their contributions were not appreciated. In either case, the enthusiasm of these individuals to participate in future studies could be jeopardized.

Leisure Service Personnel

Leisure service personnel play a vital part in the success of a community relations program. Interestingly, the employees possessing the greatest potential for influencing public opinion are those persons holding positions at the lower levels of the organizational structure. Grounds and maintenance personnel, activity leaders, activity supervisors, and office staff have substantially more contact with the general public than do most upper level administrators. Consequently, in many instances, these employees represent the front-line in terms of promoting community relations efforts.

Leisure service program directors however, should be an example to subordinates regarding conduct to be used when interacting with the public. Individuals successful in promoting positive community relations are usually persons:

1. who are courteous to other individuals at all times
2. who are easily accessible to citizens
3. who maintain an open mind and are willing to listen to various opinions
4. who follow-up on all details
5. who keep employees and citizens informed of all aspects of the community program
6. who avoid becoming embroiled in controversy
7. who are willing to mediate disputes and do so fairly
8. who view situations in an optimistic manner
9. who maintain a high level of visibility through participation in a variety of community organizations and functions

Guidelines should be developed describing the manner in which leisure service employees are expected to interact with the public. To be effective, these guidelines should be expressed in writing. Furthermore, the guidelines should be reviewed and discussed with all program personnel so that they are fully understood.

Appropriate supervision measures should be adopted and effectuated to insure that conduct guidelines are being observed. Failure to monitor compliance with accepted standards of conduct may hinder the community relations program. For example, assume that a playground supervisor failed to observe the abrasive and repugnant manner in which an activity leader treats children. In a very brief period, a successful neighborhood playground program could be virtually destroyed by the nonconforming actions of a single individual.

Employees who enjoy their work and who treat people with respect and courtesy are invaluable in helping to establish a warm and friendly atmosphere. This type of employee is a definite asset and will make a positive contribution to community relations. However, employees unable to effectively contribute to the development and maintenance of such a desirable environment should be transferred to a position which does not require them to confront the public. If this is not possible, and if skills in human relations are not developed, termination may be necessary.

Media Relations

Numerous decisions are made by media personnel which affect community leisure service programs. Decisions are made daily regarding the coverage and reporting of community events, the posture of editorial statements, the identification of feature story subjects, the amount of copy which should be cut or edited, and the selection of news releases to be published or announced.

Role of Administrator

Functioning in their respective capacities, reporters, editors, station managers, publishers, audio-visual technicians, and broadcasters, play vital roles in determining the delivery of leisure service public and community relations efforts. Therefore, it becomes the responsibility of the leisure service administrator to develop and institute appropriate measures designed to influence media representatives toward the rendering of decisions considered favorable to their program.

Role of the Leisure Service Employees

From top to bottom, leisure service employees must be apprised of the necessity and importance of fostering and sustaining solid relationships with members of the media. It must be brought to their attention that media personnel, similar to themselves, have job responsibilities and deadlines which must be met. It should be stressed that leisure service employees are to extend every assistance possible to help members of the media accomplish their jobs. For example, if a television station were dispatching a crew to film a feature story, plans should be made to meet them upon arrival, to provide sufficient parking space, and to assist with the transport of their equipment.

Providing full cooperation to media personnel usually accrues positive benefits. When treated well, most individuals tend to reciprocate in a like manner. In the case of media personnel, their appreciation is often reflected by the nature of the coverage and exposure allocated to the agency.

Developing Positive Relationships

Basic to the development of positive relationships is the extension of respect and courtesy. All media personnel encountered by leisure service employees should be afforded the utmost in courtesy and respect. They should be warmly greeted and made to feel welcome and comfortable. All leisure service employees should make a sincere attempt to remember the names of media representatives to whom they are introduced. To address an individual by name engenders a sense of importance to that person. He or she will develop an affinity for the agency much more rapidly knowing that they are known and recognized by the personnel.

Once a friendly and cooperative relationship has been developed with media personnel, it must be sustained and deepened. The following are guidelines which if observed will help to maintain the bonds of a good relationship:

1. All information given to the media should be accurate. Issuance of false or inaccurate information may prove embarrassing and could lead to a deterioration of relationships.
2. All copies submitted to the media should be clean, accurate, and available well in advance of established deadlines.
3. News releases intended for announcement and publication on a specific date should be distributed as early as possible.
4. Leisure service personnel should be punctual in keeping all appointments with members of the media.
5. All media representatives should have equal access to program information, news releases, and interviews. There should be no favoritism.
6. When a change in scheduling is made, it should be brought immediately to the attention of the media personnel. Nothing is more aggravating to media representatives than to arrive at a site to cover a scheduled event only to find that it has either been canceled, postponed, or moved to another location.

Finally, leisure service administrators should keep in mind that media personnel require and seek the same need satisfactions as does the rest of society. Realizing that the need for esteem is basic in everyone, the wise administrator will institute some form of recognition whereby the department can express its appreciation to the media personnel for their efforts and contributions to the program. This esteem-building recognition may be achieved by sending a complimentary letter to the employee and his or her employer or by staging a public ceremony. Regardless of the mode used to express the department's appreciation, the most important thing is that the individual knows that his or her efforts have been noticed and are valued.

Summary

One characteristic usually associated with successful community leisure service programs is their ability to design, institute, and sustain effective public, community, and media relations. To achieve this objective, leisure service administrators must be sensitive to the need of each segment of the community. In addition, administrators must also possess an understanding of the communication process as well as the various modes of delivery.

Public relations efforts are aimed toward providing the public with information regarding the program's goals and objectives, activities and events sponsored, and future plans. Community relations are concerned both with providing opportunities for residents to have "a piece of the action" in the decision making process and with efforts intended to create a positive image of the program within the community. Media relations focus upon the development and maintenance of a good rapport between media representatives and leisure service personnel.

Numerous vehicles exist for the delivery of public, community, and media relations efforts, ranging from public speaking to the production of 16-millimeter motion pictures. Each mode of communication possesses both positive and negative characteristics dependent upon the circumstances surrounding their intended use. Leisure service administrators are responsible for selecting the communication vehicle(s) capable of generating the greatest positive results for a given situation.

Leisure service personnel should be knowledgeable about media copy deadlines and the techniques used to develop news releases. To implement and sustain public, community, and media relations requires "teamwork." All leisure services personnel must be willing to work in a cooperative manner. When interacting with the public, leisure service employees must conduct themselves in an appropriate manner at all times. Supervisory measures must be instituted to monitor employee conduct. Individuals identified as unable or unwilling to conform to established conduct standards should be placed in positions not requiring interface with the public. If such transfers are not possible, and if the employees are unable to develop human relations skills, then it may be necessary to terminate their employment.

Administrators most successful in the area of public, community, and media relations are those who possess good human relations skills. Administrators should seek every possible opportunity to publicly acknowledge the contributions made to the leisure service program by community residents, public officials, and media representatives. This public recognition provides the individual with a "stroking" effect and helps the person in meeting his or her esteem needs.

Study Questions

1. How would you explain the process of communication and the interrelationship of the various phases?
2. What problems must be taken into consideration when constructing a public relations campaign for an urban area?
3. What are some of the desired outcomes which should be sought through a public relations effort?
4. Can you identify and describe five different media which can be used to disseminate public relations information?
5. How might a community leisure service administrator seek to develop solid, friendly departmental relationships with community residents?
6. What is the value of conducting a community survey? Are there any potential dangers associated with the use of community surveys?
7. What is the proper way to prepare a press release?
8. What is the value of developing and maintaining friendly relationships between the community leisure service department and members of the media?
9. In the leisure service personnel hierarchy, who are the persons cast into front-line roles regarding the promotion of community and media relations?

References

Bannon, Joseph J. *Leisure Resources: Its Comprehensive Planning.* Englewood Cliffs, N.J.: Prentice-Hall, Inc., 1976.

Belasco, James A.; Hampton, David R.; and Price, Karl F. *Management Today.* New York: John Wiley & Sons, Inc., 1975.

Chase, Stuart. "Executive Communications: Breaking the Semantic Barrier." *Management Review.* 46 (1957): 4.

Kraus, Richard G. *Recreation Today: Programs, Planning and Leadership.* 2nd ed. Santa Monica, Ca.: Goodyear Publishing Co., Inc., 1977.

Kraus, Richard G., and Bates, Barbara J. *Recreation Leadership and Supervision: Guidelines for Professional Development.* Philadelphia: W. B. Saunders Co., 1975.

Kraus, Richard G., and Curtis, Joseph E. *Creative Administration in Recreation and Parks.* 2nd ed. St. Louis: The C. V. Mosby Co., 1977.

Meyer, Harold D., and Brightbill, Charles K. *Recreation Administration: A Guide to Its Practices.* Englewood Cliffs, N.J.: Prentice-Hall, Inc., 1956.

Meyer, Harold D., and Brightbill, Charles K. *Community Recreation: A Guide to Its Organization.* Englewood Cliffs, N.J.: Prentice-Hall, Inc., 1964.

Newsweek. January 9 (1978).

Sessoms, H. Douglas; Meyer, Harold D.; and Brightbill, Charles K. *Leisure Services: The Organized Recreation and Park System.* Englewood Cliffs, N.J.: Prentice-Hall, Inc., 1975.

Related Readings

Artz, Robert M.; Jarrell, Temple R.; and Parker, Adah. *Publicity Handbook.* Washington, D.C.: National Recreation and Parks Association, 1968.

Banfield, E. C. *Political Influence.* New York: The Free Press of Glencoe, 1962.

Bergin, Francis J. *Public Relations.* New York: Pitman, 1976.

Blumenthal, L. Roy. *The Practice of Public Relations.* New York: Macmillan, 1972.

Canfield, Bertrand R. *Public Relations: principles, cases, and problems.* 4th ed. Homewood, Ill., R. D. Irwin, 1964.

Cutlip, Scott M., and Center, Allen H. *Effective Public Relations.* Englewood Cliffs, N.J.: Prentice-Hall, Inc., 1971.

Jefkins, Frank W. *Marketing and PR Media Planning.* New York: Pergamon Press, 1974.

Kliment, S. A. "News Release as Marketing Tool." *Architectural Record*, July, (1977): 55.

Lesly, Philip. *Public Relations Handbook.* 3rd ed. Englewood Cliffs, N.J.: Prentice-Hall, Inc., 1967.

Levine, Carol, and Levine, Howard. *Effective Public Relations for Community Groups.* New York: Associated Press, 1969.

Scherer, Daniel. "Establishing Local Press Relations." *Parks and Recreation*, October, (1967): 36.

The Planning and Delivery of Competitive Leisure Service Programs

Objectives   After reading and comprehending this chapter, you should be able to:

1. Define the concept of competition.
2. List the types of competition and select those best suited to provide for the needs of a particular situation.
3. Identify a variety of tournament structures and discuss the values and limitations of each.
4. Design tournament structures which will accommodate a variety of situations.
5. Distinguish between the differing philosophies associated with leisure service award programs.
6. Explain the merits and limitations of various types of awards.
7. Understand the need for expanding award programs to provide each participant with a sense of accomplishment.

Competition

Competition permeates most forms of human interaction, and recreational programs are no exception. In fact, competitive events usually constitute an integral facet of the average community recreation program. Competitive activities range from highly active physical sports such as football and wrestling to mental games like checkers and backgammon.

What Is Competition?

As with many concepts, competition can be characterized as either positive or negative depending upon the nature of the activity, the intensity and form of competition employed, and the specific goals and objectives of the particular activity. However, prior to assessing the merits of competitive activities, evaluators should possess an understanding of the concept of competition and the various forms it may take.

Loy (1969, pp. 4-5) defines competition as, "A struggle for supremacy between two or more opposing sides. We interpret the phrase 'between two or more opposing sides' rather broadly to encompass between man and other objects of nature, both animate and inanimate." Slusher describes competition not only in terms of opposing forces but also with reference to the eventual outcome. He states (in Fait and Billings, 1974, p. 16) that competition is, "a contention of interests, that is, it is a rivalry between opposing forces (man, animal, or nature) in which the interests of both are not mutually attainable."

Direct Competition

Slusher's definition succinctly portrays *direct competition* which, by its very nature, necessitates that for each successful competitor at least one other competitor must fail. When applied to the human domain, Gallwey (1974, p. 119) states that:

. . . competition for many is merely an arena for venting aggression; it is taken as a proving ground for establishing who is the stronger, tougher, or smarter. Each imagines that by beating the other he has in some way established his superiority over him, not just in a game, but as a man.

As viewed by Gallwey, the major problem with competition is the placing of self-images on the line. Through winning one's self-image is enhanced, whereas suffering a loss creates a deflating effect, a questioning of one's self-worth.

Viewing direct competition from another perspective, an individual may develop a negative attitude toward a particular activity, the overall recreation program, or both when denied the opportunity for continued participation because of a failure to win or if prohibited from experiencing some measure of success. And certainly the creation of an environment contributing toward the development of such an attitude is contrary to the goals and objectives of humanistically oriented programs.

Game Theory

According to Graham (1977), game theorists describe a situation in which the ratio of winners to losers is 1:1 as being a *zero sum game*, i.e., the number of winners minus the number of losers equals zero. On the other hand, game theorists refer to a situation in which the number of losers exceeds the number of winners as a *negative sum game*. Inevitably, direct competition results in either a zero or negative sum game.

Indirect Competition

Direct competition, however, is not the sole form of competition available. A second type is commonly referred to as *indirect competition*. Independent of the need to determine winners and losers, indirect competition is capable of producing a greater number of successes than failures. Consequently, in terms of the game theorists, indirect competition may potentially produce a *positive sum game*, i.e., the number of successful competitors may exceed the number of competitors encountering failure (Graham, 1977).

Positive sum conditions are highly desirable for community recreation programs as they tend to stimulate and maintain participant interest in the various activities and special events comprising the recreation program. A successful and enjoyable recreative experience enhances the probability of one's continued involvement with an activity, an involvement which possibly may last a lifetime.

Indirect competition is often associated with activities in which participants compete against nature, a standard, or some object rather than against another individual or creature. Included in this category are activities such as surfing, distance swimming, jogging, and mountain climbing. But this stereotype is not necessarily accurate. Indirect competition may also be found to exist in activities which have traditionally been considered as representative of direct competition. Such activities would include chess, golf, tennis, bridge, scrabble, and so forth.

Cooperation

In direct competition, it is the responsibility of the participants to provide their opponents with the greatest challenge possible. Followed to logical conclusion, competition may then be considered as dependent upon and identical to cooperation. In referring to such a situation, Gallwey (1974, p. 123) states that, "Each player tries his hardest to defeat the other, but in this use of competition it isn't the other person we are defeating; it is simply a matter of overcoming the obstacles he presents." Thus, in the true sense of competition none of the participants need be defeated: all benefit through their respective efforts to provide and overcome challenges. In essence, each contributes toward the development and improvement of the other. When appropriately organized and administered, activities such as chess, golf, tennis, bridge, scrabble, and frisbee may reflect elements of both direct and indirect competition. And under such conditions these activities (which traditionally have been associated with zero and negative sum games) may produce positive sum games.

Balanced Competition

In recreation programming, there are instances when the introduction of the competitive elements are clearly unnecessary and undesirable. Instructional clinics, social gatherings, community dances, and cultural and ethnic displays are examples of functions where competition is usually considered inappropriate.

Nonetheless, many other aspects of programming are based on the concepts of competition. Wise administrators will provide opportunities for program participants to engage in both direct and indirect forms of competition. Just as research has indicated that direct competition may tend to foster rather than release aggressive behavior (Harris, 1973), exclusive exposure to indirect competition may result in individuals exhibiting a fear of direct confrontation. And certainly neither outcome is desirable. The key to sponsoring a healthy competitive recreation program is in providing a balance between direct and indirect competitive opportunities.

A major thrust of leisure service programming is to provide opportunities for as many individuals as possible to engage in a wide variety of activities and special events from which, hopefully, many recreational experiences will be derived. Competitive tournaments represent a very important vehicle for providing such opportunities.

Tournaments

The sponsorship of tournaments is a frequently employed method for providing participation opportunities. Successful tournament planning involves:

1. Clientele segmentation
2. Equalizing competition
3. Tournament structure selection

Clientele Segmentation

When an activity is considered for inclusion in the total recreation program, a major factor in its acceptance or rejection relates to the population it will serve. Targeting an activity to provide for one or more groups of potential participants is referred to as clientele segmentation. To illustrate the concept: proposers of a model racing tournament must identify whether the tournament is to be targeted toward the total community or specific segments such as youths, seniors, or special populations. In most instances, activities are targeted toward multiple segments of the population, if not the entire community. Basketball programs are a fine example. In activities such as basketball, programs are usually offered for boys and girls as well as men and women and they tend to be further divided into segments for youths, teens, young adults, the over 30 group, and seniors.

Clientele segmentation is often not necessary for the successful development of "mental" activity competitive tournaments, but for the highly physical sports its is usually considered mandatory. For example, individuals of all ages are capable of successfully competing in a checkers tournament but what would happen in a basketball tournament if individuals of all ages were randomly placed in the same tournament and scheduled to play against one another? The eventual outcome should be readily apparent—disaster!

Equalizing Competition

The most successful and enjoyable tournaments are those in which equitable, well-balanced competition is evidenced. Depending upon the nature of the activity, certain administrative measures may be applied to insure, at least in part, equalized competition.

Once the process of clientele segmentation has been completed, program administrators should consider further categorization of participants. For example, in a youth model racing tournament, divisions may be established for specific age groups, that is, seven and eight year olds. In teen, young adult, and over 30 basketball programs, separate divisions may be created for participants over and under six feet tall. A community field day, blueberry pie or watermelon eating contest for youths may be divided into categories based upon both age and weight.

In other activities such as chess, tennis, swimming, and bridge, participants may be further segmented on the basis of ability. Novices, intermediates, and masters would compete in separate tournaments. Participants might be allowed to determine their own classification or the tournament director might wish to establish specific classification eligibility criteria.

The use of a handicapping system allows participants of all ability levels to compete together in the same tournament. Golf and bowling are two activities in which the use of a handicapping system is prevalent. Handicapping is a proven method for equalizing competition. Individual handicaps may be established either prior to or following tournament competition. Assignment of handicaps prior to the commencement of competition requires that the participants submit score cards (the actual number is usually left to the discretion of the tournament director) indicating recent game results. Directors should be cautious about assigning pre-tournament handicaps: first, the process is time-consuming and second, the potential for "cheating" is great. Post-tournament handicaps are established on the basis of scores recorded during the actual tournament.

Finally, program administrators can provide accommodations for specific competitive interest levels. For example, within each clientele segmentation some individuals only wish to participate in an activity, such as softball, where the intent of all involved is focused strictly on performance and winning. On the other hand, there are those participants who are much more concerned with just playing and "having a good time." It is often wise to provide separate divisions for each group.

For a step-by-step explanation of tournament development and scheduling, the reader is referred to the Appendix.

Tournament Selection

A variety of tournament structures exist. Which is best designed to fulfill the needs of a specific situation? What are the positive and negative characteristics of each? Can the various designs be modified to accommodate differing situations? To answer these questions, an examination of the characteristics, functions, and operating procedures of the various tournament designs is necessary.

The most popular and thus the most commonly employed tournament designs may be placed into the following categories:

1. Elimination
2. Challenge
3. Round Robin

Each category possesses characteristics which may be considered either desirable or undesirable depending upon the intended outcomes of the given situation.

It is the responsibility of the recreation program director to understand and evaluate the intended outcomes of a competitive program and the options available and then to select the tournament which best serves both the situation and the participant's needs. In selecting a tournament format, directors must take into consideration the nature of the activity, the desires of the participants, and the goals and objectives of the recreation program. For example, if one program goal is to provide as many participation opportunities as possible, then sponsorship of a tournament in which *continued* participation is predicated upon winning will not contribute toward achievement of that goal. On the other hand, if the focus is one of determining a champion in the least amount of time, then selection of this type of tournament would be most appropriate.

Elimination Tournaments

The primary function of an elimination tournament is implied by its name—elimination. Such tournaments are designed to systematically reduce the number of participants to the point where only one, the champion, remains. Elimination tournaments are premised on the concept of winning, since failure to win may result in automatic removal from further participation. From the elimination concept, three basic tournament designs have evolved:

1. Single Elimination
2. Double Elimination
3. Consolation

Single Elimination Tournaments

The single elimination tournament is efficiently designed to expedite the process of establishing a "winner" or "champion." This design places minimum emphasis on participation and maximum demands on winning. By definition, a single loss results in immediate termination from further participation.

Construction of a single elimination tournament is strictly dependent upon the total number of entries to be accommodated. The tournament is developed by scheduling a series of contests with the winners of each progressing to the next round of competition and the losers being terminated.

Due to the rapid termination rate (fifty percent of the participants are eliminated following completion of their first round of competition), single elimination tournaments should be employed only under limited circumstances. For instance, single elimination is an ideal method for rapidly determining an activity champion. However, the use of single elimination tournaments under normal conditions tends to flaunt the basic goal of providing maximum participation opportunities.

All elimination tournaments, regardless of total entry, share a common principal—to reduce, via the first round of competition, the number of continuing entries to a power of two, that is, 2, 4, 8, 16, 32, 64, etc. Henceforth, such numbers will be referred to as *magic numbers.*[1] Adherence to the magic number concept is extremely important because failure to do so will necessitate awarding byes to one or more entries in each competitive round of the tournament. And if such a situation were to occur, one of the three entries reaching the semi-final round of competition would receive a bye into the championship contest. To avoid a catastrophic situation of this nature, it is imperative that the magic number rule be followed.

The term *bye* is defined as a situation in which an entry is not assigned an opponent and is thereby automatically advanced into the next round of competition. The use of byes should be avoided when possible, but when necessitated their use should be restricted to the first round of competition.

In an elimination tournament, if the initial entry is not a magic number, how can it be reduced to such a number? The process is explained by the following example. Assume that a single elimination badminton tournament is to be developed and that fifteen entries have been received. The tournament must be structured in such a manner that the initial entry is reduced to a magic number at the conclusion of the first round of competition. In this particular instance, the magic number closest to—but less than—the entry of fifteen is eight. For eight entries to remain following the first round of competition, seven entries must be eliminated. Since entries are only eliminated as the result of having lost a contest, the initial round should consist of seven contests which, of necessity, requires the participation of fourteen entries. Consequently, the remaining entry must receive a bye. The byed entry along with the

1. A term created by Pat Mueller (1971).

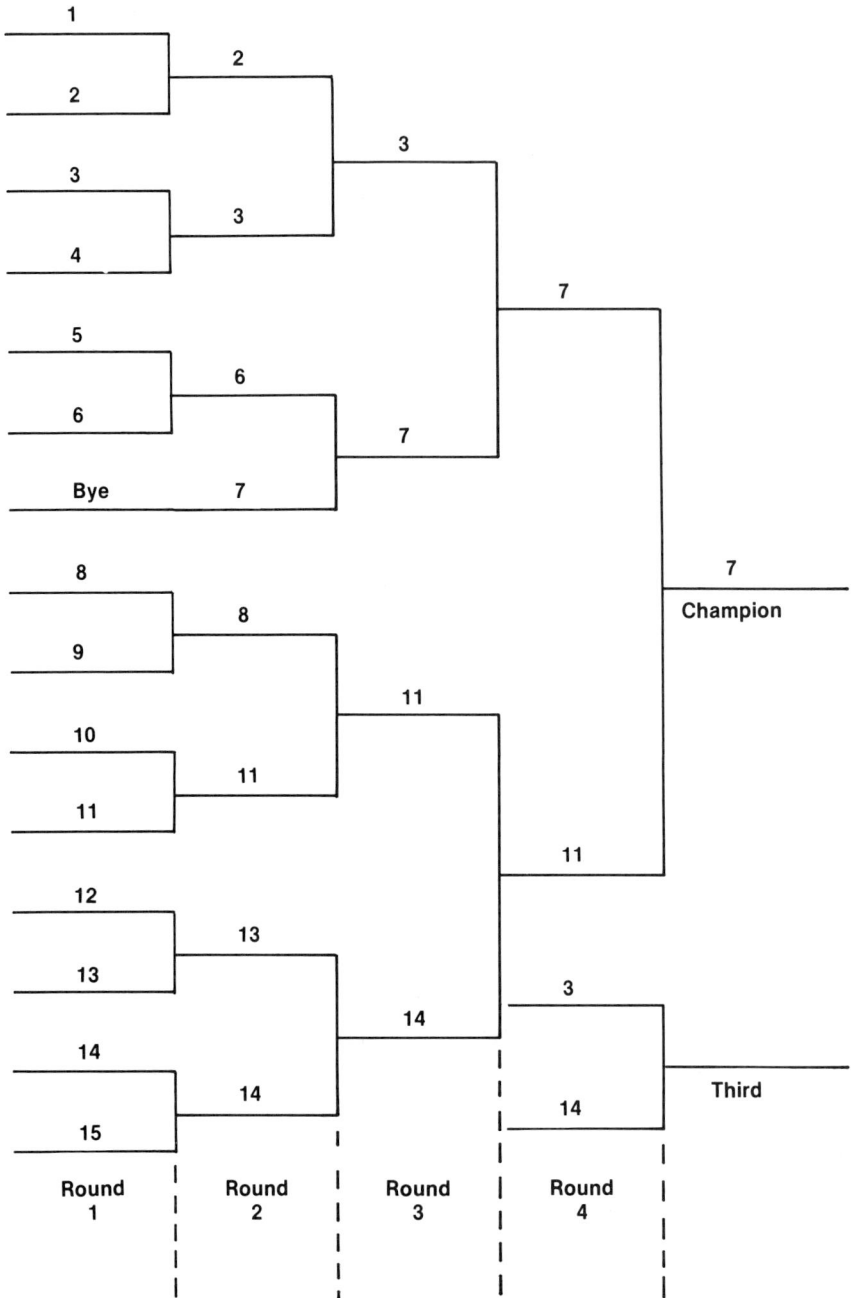

Figure 9.1   Single Elimination Tournament—Fifteen Entries

seven contest winners continues into the next round of competition and the magic number of eight has been attained.

Figure 9-1 illustrates a single elimination tournament designed to accommodate fifteen entries. Note that the single bye is located in the center of the structure and that the losers of the semi-final contests have been scheduled to compete for third place. Determination of a third place winner is an option which may be introduced into the single elimination design and as such represents the only instance whereby a defeated entry is afforded an opportunity for further competition. Often, the contest for third place is referred to as the *consolation match*.

Again, it must be emphasized that the single elimination structure offers minimum participation opportunity for over one-half of the tournament entries. Selection of this tournament is inappropriate, under most conditions, since it tends to create an atmosphere of discouragement for those participants who would prefer activity involvement on a continuing basis.

Double Elimination Tournaments

The double elimination concept is similar to that of single elimination except that the defeated entry is moved into a loser's bracket and is terminated from further competition only after being defeated for the second time. This format provides for greater participation than that available within the single elimination format (and thus is more in keeping with the goal of most recreation programs), but the primary emphasis continues to be on winning and the rapid identification of a champion. For scheduling purposes, it should be noted that a double elimination tournament requires a greater period of time to complete than does the single elimination format.

Again, irrespective of the total entry, the main purpose in the design of a double elimination tournament is to have the number of second round participants reduced to a magic number. In this case, a magic number must be arrived at in both the winner's and loser's brackets. Figure 9-2 displays a double elimination structure designed to accommodate eight entries. Note that because eight represents a magic number, the use of byes is not required in either bracket. Attention should also be paid to locating a loser from the upper-half of the winner's bracket in the lower-half of the loser's bracket and vice versa.

In the championship round, if the winner of the loser's bracket defeats the winner of the winner's bracket then both entries have a single defeat and thus a final, deciding contest must be scheduled to determine the champion. The losing entry in the final contest of the loser's bracket is usually considered as the third place finisher.

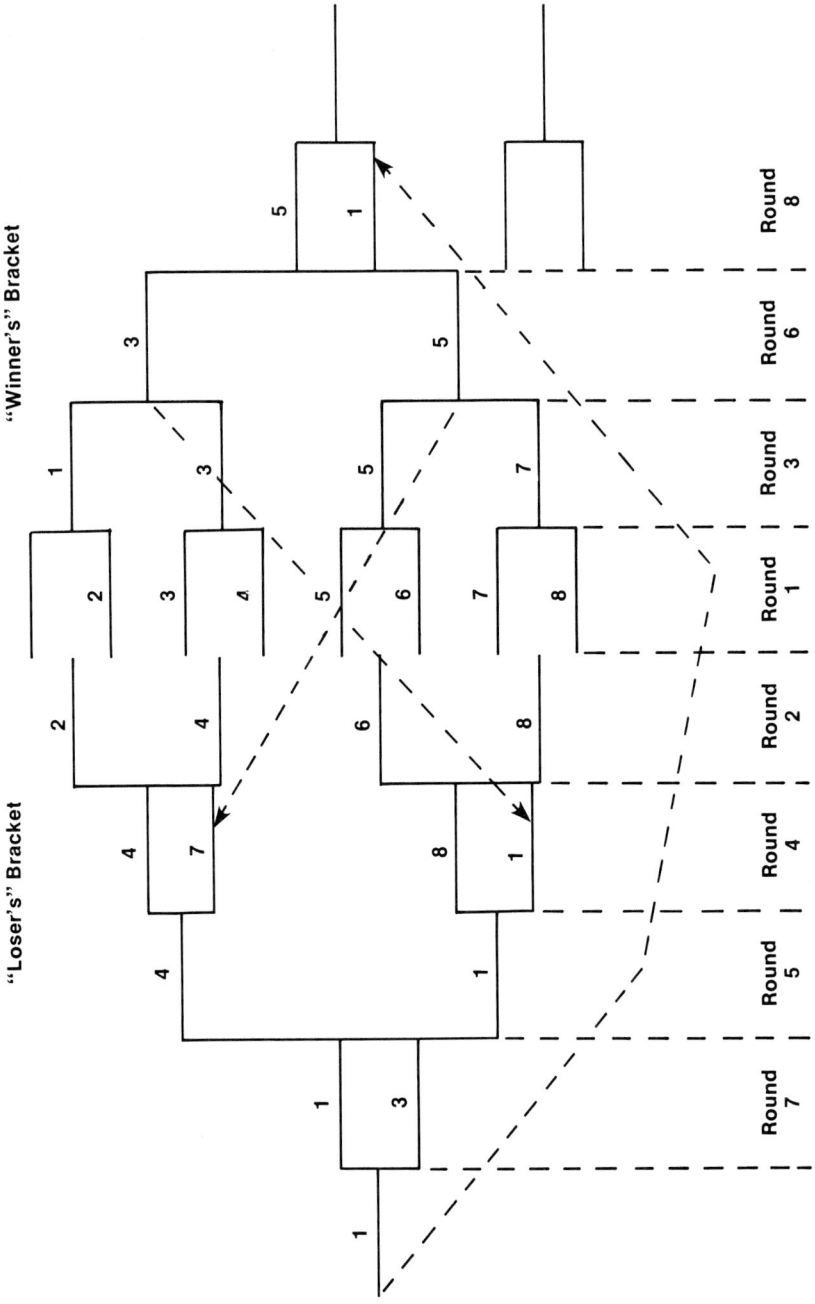

Figure 9.2 Double Elimination Tournament—Eight Entries

Consolation Tournaments

Consolation tournaments are similar to the double elimination format in that defeated entries are afforded an opportunity for continued participation. Basically, there are two types of consolation tournaments: Type A and Type B.

TYPE A CONSOLATION TOURNAMENTS

Further participation is provided only those entries losing their initial contest. Figure 9-3 illustrates a Type A consolation tournament.

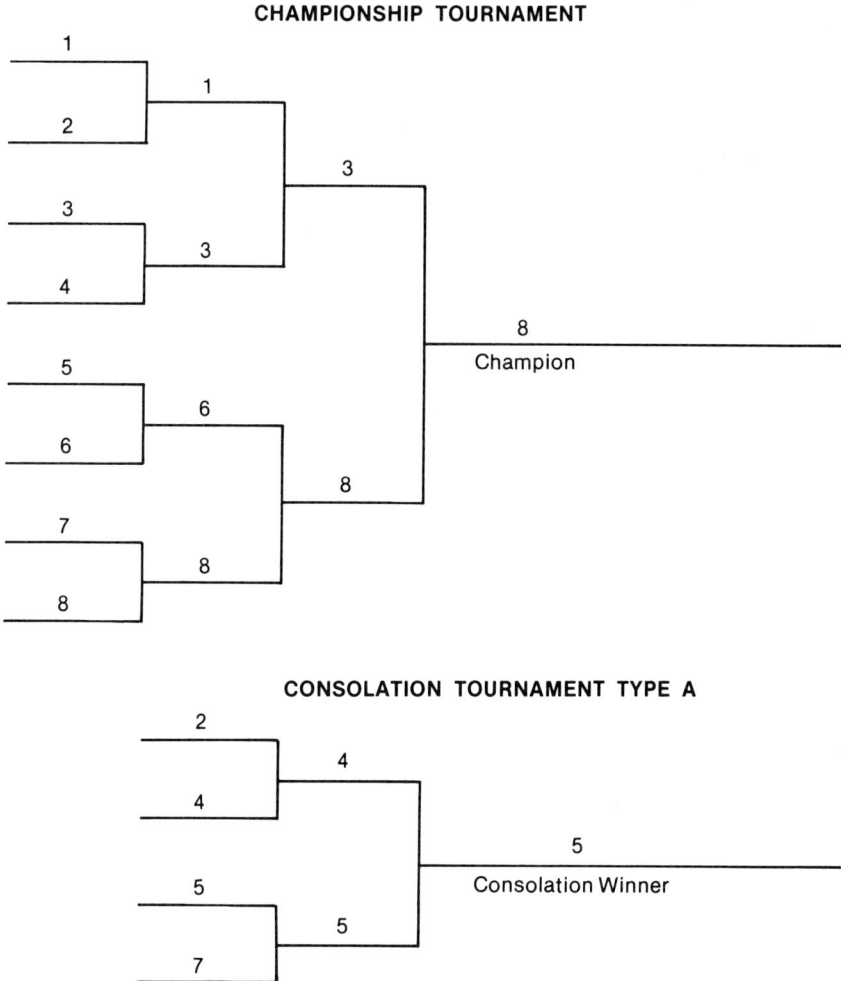

CHAMPIONSHIP TOURNAMENT

CONSOLATION TOURNAMENT TYPE A

Figure 9.3   Consolation Tournament Type A

TYPE B CONSOLATION TOURNAMENT

Type B operates much the same as the double elimination format: each defeated entry in the championship bracket, except the loser of the actual championship contest, is allowed to participate in the consolation tournament. Figure 9-4 represents a Type B consolation tournament.

Consolation tournaments possess two distinctive features. First, to qualify for participation an entry must have sustained a defeat in the

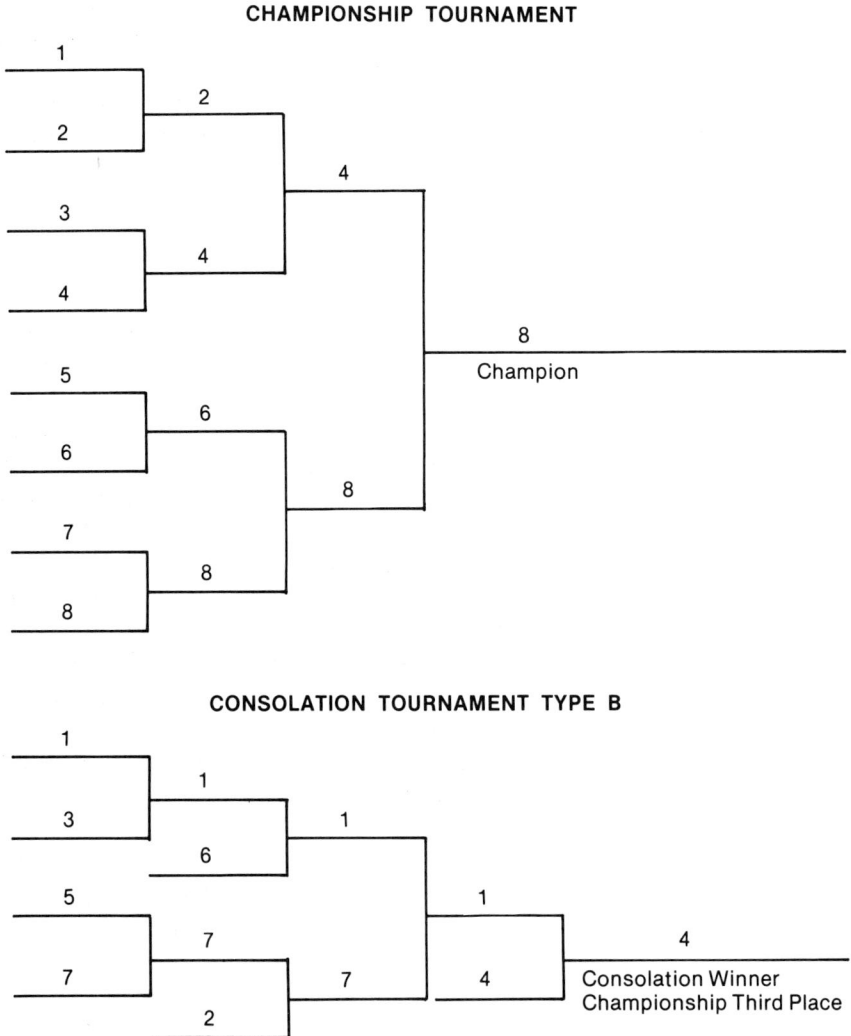

CHAMPIONSHIP TOURNAMENT

CONSOLATION TOURNAMENT TYPE B

Figure 9.4   Consolation Tournament Type B

championship bracket and second, the winner of the consolation tournament (unlike the winner of the loser's bracket in the double elimination tournament) is *not* eligible to compete for the overall championship. However, the winner of the Type B consolation tournament is normally considered to be the third place championship finisher.

Although placing strong emphasis on winning, consolation tournaments provide a greater opportunity for continued participation than that afforded by the single elimination format. A major disadvantage of the consolation tournament is that the winner of the consolation bracket is not eligible to compete for the overall championship, a situation which tends to increase the probability of forfeited contests.

Both elimination and consolation tournaments may be used for a wide range of recreational activities, not just competitive sport programs. For example, bridge, whist, chess, spelling, story telling, model racing, checkers, and backgammon tournaments are easily developed using any of the above designs.

Challenge Tournaments

How often has it been heard, "Given one more chance, I could have won!" The challenge tournament concept provides for just such opportunities. Challenge tournaments are most commonly employed in conjunction with individual and dual activities, but may also be effectively incorporated into team oriented events.

The challenge concept places greater emphasis on participation than on winning. Competitors issue and accept challenges from one another, attempting to rise to the top of the tournament structure through a series of successful challenges. However, winning is not a requisite for continued participation. Winning or losing, all entrants are provided an ongoing opportunity which only ceases with the conclusion of the tournament.

Challenge tournaments operate in the following manner. All interested individuals and teams submitting an entry are assigned a starting position within the tournament structure. Upon commencement, all entries seek to advance or maintain their respective positions. Upward mobility is achieved through the successful challenge of a team or individual possessing a position above that of the challenger. A successful challenge results in the challenger assuming the position held by the defeated opponent, who in turn must occupy the vacated lower position. In the event of an unsuccessful challenge, the participants' positions remain the same.

Two entries may not engage one another in successive challenges, regardless of the outcome of the initial encounter. Before a second challenge may be issued, one of the two participants must have engaged in at least one other contest with a third individual/team. Failure to adhere to this policy may lead to a situation whereby two entries continually challenge one another thus diminishing the upward mobility potential for other participants. If such a situation were to occur, the number of opponents available for challenge would be reduced thereby eroding, at least in part, the intent of the tournament design.

Participants are encouraged to issue and accept as many challenges as possible during the time alloted the tournament. It is important to note that prior to commencing the tournament, a termination date and time should be established and announced to each of the participating entries. At the point of conclusion, the entry residing in the uppermost position is declared the tournament winner.

Although many variations of the challenge concept exist, the two most popular structures are commonly referred to as ladder and pyramid tournaments.

LADDER TOURNAMENTS

The ladder design consists of a series of horizontal rungs placed in ascending order. Figure 9-5 illustrates the design of a ladder tournament.

Ladder Position 1   7

2   4

3   11

4   6

5   2

6   10

7   8

8   9

9   1

10   12

11   3

12   5

Note: Entry /8/ challenges entry /10/

If entry /8/ wins: If entry /8/ loses:

8   10

10   8

Figure 9.5 Ladder Tournament

Similar to a climbing ladder, the rungs are used to advance or descend from one position to another. The number of rungs may be as many or as few as desired. However, the number of entries assigned to a given ladder should be determined on the basis of two related factors: first, the amount of time allotted for the tournament and second, the probability of the entrant placed on the lowest rung having sufficient opportunity to climb to the pinnacle position within the allotted time.

Ladder tournaments operate strictly on the principle of vertical mobility: to progress an entrant must successfully challenge an opponent residing in a higher position on the ladder. Because continued participation is not predicated upon winning, won-loss records compiled during the tournament have no bearing on determining the champion. Thus, there is no need to maintain records of contest results.

PYRAMID TOURNAMENTS

The pyramid tournament derives its name from its design. As with all pyramids, the structure is supported by a broad base and it possesses sides which extend upward and inward until they come together to form a point. Pyramid tournaments may accommodate an infinite number of participants due to the expansion ability inherent in the design. To provide for additional entries, another base level need simply be added. It should be noted, however, that each added base level must contain one more entry slot than the level directly above.

Theoretically, pyramid tournaments may be as large as desired. Yet, from a pragmatic stance their size should be determined by both the time allotted the tournament and the potential of the lowest level entries being able to reach the pinnacle. Careful consideration of each criterion is vital to the success of the tournament.

A second and major advantage of the pyramid design is that it allows for challenge flexibility. Competitors have the option of selecting their opponent from any of those residing on the next higher level. Finally, this particular design eliminates the problem of assigning a single entry to the lowest level.

Figure 9-6 presents a pyramid tournament designed to accommodate a maximum of fifteen entries. Note that the lowest level contains the greatest number of entries and that with each ascending level the number of entry slots is reduced by one. It is also important to observe that for the tournament to function properly not all the entry slots need be filled. However, when the number of entries is insufficient to fill each slot, the open positions *must always* be located on the lowest level. For example, if a tournament designed to accommodate fifteen, as illustrated in Figure 9-6, only attracts thirteen entries then slots fourteen and fifteen would remain vacant. Failure to fill each of the lowest level slots does not ad-

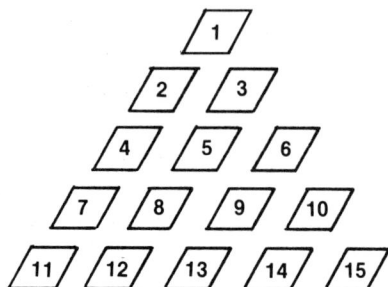

Example A:

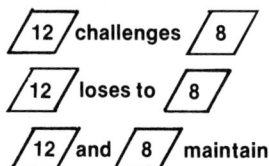 challenges

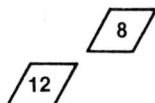 loses to

12 and 8 maintain

present positions

Example B:

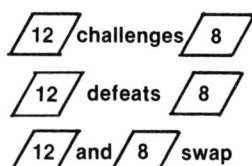 challenges

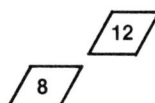 defeats

12 and 8 swap

positions

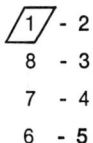

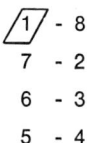

Figure 9.6 Pyramid Tournament

Round 1	Round 2	Round 3	Round 4
1 - 2	1 - 8	1 - 7	1 - 6
8 - 3	7 - 2	6 - 8	5 - 7
7 - 4	6 - 3	5 - 2	4 - 8
6 - 5	5 - 4	4 - 3	3 - 2

Round 5	Round 6	Round 7
1 - 5	1 - 4	1 - 3
4 - 6	3 - 5	2 - 4
3 - 7	2 - 6	8 - 5
2 - 8	8 - 7	7 - 6

Figure 9.7 Round Robin Tournament—Eight Entries

versely effect the tournament. In fact, additional participants may be placed in these slots during the course of the tournament.

Multiple ladder or pyramid tournaments may be conducted simultaneously. When an overall champion is desired, the winners of each tournament may be invited to compete in a championship tournament—usually consisting of a single elimination format.

Both ladder and pyramid tournaments are well adapted for use in a variety of recreational activities and are especially suited to provide for continuous participation. Yet, each possesses a major liability in that participants must constantly communicate with one another to establish times, dates, and locations to engage in issued and accepted challenges. Unfortunately, communication can frequently present a difficult task. When communication between participants breaks down or when misunderstandings arise, the quality and success of the tournament is jeopardized. Nonetheless, if providing opportunities for maximum participation is important then challenge tournaments offer an excellent means for this to occur.

Round Robin Tournaments

Round robin tournaments effectively provide organized, pre-scheduled participation opportunities. The design of this type of tournament enables each entry to compete against one another on a scheduled basis, regardless of respective won-loss records. In a round robin tournament, primary emphasis is placed on participation. Individual entries may express concern for their won-loss record, but such data exert no influence upon the tournament except with regard to position play (a concept to be discussed further in this chapter).

Design of a round robin tournament is dependent upon both the number of entries and the number of scheduled contests desired for each entry. This decision subsequently determines the maximum number of entries that a given league can accommodate.

To illustrate the process of designing a round robin structure, assume that eight entries are to be scheduled for a model racing tournament in which each entry is to be provided seven contests. To determine which entries are to compete against one another in each round of contests, list the entries in a random order. For example:

1. Flash
2. Swat
3. Fire Fly
4. Big Red

5. Buttercup
6. Nuts-n-Bolts
7. Speedo
8. Snail

In constructing the actual schedule of contests, the entry listed as number $\boxed{1}$ is placed in a stationary position around which the remaining entries rotate in a clockwise direction—rotating one position for each schedule round. Figure 9-7 portrays the development of an eight entry round robin tournament. Note that in figure 9-7 the total number of entries is an *even* number. Consequently, it is not necessary to use byes.

Round 1	Round 2	Round 3	Round 4
1 - 2	7 - 1	6 - 7	5 - 6
7 - 3	6 - 2	5 - 1	4 - 7
6 - 4	5 - 3	4 - 2	3 - 1
5 - /Bye/	4 - /Bye/	3 - /Bye/	2 - /Bye/

Round 5	Round 6	Round 7
4 - 5	3 - 4	2 - 3
3 - 6	2 - 5	1 - 4
2 - 7	1 - 6	7 - 5
1 - /Bye/	7 - /Bye/	6 - /Bye/

Figure 9.8   Round Robin Tournament—Seven Entries

Also note that in this particular example, seven rounds of competition are necessary to complete the tournament.

USE OF BYES

When leagues contain an even number of entries, the use of byes is never necessary and the number of scheduled rounds of competition will always be equal to the number of entries minus one. On the other hand, leagues consisting of an *odd* number of entries must always employ the use of byes. Furthermore, the number of competition rounds will always be equal to the number of desired contests plus one. In leagues with an odd number of entries, a different entry receives the bye in each round of competition.

Contest pairings are determined in leagues with an odd entry by placing the /Bye/ in a stationary position and rotating the entries around it in a clockwise direction, moving one position for each scheduled round of competition. Figure 9-8 demonstrates the scheduling process for a seven entry league. Observe that although each entry is scheduled for only six contests, the use of byes necessitates that the number of competition rounds be equal to the number of desired contests plus one, in this instance seven.

Establishing the Number of Contests

The number of contests to be scheduled for each participant is often determined prior to actual receipt of the tournament entries. In such instances, how may a recreation program director insure that each participant will be scheduled for the desired number of contests? One method effectively employed is to assign to each league only the exact number of entries necessary to produce the desired number of contests. For this method to effectively function, tournament entries are often restricted to multiples of the maximum league entry. To illustrate, if it were determined that each participant should be scheduled for seven contests, then eight would constitute the maximum league entry. Thus, to insure that each league will contain a maximum entry the total tournament entry would be restricted to a multiple of eight, that is 8, 16, 24, 32, etc.

But, the introduction of a policy limiting entries violates a basic principle of recreation programming: to provide within the constraints of time, finances, and facilities maximum participation opportunity. If this fundamental principle is to be honored, how then may the number of scheduled round robin tournament contests be equated for each entry when often the total entry received is either greater or less than a multiple of the established maximum league size?

There is a method for resolving such problems. Once the total tournament entry has been received, as many leagues as possible containing the maximum entry should be established. The remaining entries should be then grouped together to form a final, less than maximum league. It is extremely important to note, however, that under no circumstances should a league be created containing less than one-half of the maximum entry. When the number of remaining entries constitutes less than one-half the maximum league entry, an established maximum entry league must be dissolved and combined with the remaining entries. In this way, two less than maximum leagues may be formulated—each containing an entry equal to or greater than one-half the maximum entry.

Round robin scheduling techniques applied to leagues with less than the maximum entry fail to produce the desired number of contests for each participant. To demonstrate the point: if entries are to participate in seven contests then all leagues containing eight entries will automatically produce the desired schedule. However, a seven entry league in the same tournament will only provide each entry with six contests. To rectify unequal situations of this nature, some means must be employed to produce the seventh contest. One practical method for achieving this goal is through the use of a technique referred to as position play.

Position Play

The term *position play* is used to describe a scheduling technique whereby the won-loss records of league entries are used to determine contest opponents. Position play is usually introduced at the conclusion of a tournament and is normally employed to provide scheduled contests for leagues which, through normal round robin scheduling, fail to produce the desired number of contests per participant.

Position play functions in a rather simple manner. At a point just prior to the scheduling of position play contests, the won-loss records of the league teams are rank-ordered. Any rank-order ties are dissolved on

Randomly Assigned Entry Number	Entry Name	Won-Loss Record	Rank-Order
1	Apples	5 - 0	1
2	Grapes	3 - 2	3
3	Oranges	0 - 5	6
4	Peaches	4 - 1	2
5	Bananas	1 - 4	5
6	Pears	2 - 3	4

Position Play Schedule
Based Upon Rank-Order

1 vs 2		Apples vs Peaches
3 vs 4	Therefore	Grapes vs Pears
5 vs 6		Bananas vs Oranges

Figure 9.9   Position Play

the basis of predetermined criterion, that is, total offensive points, total pin fall, etc. If a tie persists, a second criterion or a flip of a coin may be used to decide the issue.

As shown in Figure 9-9, position play opponents are determined by placing the entries into the position play slots corresponding to their rank-ordered position. Because position play tends to create great interest among participants, it should normally be reserved for the final round of competition. Frequently, first place entries have only one more recorded victory than the second place entries. Thus, the position play presents an opportunity for those in second place to challenge and possibly defeat the league leader thereby creating a tie for the league championship. When such a situation occurs, a final and deciding championship contest must be scheduled.

Because byes must be employed in round robin and position play scheduling for leagues containing an odd number and less than maximum entry, it becomes impossible to equate the number of scheduled contests for each league entry. This unfortunate result can not be avoided because, in effect, the entry receiving the bye in the position play is really being denied the opportunity to participate due to the lack of an opponent. In fact, when position play is introduced more than once in an odd entry league schedule, it is possible that the same entry may receive the bye each time because of its rank-order position at the time of determining position play opponents.

Double Round Robin Tournaments

A double round robin tournament simply represents a repetition of the single round robin scheduling format. Under certain conditions a double round robin will provide the desired number of contests for a less than maximum league. When such circumstances occur the double round robin is an excellent technique for equalizing league play.

Special Consideration in Awarding Byes

At best, the awarding of byes is a difficult task and one that is often subject to criticism. Most criticism tends to be generated when byes are incorporated into an elimination tournament format. The selection of criteria to identify which entries are to receive byes represents a significant issue. In an effort to provide insulation against charges of favoritism, bias, and discrimination recreation administrators are strongly advised to establish bye awarding criteria prior to the commencement of an activity and only after a thorough examination of the potential ramifications of each criterion.

Inasmuch as the greatest bye awarding problems are usually centered around elimination tournaments, a review is in order. For the most part, elimination tournaments may be divided into three categories: general tournaments, tie dissolving tournaments, and championship tournaments.

The assignment of byes in a general elimination tournament is usually accomplished through one of two popular methods. The first involves assigning the bye to the entry having compiled the best won-loss record in a prior tournament, or to the entry perceived by the director (or a committee) as possessing the greatest championship potential. The second method consists of simply awarding all byes on a random basis; a method much more defensible than the first.

Records compiled in previous tournaments frequently have little, if any, significant value in predicting future success or failure. Thus, data of this nature are often (and should be) considered invalid as a bye awarding criterion. For general elimination tournaments, it is recommended that byes be awarded strictly on a random basis.

League of four entries, each to play six contests

Round 1	Round 2	Round 3
/1/ - 2	/1/ - 3	/1/ - 4
3 - 4	4 - 2	2 - 3

Round 4	Round 5	Round 6
/1/ - 2	/1/ - 3	/1/ - 4
3 - 4	4 - 2	2 - 3

Note: Rounds 4, 5, and 6 are simply a repeat of Rounds 1, 2, and 3.

Figure 9.10 Double Round Robin Tournament

From another perspective, however, the awarding of byes in a tournament specifically designed to dissolve a tie should not necessarily be made on a random basis. For example, if three entries are tied for a league championship and during the course of the tournament Entry A defeated both Entries B and C, then Entry A should automatically receive the bye. The winner of Entries B and C's contest would then challenge Entry A for the championsip. However, if no differing criteria existed between the tied entries or if tie breaking criteria had not been established prior to the start of the tournament, then it would be only appropriate for all byes to be awarded on a random basis.

Some recreation program directors prefer statistical data to any other form of criteria for identifying bye recipients. Use of these criteria, however, may potentially produce some unnecessary, undesirable, and rather serious effects. It can, for example, cause too much emphasis to be placed on the cumulative results of each contest. Aware that statistical data will be used to determine the awarding of byes, entries may consciously strive to generate the highest (or lowest dependent upon the criterion) results from each contest. To this end, many entries may restrict participation to their best contestants. And often in the pursuit of statistics, sportsmanship and fair play are forgotten—a situation which can easily lead to undesirable and possibly dangerous confrontations between participants. In addition, participation in an activity may come to be perceived as a form of work rather than a recreative opportunity. Winning and winning big may become the primary objective. And surely recreational tournaments are neither designed, instituted, promoted, nor conducted to spawn such results.

In a championship tournament, the awarding of byes constitutes a vital decision making process, one which may ultimately contribute heavily toward determining the eventual champion. In this type of tournament, many directors tend to favor awarding byes to those entries possessing the best won-loss records or to the defending champion. The fact of the matter is that for a director (or even a committee) to attempt to compare and rank-order the won-loss records of entries, each the champion of a respective league, is as foolish and invalid as attempting to compare apples and oranges. In a similar vein, the fact that an entry may be the defending champion suggests nothing about its current ability compared to the other entrants and therefore should have absolutely no bearing upon the awarding of byes. The only method justifiable, and thus recommended, is to award byes in a championship tournament strictly on the basis of chance.

But how may byes be awarded on a chance (random) basis? One efficient and fair technique involves the use of random-ordered numbers, each representing a tournament entry. To employ this technique a Table of Random Numbers (usually found in most statistics books) is required.

The initial step of the process consists of randomly generating numbers one through whatever number of entries are to be included in the tournament. The randomly generated numbers are then recorded, in the sequence obtained, on the tournament structure.

The next step requires an arbitrary listing of the tournament entries followed by a second generation of random-ordered numbers. Numbers from the second set are then assigned, in their generated order, to the listed tournament entries. In the final step each entry is placed into the tournament slot bearing the corresponding number.

Awards

A benchmark of contemporary society is its penchant to recognize achievement, both individual and collective. As a population, we are continually exhorted to win, to continually strive for success. And once success has been acquired, we are conditioned to anticipate receipt of some form of external recognition. The concept of recognition has a strong association with many of the activities commonly sponsored by the average leisure service agency.

Philosophical Conflicts

Controversy has historically existed regarding the incorporation of awards into leisure service programs. Opponents argue that leisure activities should be designed to allow the participants the opportunity to gain a positive experiences and that this in itself should represent ample reward for having participated, for having achieved. Proponents of this philosophy further argue that goal attainment automatically produces an intrinsic reward—a personal feeling of success, a sense of accomplishment and satisfaction that does not necessitate external recognition. Furthermore, opponents contend that awards tend to foster an attitude of participation simply to gain a "prize" rather than participating purely for the sake of the activity and the enjoyment it provides. Finally, award opponents believe that leisure service programs should provide an escape from the pressures of the "everyday world" and that the concepts of a humanistically oriented program become obstructed if the quest for achievement—to win, to succeed—becomes overemphasized as the result of the introduction of an external award program.

Award proponents, on the other hand, argue that leisure service activities represent a special facet of life—a facet designed to educate and prepare participants (especially youth) to cope successfully with life's various problems. Therefore, it is held that the recreation program environment should replicate those conditions evidenced and encountered in everyday life. Thus, award programs are encouraged because to withhold them would create an environment alien to that existing in most other aspects of "real" life. Proponents argue that leisure activities should assist participants in acquiring habits of extraordinary effort and a spirit of achievement—attributes necessary if one is to succeed in life. For individuals of this persuasion, the striving for awards and the associated external recognition is viewed as an excellent method for producing a success oriented population. Extrinsic rewards represent a key motivator for participation and extraordinary performance. Proponents contend that failure to provide awards tends to dampen interest thereby reducing incentives for participation in the various activities and the motivation for superior performance.

Awards are a traditional and useful part of most community recreation programs. When used skilfully they can enhance the human results of these programs without incurring the liabilities which accompany many awards programs. To avoid potential negative aspects of awards, policies must be devised carefully.

Developing an Awards Program

Prior to incorporating awards into a program, several important questions must first be resolved. For what are awards to be presented? What criteria will be used to select recipients? What form will the award take? When should they be presented? Should awards be used to generate publicity?

AWARDS FOR WHAT?

The initial problem is one of determining the areas for which awards will be presented. In addition to the traditional award categories, program administrators are encouraged to establish awards for such things as sportsmanship, participation, and other value oriented areas appropriate to the specific activity. For example, all community field day participants might be presented a ribbon in recognition of their participation. Adoption of this type of awards program (even though additional awards may be presented to those individuals achieving in the various events) provides recognition to each and every person for their efforts. Likewise, the number of special award categories could be expanded so that a greater number of participants (ideally all) emerge as "winners." To illustrate the point, in a bicycle decorating contest sufficient award categories could be devised to provide each entry with an award for having a first, second, or third place bicycle. In this way no participant is left out, no participant's efforts go unrecognized. The major point is that as long as awards are part of a program, administrators should strive to enable as many participants as possible to share in the external expression of achievement.

AWARD CRITERIA

Award categories having been selected, the next problem is to determine those criteria to be employed in identifying recipients. It is extremely important that all award selection criteria be established prior to commencement of the activity. Program directors should state award criteria in writing and make copies available to participants upon request. The availability of written criteria will help avoid potential complaints of bias, unfairness, and so on. Prudent administrators will insure that "secret" criteria neither exist nor enter into the decision making processes.

JUDGING CRITERIA

It is of equal importance that award criteria be clearly defined for all activities employing a judge or team of judges and that printed copies of the criteria be made available to the judge(s) well in advance of the contest or event. Failure to provide such guidelines may result in unfair, erroneous, inconsistent judging—judging which although done in good faith could nonetheless destory the credibility of the particular activity and inflict severe damage upon the reputation of the entire recreation program.

TYPES OF AWARDS

Awards may range from simple ribbons to elaborate trophies. Which type should be selected? The answer to this question is situational and dependent upon several factors including the nature of the activity, the nature of the participants, and the philosophies possessed by the program director and the sponsoring institution or agency. And of course, budgetary considerations play an important role in determining the types of awards featured by a program. Some of the more popular forms of awards include:

1. Ribbons
2. Certificates
3. Pins and tie tacks
4. Key rings
5. Mugs and trays
6. Personal attire (ties, jackets, sweaters, t-shirts)
7. Gift certificates
8. Photographs
9. Plaques and trophies
10. Medals

There is no single "best" type of award. Some program directors prefer plaques, small trophies, or medals while others opt for utilitarian items such as mugs, trays, or t-shirts. For group activities, photographs usually enjoy a measure of popularity. Astute administrators will conduct a participant survey to ascertain award preferences. A survey may reveal that different types of awards are preferred by different segments of the program's clientele. Younger participants have a tendency to select plaques and trophies, whereas more mature segments often prefer utilitarian items.

PERSONALIZED AWARDS

From a humanistic perspective, personalized awards are always encouraged. For example, plaques or trophies which provide a plate on which to engrave the name of the recipient are preferable to the nonidentifiable type. Ribbons with an attached identification tag and individual or group photographs are highly desirable.

Purchase of Awards

Program directors are advised to acquire awards as early as possible, preferably prior to the commencement of the activity. Adherence to this policy will insure sufficient time to rectify incorrect shipments or damaged, imperfect articles. Nothing is more discouraging than to receive an awards shipment just prior to the time for presentation and to discover that the wrong order has been sent or that the quality is unacceptable.

Presentation of Awards

When should awards be presented and in what manner? These two questions tend to evoke a variety of responses. Again, there is no single approach which fits every situation. Some recreation administrators prefer to present awards immediately following the conclusion of an activity while others are prone to wait until a formal presentation ceremony can be held. Dependent upon the philosophy of the sponsoring agency and the program director, the award ceremony may either be simple or elaborate: it may range from simply handing out the awards to the presentation of formal speeches.

Since the excitement of having achieved a desired result is greatest at the moment of success, it is recommended that awards be presented as close to that moment as possible. It is during this period that personal recognition usually has the most impact and meaning to the individual recipients. It is further recommended that the ceremony be kept brief and to the point. Excited award recipients are usually not interested in listening to long speeches nor participating in lengthy functions.

Although usually held at a time somewhat removed from the conclusion of an activity, the presentation of awards at an elaborate banquet or assembly is quite popular and does have merit. Some individuals may consider the award ceremony to be a bore because the thrill of accomplishment has worn off. For others, however, the ceremony serves as an opportunity to rekindle the emotions associated with achievement. In addition, award ceremonies provide an opportunity for recipients to receive recognition not only from their fellow competitors but also from their family, friends, and the community in general.

Award Publicity

Publicity is usually generated through the availability and presentation of awards, whether desired or not. The problem to be resolved, therefore, is one of determining the type and amount of publicity that should be generated. Yet, as is so often true, the solution is not easily achieved. The philosophies held by the program administrator, sponsoring agency or institution, and the media personnel each play an important role in determining the nature and extent of publicity attributed to the awards program.

Some recreation administrators and agencies seek to gain maximum program visibility and publicity through the promotion of awards and recipients via internal and external media. Operating under such a philosophy, their photographs, press releases, and other communication materials tend to focus on the "quest for excellence" and "hailing of the victor." Yet, when handled in a responsible and proper manner this type of publicity can prove to be beneficial to both the participant and the agency.

Other administrators, on the other hand, might be more inclined to treat award publicity in a different fashion. Rather than having the publicity focus on the achiever or the award, the communications issued by these administrators might cast attention toward the benefits derived by all those who participated in the program.

To minimize exploitation of achievement, competition, and winning, program administrators often invite members of the local media to a meeting for the purpose of explaining the philosophical goals and objectives upon which the community's recreation program is premised. Through such a meeting, the recreation administrator should attempt to enlist the support of the media personnel in promoting the various activities and special events in a manner reflecting the program's philosophy.

Summary

Competitive recreation activities constitute an important and integral portion of the overall community program. Consequently, the successful planning and delivery of competitive programs represents a serious and important undertaking—one primarily dependent upon the goals and objectives established by the sponsoring agency or institution, and the program administrator's knowledge of competition, tournaments, award programs, and the application of a humanistic philosophy to competitive activity programs.

Direct competition with its resulting zero sum and negative sum games is the most common form of competitive tournament programming. However, for a balanced program indirect competition is extremely important. Without competitive balance, the needs of a large segment of the community population will possibly not be met.

Although most tournaments are designed to accommodate direct competition, elements of indirect competition may concurrently be introduced. Activity programs which promote positive sum games should receive wide support from administrators. Although elimination tournaments are the most expedient for determining a winner or champion, challenge and round robin tournaments are best for providing continuous participation.

Recognition for achievement is a trademark of contemporary society and award programs usually enjoy a prominent position in most community recreation programs. To avoid the potential negative aspects associated with awards, policies must be very carefully devised. It is recommended that the number of award categories and recipients be greatly expanded. Awards need not be of a highly extrinsic value, rather they serve as a means for providing recognition to as many individuals as possible for their efforts expended and their achievements.

Study Questions

1. How would you define the concept of competition?
2. How might you describe the various forms of competition; their values, and liabilities?
3. How do game theorists define the terms: "positive sum game," "negative sum game" and "zero sum game"?
4. In designing a competitive tournament, what types of considerations should be included in the planning process?
5. What are the assets and liabilities associated with the various tournament structures commonly employed in leisure service programs?
6. What is the "magic number" concept?
7. How is a double elimination tournament designed to accommodate twelve entries?
8. What is the design of a round robin tournament for a seven entry league with each entry being scheduled for eight contests?
9. Are there philosophical conflicts commonly encountered when planning a leisure service award program? If so, what are they?
10. As a leisure service administrator, how would you design, implement, and administer an effective awards program?

References

Gallwey, W. Timothy. *The Inner Game of Tennis.* New York: Random House, 1974.

Graham, Peter J. "Intramural Sports Programs: The Role of Competition." *NIRSA Journal* 1 (1977): 21-24.

Harris, Dorothy V. *Involvement in Sport: A Somatopsychic Rationale for Physical Activity.* Philadelphia: Lea & Febiger, 1973.

Loy, John W. "The Nature of Sport: A Definitional Effort." *Quest* 10 (1968): 1-15.

Mueller, Pat. *Intramurals: Programming and Administration, 4th ed.* Englewood Cliffs, N.J.: Prentice-Hall, Inc., 1971.

Related Readings

Alley, Louis E. "Athletics in Education: A Double Edged Sword." *Phi Delta Kappan* October (1974): 102-105, 113.

Campbell, David H. "On Being Number One: Competition in Education." *Phi Delta Kappan* October (1974): 143-146.

Cheek, Neil H., and Burch, William R. *The Social Organization of Leisure in Human Society.* New York: Harper & Row, 1976.

Fait, Hollis F., and Billings, John E. "Reassessment of the Values of Competition." In *Issues in Physical Education,* edited by George F. McGlynn. San Francisco: National Press, 1974.

Gardner, John W. *Excellence.* New York: Harper & Row, 1961.

Kleindienst, Viola, and Weston, Arthur. *Intramural and Recreation Programs for Schools and Colleges.* New York: Appleton-Century-Crofts, 1964.

Lowe, Benjamin. *The Beauty of Sport: A Cross-Disciplinary Inquiry.* Englewood Cliffs, N.J.: Prentice-Hall, Inc., 1977.

Murphy, James F.; Williams, John G.; Niepoth, E. William; and Brown, Paul D. *Leisure Service Delivery System: A Modern Perspective.* Philadelphia: Lea & Febiger, 1973.

Program Scheduling and Administrative Records

Objectives   After reading and comprehending this chapter, you should be able to:

1. Develop a variety of schedule calendars.
2. Explain the rationale for maintaining administrative records.
3. Explain the problems associated with the collection and use of qualitative and quantitative data.
4. List and describe the data collecting techniques used in the administration of leisure service programs.
5. Discuss the need for preciseness in the definition and use of statistical terminology and data.
6. Identify the problems which may arise from the collection and publication of participant performance data.

Introduction

Once those activities to be included in the total recreation program have been selected, attention must be given to developing program calendars, determining the various types of administrative records to maintain, and electing the recording formats.

At times, each of the above tasks may appear rather mechanical and mundane. Nevertheless, collectively they represent critical factors in program administration and subsequently require a substantial investment of time. Evaluation, decision making, and planning efforts expended on program scheduling and administrative records often produce some of the strongest influences related to the success or failure of programs.

Scheduling

Scheduling processes vary according to activities. However, common practice suggests that scheduling should not commence prior to the selection of all program activities. This is not to say that additional activities are prohibited from being added at a later date. Additions are always possible. However, post-schedule additions must be limited to open dates and the availability of facilities. In addition, the alteration of an established program schedule is both costly and time consuming and may possibly result in unnecessary confusion for participants and administrative staff alike.

Although many types of schedules exist, for all practical purposes they may be classified into two categories:

1. Activity calendars
2. Schedules for specific events or programs

To insure smooth continuity throughout the implementation stage, both calendars and schedules must be carefully planned and, once constructed, double-checked for accuracy.

Activity Calendars

Activity calendars represent a mapping of activities and special events planned for a given period of time. Calendars may be constructed for a year, season, month, or week. Depending on the desired purpose, the calendar may include information pertaining to the dates, times, users, and locations of scheduled activities.

Through the use of a calendar, scheduling conflicts can readily be identified and remedied prior to program completion. For example, if a rug hooking program and a backgammon tournament were both scheduled for the same facility at the same time, the conflict would immediately appear on the calendar. Once evidenced, the problem can be easily resolved by rescheduling one of the two activities for a different time, location, or day. Activity calendars are also helpful in visualizing potential problems such as the scheduling of two large participation activities in an overlapping manner. The effort required to attract the desired percentage of potential participants to a given activity increases when the individuals sought are already engaged in another program. Therefore, for the benefit of both the program and the participant, the wise administrator will eliminate most overlapping. On the other hand, if it were evidenced that a number of *specific* interest activities were being offered at the same time (activities such as bridge, pottery, squash, and rock collecting) then most likely no corrective action need be taken. The probability of creating interest conflicts through the scheduling of specialized interest activities at the same time is usually minimal.

An important value of a carefully developed activity calendar is its ability to display, at a single glance, all of the ongoing activities for a specific time span. This asset may be enhanced through the use of colors to identify, locate, and distinguish activities designed for specific groups. For example, boys' activities might be recorded in red; girls' in green; men's in blue; women's in orange; senior citizens' in purple; those open to all in black, and so on.

To illustrate the color coding technique, assume that basketball programs were to be offered independently for boys, girls, men, and women. The word **BASKETBALL** would be printed on the activity calendar followed by a series of rectangles ⬚ containing the colors representative of the clientele to be served by each individual segment of the total program. In this instance, red, green, blue, and orange rectangles would be displayed following the name of the activity.

Color coding may also be used to identify clientele to be served by special event programs as well as programs designed to serve jointly more than one segment of the community population. For example, a special event specifically designed for senior citizens would be referenced by a purple rectangle, whereas a musical concert aimed at the total population would be designated by a black rectangle. Coed activities or those planned for joint participation by two or more segments of the clientele may be indicated through the use of two or more colors in a single rectangle. An adult coed stamp collecting program would be identified by a rectangle, ⊏▭▭▭⊐ , colored half blue and half orange. A father and son camping program would be represented by a red and blue rectangle.

Only when the complete list of activities and special events has been established should the recreation director commence developing the various activity calendars. Once the activity program has been solidified, the director must then make a decision regarding the type of calendar that will best provide for the needs of the program participants and administrative personnel. Often a series of annual, seasonal, monthly, and weekly calendars are produced to accommodate the differing requirements of programmers, supervisory personnel, and participants.

Annual Calendars

Construction of an annual calendar is usually not a difficult task since it generally contains little detailed information. Annual calendars are primarily designed to graphically display periods of time within a given year that programs are to be offered. Figure 10-1 presents an example of an annual calendar. Observe that certain activities appear more than once. This occurs when a particular activity is to be offered to the same or different groups during several periods of the year. Multiple colors are used to identify those activities designed for joint participation by two or more specific population segments (as earlier explained). This coding technique can be used to advantage with the annual calendar format.

Seasonal Calendars

The seasonal calendar is a second and popular design. Many special events and recreational activities are associated with a particular time of the year and tend to commence and conclude within the appropriate season. Although quite similar to the annual format, the seasonal calendar is slightly more advanced. In addition to presenting the activities offered,

Figure 10.1 Annual Calendar Schedule

Facility	Jan	Feb	March	April	May	June	July	Aug	Sept	Oct	Nov	Dec
Senior Citizen's Club												
Swimming (General)			(Indoor Pool)				(Outdoor Pool)				(Indoor Pool)	
Swimming (Competitive)			Boy's Girl's Men's Woman's						Boy's Girl's Men's Women's			
Special Events									Boy's Girl's Co-ed—Youths Men's Women's Co-ed—Adults			
Softball												
Playgrounds						(Close of School—Labor Day)						
Arts & Crafts						(Playground Theatre Program)						
Theatre												
Basketball			Boy's Girl's Men's Women's						Boy's Girl's Men's Women's			

the calendar also indicates the times and days that each activity is scheduled for a given facility.

Monthly and Weekly Calendars

Monthly and weekly calendars are developed in much the same manner as the seasonal format with one major difference: by definition, the time parameters are tightly restricted. Figure 10-2 illustrates a swimming facility monthly calendar. Note that two activities are never scheduled concurrently for the same space.

In addition to displaying the types and times of scheduled activities, monthly calendars are also beneficial in the planning of administrative functions such as:

1. Assignment of supervisory personnel
2. Payroll projection and development
3. Facility maintenance and repair programs

Other managerial functions may also be facilitated through the use of this particular calendar format.

Another attribute of the monthly calendar is that it may serve as a valuable publicity instrument. Monthly calendars are easily mass produced in a single color (the cost of multiple color reproductions is usually prohibitive) and may be distributed to the program participants. By providing periodic information regarding new activities, entry deadlines, and planned changes in the normal schedule of operations, the monthly calendar becomes an excellent public relations and communication vehicle.

Weekly calendars, on the other hand, are generally employed when:

1. Activities are scheduled in the same pattern for an extended period of time
2. Notice need be given of planned interruptions of programs and/or facility usage
3. Weekly schedules vary considerably in activity offerings

To produce and distribute a weekly calendar on a one-time basis is effective if the schedule of activities remains the same each day and/or week for an extended period of time. When adopted for this purpose, the weekly calendar tends to exhibit characteristics normally associated with the annual or seasonal calendar, except that the weekly calendar contains a greater amount of detailed information.

Weekly calendars may also be utilized to inform both staff and participants of planned program changes and/or disruptions. When used for this purpose, it is vital that those activities scheduled to undergo change and/or disruption be clearly identified. For example, the closing of a

Facility	M	T	W	T	F	S	S	M	T	W	T	F	S	S	M	T	W	T	F	S	S	M	T	W	T	F	S	S	
	1	2	3	4	5	6	7	8	9	10	11	12	13	14	15	16	17	18	19	20	21	22	23	24	25	26	27	28	29

Swimming Pool

Public School Classes
8:30 AM-2:30 PM

General Swimming
10:00 AM-12 Noon
1:00 PM-4:00 PM
3:00 PM-4:00 PM

Competitive Swimming
Boys & Girl's
4:00 PM-5:30 PM
Men's
7:00 PM-8:00 PM
Women's
7:00 PM-8:00 PM

General Swim
(Adults Only)
8:00 AM-9:30 PM

Pool Reserved for
Private Splash Parties
(Rentals)
7:30 PM-10:00 PM

Figure 10.2 Monthly Calendar Schedule

game room to install new equipment or the suspension of the entire program of operations due to a holiday needs to be highlighted. Highlighting may be accomplished through the use of bold or upper case print, underscoring, or the placement of distinctive boarders around the area containing the important information. The use of one or more of these techniques will attract the reader's attention—and that is exactly the outcome desired.

Failure to highlight or distinguish program alterations and/or disruptions may actually defeat the purpose of the announcement. In fact, the failure to communicate effectively with the program participants and staff may prove to be counter productive: the level of confusion may be increased rather than diminished by the announcement.

Administrative Records

The development and careful maintenance of a system of administrative records—one designed to collect, document, and preserve data—is considered essential by many program agencies and directors. A myriad of data categories exist. The variety or records maintained by some recreation agencies is simply mind boggling. Extensive data collection, nonetheless, has a distinctive appeal to our quantitatively oriented society. These records are often essential for the justification and management of the programs.

It should be noted at the onset that maintaining administrative records is not to be confused with the process of program evaluation. As discussed in Chapter Three, the process of evaluation consists of more than simply collecting quantifiable data, although such data do represent an ingredient in the evaluative process.

Recreation program data may range from the simple tabulation of program participants to the development of elaborate, sophisticated computerized programs designed to produce detailed individual and group performance statistics. For purposes of this chapter, only those records classified as *administrative statistics* and *individual* or *team performance statistics* will be discussed.

Administrative Statistics

Administrative statistics refer to data illustrating or documenting achievement (or the lack thereof) of specific activity goals and objectives. However, as previously mentioned, such data are not to be confused with qualitative assessments.

Examples of administrative data include but are not limited to:

1. The number of entries in an activity
2. The number of participants in an activity

3. The number of events/contests scheduled, forfeited, postponed, and fulfilled
4. Total annual program participation
5. The collective and individual hours that facilities have been made available for participation
6. Total number of staff hours expended
7. Total number of volunteers used in the program
8. Total volunteer hours contributed

Each of the above categories represents an area of *quantifiable data.* Observe that data such as activity evaluations submitted by participants are not listed. Lack of such data should not be considered unusual, however, as only during recent years has consideration been given to evaluating the humanistic goals and objectives of recreational programming. The concepts associated with participant evaluations are discussed in Chapter Three.

Among program directors, is the collection of administrative data considered to be important? The answer must be an unqualified—Yes! To illustrate its importance, try to identify program directors who fail to collect such data. The task would be extremely difficult, if not actually impossible to accomplish.

Information generated by the collected data and the resulting administrative statistics may be used by program directors for a variety of purposes:

1. To ascertain program status in terms of growth to guide future program planning
2. To establish a basis for predicting equipment replacement
3. To assist in facility maintenance program planning
4. To forecast future facility and scheduling requirements
5. To predict future staff and volunteer requirements
6. To justify existing or requested personnel and budget allocations

The availability of administrative data can be a valuable asset to program directors. However, the fact that statistics, in and of themselves, represent nothing more than a collection of numerical tabulations can not be overemphasized. By no stretch of the imagination should these data be considered as the only criteria available for use in evaluating the overall success (or failure) of recreational activities and programs.

Unfortunately, for many program directors, quantity is often identified or defined as being virtually identical to quality. Activity and program evaluations limited to quantity assessments often reflect a situation in which little or no effort has been expended toward the development of humanistic goals and objectives. As previously noted, goals and objectives representative of the humanistic programming philosophy may occasionally be adopted, but often are rarely evaluated due to either a lack of interest or an inability to develop and implement the necessary evaluative criteria. Therefore, quantitative data are relied upon for assessing the level of achievement attained.

Program directors are, nonetheless, encouraged to maintain program participation/attendance data as often such documentation represents the only means available (especially in the absence of qualitative data) to justify or defend activity programs, requests for increased personnel and budgetary allocations, facility development plans, and so forth at the institutional or agency administrative level. One word of caution, however, with respect to the use of such data; paramount concern must be directed toward the development and strict maintenance of accurate data collection and reporting procedures. The failure to institute such controls may result in erroneous program status reports.

The use of quantitative data can be abused. How often have recreation programs received praise for the high quality of their activities— quality assumed to exist simply because of the growth experienced in the number of participants? Yet, such abuse should not be considered surprising. Our society has been subjected to an overriding premise that growth represents success. Thus, it is reasonable to assume that the end result of such "mental conditioning" is the automatic equating of most positive numeric growth indices with success. In recreation programs such success would indicate that the program has provided for the needs, wants, and desires of the program's participants. Yet, such deductions are speculative at best.

Although program evaluations based *strictly* on quantitative administrative data must be regarded as totally unfounded and invalid (at least from a scientific posture), they are frequently used by recreation administrative personnel. And, unfortunately evaluations based upon such data are rarely challenged as to their accuracy.

Statistics should not be viewed unequivocally as negative. When sensibly employed they can be extremely helpful. For example, how would a program director justify either the elimination or continuation of an activity designed to attract and provide for the needs of a large number of people if data were not available to substantiate the percentage of the target population attracted? Obviously, without quantitative data, program administrators would be at a disadvantage in documenting their efforts.

Viewed from a different perspective, programmers must be cautious not to recommend the continuation or elimination of an activity strictly on the basis of numerics. Some special event programs and certain activities such as chess, whist, poetry reading, stone rubbing, and so forth may be included in the total scheme of a community recreation program with full knowledge that only a small number of individuals will be attracted to each event. If interest indicators and activity evaluations are restricted to quantitative analysis, then the probability of limited interest activities receiving a numerical evaluation high enough to warrant retention would be remote.

At this point in the discussion, it should be clear that administrative data must be gathered for specific purposes and used only to support those purposes. The next area of exploration relates to the types of data commonly collected and collection methods.

The most common method of collecting data is through *manual tabulation*. Even though computers have proven quite efficient in handling such tedious, time-consuming, and often costly administrative chores, they are usually only found in the largest and most sophisticated recreation agencies.

Consequently, the manual process of tabulating and assimilating data remains quite prevalent. In reality, the actual manual collection process is relatively simple in terms of procedural steps. For example, if a director wished to determine the number of entries received for a particular activity, each of the submitted entry sheets would be hand counted to produce the total. Other statistics such as the number of events scheduled, postponed, played, or forfeited could be obtained through similar manual computations.

Statistical Terminology

To minimize the potential for confusion in the discussion that follows, the following terms commonly used in reference to recreation program administrative data need to be defined:

Entries — Individuals or groups submitting a request to be scheduled for participation in an activity.

Participant — Those persons entered in an activity either as an individual or group member who participate in the activity at least once.

Total number of participations — The total number of times each individual participates in a specific activity; or, the collective number of participations by each individual in the total activities offered by the program. (Note: When this term is used, it must be specified as to whether it is referencing a specific activity or the total program. Also, the span of time must be stated.)

To illustrate the use of the terms: Fifteen *entries* were received for a pet show of which twelve appeared on the day of the contest. From the twelve *participants,* seven were selected as finalists and were included in the championship event the following day. At the conclusion of the pet show, there were nineteen total participations by the twelve participants.

Chapter 10

Recreation administrators should exercise care in the use of statistical terminology. When employed, it must be stated in a clear and precise manner. As the above definitions illustrate, several of the terms are similar in pronunciation and spelling, but quite different in their respective meanings. Unfortunately, some statistical terms are often used in the wrong context. For example, program directors are frequently guilty of issuing statements such as the following: "On the average, over the period of a year, one thousand people use our game room weekly." To the average person, this statement is usually interpreted to mean that in a given week one thousand *different* individuals make use of the game room. Is this what the director meant to imply? Probably not. Most likely what the director meant to convey was that through multiple participations, by an unknown number of individuals, an aevarge of one thousand participations was recorded per week.

In his book, *How to Lie with Statistics*, Darrell Huff (1954) presents a number of examples in which statistical data have been twisted to support contentions which, in fact, are not validated by the data. Many administrators indulge, either knowingly or unwittingly, in similar deceptive practices. This occurs when statistical terms are used in an improper context or through the issuance of statements susceptible to misinterpretation. To avoid criticism and suspicion in using statistical data, program directors should collect accurate information and be extremely careful to present all data in a clear, precise, defined, easily understood format. Following such guidelines, the potential for misrepresentation of data should be reduced to an absolute minimum.

Types of Administrative Data Collected

What types of administrative data should program directors consider gathering? Some of the traditionally collected data and their value are presented below:

1. *Total entries* — The primary purpose of collecting these data is to develop an accurate accounting of the entries submitted. Directors also use this statistic to determine the drop-out rate prior to commencement of the activity. When high drop-out rates are evidenced, an investigation to identify the contributing factors may be warranted.
2. *Total events scheduled, forfeited, and completed* — This statistic is often used to demonstrate the growth (or lack thereof) of an activity, facility usage, and forfeit rate percentage.
3. *Total activity/program participants* — A desirable statistic because it provides information relative to the number of participants and percentages of the total community population attracted to a particular activity.

4. **Total activity/program participations** — This statistic represents the collective number of participations recorded by each participant in either a specific activity or the total program. Because this statistic tends to produce large, impressive numbers, its use has become quite popular.
5. **Total hours of facility availability** — The value of this statistic is its ability to demonstrate the availability of a given facility (or all facilities on a collective basis) for the conduct of both scheduled and unscheduled activities.
6. **Staff/participant ratios** — In an age of accountability, personnel resource allocation information becomes extremely important, especially if cost analysis studies are to be undertaken.

Data Collection Methods

Collection methods and the design of recording forms are usually left to the discretion and imagination of the agency or institution. A key to successful record keeping is the development of a simplified data collection system utilizing clear, easily understood recording forms. For example, to collect game room participation data, access to the facility might be restricted to a single entrance. Upon entering, each person would be required to provide the information requested on a *sign-in sheet.* Through use of this technique, a single supervisor is able to control access to the facility while at the same time insuring the maintenance of an accurate facility usage and participation record.

Displayed in Figure 10-3 is a basic sign-in sheet which is adaptable for use in a variety of situations — in this instance a game room. While examining Figure 10-3 note that:

1. Sign-in lines are numbered in consecutive order; a feature that assists in tabulating the total number of participations.
2. Participants are requested to PRINT FULL NAMES. Unreadable signatures and/or the use of nicknames tend to be reduced through the use of this procedure.
3. Participants are requested to record entry and departure times. These data may be used at a later date in conjunction with facility usage studies.
4. Provision of space for first-time users to record their program identification numbers. Note: If data are desired relating to total facility usage by each individual, then all individuals must record their identification number *each time* they use the facility.

For those programs using computers to maintain participation records, the use of an optical scan form could be highly efficient. *Optical scan forms* are designed to be machine-read and processed for computer

Southridge Recreation Department
Participation Record

Facility: Game Room _____   Date: _____

| Name | Time | | Identification Number |
	Entering	Leaving	
1.			
2.			
3.			
4.			
5.			
6.			
7.			
8.			
9.			
10.			
11.			
12.			
13.			
14.			
15.			
16.			
17.			
18.			
19.			
20.			

Figure 10.3   Facility Sign-in Sheet

use. This procedure eliminates the need for manual tabulations or key-punching of data.

The optical scan method of collecting data operates in the following manner:

1. Using a no. 2 pencil or less, each participant completes the optical scan form.
2. Each day (or when desired) the completed forms are processed by an optical scan reader which automatically keypunches the informa-tion on to computer cards.

3. The keypunched computer cards are then stored until a participation record is desired. At that time, the entire collection of cards is processed by the computer. Requested statistical data will be tabulated and recorded on a computer printout sheet.

An example of an optical scan form is shown in Figure 10-4. Note the minimal amount of information requested. All numerical information is obtained by recording the digits and then filling in the corresponding bubbles with a pencil. In our quantitatively oriented society, even the youngest school child is capable of completing this process.

Aside from its efficient ability to process daily and accumulated participation counts, the optical scan system is also capable of providing data relative to the number of individual participants as well as the number of times each participant has made use of each facility. Information of this nature is obtained through the use of a basic computer operation which sorts the keypunched cards into alphabetical or identification number sequence (depending upon the organizational format specified in the computer program). Through use of the proper program, the computer will produce printouts listing each individual participant and the number of times he or she used each facility.

Other computer programs can produce printouts displaying the day by day usage for each facility. Such data are valuable when conducting participation flow studies. Having daily participation figures listed on a single sheet for each facility allows for easy comparisons. Finally, if facility entry and departure times are carefully maintained, studies aimed at determining the greatest periods of usage for each facility and the average amount of time spent per participation may be conducted using the computer.

The methods most commonly used in collecting data, however, include head counts and the employment of entrance turnstiles or electronic eyes. Counting heads requires a supervisor to maintain an accurate record of the number of individuals entering a facility. The advantage to the turnstyle or electronic eye method is that it eliminates the need to station a supervisor at the entrance location. Obviously, neither method is as accurate as the sign-in system nor as reliable in providing accurate data relative to the number of different facility users.

Activities employing score cards on which participants list their names will automatically generate participation records. Usually the score cards are collected following completion of each event so that individual and/or group statistical data may be recorded on appropriate forms. Participation data may be collected by checking off on *master participation lists* the names of each participant recorded on each

Southridge Recreation Department

Participation Record

Facility: __Game Room__

	Code:	0	1
	0	(●)	( )
01 Game Room	1	( )	(●)
02 Gymnasium	2	( )	( )
03 Swimming Pool	3	( )	( )
04 Quiet Room	4	( )	( )
05 Arts & Crafts Room	5	( )	( )
06 Music Room	6	( )	( )
07 Senior Citizen's Center	7	( )	( )

Participants: Please fill-in the requested information and return the completed form to the attendant at the facility entrance. THANK YOU FOR YOUR COOPERATION.

Full Name (Please Print)

George E. Gregory

Date: __1 2 / 0 8 / 7 7__

0	( ) ( ) (●) ( ) ( ) ( )
1	(●) ( ) ( ) ( ) ( ) ( )
2	( ) (●) ( ) ( ) ( ) ( )
3	( ) ( ) ( ) ( ) ( ) ( )
4	( ) ( ) ( ) ( ) ( ) ( )
5	( ) ( ) ( ) ( ) ( ) ( )
6	( ) ( ) ( ) ( ) ( ) ( )
7	( ) ( ) ( ) ( ) (●) (●)
8	( ) ( ) ( ) (●) ( ) ( )
9	( ) ( ) ( ) ( ) ( ) ( )

Identification Number - Record the digits and then fill-in the appropriate bubbles using the provided pencil.

__0 3 2 - 3 0 - 0 5 9 1__

0	(●) ( ) ( ) ( ) (●) (●) ( ) ( ) ( ) ( )
1	( ) ( ) ( ) ( ) ( ) ( ) ( ) ( ) ( ) (●)
2	( ) ( ) (●) ( ) ( ) ( ) ( ) ( ) ( ) ( )
3	( ) (●) ( ) (●) ( ) ( ) ( ) ( ) ( ) ( )
4	( ) ( ) ( ) ( ) ( ) ( ) ( ) ( ) ( ) ( )
5	( ) ( ) ( ) ( ) ( ) ( ) (●) ( ) ( )
6	( ) ( ) ( ) ( ) ( ) ( ) ( ) ( ) ( ) ( )
7	( ) ( ) ( ) ( ) ( ) ( ) ( ) ( ) ( ) ( )
8	( ) ( ) ( ) ( ) ( ) ( ) ( ) ( ) ( ) ( )
9	( ) ( ) ( ) ( ) ( ) ( ) ( ) ( ) (●) ( )

Time Entering

__0 9 : 1 5__ AM (●) PM ( )

0	(●) ( ) ( ) ( )
1	( ) ( ) (●) ( )
2	( ) ( ) ( ) ( )
3	( ) ( ) ( ) ( )
4	( ) ( ) ( ) ( )
5	( ) ( ) ( ) (●)
6	( ) ( ) ( ) ( )
7	( ) ( ) ( ) ( )
8	( ) ( ) ( ) ( )
9	( ) (●) ( ) ( )

Time Leaving

__1 1 : 3 0__ AM (●) PM ( )

0	( ) ( ) ( ) (●)
1	(●) (●) ( ) ( )
2	( ) ( ) ( ) ( )
3	( ) ( ) (●) ( )
4	( ) ( ) ( ) ( )
5	( ) ( ) ( ) ( )
6	( ) ( ) ( ) ( )
7	( ) ( ) ( ) ( )
8	( ) ( ) ( ) ( )
9	( ) ( ) ( ) ( )

Figure 10.4 Optical Scan Form

Players Names (List in alphabetical order)	Contest Dates					Total number of participations
	11/4	11/6	11/11	11/13	11/18	
1. Anthony, Alan	✓	✓	✓		✓	4
2. Bond, William	✓		✓	✓	✓	4
3. Carr, Irene	✓	✓	✓	✓	✓	5
4. Collins, Janet	✓	✓	✓	✓	✓	5
5. Collins, Peter		✓	✓		✓	3
6. Gregory, George	✓	✓	✓	✓	✓	5
7. James, Paul	✓	✓	✓	✓	✓	5
8. Judd, Sandra	✓	✓		✓	✓	4
9. Kilduff, Alice	✓	✓	✓	✓	✓	5
10. Krupp, Hans	✓	✓				2
11. Lane, John	✓	✓	✓		✓	4
12. Lowence, Milt	✓	✓	✓	✓	✓	5
13. Moulton, Bruce		✓	✓	✓	✓	4
14. Muller, Man	✓	✓	✓	✓	✓	5
15. Nagele, Mary			✓	✓		2
16. Novak, Wallace	✓	✓	✓	✓	✓	5
17. Nutone, Linda	✓	✓	✓	✓		4
18. Peters, Thomas	✓	✓	✓	✓	✓	5
19. Queen, Thomas	✓	✓	✓		✓	3
20. Watkins, Gordon	✓	✓	✓	✓	✓	5
Daily Participation	17	17	18	15	17	84
Total Participation	17	34	52	67	84	

Figure 10.5 Team Participation

score card. Figure 10-5 represents a master participation recording form. Several of the form's features deserve close observation. Note that:

1. The lines for recording participants' names are numbered in sequence.
2. Names are listed in alphabetical order.
3. Separate columns are provided for each event date.
4. Participations are recorded by placing a check mark opposite the participant's name in the appropriate column for the event date.
5. At the bottom of each column, space is provided to record the total participation of that date as well as the accumulated participation.
6. Following the final event date, a column is provided for recording the total number of participations for each individual.

7. Space is provided at the top of the form to record the number of individual entries, the number of actual participants, and the total number of participations. Note: easy access to this type of information is helpful when data are collected to develop periodic or annual reports.

Similar participation recording forms may be developed for use with dual and individual activities as well as group events. In addition, facilities scheduled for "open," "free," or "unstructured" activity programs may employ a master participation recording form. As illustrated in Figure 10-6, daily participation tallies are recorded on the master form to provide an accumulated participation record.

Master recording forms are especially desirable because of their ability to display at a single glance either participation generated on a given day or the accumulated total for any specific point in the recording period. For those directors primarily concerned with the quantitative growth or decline of their programs, master participation forms are ideally structured to provide such information in a simple format.

Annual Reports

It is customary at the conclusion of a fiscal or calendar year for directors to submit an annual report to their governing body. *Annual reports* usually contain data pertaining to each facet of the total program's operation. These data are accompanied by statements indicating the accomplishments and/or failures experienced during the reporting period. Although some directors take pride in their ability to develop voluminous, complex reports, most recreation administrators prefer to submit brief reports containing all of the necessary information about the operation of the program.

To paraphrase a saying, "A single statistical table can say more than a thousand words." For this reason, recreation directors tend to incorporate statistical records into their reports when possible. Figure 10-7 portrays an annual report table specifically designed for presentation of data relative to a single phase of the overall recreation program—team activities. Similar tables may be created to illustrate data generated by individual activities, special events, and general facility usage. Note that in Figure 10-7 comparisons are made between current data and historical data reported the previous year. Such tables are capable of transmitting a considerable amount of information about the operation of the program and its growth status (but not necessarily its quality status). This is especially true when current data are contrasted with previous report statistics.

Southridge Recreation Department

Facility: <u>Game Room</u>

Date	Daily Participation	Total Participations
February 1	78	78
2	64	142
3	71	213
4	68	281
5	54	335
6	69	404
7	81	485
8	73	558
9	64	622
10	76	698
11	84	782
12	56	838
13	31	869
14	62	931
15	69	1,000
16	73	1,073
17	57	1,130
18	67	1,197
19	48	1,245
20	54	1,299
21	59	1,358
22	62	1,420
23	39	1,459
24	57	1,516
25	72	1,588
26	59	1,647
27	64	1,711
28	66	1,777

Figure 10.6   Master Facility Usage Participation Record

ANNUAL REPORT OF TEAM ACTIVITIES

ACTIVITY	Total Entry	Pre-vious Year	% Change	Total Parti-cipants	Pre-vious Year	% Change	Con-tests Sched.	Pre-vious Year	% Change	Total For-feits	Pre-vious Year	% Change	Total Partici-pations	Pre-vious Year	% Change	Total Staff Hours	Pre-vious Year	% Change	Total Volunteer Staff	Pre-vious Year	% Change
FLAG FOOTBALL	27	23	17.4	396	321	23.4	73	63	15.9	8	6	33.3	1584	1220	29.8	307	274	12.0	16	13	23.1
BASKETBALL	38	36	5.6	368	351	4.8	100	95	5.3	3	7	-57.2	1546	1369	12.9	268	256	4.7	16	13	23.1
VOLLEYBALL	74	58	27.6	729	556	31.1	190	150	26.7	14	11	27.3	3500	2502	39.9	270	248	8.9	16	13	23.1
TENNIS MIXED DOUBLES	29	30	-3.4	58	60	-3.4	29	30	-3.4	8	4	200.0	42	52	-20.1	15	15	..	..	..	..
SOFTBALL	43	41	4.9	600	588	2.0	113	103	9.7	9	12	-25.0	2820	2705	4.3	310	276	12.3	18	15	20.0
TUG-O-WAR	12	7	71.4	112	83	35.0	33	21	57.2	4	2	200.0	459	382	20.2	20	15	33.3	3	0	300.0
BADMINTON MIXED DOUBLES	18	12	50.0	36	24	50.0	18	12	50.0	2	0	200.0	32	24	33.3	10	10	0.0	..	..	..
SOCCER	16	11	45.5	203	177	14.7	43	31	38.7	3	3	0.0	934	779	19.9	130	110	18.2	8	3	266.7
TOTALS	257	218	17.9	2502	2160	15.8	599	505	18.6	51	45	13.3	10917	9033	20.9	1330	1204	10.5	77	57	35.1

Figure 10.7 Annual Report of Team Activities

Individual and Group Statistics

The interest of current society in statistical data is demonstrated daily. For evidence, one need go no further than the nearest major newspaper. A cursory review of the sport or financial pages will reveal that a significant number of column inches have been devoted to the printing of statistics. As commercial, profit oriented enterprises, newspapers certainly would not allocate such a large percentage of non-revenue producing column space to such data if it were not believed (and validated) that data of this nature were highly sought by the readership and thus responsible for sales.

Astute directors, aware of the desire for the maintenance and publication of personal and group performance data, should make the resources available to publish such data. Allocation of resources to support projects of this nature may be justified on the basis that the end product provides for the expressed needs and desires of the program clientele. Such resource investments may also be defended on the basis of public relations and program publicity.

On the other hand, program directors who publish performance data should be alert for manifestations of a "win at all cost" attitude. The introduction and subsequent spread of such an attitude can rapidly create a destructive atmosphere for both the participants and total program alike. To avoid, at least in part, the opportunity for attitudes of this nature to develop, program directors may be well advised to collect, publish, and disseminate only the most basic of individual and group statistics.

Types of Individual/Group Statistical Data

Assuming that group and individual statistical data will be collected, decisions must be made with respect to what types of data are to be collected and the methods to be used in obtaining them. For the most part, these decisions are primarily dependent upon the nature of the activity and the philosophy of both the agency and the director. In a touch football program, for example, an extensive number of categories exist for data collection (professional and collegiate sport statisticians appear to be continually adding new categories to an already lengthy list). Routinely collected data are related to:

Group

1. Won—loss record
2. Offensive and defensive records
3. League standings

Individual

1. Number of touchdowns scored
2. Total points scored
3. Number of tags
4. Number of pass receptions
5. Number of passes thrown/completed
6. Number of passes intercepted
7. Number of yards gained

The list could go on and on. In the final analysis, it is the responsibility of program director and the sponsoring agency or institution to select the statistics to be maintained.

BOWLING LEAGUE STANDING SHEET

TEAM STANDINGS	WON	LOST	PCT.	PINFALL	AVE.
ROCKETS ***	70.5	43.5	.618	31703	812
SILENT FIVE	66.0	48.0	.579	29393	753
MISFITS	60.0	54.0	.526	26924	690
BIT BUSTERS	56.5	57.5	.496	28196	722
CAMPUS CENTER	55.5	58.5	.487	27220	697
D. O. M.	51.5	62.5	.452	27933	716
CHEMISTRY	49.0	65.0	.430	27967	717
RAIDERS	46.5	67.5	.408	27188	697

1ST HIGH TEAM, 3-GAMES	ROCKETS ***	2552	1ST HIGH, TEAM GAME	ROCKETS ***	901
2ND HIGH TEAM, 3-GAMES	SILENT FIVE	2489	2ND HIGH, TEAM GAME	SILENT FIVE	895
3RD HIGH TEAM, 3-GAMES	BIT BUSTERS	2294	3RD HIGH, TEAM GAME	RAIDERS	825
1ST HIGH IND 3-GAMES	BARBER	612	1ST HIGH IND. GAME	JOHNSON	229
2ND HIGH IND 3-GAMES	LYMAN	594	2ND HIGH IND. GAME	DUPREY	221
3RD HIGH IND 3-GAMES	ROZANSKI	573	3RD HIGH IND. GAME	ROZANSKI	218

INDIVIDUAL AVERAGES

NAME	HDCP	TOTAL PINS	GAMES	AVE.	NAME	HDCP	TOTAL PINS	GAMES	AVE.
D. O .M.					**BIT BUSTERS**				
TURNAO	33	3690	27	136	MAZIARZ	23	4941	33	149
MAWSON	15	5747	36	159	LORD	31	5403	39	138
CULBERTSON	15	6251	39	160	PETITTO	35	4011	30	133
GATSLICK	30	4195	30	139	ROZANSKI	21	5924	39	151
POWERS	50	334	3	111	LYMAN	17	5194	33	157
PROGULSKE	35	1192	9	132	WOZNIAK	30	845	6	140
COLE, J.	33	3259	24	135	**CAMPUS CENTER**				
CHEMISTRY					LACOMBE	20	5050	33	153
BERNASCONI	26	4811	33	145	YOUNG	34	4036	30	134
OBERLANDER	33	4080	30	136	TILLEY	49	3789	33	114
SHORT	42	2242	18	124	JACKSON	36	396	3	132
CURRAN	20	5517	36	153	SOLOMON	21	4582	30	152
POLLARD	21	4248	28	151	MASIALIZ	18	2342	15	156
NOVAK	32	2329	17	137	DUPREY	11	2476	15	165
MARCUS	27	2145	15	143	KIRBY	42	2599	21	123
MILLER	21	1835	12	152	**RAIDERS**				
SILENT FIVE					OLZEWSKI	46	356	3	118
WORTMAN	24	4454	30	148	SMITH	30	4651	33	140
GRAHAM	22	5858	39	150	JUSAIWICZ	41	4515	36	125
KLAR	20	4140	27	153	BROEKHUIZEN	32	4551	33	137
SIMPSON	24	4785	33	147	MARCHANT	21	5954	39	152
JOHNSON	11	6445	39	165	SYSKO	25	5279	36	146
AYRES	35	2768	21	131	BARAN	33	410	3	136
VANDERZWAGG	28	852	6	142	PAPIPO	39	767	6	127
ROCKETS *					**MISFITS**				
VLACH, E.	17	4259	27	157	MELACASA	33	3672	27	136
BOYER	12	4900	30	163	BROOKS	45	3226	27	119
PARKINSON	25	4404	30	146	SCOTT	27	5165	36	143
PAGE	7	5118	30	170	COMO	27	5218	36	144
BARBER	0	4324	24	180	LOS	16	1904	12	158
VLACH, F.	3	4685	27	170	HORN	36	4357	33	132
DAY	21	3178	21	151	SYKES	15	957	6	159
MEADE	21	915	6	152	WHITE	3	529	3	176

Figure 10.8   Bowling League Standing Sheet

Possession of individual and group performance statistics makes it possible to establish "annual" and "all-time" records. For example, in ten pin bowling an honor might be established for recording the highest single game score, the highest triple game score, or the highest total pin fall average. Also, it is not uncommon for groups compiling the best single and triple games scores to be recognized.

Figure 10-8 exhibits a bowling data sheet containing both individual and group statistics. To expedite data collection, participants are provided score cards. In bowling, as with many activities, the program director is completely dependent upon the participants for the accurate recording of data on the score cards.

Once the first set of categorical statistics has been obtained, it becomes possible for "new" and "all-time" records to be established. The decision whether to promote or discourage the collection of these types of data rests with the program director or recreation commission. However, caution is urged regarding the potential for creating undesirable attitudes if the concepts of winning and establishing records become overemphasized. Recreation program directors must be prepared to encounter and effectively deal with volatile and potentially dangerous situations if the competitiveness exhibited by participants is allowed to escalate in an uncontrolled manner. The failure to recognize and successfully cope with the problems of this nature may result in the creation of an environment in which once healthy viable activity programs begin to wither and deteriorate.

Summary

Leisure service administrators should commence the processes of activity scheduling only after all decisions have been made regarding the various activities and special events that will constitute the overall program. Activity calendars are considered valuable assets for scheduling, identifying, and publicizing activities and special events. In addition, they often serve as important communication vehicles for the dissemination of information relative to facility availability, schedule changes, and planned interruptions in program operations. Annual, seasonal, monthly, and weekly calendars each possess unique as well as common characteristics. Often, program directors will employ a variety of calendars to provide for the differing needs of the program participants and administrative staff.

Administrative records should be maintained for all programs. An extensive variety of statistical categories exist for which administrative and performance data may be collected and processed. Decisions regarding the types and methods of collecting and recording data usually rest with the agency or institution. Although computers are extremely efficient in the tedious and often time-consuming process of collecting and analyzing data, they tend to be found only in large, sophisticated programs. In most instances, statistical data are collected and tabulated manually.

Measures of quantity rather than quality represent the majority of data categories maintained. Consequently, caution must be exercised not to evaluate the success or failure of activity programs and special events strictly on the basis of quantified documentation.

Methods of collecting and recording data must be designed to insure accuracy. When reporting data analysis, it must be accomplished in a clear, precise, and defined manner so that the risk of misinterpretation is reduced to the lowest level.

Finally, when individual and/or group performance data are published or when "leading" or "all-time" records are established, program directors must be alert to detect and eliminate any manifestations of a "win at all cost" attitude exhibited by program participants. Failure to immediately control such problems could prove detrimental for both the program and participants alike.

Study Questions

1. What types of calendars are used in community leisure service programs? Describe each.
2. Of what value is the maintenance of administrative records?
3. What are the strengths and liabilities of administrative statistics and of performance statistics?
4. What methods are employed to collect statistical data?
5. How may technology be applied to the maintenance of leisure service administrative records?
6. What problems, if any, might the collection and publication of individual and group performance statistics create?

References

Huff, Darrell. *How to Lie with Statistics*. San Francisco: Norton, 1954.

Related Readings

Bannon, Joseph J. *Leisure Resources: Its Comprehensive Planning*. Englewood Cliffs, N.J.: Prentice-Hall, Inc., 1976.

Kleindienst, Viola K., and Weston, Arthur. *Intramural and Recreation Programs for Schools and Colleges*. New York: Appleton-Century-Crofts, 1964.

Lutzin, Sidney G. and Storey, Edward H. (eds.) *Managing Municipal Leisure Services*. Washington, D.C.: International City Management Association, 1973.

Meyer, Harold D., and Brightbill, Charles K. *Recreation Administration: A Guide to its Practices.* Englewood Cliffs, N.J.: Prentice-Hall, Inc., 1956.

Murphy, James F. *Recreation and Leisure Service.* Dubuque, Ia.: Wm. C. Brown Co. Publishers, 1975.

Murphy, James F., and Howard, Dennis R. *Delivery of Community Leisure Services: An Holistic Approach.* Philadelphia: Lea & Febiger, 1977.

Murphy, James F.; Williams, John G.; Niepoth, E. William; and Brown, Paul D. *Leisure Service Delivery System: A Modern Perspective.* Philadelphia: Lea & Febiger, 1973.

Rodney, Lynn S. *Administration of Public Recreation.* New York: The Ronald Press Co., 1964.

Tanur, Judith M. (ed.) *Statistics: A Guide to the Unknown.* San Francisco: Holden-Day, Inc., 1972.

Leisure Service and the Law

Objectives After reading and comprehending this chapter, you should be able to:

1. Explain the legal basis for leisure service programs.
2. Discuss the concepts of contractual and tort liability.
3. Describe the conditions constituting negligence, the strategies used to defend against charges of negligence, and the methods employed to avoid involvement in liability litigation.
4. Explain some of the legal considerations related to the employment, assignment, and evaluation of personnel.
5. Identify and discuss several legislative acts which provide resources for the funding of leisure service related grants.
6. Name recent federal legislative enactments which have had a significant impact upon the programming responsibilities of leisure service departments.
7. Recognize the need to meet legal responsibilities and to consult with legal counsel on all matters requiring legal clarification or interpretation.

Introduction

The administration of leisure service programs has become increasingly complex with the proliferation of laws and regulations affecting community programs. In this chapter a variety of legal considerations and legislative enactments are introduced. It is not the purpose of this chapter to provide answers to all the legal questions related to the administration of community programs; rather, the chapter is designed to provide basic information concerning legal responsibilities and legislative enactments directly affecting leisure service programs. A further goal is to stimulate an awareness of the need to seek professional counsel on all issues requiring clarification.

Legal Basis for Community Programs

Historically, parks in the United States have been established and administered under the purview and legal jurisdiction of governmental bodies, either at the federal, state, county, special district, or local level. In contrast, not until late in the nineteenth century did governments begin to assume responsibility for the provision of recreational opportunities for their constituents. Prior to that time, the only leisure activities and events available to the general public were those sponsored by charitable agencies and private individuals.

Today, all tax supported leisure service programs gain their authority through state and local legislation. The Tenth Amendment of the United States Constitution leaves to the individual states any powers not reserved for the federal government or specifically prohibited to the states. Thus, since the right to establish and regulate leisure service programs is neither given to the federal government nor denied the states, such power reverts to the states.

States are empowered to delegate the administration of certain functions to local units of government. For example, the state is responsible for educating the public. However, each state has delegated the responsibility for providing and administering public education to each of its local communities or special school districts. In similar fashion, state governments have delegated the power to establish and maintain leisure service programs to local communities and special districts.

Types of Legislation

States delegate power through legislation which may be either mandatory or enabling in nature. *Mandatory legislation* requires compliance with the provisions contained in the legislative act. *Enabling legislation* is statutory law that allows or permits rather than requires or mandates. Leisure service programs are usually authorized under enabling legislation. Such legislation permits but does not compel local governments and special districts to develop leisure service programs, provide leadership, and to acquire and maintain the facilities necessary to support such programs.

State enabling legislation is usually written and enacted in a manner which encompasses all governmental units and special districts under its provisions. Such laws generally contain specific instructions relating to the creation of leisure service boards or commissions, the method of member appointment, committee size, and the committee's responsibilities and authority.

Communities electing to establish a leisure service program must comply with the requirements set forth in the enabling legislation. This does not mean, however, that local communities are precluded from enacting their own rules and regulations governing program operations. To the contrary, most states allow local communities to enact their own rules and regulations through *home rule legislation* as long as they neither conflict with nor undermine existing federal, state, county, or local statutes.

Program Status

Most community leisure service programs are characterized as legitimate *governmental functions* designed to provide services necessary to meet important public needs and interests. However, those programs which charge clients fees to participate in activities and events may be classified as *proprietary functions* rather than governmental. Program administrators are advised to consult with legal counsel regarding particular state statutes defining program status.

Fee Charging

The number of programs in which user fees are charged has increased in recent years. In most instances, user fees are instituted to defray or underwrite the expense of providing a particular activity or event. Frequently, activities and events for which fees are charged would not be provided unless the participants were willing to underwrite, at least in part, the financial obligations incurred.

The practice of instituting user fees is perfectly legitimate so long as it does not conflict with statutes prohibiting such charges. However, the levying of user fees does give rise to several legal questions. Two common questions are: (1) does charging a user fee alter the leisure service program's classification status? (2) does the charging of a user fee obligate the program's administration to provide participants with a greater degree of care and safety than that normally rendered?

In response to the first question, whether a program's classification status shifts from governmental to proprietary depends upon the circumstances surrounding the charging of fees. Unless a governmental program assesses a fee for the express purpose of generating a profit, its classification status generally will not be altered. For example, if the charges assessed participants in a camping program were used to pay for and replace equipment and supplies used in the program, the program's classification status would probably not be subject to alteration. But, if the fees charged were designed to produce a profit and the funds were to be used for purposes not related to the camping program, then the motives behind the fee assessment would be suspect and the program's classification status could be subject to change.

The answer to the second question is quite clear. Leisure activity sponsors, both governmental and proprietary, are responsible for the development, implementation, and enforcement of rules and regulations designed to insure adequate care and safety for the participants. This responsibility is not affected by the absence or establishment of user fees, and one is always vulnerable to legal suits in cases of alleged negligence.

Program administrators should be aware, however, that judges and juries tend to expect that a greater degree of care and safety be exercised in instances where participants have been charged a fee.

Legal Terminology

For leisure service administrators to understand their responsibilities related to the concept of liability, a knowledge of certain legal terms is mandatory. Terms commonly associated with legal liability have been defined by Black's Law Dictionary (1968) as follows:

Tort   A legal wrong committed upon the person or property independent of contract. It may be either (1) a direct invasion of some legal right of the individual; (2) the infraction of some public duty by which special damages accrue to the individual.

Defendant   The party against whom relief or recovery is sought in action or suit.

Plaintiff   A person who brings an action; the party who complains or sues in a personal action and is so named on the record.

Liable   Bound or obligated in law or equity; responsibility; chargeable; answerable; compellable to make satisfaction, compensation, or restitution.

Negligence   The omission to do something which a reasonable man, guided by those ordinary considerations which ordinarily regulate human affairs, would do, or the doing of something which a reasonable and prudent man would not do.

Contributory Negligence   Any want of ordinary care on the part of the person (or on the part of another whose negligence is imputable to him), which combined and concurred with the defendant's negligence, and contributed to the injury as a proximate cause therefore, and as an element without which the injury would have not occurred.

Nuisance   That class of wrongs that arise from the unreasonable, unwarrantable, or unlawful use by a person of his own property, either real or personal, or from his own improper, indecent, or unlawful personal conduct, working an obstruction of or injury to the right of another or of the public, and producing material annoyance, inconvenience, discomfort, or hurt, that the law will presume might result in damage.

Assumption of Risk   Exists where none of the fault for injury rests with plaintiff, but where the plaintiff assumes consequences of injury occurring through fault of defendant, person, or fault of no one.

Legal Liability

Legal liability is the one area of law of which most leisure service administrators are aware. *Liability* is a concept that infers the existence of certain responsibilities between two or more persons (individuals, corporate structures, associations, and all legal entities). This concept further implies that any person failing to properly and adequately fulfill his or her responsibilities because of *negligence* must provide compensation to those affected by such failure. Before a lawsuit can be won, according to Prosser (1941, p. 8), the following elements are required:

1. A duty or obligation, recognized by the law, requiring the actor to conform to a certain standard of conduct for the protection of others against unreasonable risk.
2. A failure on his part to conform to the standard required.
3. A reasonably close causal connection between the conduct and the resulting injury.
4. Actual loss or damage resulting to the interests of another.

There are several types of legal liability. But for purposes of this chapter only contractual and tort liability will be reviewed. It should be kept in mind that liability suits generally stem from action considered negligent because (Colgate, 1978, p. 45):

1. It is not properly done, appropriate care is not employed by the actor.
2. The circumstances under which it is done create risks, although it is done with due care and precaution.
3. The actor is indulging in acts which involve an unreasonable risk of direct and immediate harm to others.
4. The actor sets in motion a force, the continuous operation of which may be unreasonably hazardous to others.
5. The actor creates a situation which is unreasonably dangerous to others because of the likelihood of the action of third persons or of inanimate forces.
6. The actor entrusts dangerous devices or instrumentalities to persons who are incompetent to use or to care for them properly.
7. The actor neglects a duty of control over third persons who by reason of some incapacity or abnormality he knows to be likely to inflict intended harm upon others.
8. The actor fails to employ due care to give adequate warning.
9. The actor fails to exercise proper care in looking out for persons whom he has reason to believe may be in a danger zone.
10. The actor fails to employ appropriate skill to perform acts undertaken.
11. The actor fails to take adequate precautions to avoid harm to others before entering upon certain conduct where such precaution is reasonably necessary.
12. The actor fails to inspect and repair instrumentalities or mechanical devices used by others.
13. The actor's conduct prevents a third person from assisting persons imperiled through no fault of his own.

Leisure service administrators must keep in mind that the above list is not all-inclusive and that each instance of suspected negligence must be determined on the basis of the particular circumstances surrounding its occurrence.

Contractual Liability

According to van der Smissen (1968, p. 50), contractual liability "involves a single, limited interest protected by the law and based on the premise of the parties, such as contracting to purchase some goods or perform a service." Under normal circumstances, leisure service personnel, as individuals, are not liable in damages for breaches of contracts entered into in the name of the leisure service agency, unless an individual makes a promise to assure personal responsibility.

Leisure service administrators should, nonetheless, be cognizant of the state legislation which empowers them to enter into contractual agreements. For example, in most states laws exist which prohibit contracts exceeding a stipulated amount from being awarded prior to public solicitation of contract bids.

The reason that administrators are not personally held liable in contractual disputes, according to Lutzin and Storey (1973), is because they serve in the capacity of "agents" for the legal entity. Thus, when entering into contractual obligations, they do so not as individuals but as representatives of the entity and therefore are not bound by the contractual agreements entered into in their professional capacity. However, an "agent" must assume personal responsibility for actionable events resulting from fraudulent or deceitful conduct.

To illustrate the differing aspects of obligation under contractual liability, assume that a leisure service supervisor placed an order, without benefit of bid, for several "special" park benches each to display the community's seal. Upon receipt of the contract, the vendor constructs and prepares to deliver the benches. In the intervening period, however, the supervisor decides against the benches and thus refuses to accept their delivery. The manufacturer subsequently initiates a legal suit against the department.

If under the statutes governing the operation of the leisure service program, the supervisor was authorized to enter into contractual agreements as an "agent," then the supervisor would not be personally liable for payment to the vendor. Rather, the responsibility would revert to the agency on whose behalf the supervisor acted. On the other hand, if the supervisor had not been authorized to enter into such a contractual agreement yet knowingly did so, or if the supervisor knew that the contract should have been subject to public bid prior to being awarded but knowingly violated this regulation, then the probability is high that the supervisor would be held personally responsible for providing payment to the vendor.

Tort Liability

This concerns a wide variety of civil, non-criminal wrongs for which the injured person or property is entitled to compensation. In leisure services, van der Smissen (1968, p. 51) notes that, "Almost all of the cases involving torts arising out of the operation of municipal and school facilities and programs are brought on the basis of negligence." For example, a large percentage of cases are based on the contention that an activity leader or supervisor failed to exercise proper care which ultimately led to the plaintiff being injured. This is the number one cause of liability suits in the leisure service field.

Negligence must be proven to substantiate liability in cases when a person or property sustains injury or damage. However, many local, county, and state governments continue to operate under the old legal concept of *governmental immunity.* Derived from the old English common law, this concept is premised on the theory that, *"the king can do no wrong."* In 1907, Justice Holmes noted the existence of this concept in the American legal system when he stated:

A sovereign is exempt from suit, not because of an absolute theory, but on the logical and practical ground that there can be no legal right as against the authority that makes the law on which the right depends. (Kawananakoa v. Ploybank, 205 US 349)

Although municipal and other governmental entities may be immune from tort liability suit, their employees are not. All government employees are subject to the laws of tort and as such are held legally accountable for any negligent acts which may arise and result in injury or damages to another person or property.

Leisure service administrators should explain the concept of tort liability to their subordinates and emphasize the fact that they are personally responsible for their actions. It is most important that leisure service employees be appraised of their financial responsibilities in the event that they may be adjudged personally negligent in a liability suit.

Indemnification

In many states, legislation has been enacted allowing individual governmental entities to indemnify their employees. *Indemnification* means that an individual is relieved from personal responsibility for payment of an award made to a plaintiff in a liability suit. Rather, the employer (or the employer's insurance agency) assumes responsibility for the award payment. Indemnification does not, of course, free the individual from the responsibility for personal conduct. Indemnified individuals are only freed from the personal obligation of payment.

In most states where indemnification statutes exist, they have, unfortunately, been recorded in the form of enabling acts. In Massachusetts, for example, indemnification for public school teachers is mandatory, but for municipal employees the indemnification statute is written as permissive legislation. Consequently, very few governmental agencies in the Commonwealth of Massachusetts have taken the initiative to assume financial obligations resulting from negligence on behalf of their employees. Thus, in Massachusetts, as in most states, the majority of government employees continue to be personally responsible for any and all financial ramifications resulting from their negligent acts.

Leisure service administrators concerned about the welfare of their subordinates should make it a point to inform each employee, in writing, of his or her indemnification status. If an employee is not indemnified, he or she should be advised of the importance of obtaining sufficient personal liability insurance coverage. When indemnification is afforded the employee should be told the maximum amount of coverage provided.

Insurance

Insurance to protect against business related tort liability may be obtained from several sources. Persons owning homes or residing in apartments can request that a rider be attached to their homeowner's or apartment dweller's insurance policy. Separate liability insurance policies are also available from insurance agencies. In addition, many professional associations offer liability insurance policies to their membership on an annual subscription basis.

The cost of purchasing liability insurance tends to be relatively inexpensive. No individual engaged in the leisure service profession should be without the protection of liability insurance. In fact, it is a wise practice, even for those protected by indemnification, to obtain a personal liability insurance policy. The additional coverage afforded by such a policy can be extremely beneficial if a situation arises whereby the plaintiff's award exceeds the financial limits provided by the indemnification statute (or policy). In other words, if the financial award to the plaintiff exceeds the amount of coverage provided by the agency for a given incident the differential would have to be paid out of pocket. The purchase of a personal liability insurance policy would help protect against such an occurrence.

Liability Defense

Immediately upon notification that a tort liability suit has been filed, the first step for those named in the suit is to contact legal counsel beginning with the agency's attorney, if one exists. Defendants (or potential defendants) should not discuss any aspect of a tort case with anyone other than their legal counsel.

Governmental Immunity

The legal defense for an individual charged with negligence can be constructed from one or more perspectives. Typically, the defense employed by government agencies named in tort liability suits is premised on the concept of *governmental immunity.* However, as previously noted, such immunity does not apply to government employees.

Contributory Negligence

A defense founded on the concept of *contributory negligence* is often introduced when evidence can be shown to substantiate the fact that the plaintiff or a third-party contributed to the event(s) leading to the contested injury or damage. The plaintiff may be barred from recovery of damages if it can be proven that his or her negligent action contributed substantially to the injury or damage sustained. In such cases, even if only partial negligence can be attributed to the injured party, the amount of damages (money) awarded the plaintiff may be substantially reduced.

It should be noted that in recent years, the plaintiff's degree of contributory negligence has become a critical factor in judicial decisions. At one time it was only necessary for the defense to show that the plaintiff was, in fact, negligent, regardless of the degree of contributory negligence. Today, however, the courts are examining the plaintiff's contributory negligence much more closely. Evidence of minor contributory negligence is no longer considered sufficient to bar the plaintiff from recovery for injuries and damages. For example, at one time if a person gained access to a gymnasium through "breaking and entry," and was subsequently injured because of a faulty piece of equipment, the individual would have been barred from seeking recovery for injuries. Currently, however, the plantiff's contributory negligence, as exhibited by the "breaking and entering," would be weighed by the court, but such negligence would not absolve the defendant's negligence relative to the alleged defective piece of equipment which was the proximate cause of the plaintiff's injuries.

To illustrate the defense concept of contributory negligence, assume that a leisure service aquatic director is sued by an 18 year old male for back and neck injuries allegedly sustained while using the diving board at the community swimming pool. The plaintiff contends that the injury was the direct result of the aquatic director's failure to insure that the diving board, when wet, provided sufficient traction to prevent slipping. The plaintiff claims that his injuries were caused by a fall on the wet, slippery board. The contested accident occurred at 11 p.m., three hours after the swimming pool had been closed and secured for the evening.

The defendant's defense would be based upon the concept of contributory negligence. An attempt would be made to demonstrate that the plaintiff contributed to his own injury by having scaled a 10-foot fence to gain access to the diving board. It would be stressed that through the plaintiff's illegal trespass, he contributed in a major way to the contested accident. In addition to providing evidence negating the plaintiff's claim that the diving board failed to provide sufficient traction when wet, the defense would attempt to illustrate that had it not been for the plaintiff's negligent action which placed him at the scene of the accident, the accident would have never occurred.

On the other hand, if the plaintiff had not scaled the fence, but had walked unimpeded through an unlocked gate, then a defense based upon contributory negligence might not be quite as effective. The fact that the swimming pool gate had been left unlocked would certainly increase the defendant's degree of negligence while significantly reducing the plaintiff's.

Leisure service administrators should keep in mind that the younger the plaintiff, the more difficult it is to establish contributory negligence. Judges and juries tend to be very sympathetic toward youthful plaintiffs.

Act of God

A third defense tactic is to attribute the cause(s) of the plaintiff's injury or damage to an *act of God.* Acts of God refer to those situations created by and related to the elements over which humans lack control. As an example, consider the situation in which a youngster sustains a severe head injury when struck by a metal sign, located in a municipal park, which had been ripped from its mount by a severe, unusual gust of wind.

If the youngster (or parents) initiated a law suit to recover damages, the defendant's defense would be premised on the fact that the injuries sustained by the plaintiff were the direct result of an act of God. The defense would argue that the defendant had absolutely no control over the circumstances which produced the unfortunate results. The defense would attempt to demonstrate that the sign had been securely fastened to its mount and under all "normal" conditions was perfectly safe. It would be further argued that the intense gust of wind which ripped the sign from its mount was very unusual for the area and certainly an unforeseen condition, one over which the defendant had absolutely no control. Subsequently, it would be argued that the conditions which gave rise to the plaintiff's injuries could be attributed to neither the plaintiff nor the defendant and therefore could only be explained as an act of God or a "no fault" occurrence.

Assumption of Risk

A fourth defense strategy is based upon the grounds that the plaintiff knowingly and willingly entered into a set of conditions where the potential for injury or damage was high. Referred to as an *assumption of risk,* this form of defense is of particular importance given the recent increase in the number and the popularity of high-risk recreational activities. When employing this strategy, the defense must be able to demonstrate that the plaintiff did, in fact, elect to participate in the activity in spite of the known dangers inherent in the activity.

To illustrate, assume that a rock climber files suit against the leader of a climbing expedition for ankle injuries suffered in a climbing accident. Basing a defense upon the assumption of risk principle, the leader would contend that rock climbing accidents (no matter how unfortunate) do occur and that the plaintiff would logically be aware of the high risk involved. The defense would argue that even with this information, the plaintiff willingly pursued the activity and knowingly entered into a potentially hazardous situation.

From another perspective, the defense could argue that the plaintiff's injuries were caused by his or her failure to secure an adequate hand or foothold, thereby causing the accident. It would be emphasized that the climber had been attached to a safety rope which subsequently prevented the accident from producing a more severe injury. The defense would also note that the defendant sought to prevent such accidents from occurring by teaching proper climbing techniques and by requiring all rock climbers to be attached to and make use of safety ropes.

Leisure service administrators should note, however, that the assumption of risk concept has undergone close review by the courts in recent years and that its once broad application has been somewhat constricted. Assumption of risk by an individual should not be construed to imply that sponsors of activities and events are absolved from any or all responsibility for providing participants with adequate care and safety. Quite the opposite is true.

For example, in skiing it is not uncommon for participants to lose their balance and fall. Skiers of all ability levels fall at one time or another. Under normal conditions, a skier's fall is considered a part of the activity and thus a part of the assumed risk. But, if a skier falls and sustains an injury because the ski trail was not maintained in a manner consistent with commonly accepted industry standards, then the ski area's management probably would not be successful in waging a defense based upon assumption of risk. In this particular instance, the plaintiff's claim of negligence on the part of the defendant would likely prevail.

Tort Liability Preventive Measures

A major challenge for leisure service administrators is that of developing and implementing measures designed to prevent situations which might lead to tort liability suits. There is a saying that, "If accidents gave warnings, there wouldn't be any." The saying is probably quite true; but, accidents do not give warnings and thus it becomes necessary to institute measures designed to eliminate, or at least minimize, the potential for their occurrence.

Successful accident prevention efforts not only help to maintain a positive image of the leisure service program, but should also provide strong measures of protection for employees with respect to their becoming involved in negligence suits. At the same time, the successful implementation of accident prevention measures affords participants with safe and healthy environments in which to engage in leisure pursuits.

Periodic Reviews

Leisure service administrators should periodically review programs to insure that the highest level of accident prevention measures is being employed and maintained. One area of concern should be with the types and quality of equipment used in the program. All equipment should be of the best quality available given the constraints of budget allocations. Equipment purchase decisions, unfortunately, cannot be made using price as the sole criterion; the most expensive item is not always the best nor is the least expensive necessarily the poorest. Under no circumstances should equipment be purchased simply because it is the least expensive. To provide maximum protection against a tort liability suit, all equipment purchased should be selected on the basis of its quality, its safety, its projected serviceability, and its cost.

All equipment and facilities should be subjected to periodic routine inspections to ascertain that they meet minimum safety standards and to detect existing or potential safety habards. Hazards detected should either be reduced to minimum danger levels or, better yet, eliminated. Program administrators should require activity leaders and supervisors to conduct daily inspections of their facilities and equipment. All problems and potential hazards should be reported immediately. Participants should be restricted from using hazardous equipment and facilities until corrective measures have been taken. Hazard complaints should be kept on file along with records indicating the corrective actions taken.

For example, playground leaders should be required to inspect playing fields, sandboxes, and other play areas on a daily basis to insure that they are free of glass, rocks, or any other foreign objects which might cause injury to participants. Furthermore, all playground equipment should be examined daily to insure that it is in proper condition and functioning well.

Accident Records

Administrators should maintain accurate records of the number and types of accidents associated with each activity and event sponsored. Based upon these data, decisions can be formulated regarding the continuence or deletion of specific activities or events. For example, many administrators have decided to prohibit the use of trampolines due to the high incidence of accidents attributed to this particular piece of apparatus.

This type of injury data is also helpful in determining whether or not the procedures employed to govern the conduct of certain activities need to be altered. As an illustration, an analysis of touch football injury records may reveal that the greatest number of injuries occur on kick-offs and attempted fumble recoveries. Based upon such data, it would appear that the most fruitful method for reducing the number of injuries might be to change the rules concerning kick-offs and fumble recoveries. In the Amherst, Massachusetts Youth Football League, for example, runbacks are not permitted following kicks of any kind.

Employee Qualifications

High qualification standards for employment should be established and adhered to in the selection of activity instructors and facility supervisors. Employment qualifications for life guards, for example, should require that candidates, at the minimum, possess a senior life-saving certificate issued by the Red Cross. Preference should be given to applicants possessing a water-safety instructor's certificate.

Likewise, candidates for employment as supervisors of gymnastic-related activities should be required to secure a written statement from a recognized "expert," usually a gymnastic coach or teacher, verifying that the candidate possesses the knowledge and experience necessary to successfully fulfill the responsibilities associated with the role of a gymnastic supervisor. Failure to provide such a document should eliminate the candidate from further employment consideration.

All employee qualification documents should be photocopied and kept on file. Expiration dates should be noted for all qualifications requiring periodic renewals. Employees failing to present evidence of renewed certification should be terminated or suspended effective the date of expiration, and not reinstated until evidence of the renewed certification is presented. The maintenance of employee qualification records may prove quite beneficial in the event that a tort liability suit is filed against the leisure service administrator or a particular employee.

Liability Waivers

One method used (erroneously) to avoid liability suits is that of requiring participants to sign waivers stating that the agency is released from any responsibility for injuries or damages sustained while participating in a particular event or activity. Used in conjunction with children's programs, these waivers are commonly referred to as *parental permission slips.*

Parental permission slips from a legal perspective are not worth the paper they are printed on. They do serve, however, as an excellent means of informing parents about the particular activities and events in which their youngsters are interested.

In the past, the use of parental permission slips or liability waivers were effective in preventing many law suits because those signing such documents believed that they had incurred, at the very least, a moral obligation not to hold the potential defendant responsible for any injuries or damages which might be sustained. The fact of the matter, however, is that an individual must always be held accountable for his/her negligent acts that cause injury or damage to another or to property. Furthermore, parents can not sign away the rights of their youngsters to seek recovery for injuries or damages suffered as the result of a negligent action. Thus, even if a youngster's parents had signed a waiver and elected not to pursue legal action seeking recovery, the youngster upon reaching *legal age* (which varies from state to state) may initiate his or her own liability suit.

The use of parental permission slips or liability waivers as a method of attempting to avoid responsibility for negligent acts is not condoned. The public should not be subjected to acts of deceit nor should leisure service administrators attempt to abrogate their (or others') legal responsibilities.

Program and Facility Development Legislation

Not all legislation focused toward leisure service programs is concerned with litigation. Program directors should be aware of the wide variety of federal and state enactments designed to assist with the development of leisure service programs and facilities, either through financial or advisory help. The following federal public laws (PL) represent but a few of the many significant pieces of legislative that have a direct effect upon leisure service programs.

The *Land and Water Conservation Fund Act of 1965* (PL 88-578), amended in 1968 by PL 90-401, contains provisions for grants to be made available to cover up to 50 percent of the costs of projects (state, federal, or a sub-division thereof) designed to plan, acquire, and develop outdoor recreation areas and facilities. All projects seeking to qualify for funding through this act must first be in accord with their state's overall plan.

The *Open Space Land Program* created by *Title VII of the Housing Act of 1961* (PL 87-70) was amended by the *Housing and Urban Development Act of 1965* (PL 89-117). Under provisions of this act, communities may be assisted in the acquisition and development of urban openspace lands and for the creation of small parks in built-up areas. The act allows the federal government to assume up to 50 percent of the cost to local agencies for such undertakings.

The *Watershed Protection and Flood Prevention (Small Watershed) Act of 1954* (PL 83-566), amended by the *Food and Agricultural Act of 1963*, enables the Soil Conservation Service to share with state and local agencies up to half the cost of construction, land rights, and minimum basic facilities needed for recreation programs.

Administered under the Department of Agriculture, the *Greenspan Program,* part of the *Cropland Adjustment Program* (PL 89-321), offers state and local government agencies financial aid to acquire cropland for the preservation of open space and the retention of natural beauty, or for the development of wildlife or recreation facilities. This act is of particular benefit to rural areas.

Section 701 of the Housing Act of 1954 (PL 83-560) allows for the awarding of grants to provide for up to two-thirds the costs of all aspects of comprehensive urban planning, including recreation. Administratively, this act falls under the jurisdiction of the Department of Housing and Urban Development.

Section 704 of the Housing and Urban Development Act of 1965 (PL 89-117) enables the Secretary of Housing and Urban Development to authorize grants to local public agencies to acquire sites for the future construction of public facilities, including recreational facilities.

The *Urban Beautification and Improvement Program* under Title I of the Housing Act of 1949 (PL 81-171) provides for the issuance of grants to cover up to two-thirds of the cost of acquisition of park and playground lands which are part of an urban renewal project. Section 703 of the act provides for grants up to two-thirds of the costs of community-renewal planning that assesses present and future recreational and park needs.

The *Older American Act of 1965* (PL 89-73) authorizes the Administration on Aging section of the Department of Health, Education, and Welfare to issue grants up to 75 percent for community planning and coordinating programs for existing centers conducting recreational and other leisure time activities for older people. This act, however, does not provide for any construction costs.

Having reviewed the above federal enactments, it should be apparent that numerous pieces of legislation have been passed to assist urban, suburban, and rural communities develop and improve their leisure service programs and facilities in a variety of ways. Leisure service administrators wishing to share in the benefits afforded by these assistance programs must prepare and submit proposals in search of grant awards.

Project Funding Sources

Leisure service administrators in search of funding for projects are advised to contact their state and/or regional recreation directors for information regarding the availability of grants and other funds. Another method for identifying potential funding sources is to conduct a computer search. Data concerning all federal assistance programs are currently stored in a computer data bank referred to as the Federal Assistance Program Retrieval Program (FAPRS). This data bank contains key information about each existing assistance program, such as the types of projects which qualify for funding, the maximum amounts of grants, the agency responsible for administering the program, and other pertinent data.

Utilization of the FAPRS computerized search technique requires that the project for which funding is sought be completely formulated. This is necessary so that specific information can be extracted and used to identify sources for which the project meets the established funding qualifications.

Users of the FAPRS search technique should be advised that it is not uncommon for grant programs to have their qualification requirements altered after the program has been established. Thus, it is quite possible that the computer-generated grant information may be inaccurate. Consequently, it is highly recommended that once potential funding sources have been identified, the administering agency be directly contacted to insure the accuracy of the qualification requirements. Subscribing to this verification procedure may prevent the expenditure of valuable energies and resources on the development of grant proposals which have absolutely no chance for receiving funding approval.

Employment Legislation

A third area of legislative concern for the administrator is that related to the employment of personnel. During the course of the past century, numerous federal and state statutes have been enacted for the express purpose of insuring certain employee benefits and rights. It behooves administrators responsible for the hiring and supervision of leisure service personnel to possess an understanding of employment related legislation.

Only in the last half of the twentieth century have municipal employees received the right to organize for the purposes of negotiating wages and the conditions of employment. Today, however, the terms "union," "professional association," and "collective bargaining" are an integral part of municipal employee parlance. In the eyes of municipal employees, as well as for all other professional and trade groups, the individual providing leadership to the agency is viewed as being a representative of management. Consequently, it is this person who employees hold responsible for fulfilling all the provisions encumbered under the rubric of fair labor practices. Leisure service program administrators are viewed by their subordinates as members of the management team.

Federal Labor Enactments

Numerous rules and regulations pertaining to labor have been enacted by federal, state, and local governments. Federal enactments have, however, had the greatest impact. According to Sterle and Duncan (1973, p. 133), "Some of the most important federal laws that affect the recreation supervisor are the National Labor Relations Law, the Civil Rights Law, the Federal Wage and Hour Law, and the Equal Pay for Women Act."

Labor Relations

The *National Labor Relations Law,* passed by Congress in 1935, has since been subjected to several amendments. Probably the two best known are the Taft-Hartley Act and the Landrum-Griffen Act. Through the National Labor Relations Law *both* labor and management are prohibited from engaging in specific practices. For example, management is barred from disrupting the rights of employees to form, join, or assist labor organizations or to bargain collectively. On the other hand, labor organizations are restricted from coercing employee membership or to issue threats if they fail to affiliate.

Sterle and Duncan (1973) also note that management representatives may issue statements in opposition to the union and may comment on the risks that employees will assume should they choose to be represented by a union. But, under no circumstances are management representatives permitted to make any declarations which can be construed as a threat to the economic stability of the employee as related to his or her potential union affiliation.

Civil Rights in Employment

The *Civil Rights Act of 1964,* amended in 1972 by PL 92-261, represents a significant, far-reaching piece of legislation. Every federal, state, and local government agency throughout the nation is subjected to the provisions of this act. The primary purposes of the act are:

to enforce the constitutional right to vote, to confer jurisdiction upon the
district courts of the United States to provide injuncture relief against
discrimination in public accommodations, to authorize the Attorney General
to institute suits to protect Constitutional rights in public facilities and public
education, to extend the Commission on Civil Rights, to prevent discrimination
in federally assisted programs, to establish a Commission on Equal Employment Opportunity (EEOC), and other purposes. (Civil Rights Act of 1964,
p. 1)

Title VII of the act bars discrimination on account of a person's race, color, religion, sex, or national origin. Employers failing to conform to this act are subject to the loss of all federal program and contract funding. Economic sanctions tend to be very effective in getting public agencies, at least those relying upon federal monies, to conform to the law.

The sections of the act which pertain to the administration of community leisure service programs, as summarized by Reynolds and Hormachea (1976, pp. 188-189), are:

1. Any locality with 25 or more employees is subject to the Act.
2. Exemptions (Sec. 702): employment of aliens outside any state or a bona fide occupational qualification (BFOQ) where an employer can prove a particular religion, sex, or national origin is absolutely essential to the normal operations. Very few, if any, exemptions are considered valid. However, hardship cases may be submitted to EEOC for consideration.[1]
3. Unlawful employment practices for an employer (Sec. 703) are:
   a. To fail or refuse to hire or to discharge any individual, or otherwise to discriminate against any individual with respect to his compensation, terms, conditions, or privileges of employment.
   b. To limit, segregate, or classify his employees or applicants for employment in any way which would deprive or tend to deprive any individual of employment opportunities or otherwise affect his status as an employee.[2]
   c. To discriminate in employment practices, training and retraining because of race, color, religion, sex, or national origin except as may be especially exempted (BFOQ).
4. Section 704 prohibits employers from discriminating against any employee because he has opposed an unlawful practice or made a charge, testified,

1. See *Rosenfeld v. Southern Pacific Co.* 444 F 2d 1219 (1971) and *Griggs v. Duke Power Co.* 401 US 424 (1971).
2. See *Fronterio v. Richardson.* 93 S Ct. 1764 (1973).

assisted or participated in any manner in an investigation, proceedings, or hearings under this title, or from printing, publishing, or causing to be published any notice or advertisement relating to employment indicating any preference, limitation, specification, or discrimination based upon race, color, religion, sex, or national origin except bona fide occupational qualification for employment.

Leisure service administrators must also be cognizant of state statutes relating to civil rights. Many states have enacted such legislation. Federal authorities have been lenient in allowing sufficient time for state statutes to become operationalized. Yet, in instances where it becomes evident that such legislation is either lacking or not being enforced, federal authorities will intervene.

Terms of Employment

The *Federal Wage and Hour Law,* more correctly known as the Federal Labor Standards Act, mandates that in all but certain industries employees must be compensated at a minimum established salary per hour. In addition, employees are expected to work no more than 40 hours per week (there are, however, exemptions to this regulation). For all labor in excess of the 40-hour standard, employees must be compensated at the rate of at least one and one-half times the minimum salary in effect.

Leisure service personnel responsible for establishing employee work schedules and preparing employee payrolls should keep informed of the minimum wage standards and the rules and regulations governing these areas. Program directors should also be aware that in addition to federal guidelines there are also state and local regulations which must be adhered to.

Discrimination

The Fair Labor Standards Act was amended in 1963 by the *Equal Pay Act.* This amendment prohibits employers from paying employees of one sex less compensation than employees of the opposite sex when the job requires equal skill, effort, and responsibility and is performed under similar working conditions.

The *Equal Employment Opportunity Act* (EEO), enacted in 1972, further strengthened the Equal Pay Act. In addition to covering employees in the private sector, the act, as it presently stands, affords protection to, "state and municipal employees, teachers and administrative personnel of private and public institutions." (Sterle and Duncan, 1973, p. 135)

Leisure service employees responsible for personnel actions should possess a working knowledge of the provisions contained in Title VII as well as the regulations and guidelines established by the Equal Employment Opportunity Commission. Of greatest importance to leisure service administrators are those noted by Reynolds and Hormachea (1976, p. 192):

1. Qualifications and personnel actions must be based entirely on realistic requirements or doing the job.
2. Activities which tend to favor or discriminate against a class are prohibited.
3. Illegal employment practices include pencil and paper testing of applicants as a basis for selection; qualifications or tests that adversely affect a class and not specifically related to performance on the job; prehire inquiries not related to selection for the job such as age, religion, national origin, photograph, number of children, marital status, arrests (criminal convictions cannot be used as a reason to refuse employment if they are unrelated to the job—example, a clerk convicted for speeding); testing procedures which have not been validated by EEOC; and the same questions not being asked of all applicants.

Leisure service administrators must also be careful not to discriminate against a person because of age. The *Age Discrimination Act of 1967*, administered by the Wage and Hour Division of the Department of Labor, forbids discrimination of any nature against persons between the ages of 40-65. With the passage of legislation prohibiting mandatory retirement of persons prior to age 70, this act will probably be amended in the near future to prohibit discrimination against any person between the ages of 40-70.

Affirmative Action

Finally, as employers, leisure service administrators must be concerned with the requirements of *Affirmative Action*. In 1965, President Johnson issued *Executive Order 11246* which was later amended by *Executive Order 11375*. The Executive Orders required all federal contractors and sub-contractors to develop and implement affirmative action programs. In essence, this means that, "new [employee] recruiting practices must be developed whenever evidence indicates that the old methods have resulted in attracting a low representation of women and minority applicants." (Graham, 1976, p. 30)

Bulwik and Elicks (1972, pp. 6-7) list the following guidelines for determining whether minority groups and women are under-represented:

1. The percentage of minority and female work force as compared with the total work force in the immediate area.
2. The general availability of minority group members and women with requisite skills in the immediate work area.
3. The availability of members of minority groups and women with requisite skills in an area in which a contractor can reasonably recruit.

4. The availability of women and minority group members seeking employment in the labor or recruitment area of the contractor.
5. The availability of promotable or transferable minority group and female employees within the contractor's organization.
6. The existence of training institutions capable of training members of minority groups and women in requisite skills.
7. The degree of training which the contractor is reasonably able to undertake as a means of making all job classes available to women and members of minority groups.

When an employer detects an employment pattern deficiency, that is, a situation in which too few women and/or minority group members are employed, or are assigned to positions below their capabilities, the law requires that an affirmative action recruitment, employment, and promotional plan be devised, approved by the EEOC, and implemented. The design of an affirmative action plan must be such that it will initially reduce and then eventually eliminate employment disparities caused by past discriminatory practices.

Equal Opportunity

The sixties and seventies, in the history of the United States, will probably be recognized as years in which tremendous gains were achieved toward insuring equality for all segments of society. During this period, numerous federal and state legislative statutes were passed mandating that each citizen must be afforded an equal opportunity, regardless of sex, race, color, religion, or national origin. With respect to leisure services, several key pieces of legislation enacted during this period were the Civil Rights Act of 1964, Title IX of the Educational Amendments of 1972, and the Education for the Handicapped Act of 1975.

Each of these laws affect community recreation programs, either directly or indirectly. To successfully comply with the mandates and spirit of each of these laws, leisure service administrators must first be knowledgeable regarding the specifics of the legislation and second, must develop and institute appropriate compliance measures.

Civil Rights in Programming

The *Civil Rights Act of 1964,* amended in 1972 by PL 92-261, as previously noted, represents one of the most significant pieces of social legislation in the twentieth century. According to Reynolds and Hormachea (1976, p. 189), the Civil Rights Act affects leisure service administrators in two ways:

First, he must provide equal and fair treatment of citizens and participants. This involves equal protection of the law, freedom of speech, freedom of assembly, unrestrained use of public areas without harrassment or invasion of the individual's privacy, freedom from unreasonable searches and seizures, maintaining appropriate conduct of staff, protecting the rights and privileges of everyone, even informing the individuals taken into custody of their legal rights and privileges including the right to be silent. Second, he must provide equal, fair treatment and equal opportunities for employees as outlined by this Act.

The effects of this law in terms of employment have been discussed earlier. The law also has a profound impact upon a second aspect of leisure service administration—programming. The Civil Rights Act prohibits any and all forms of discrimination related to sex, color, religion, race, or national origin. Therefore, to comply with this legislation, no activity or event sponsored within leisure service programs can be discriminatory in terms of participation eligibility.

Moreover, each activity and event must be made accessible to all members of the population segment to whom they are directed. For example, activities and events aimed toward teenagers cannot be restricted to only black or only white youths. In the same vein, no activity or event can be limited to Irish or Greek teenagers nor can participation be restricted to only Catholic or Jewish residents. Thus, to comply with the Civil Rights Act, participation in a Spanish Heritage Festival must be open to all residents wishing to participate, not just those who are of Hispanic background.

In a like manner, facilities must be made reasonably accessible to all members of the community. Furthermore, rules and regulations governing the use of facilities must be enforced in an equitable manner; one group must not be required to adhere to the rules and regulations in a strict and precise manner while another group is virtually allowed to ignore the same policies.

Failure to abide by the spirit and mandates of the Civil Rights Act may precipitate legal remedies being sought through complaints filed in federal district courts. To preclude the need for such action, every aspect of the community program should be designed in such a manner that all members of the community are accommodated on an equitable basis. Discrimination of any nature must be avoided, and it becomes the responsibility of the administrator (both morally and legally) to insure that such is the case.

Discrimination by Sex in Programming

Within the United States, participation by females in physically active leisure pursuits has been traditionally frowned upon.

Women and girls have been characterized by the Victorian image—physically weak, dependent upon the male, and abhorred by the thought of engaging in physical competition amongst themselves. Consequently, until recent years, few opportunities for women and girls to engage in sport and athletics have been provided by society. (Graham, 1975, p. 239)

Over the years, leisure service programs have perpetuated this sociological stereotype by providing active, physically demanding events and activities for males while sponsoring passive activities for females.

Today, however, females no longer accept passive roles. They demand the opportunity to participate in all activities and events on an equal basis with their male counterparts. This demand (already supported by the Civil Rights Act) has received additional support from the passage of *Title IX*, a part of the *Educational Amendments of 1972*. Title IX reads as follows:

No person in the United States shall, on the basis of sex, be excluded from participating in, be denied the benefits of, or be subject to discrimination under any education program or activity receiving Federal financial assistance . . . .

Although Title IX is focused on educational programs, it does nonetheless present indirect, but far-reaching, implications for the conduct of leisure service programs. Under the requirements of Title IX, all programs sponsored or endorsed by an educational district in receipt of federal financial assistance (there are some specific exceptions) must comply with the mandates prohibiting discrimination on the basis of sex. Consequently, to protect their own interests, school administrators must insure that all agencies allowed to use school facilities are in compliance with Title IX. The penalty for school districts failing to comply with and abide by the mandates of Title IX is loss of all federal financial assistance.

Most municipal programs make use of school facilities (or at least they should). Subsequently, policies governing their operation must be free from any and all sex-related discrimination. Failure to comply may force school authorities to deny the use of school facilities for leisure service activities and events. For many programs, the use of school facilities is essential to their successful operation. Such a program, if prohibited from using school facilities, would be rendered inoperative or totally ineffective in delivering leisure services.

Another very important reason why leisure service administrators should strive toward insuring that their programs comply with the standards established by Title IX is premised upon a moral and humanistic foundation. One of the basic goals of many agencies is to provide each individual with numerous and varied opportunities to achieve a "recreational experience." By subscribing to this goal, leisure service administrators assume the moral obligation to provide each individual with such opportunities on an equitable basis, regardless of sex. And only through such freedom to participate will each individual be afforded the maximum opportunity to fulfill his or her needs as described by Maslow's Hierarchy of Needs.

To insure that sex-related discrimination does not exist is a task which requires an examination of the total spectrum on a program's operation. For example, both the type and quality of equipment and supplies used in male and female programs must be of equal quality and available in equal quantity; if coaching and instruction is provided for one sex, it must be available, upon demand, to the other; in activities and events requiring officiating, the number and quality of officials must be equitable; and, the scheduling of facilities must afford each sex an equal amount of "prime time."

Title IX also requires that playing areas and meeting rooms be provided on an equitable basis. The quality and maintenance of all playing facilities must be the same for both sexes. The law requires that showers, toilets, and locker accommodations be equitable, but also allows these facilities to be provided on a sex-segregated basis.

Another area related to Title IX concerns the rules and regulations governing eligibility for participation. All participation qualification standards must be applied equally for males and females. Eligibility requirements aimed toward a single sex are not permissible. The problem of rules and regulations restricting the participation of a single group have been addressed by the courts and their rulings have established "precedents" for the prohibition of qualification standards not applied equally to both sexes.[3]

Leisure service administrators must also resolve the question related to mixed-sex participation. Traditionally, certain activities have been sponsored on a "co-rec" basis—males and females participating together. But, tradition has also dictated that other activities, especially those involving "contact," be restricted to single-sex participation. For example, in the United States males have been restricted from field hockey, whereas females have been excluded from football and ice hockey.

However, sex-related participation restrictions have been successfully challenged. In numerous cases, arguments that participation restrictions based solely upon sex are discriminatory and therefore unconstitutional have been upheld by the courts.[4] Consequently, the wise leisure service administrator should institute appropriate measures to

3. See *Rosenfeld v. South Pacific Co.* 444 Fed. 1219 (1971).
4. See *Hass v. South Bend Community School Corporation.* 289 N.E. 2d 495 (1972), *Hollander v. The Connecticut Interscholastic Athletic Conference.* N. 12-49-27, Conn. Sup. Ct. (1971), *Morris v. Michigan State Board of Education.* 474 F 2d 292 (1973) and *Reed v. Nebraska School Activities Association.* 341 F. Supp. 258 (1972).

insure that both sexes are protected from participation eligibility rules which discriminate on the basis of sex. Through such efforts, the administrator will not only insure each individual his or her right to equal treatment, but each individual will be afforded maximum opportunities to pursue a "recreational experience."

Legislation Related to Handicapped Persons

Handicapped persons represent a segment of society which for too long has been a forgotten minority. Like other segments of the population, handicapped persons have needs which must be satisfied. Unfortunately, this group's leisure needs have never been adequately addressed nor provided for by the average community program.

Handicapped Population

The number of handicapped persons in the United States has increased significantly in recent years. This rapid escalation can be attributed, at least in part, to the increasing number of maiming accidents recorded annually. Also, advancements in medical technology have enabled physicians to save the lives of many persons who in the past would have succumbed to the mutilating injuries sustained. In addition, military actions, such as the Viet Nam Conflict, have produced a tremendous number of handicapped individuals.

Educational Legislation

The escalation in the number of handicapped persons has brought about a concomitant awareness of the lack of public programs and facilities designed to accommodate and provide for the needs of this special population. Public recognition of the plight of the handicapped culminated with the passage of the *Education for the Handicapped Act of 1975* (PL 94-142).

Like Title IX, the Education for the Handicapped Act is focused upon education. However, it has brought a great deal of national and local attention to the need to develop and implement a variety of other programs for handicapped individuals. The need for such programs is especially true in the area of leisure services. According to the findings of the National Institute on New Models for Recreation and Leisure for Handicapped Children and Youths, as noted by Nesbitt (1977, pp. 10-11):

The fundamental goal of community recreation for handicapped is to enhance function and fulfillment for the handicapped individual at the highest level possible through play, recreation, and leisure.

The basic objectives of community recreation for the handicapped are:

1. Achievement of enjoyment, satisfaction, or fulfillment by the participant at the highest level possible.
2. Achievement of equality of opportunity in leisure, the arts, recreation, park, and culture by the participant who is handicapped.
3. Achievement of a normal life style (normalization) by the participant who is handicapped based on individual needs, interests, and desires.

Grants

Grant monies are available through PL 94-142 to fund programs designed to provide leisure services to the handicapped. Both therapeutic and "mainstream" recreation programs qualify for funding under the guidelines of this art. To assist with the financial aspects of developing and implementing new programs for the handicapped, leisure service program administrators should become knowledgeable regarding the funding provisions of PL 94-142 and should construct and submit a grant proposal.

Architectural Barriers

Recently, both state and federal governments have placed increased emphasis upon the need to eliminate architectural barriers which prevent the physically handicapped from gaining access to public facilities. Legislation has been enacted by the federal government and many state legislatures requiring all new public construction projects assisted by government monies to incorporate architectural standards designed to enable easy access for the handicapped. In addition, many existing public facilities are being required to make structural alterations designed to accommodate the needs of the physically handicapped citizen.

In Massachusetts, for example, the Department of Public Safety has published a document pertaining to the architectural standards adopted by the Commonwealth to make public facilities accessible to, functional, and safe for the use of physically handicapped citizens. All new construction of public facilities must conform to these standards and regulations and, when possible and feasible, existing structures must make structural modifications to eliminate or reduce architectural barriers.

In reference to recreational facilities, the Massachusetts *Rules and Regulations of the Architectural Barriers Board* (1977, p. 48) states the following:

A *means of egress* in a building containing recreational facilities from the street to all such facilities shall be accessible.

Swimming pools open to the public shall be accessible
   Entrance to such pools shall be made available to the physically handicapped by means of either a ramp with a non-slip surface

extending into the pool toward the shallow end thirty (30) inches wide, clear, with railings on each side, with a slope not exceeding one-in-six (1:6), or by a removable or portable sling-lifting device.

Such pools shall provide and maintain an unobstructed *means of egress* around the pool not less than forty-eight (48) inches wide. Such area shall have a surface that is non-slip.

Bowling alleys on floors otherwise accessible shall provide at least two (2) adjacent lanes accessible to wheelchairs.

Locker rooms in a building open to the public shall be located so as to be accessible by an unobstructed means of egress to at least five (5) percent of the lockers.

Shower facilities adjoining rooms shall be accessible.

Locker room and shower *floor* shall have a surface that is non-slip.

Parks, campsites, and roadside parks: If the sidewalk, walk or walkway in the park, camp, or roadside park is a means of passage through the area and not passage solely to the recreation facility, then these regulations apply.

Spectator facilities shall provide seating capacity to be accessible and on a level area for those in wheelchairs. Such area may have removable seating.

Administrators should be aware of *The Architectural Barriers Act of 1968* (PL 90-480), which mandates that any new public facility funded to any degree by federal monies must be fully accessible to all handicapped individuals. Also, the *1973 Rehabilitation Act, Section 504* (PL 93-112), states that:

No otherwise qualified handicapped individual in the United States . . . .
shall, solely by reason of his handicap, be excluded from participating in, be denied the benefits of, or be subject to discrimination under any program or activity receiving Federal assistance.

Role of the Administrator

Directly or indirectly, many leisure service programs derive benefits from federal monies. Therefore, the astute program administrator will insure that measures are taken to institute leisure service programs designed to either incorporate (mainstream) the handicapped, or to provide special programs and/or services to meet the needs of this special population, or both. In addition, administrative action should be initiated to eliminate architectural barriers which prevent physically handicapped individuals from gaining access to leisure service facilities.

Public facility construction projects failing to eliminate architectural barriers, thereby restricting or prohibiting access to the facility for physically handicapped individuals, have been successfully challenged in the courts.[5] Therefore, leisure service administrators should personally verify that construction plans for all new facilities are designed in strict compliance with both federal and state rules and regulations.

Summary

All municipal leisure service programs derive their authority from state enabling legislation. Under most circumstances, programs are considered governmental functions. However, if user fees are charges, the program's classification status may be subject to change.

Leisure service administrators should be knowledgeable regarding contractual and tort liability. All leisure service employees should be advised of their indemnification status and informed of their personal financial responsibility for liability judgments awarded to plaintiffs.

Leisure service personnel should be instructed to implement measures designed to avoid accidents and potential liability suits. All leisure service facilities should be continually examined for hazardous conditions. Upon detection, such conditions should be either eliminated or corrected. The rules and regulations pertaining to all phases of the operation should periodically be reviewed and revised in an effort to provide participants with safe environments in which to pursue leisure activities.

Numerous pieces of federal and state legislation have been enacted containing provisions for granting monies to assist with various leisure related projects. Program directors should be aware of these enactments and when appropriate should submit grant proposals in search of project funding.

Those responsible for hiring, assigning, and evaluating personnel should be cognizant of labor laws pertaining to such actions. These laws have experienced significant changes in recent years.

The sixties and seventies will be recognized as a period in the history of the United States in which the social conscience of the nation focused upon the need to insure each citizen's right to an equal opportunity. Probably the most significant enactments during this period, at least from the perspective of leisure services, were the Civil Rights Act of 1964, Title IX of the Educational Amendments of 1972, and the Education for the Handicapped Act of 1975. Leisure service administrators should be knowledgeable regarding the impact that these enactments have had upon recreation and the measures required to bring their program's into compliance.

5. See *Urban League v. WMATA.* Civil No. 776-72 U.S. D. Ct., D.C. (1973); *Disabled in Action of Baltimore,* et al. *v. Hughes, et al.* Civil Action No. 74-1069-HM, U.S. D. CT., Md (1974); and, *Friedman v. County of Cuyahoga.* Case No. 895961 Court of Common Pleas, Cuyahoga County, Ohio (1972).

Above all, administrators must be constantly aware of their obligation to understand, meet, and enforce a host of legal responsibilities. The wise administrator will seek the advice of legal counsel on *all* matters requiring legal clarification.

Study Questions

1. What do the terms governmental function and proprietary function mean? Does one classification have an advantage over the other?
2. From what source(s) do municipal leisure service programs derive their legal authority?
3. What conditions must be present for a person to be held liable for the injuries and/or damages sustained by another person or property?
4. As a leisure service administrator, what advice would you give to your subordinates concerning avoidance of liability suits?
5. What does the term indemnification mean? Of what value is it?
6. How might financial and planning assistance be secured from outside agencies for the development and implementation of various community leisure service facilities and programs?
7. What does the acronym FAPRS stand for? How might this be of value to a leisure service administrator?
8. What aspects of labor law should leisure service administrators responsible for personnel employment, assignment, and evaluation be aware?
9. How have federal and state legislative enactments affected leisure service programming patterns?
10. How should leisure service programs attempt to provide for the needs of the physically handicapped? How might assistance with the development and implementation of handicapped programs be secured?

References

Black, Henry C. *Black's Law Dictionary*. 4th ed. St. Paul, Minn.: West Publishing Company, 1968.
Bulwik, H. C., and Elicks, S. R. *Affirmative Action for Women: Myth and Reality*. Berkeley, Ca.: University of California, 1972.
Civil Rights Act of 1964. 42 USC 2000.
Colgate, John A. *Administration of Intramural and Recreational Activities: Everyone Can Participate*. New York: John Wiley & Sons, Inc., 1978.
Graham, Peter J. "Title IX: Human Rights in School Sport." *26th Annual Conference Proceedings of the National Intramural-Recreational Sports Association* (1975): 238-251.

Graham, Peter J. "Affirmative Action: Its Effect Upon Intramural-Recreational Sports Department Employment Policies." *27th Annual Conference Proceedings of the National Intramural-Recreational Sports Association* (1976): 29-43.

Kawanananaka v. Ploybank, 205 US 349.

Lutzin, Sidney G., and Storey, Edward H. *Managing Municipal Leisure Services*. Washington, D.C.: International City Management Association, 1973.

Massachusetts, Commonwealth of. *Rules and Regulations of the Architectural Barriers Board*. Boston: Author, 1977.

Nesbitt, John A. *Regional Institute Newsletter*. Washington, D.C.: National Institute, Community Recreation for Handicapped, No. 9-9-9-9, September, 1977.

Prosser, William L. *Handbook of the Law of Torts*. St. Paul, Minn.: West Publishing Company, 1941.

Rehabilitation Act of 1973, Section 504 (PL 93-112).

Reynolds, Jesse A., and Hormachea, Marion N. *Public Recreation Administration*. Reston, Va.: Reston Publishing Company Inc., 1976.

Statute 42, United States Code, Section 1983.

Sterle, David E., and Duncan, Mary R. *Supervision of Leisure Service*. San Diego: San Diego State University Press, 1973.

Title IX of the Educational Amendments of 1972, 20 USC 1681-86.

van der Smissen, Betty. *Legal Liability of Cities and Schools for Injuries in Recreation and Parks*. Cincinnati: The W. H. Anderson Company, 1968.

Related Readings

Appenzeller, Herb. *From Gym to Jury*. Charlottesville, Va.: The Michie Company, 1970.

Appenzeller, Herb. *Athletics and the Law*. Charlottesville, Va.: The Michie Company, 1975.

Bureau of Outdoor Recreation. *Outdoor Recreation Research: A Reference Catalog*. Washington, D.C.: U.S. Government Printing Office, January, 1970.

Dunn, Diana R., and Gulbis, John M. "The Risk Revolution." *Parks & Recreation*, August (1976): 12-17.

Jensen, Clayne R. *Outdoor Recreation in America: Trends, Problems, and Opportunities*. 2nd ed. Minneapolis, Minn.: Burgess Publishing Company, 1973.

Kleindienst, Viola K., and Weston, Arthur. *The Recreational Sports Program: Schools, College, Communities*. Englewood Cliffs, N.J.: Prentice-Hall, Inc., 1978.

Meyer, Harold D., and Brightbill, Charles K. *Recreation Administration: A Guide to its Practices*. Englewood Cliffs, N.J.: Prentice-Hall, Inc., 1956.

Rankin, Janna. "Legal Risks and Bold Programming." *Parks & Recreation*, July (1977): 47-48; 67-69.

Rodney, Lynn S. *Administration of Public Recreation*. New York: The Ronald Press Company, 1964.

Appendix
Tournament Development and Scheduling

Tournaments often represent one of the more complex phases of the recreation program planning process. This perception arises out of the numerous variables which must be considered and effectively dealt with to insure a successful tournament.

Tournament Selection

As discussed in Chapter Nine, tournament format selection should be based upon and should reflect the particular purpose of the tournament. Once the appropriate tournament structure has been selected, what are the variables which must be taken into account? The following list, although certainly not all-inclusive, presents some of the major areas of concern:

1. The number of available facilities (fields, courts, tables, pools, rooms, alleys, etc.)
2. The number of hours each facility is available per day
3. The number of days each facility is available
4. The number of days or schedule dates required for practices, clinics, scheduled contests, rescheduling of postponed contests, tie breakers, and championship contests
5. The maximum number of entries that can be accommodated given the available facilities and the time frames allotted for their use
6. The number of contests to be scheduled for each entry
7. The amount of time that participants can devote to involvement in the activity

Only after decisions have been established on these matters should administrators proceed with the tournament schedule development.

To illustrate the various facets involved in the development and scheduling of a tournament, assume that a coed softball tournament is to be constructed.[1] Further assume that the tournament sponsors have established the following:

1. A round robin schedule format will be used with the league winners participating in a single elimination championship tournament.

---

[1]. The same development and scheduling procedures may be applied to all tournaments (bowling, volleyball, chess, bridge, backgammon, etc.).

2. Six softball diamonds will be available for tournament use Monday through Friday from 4-6 pm for a period not to exceed six weeks.
3. Each team will be allowed to participate in at least one practice game prior to the start of the actual tournament.
4. Each team is to be scheduled for seven league contests.
5. When possible, reasonable scheduling preferences will be honored.

Tournament Calendar

Given the above operational guidelines, the first step in constructing the tournament schedule is to create a calendar displaying the six weeks during which the tournament will be conducted. Once constructed, the dates reserved for practice games and championship play-offs should be noted on the calendar. The remaining dates may then be used for scheduling the round robin contests. However, schedulers must be cautioned to provide some facility time for league tie-breakers and the rescheduling of postponed contests.

In this particular example, it is recommended that the first week be reserved for practice games and the last for the championship tournament. Dates for rescheduled contests and tie breakers can be interspersed throughout the calendar as the league schedules are developed. Tie-breakers can usually be scheduled following conclusion of the round robin schedules. But, it must be stressed that rescheduling time is usually required throughout the period allotted to round robin scheduling because of postponements resulting from inclement weather or participant requests.

Facility Schematic

Development of a schematic displaying the times that each facility is available on a weekly basis represents the next step. Based upon our example, Figure A-1 shows that fields one through six are available Monday through Friday from 4-6 pm each week. After tabulating the number of fields available each week (60), it is established that one hundred twenty teams can be scheduled to play one game per week or sixty teams to play twice a week.

Given that the first and last week of the tournament's allotted time has been reserved for practice games and championship play-offs respectively, only four weeks (twenty schedule dates) remain in which to schedule the round robin contests. And knowing that each team is to participate in seven contests, it becomes evident that to accomplish this task each team will have to be scheduled for two games per week. Thus, the maximum entry that this particular tournament can accommodate is limited to sixty.

Time	Field	Monday	Tuesday	Wednesday	Thursday	Friday
4:00 PM	1					
	2					
	3					
	4					
	5					
	6					
5:00 PM	1					
	2					
	3					
	4					
	5					
	6					

Figure A.1   Schedule Schematic

League Construction

After the tournament has been publicized and the entries received, the next step involves the construction of leagues. To continue with our example, assume that forty-six softball entries have been received. How can these forty-six entries be arranged into round robin leagues which will produce seven contests per entry? At first glance, a logical approach would appear to be to construct as many eight-team leagues as possible with the remaining entries being grouped together to constitute a smaller league. This approach would appear reasonable since each entry in an eight-team round robin league would be scheduled for seven contests (as was illustrated in Chapter Nine). Thus, if this approach were selected five eight-team leagues and one six-team league could be formulated.

Effective Facility Utilization

However, before establishing any league structure, consideration must be given to another important scheduling criterion: How effectively will the proposed league structure utilize the available facilities? A review of the schematic (Figure A-1) will help in resolving the question. Again note that six softball diamonds are available for use both hours. An

<table>
<tr><th>Time</th><th>Field</th><th>Monday</th><th>Tuesday</th><th>Wednesday</th><th>Thursday</th><th>Friday</th></tr>
<tr><td rowspan="6">4:00 PM</td><td>1</td><td rowspan="4">League A 8 Teams</td><td rowspan="4">League D 8 Teams</td><td rowspan="4">League A 8 Teams</td><td rowspan="4">League D 8 Teams</td><td rowspan="6"></td></tr>
<tr><td>2</td></tr>
<tr><td>3</td></tr>
<tr><td>4</td></tr>
<tr><td>5</td><td rowspan="4">League B 8 Teams</td><td rowspan="3">League F 6 Teams</td><td rowspan="4">League B 8 Teams</td><td rowspan="3">League F 6 Teams</td></tr>
<tr><td>6</td></tr>
<tr><td rowspan="6">5:00 PM</td><td>1</td><td rowspan="6"></td></tr>
<tr><td>2</td><td>Open</td><td>Open</td></tr>
<tr><td>3</td><td rowspan="4">League C 8 Teams</td><td rowspan="4">League E 8 Teams</td><td rowspan="4">League C 8 Teams</td><td rowspan="4">League E 8 Teams</td></tr>
<tr><td>4</td></tr>
<tr><td>5</td></tr>
<tr><td>6</td></tr>
</table>

[shaded box] = Split time league scheduling

Figure A.2 Split Time Scheduling

eight-entry round robin league schedule will require the use of four fields for each schedule date. Subsequently, two of the six fields will remain vacant each hour unless another league is scheduled in such a manner that two of its games are played during one hour and the remaining two during the second time frame. For example, two contests could be scheduled for fields 5 and 6 at 4 pm and two played at 5 pm on fields 1 and 2. Figure A-2 displays the split time scheduling pattern.

Consistent Scheduling Patterns

The above scheduling pattern is certainly workable but its implementation would undoubtedly create confusion for numerous participants because of the continual change in contest starting times for those entries in the split-schedule league. Thus, *when possible all leagues should be scheduled for the same hour and on the same days throughout the tournament.* Adherence to this policy will help avoid confusion which could ultimately lead to late starts, forfeits, and/or the necessity to reschedule contests.

Efficient League Scheduling

Methods of making the best possible use of facilities must at all times be sought and implemented. With respect to the softball tournament, would it be possible to structure six seven-team leagues and one four-team league? The answer is yes. Seven-team leagues, although needing an additional schedule date because of the odd number, only require the use of three fields per schedule date. Consequently, two leagues can be scheduled at the same hour with all six fields being effectively utilized. By adopting this league formulation pattern, four leagues could be scheduled on a Monday-Wednesday sequence and four on a Tuesday-Thursday basis. Fridays would then remain available for the scheduling of postponed contests and league tie-breakers.

Developing the Schedule of Contests

The problem of actually developing the seven scheduled contests for each entry is next to be solved. As recalled from Chapter Nine, a seven-team round robin league will produce six scheduled contests for each entry and will require seven scheduling dates (the seventh necessitated because of the odd entry which mandates the use of a bye in each schedule round). To provide the seventh contest, a position play must be introduced at the conclusion of the round robin. In the case of the four-team league, a double round robin scheduling format will produce six contests for each entry. Again, a position play inserted at the conclusion of the round robin will provide the seventh contest.

Tournament schedulers should be alert to the fact that one entry in each of the seven-team leagues will not receive an opportunity to actually play a seventh contest due to the necessity of using a bye in the position play. However, in the current example, this problem can be eliminated with just a little extra imagination and planning on the part of the scheduler. Because there are six seven-entry leagues each of the last rank-ordered teams at the conclusion of the round robin tournament can be paired off to create three additional contests—contests which can be scheduled for the same date that the remainder of the tournament entries participate in position play. When possible, it behooves recreation administrators to use their imagination in creating greater participation opportunities for *all* tournament entries.

Assigning Entries to Leagues

Since the best league numerical structure has been established, the next problem focuses on the question of which teams are to be assigned to which leagues. The initial step is to separate into groups those entries indicating a need for special scheduling consideration and those which can be scheduled at any time. Entries requiring special scheduling should be further divided into groups according to the nature of their request; for example, all entries to participate on Thursdays should be grouped together as should those indicating a preference for a Monday-Wednesday 4 pm schedule sequence.

Once the sorting process has been accomplished, the special consideration groups should be then placed into seven-team leagues. If entries remain or if the initial group numbered less than seven entries, entries from the "schedule anytime" group should be added to complete the league. The last four entries will comprise the final league.

League Identification Card and Tournament Schedule List

Having formulated the leagues, each league's entries should be clipped together along with a card on which space is provided to list the following information:

1. The name of the league
2. The number of teams in the league
3. Special scheduling required
4. The assigned schedule days, time, and field numbers

Names should then be assigned to each league and recorded on the appropriate card. Next, a tournament schedule list, similar to that exhibited in Figure A-3, should be constructed using the information recorded on the cards attached to each league's entries.

Referring to the tournament schedule list observe that the National league is unable to participate on Thursdays and therefore must be scheduled for a Monday-Wednesday sequence. Scanning the schemantic (Figure A-1) note that the National League's request can be accommodated by scheduling it for Mondays and Wednesdays at 4 pm using fields 1, 2, and 3. If the schedule sequence is acceptable, appropriate notation should be made on both the schematic and the card attached to the league's entries.

Upon further reference to Figure A-3, observe that the American League may be scheduled for any day but only at 4 pm. A review of the schematic (Figure A-1) reveals that the scheduling choices available to the American league at 4 pm include:

Mondays and Wednesdays, fields 4, 5, and 6
Tuesdays and Thursdays, fields 1, 2, and 3
Tuesdays and Thursdays, fields 4, 5, and 6

When it has been decided where to locate the American League, the appropriate notations must be again recorded. This assignment procedure is repeated for each league.

#	League Name	# Teams	# Fields Required	Special Requests
1	American	7	3	Schedule any day—4 pm only
2	National	7	3	Do not schedule on Thursdays
3	Midwest	7	3	None
4	Eastern	7	3	None
5	Western	7	3	Do not schedule on Mondays or Fridays
6	Northern	7	3	None
7	Southern	4	2	None

Figure A.3   Tournament Schedule List

The use of a scheduling schematic is extremely helpful especially in terms of avoiding errors such as scheduling two leagues for the same days, times, and fields. However, the precise transfer of information contained on the schematic to the cards attached to the league's entries is even more important. Errors committed in the transfer process will automatically negate the value of the schematic.

Scheduling Officials

Figure A-4 represents a completed schematic displaying the scheduling pattern for each team in the coed softball tournament. In examining Figure A-4 note that the Southern league (a four-team league) only requires the use of two fields per schedule date and therefore was purposely scheduled at 4 pm on fields 4 and 5. This particular time was selected to facilitate the scheduling of tournament officials. When possible, officials should be assigned more than one contest on each date scheduled. There will be occasions, however, when only single contest assignments are possible. In these instances every effort should be made to minimize the number of officials affected.

Using the softball tournament as an example, it can be demonstrated that with good planning the problem of single contest assignments can be minimized. If all six softball fields were to be scheduled at 4 pm then

Time	Field	Monday	Tuesday	Wednesday	Thursday	Friday
4:00 PM	1					
	2	National	Western	National	Western	
	3					
	4		Southern		Southern	
	5	American		American		
	6					
5:00 PM	1					
	2	Eastern	Midwest	Eastern	Midwest	
	3					
	4					
	5	Northern		Northern		
	6					

Figure A.4   Completed Schedule Schematic

six sets of officials (two officials per set) would be required. And if the schedule were such that the following hour (5 pm) three contests were to be played, then only three sets of officials would be necessary. This scheduling procedure results in three of the six sets of officials receiving a single game assignment.

On the other hand, employing a little planning foresight this problem could be reduced in scope by scheduling only five contests at 4 pm (a seven-team league and the four-team league) which would necessitate the assignment of only five sets of officials. A seven-team league scheduled for the 5 pm slot would require three sets of officials. Thus, only two sets of officials would receive single contest assignments—a reduction of fifty percent over the original scheduling pattern.

Rough Draft Schedules

The construction of a rough draft of the schedule represents the next task. Rough draft schedules are completed for each league in the tournament and should be developed on a form specifically designed for this purpose. To actually schedule each league's round robin contests, the scheduler should first record the name of the league and the names

ROUGH DRAFT SCHEDULE

Name of League: __American__

Teams

1. Bucks	5. Tigers
2. Lions	6. Ducks
3. Bears	7. Hounds
4. Cats	

Date	Time	Field		Date	Time	Field	
July 5	4:00 PM	4	Bucks - Lions	July 19	4:00 PM	4	Cats - Tigers
		5	Hounds - Bears			5	Bears - Duck
		6	Ducks - Cats			6	Lions - Hounds
July 7		4	Hounds - Bucks	July 21		4	Bears - Cats
		5	Ducks - Lions			5	Lions - Tigers
		6	Tigers - Bears			6	Bucks - Ducks
July 12		4	Ducks - Hounds	July 26		4	Lions - Bears
		5	Tigers - Bucks			5	Bucks - Cats
		6	Cats - Lions			6	Hounds - Tigers
July 14		4	Tigers - Ducks	July 28		4	Position Play* 1 - 2
		5	Cats - Hounds			5	3 - 4
		6	Bears - Bucks			6	5 - 6
							7 - Bye

*In the position play, the 7th ranked team will be scheduled for a game against the 7th ranked team from the National league at a date, time, and field to be announced.

Name of Scheduler: _George Gregory_

Figure A.5   Rough Draft Schedule

of the individual teams on the form, and then the scheduling procedures outlined in Chapter Nine should be followed.

An example of a completed rough draft schedule is illustrated by Figure A-5. Particular attention should be paid to the space provided for the scheduler's signature located at the lower right side of the form. Schedulers' names are requested so that when an error or series of mistakes are evidenced the responsible person can easily be identified. Knowledge that they will be held accountable for their errors tends to increase the care and accuracy exercised by schedulers.

Master Schedule Development

With the completion of each league's rough draft schedule it should be transcribed onto a master schedule similar to that displayed in Figure A-6. (See p. 316 and p. 317). Because the coed softball tournament requires only the development of a single tournament, no need exists to introduce a master schedule recording color code system. However, had several tournaments been developed (that is, men's, women's, and coed) then the recording of the contests related to each specific tournament in a different color would prove very helpful for purposes of identification.

Reproduction and Distribution of League Schedules

Upon its completion, the master schedule must be double-checked for accuracy and any errors detected must be immediately corrected. The rough draft schedules should then be prepared for reproduction so that multiple copies can be produced (Xeroxed, mimeographed, etc.). Again, the need for accuracy when transcribing data from the rough draft schedule must be emphasized. It is of paramount concern; a single error is capable of generating considerable frustration and confusion for both the participant and the program administrators. The dissemination of erroneous information may produce late starts, forfeits, or at the very least, a significant amount of rescheduling and communication problems— each of which serves only to diminish the quality and potential success of the program.

Reproductions of the league schedule should be distributed to each of the participating entries (within a given league), posted in appropriate locations, and included in the tournament record book, if records are to be maintained. Master copies should be preserved and filed for future reference.

Practice Schedules

A practical and wide-spread policy of many recreation program planners is one of providing sufficient opportunity for participants to engage in practice games, scrimmages, or strategy sessions prior to the start of the tournament. Entries may conduct their practice sessions either independently or in conjunction with another unit. To insure an equal amount of facility usage afforded each entry, administrators often require that facility reservations be made. Generally, a maximum is placed on the number of reservations allowed each entry.

Providing facility time for pre-tournament practices allows participants an opportunity to organize their teams and to become familiar with the facility and its environment. Such opportunities also provide for that often needed chance to "remove the rust" and to "sharpen" individual skills and team coordination.

When facilities are limited and a large number of program entries is anticipated, recreation administrators are advised to initiate a reservation system for the scheduling of practice sessions. A practical suggestion is to have the reservation system administered by just one or two staff members and to specify a single location where reservations may be secured. By allowing just a few individuals the power to issue reservations, the probability of enforcing established maximum practice time limits will be enhanced. The issuance of reservations at a single location helps to reduce confusion among participants as to where a reservation may be secured. It also eliminates the potential for duplicate reservations being issued for the same facility during the same day and time. Without controls of this or a similar nature, serious problems could arise. Problems of frustration, inequity, and confusion experienced during the organizational stages of activity programs only serve to deteriorate the quality of the endeavor.

Championship Tournament Scheduling

In many recreation programs multiple league tournaments usually culminate with a championship tournament in which each league winner participates. Single elimination is the most popular format for this type of tournament. Although at cross purposes to the round robin tournament concept (in terms of promoting participation), the single elimination format is an efficient champion producing vehicle. In our coed softball example, seven league winners will qualify for the championship play-offs. Using the guidelines presented in Chapter Nine, a seven-entry single elimination tournament structure must be developed and the qualifying entries must be assigned to specific tournament slots.

Before designating playing dates for the championship contests, the tournament master schedule should be consulted. Schedulers must always anticipate the need for extending the completion date for round robin and position play contests due to postponements and rescheduling. It must also be assumed that league play may conclude with two or more

Time	Field	MON June 28	TUES June 29	WED June 30	THURS July 1	FRI July 2
4:00 P.M.	1					
	2					
	3	FIELDS RESERVED ──────────────────────────►				
	4					
	5					
	6					
5:00 P.M.	1					
	2					
	3	FOR PRACTICE SESSIONS ───────────────────►				
	4					
	5					
	6					

Time	Field	MON July 5	TUES July 6	WED July 7	THURS July 8	FRI July 9
4:00 P.M.	1	Oranges—Apples	Peas—Beans	Bananas—Oranges	Corn—Peas	
	2	Bananas—Pears	Corn—Carrots	Berries—Apples	Celery—Beans	
	3	Berries—Grapes	Celery—Peppers	Plums—Pears	Beets—Carrots	
	4	Bucks—Lions	Bruins—Wings	Hounds—Ducks	Bruins—Aces	
	5	Hounds—Bears	Aces—Knicks	Bucks—Lions	Knicks—Wings	
	6	Ducks—Cats		Tigers—Bears		
5:00 P.M.	1	Atlantic—Pacific	Blue—Green	North—Atlantic	Gray—Blue	
	2	North—Indian	Grey—Red	Arabian—Pacific	Black—Green	
	3	Aegean—Baltic	Black—Yellow	Aegean—Indian	White—Red	
	4	Elm—Maple		Birch—Elm		
	5	Birch—Spruce		Willow—Maple		
	6	Willow—Pine		Oak—Spruce		

Time	Field	MON July 12	TUES July 13	WED July 14	THURS July 15	FRI July 16
4:00 P.M.	1	Berries—Bananas	Celery—Corn	Plums—Berries	Beets—Celery	
	2	Plums—Oranges	Beets—Peas	Grapes—Bananas	Peppers—Corn	
	3	Grapes—Apples	Peppers—Beans	Pears—Oranges	Carrots—Peas	
	4	Ducks—Hounds	Bruins—Knicks	Tigers—Ducks	Bruins—Wings	
	5	Tigers—Bucks	Wings—Aces	Cats—Hounds	Aces—Knicks	
	6	Cats—Lions		Bears—Bucks		
5:00 P.M.	1	Arabian—North	Black—Gray	Aegean—	White—Black	
	2	Aegean—Atlantic	White—Blue	Baltic—North	Yellow—Gray	
	3	Baltic—Pacific	Yellow—Green	Indian—Atlantic	Red—Blue	
	4	Willow—Birch		Oak—Willow		
	5	Oak—Elm		Pine—Birch		
	6	Pine—Maple		Spruce—Elm		

Figure A.6 Co-ed Softball Tournament Master Schedule

Time	Field	MON July 19	TUES July 20	WED July 21	THURS July 22	FRI July 23
4:00 P.M.	1	Grapes—Plums	Peppers—Beets	Pears—Grapes	Carrots—Peppers	
	2	Pears—Berries	Carrots—Celery	Apples—Plums	Beans—Beets	
	3	Apples—Bananas	Beans—Corn	Oranges—Berries	Peas—Celery	
	4	Cats—Tigers	Bruins—Aces	Beans—Cats	Bruins—Knicks	
	5	Beans—Ducks	Knicks—Wings	Lions—Tigers	Wings—Aces	
	6	Lions—Hounds		Bucks—Ducks		
5:00 P.M.	1	Baltic—Aegean	Yellow—White	Indian—Baltic	Red—Yellow	
	2	Indian—Arabian	Red—Black	Pacific—Aegean	Green—White	
	3	Pacific—North	Green—Gray	Atlantic—Arabian	Blue—Black	
	4	Pine—Oak		Spruce—Pine		
	5	Spruce—Willow		Maple—Oak		
	6	Maple—Birch		Elm—Willow		

Time	Field	MON July 26	TUES July 27	WED July 28	THURS July 29	FRI July 30
4:00 P.M.	1	Apples—Pears	Beans—Carrots	National Position Plan 1-2	Western Position Plan 1-2	RESERVED FOR RESCHEDULED GAMES
	2	Oranges—Grapes	Peas—Peppers	3-4	3-4	
	3	Bananas—Plums	Corn—Beets	5-6	5-6	
	4	Lions—Bears	Southern Position Plan	American Position Plan 1-2		
	5	Bucks—Cats	1-2	3-4		
	6	Hounds—Tigers	3-4	5-6		
5:00 P.M.	1	Pacific—Indian	Green—Red	Eastern Position Plan 1-2	Midwest Position Plan 1-2	AND TIE BREAKERS
	2	Atlantic—Baltic	Blue—Yellow	3-4	3-4	
	3	North—Aegean	Grey—White	5-6	5-6	
	4	Maple—Spruce		Northern Position Plan 1-2		
	5	Elm—Pine		3-4		
	6	Birch—Oak		5-6		

Time	Field	MON August 2	TUES August 3	WED August 4	THURS August 5	FRI August 6
4:00 P.M.	1	RESERVED FOR RESCHEDULED GAMES →		CHAMPIONSHIP →		
	2					
	3					
	4					
	5					
	6					
5:00 P.M.	1	AND TIE BREAKERS →		PLAYOFFS →		
	2					
	3					
	4					
	5					
	6					

Figure A.6   Co-ed Softball Tournament Master Schedule—Continued

entries tied for first place, a situation usually resolved through the use of tie-breaking contests. Therefore, it is recommended that a minimum of two schedule dates be left open between the anticipated completion of the round robin-position play tournament and commencement of the championship play-offs. These two playing dates should be recorded on the master schedule as being reserved.

Caution must also be taken to provide at least one schedule date to accommodate postponements in the championship tournament itself. Finally, care must be exercised by schedulers to insure that the tournament will conclude within the time frame allotted for the program. Nothing is more frustrating than to have two activity schedules in conflict over the use of the same facility, one attempting to conclude while the other seeks to commence.

Officials and Staff Assignment Schedules

Programmers must also direct their attention toward the need to schedule game officials and program staff. In many recreation programs a large segment of planned activities do not require the services of officials. However, activities such as basketball, softball, football, and soccer have traditionally been conducted with the assistance of officials. Yet, this is not to say that programs of this nature cannot be conducted without the provision of officials. To the contrary—there are numerous instances when officials are neither needed nor employed.

Nevertheless, when officials are employed, at least two problems must be resolved. First, prospective officials must be recruited and trained. And second, when all the officials have been identified and employed they must then be individually scheduled for game assignments. Similar to league scheduling, game assignment schedules must be developed and distributed to each official.

Assignment schedules for officials should be established immediately following the completion of the master contest schedule. To aid in the assigning of officials, each official should be required to complete a form indicating days available for employment. The next step is to create a master assignment schedule for officials similar to that displayed in Figure A-7. Recorded on the master schedule for each schedule date should be the names of the official(s) assigned to each contest.

Individual assignment schedules can be prepared once the official's master schedule has been completed. The individual schedule, as illustrated in Figure A-8, should contain the name of the official and the date, time, location, and names of the competing entries for each contest assigned. Accompanying the individual schedule should be a list of the names, addresses, and telephone numbers of all regular and substitute officials. A list of this nature is quite valuable when an assigned official, for one reason or another, must find a replacement.

		Fields						Extra Official
		1	2	3	4	5	6	
Day	Time							
Mon	4:00 PM							
	5:00 PM							
Tues	4:00 PM							
	5:00 PM							
Wed	4:00 PM							
	5:00 PM							
Thurs	4:00 PM							
	5:00 PM							
Fri	4:00 PM							
	5:00 PM							

Figure A.7   Master Schedule of Officials Assignments

As soon as officials receive their assignments, they should be required to immediately report any conflicts with other personal commitments. If assignment conflicts exist, they must be corrected as rapidly as possible. Once an activity program has commenced some recreation administrators have a policy of not allowing officials to alter their schedules—unless for an exceptional reason and providing that the requesting official takes personal responsibility for securing a qualified substitute.

Nonetheless, it is inevitable that instances will occur, for a variety of reasons, when an official is unable to fulfill a commitment. It is therefore recommended that for each schedule date one extra official be assigned. If all of the regularly assigned officials report for their contests, the extra official can be allocated supervisory responsibilities while

Activity: <u>Coed Softball</u>   Name: <u>Steve LeClere</u>

Assignments   Location: <u>Softball Fields</u>

Date	Time	Field/Court
7/5	4:00 PM	1
	5:00 PM	1
7/6	4:00 PM	4
7/12	4:00 PM	1
	5:00 PM	1
7/13	4:00 PM	3
	5:00 PM	3
7/19	4:00 PM	2
	5:00 PM	2
7/20	4:00 PM	5
7/26	4:00 PM	6
	5:00 PM	6
7/27	4:00 PM	2
	5:00 PM	2

Figure A.8   Individual Officials Schedule

continuing to be available to replace a colleague sustaining an injury or illness and unable to complete an assignment.

Premised on much the same rationale, staff members should be scheduled and assigned their duties dependent upon the demands required by the activities being conducted. Development of assignment schedules for part-time employees is especially relevant. In most recreation programs, the functions of part-time employees are directly related to the requirements of the activities being sponsored and, therefore, are subject to frequent changes and alterations. For these reasons, part-time personnel serving as supervisors, statisticians, equipment managers, trainers, and so forth, require advance knowledge of changes in their work schedules. Lacking such information, it becomes extremely difficult for these individuals to make the necessary adjustments in their non-work schedules.

Index

evaluation, 179-181
interviewing, 173
limitations, 167-168, 169
motivation, 164
qualification standards, 169
reassignment, 168
recognition, 181-183
recruitment, 169, 170, 172
resource file, 172

roles, 164-166
screening, 172-173
supervision, 177-179
termination, 168
training, 136, 175-177
use of media, 170
value, 92, 111, 166-167

Zeigler, E., 183